December 2018

To Skip

Merry Christmas wishes from
us all - happy reading!

Betsy

Annie

NIKKI

JOE

FOUNDING MARTYR

FOUNDING MARTYR

The Life and Death of
Dr. Joseph Warren,
the American Revolution's
Lost Hero

CHRISTIAN DI SPIGNA

CROWN
NEW YORK

Library of Congress Cataloging-in-Publication Data
Names: Di Spigna, Christian, author.
Title: Founding martyr : the life and death of Dr. Joseph Warren, the
American Revolution's lost hero / Christian Di Spigna.
Description: First edition. | New York : Crown Publishers, 2018.
Identifiers: LCCN 2017057934 (print) | LCCN 2017058311 (ebook) |
ISBN 9780553419337 (ebook) | ISBN 9780553419320 (hardcover) |
ISBN 9780553419344 (trade pbk.)
Subjects: LCSH: Warren, Joseph, 1741–1775. | Massachusetts—History—Revolution,
1775–1783—Biography. | United States—History—Revolution, 1775–1783—Biography. |
Boston (Mass.)—History—Revolution, 1775–1783. | Soldiers—Massachusetts—
Biography. | Physicians—Massachusetts—Boston—Biography.
Classification: LCC E263.M4 (ebook) | LCC E263.M4 W235 2018 (print) |
DDC 973.3092 [B]—dc23
LC record available at https://lccn.loc.gov/2017057934

ISBN 978-0-553-41932-0
Ebook ISBN 978-0-553-41933-7

PRINTED IN THE UNITED STATES OF AMERICA

Book design by Andrea Lau
Title page painting by John Trumbull
Maps by Jeffrey L. Ward
Jacket design by Elena Giavaldi
Jacket art: *Joseph Warren* by John Singleton Copley, 1765,
oil on canvas © 2018 Museum of Fine Arts, Boston

10 9 8 7 6 5 4 3 2 1

First Edition

For my moon and my stars, Ava Elizabeth and Jen

CONTENTS

WARREN'S MASSACHUSETTS

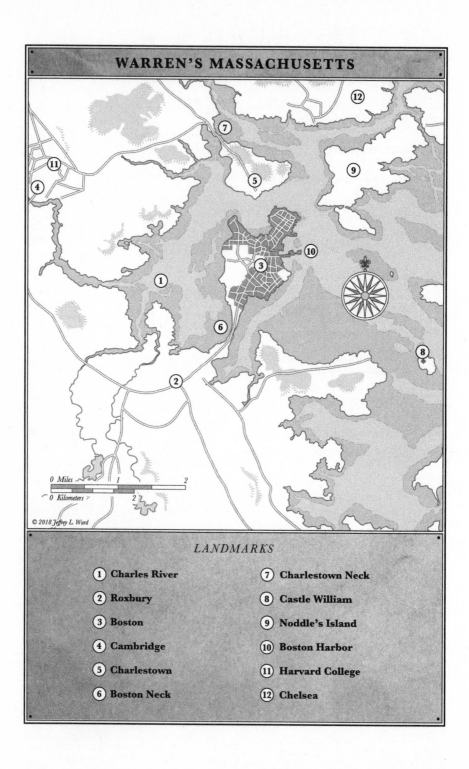

LANDMARKS

1 Charles River   7 Charlestown Neck

2 Roxbury   8 Castle William

3 Boston   9 Noddle's Island

4 Cambridge   10 Boston Harbor

5 Charlestown   11 Harvard College

6 Boston Neck   12 Chelsea

© 2018 Jeffrey L. Ward

0 Miles   1   2

0 Kilometers   2

WARREN'S BOSTON

Charlestown

Charles River

2

NORTH
END

11

4   10

3

6

7

Boston

5   1

8

9

SOUTH
END

12

Boston Harbor

13

0 Miles   .25   .5
0 Kilometers   .5

© 2018 Jeffrey L. Ward

LANDMARKS

1 Location of Warren's house, 1761–62

2 West Boston estate (purchased 1770)

3 Green house (rented circa 1770–72)

4 Chardon house (rented circa 1774–75)

5 Dr. James Lloyd's House

6 Brattle Street Meetinghouse (Warren's church)

7 Town House (near site of Boston Massacre)

8 Old South Meeting House

9 Boston Common

10 Green Dragon Tavern

11 Copp's Hill

12 Long Wharf

13 Griffin's Wharf
(site of Boston Tea Party)

BATTLE OF BUNKER HILL

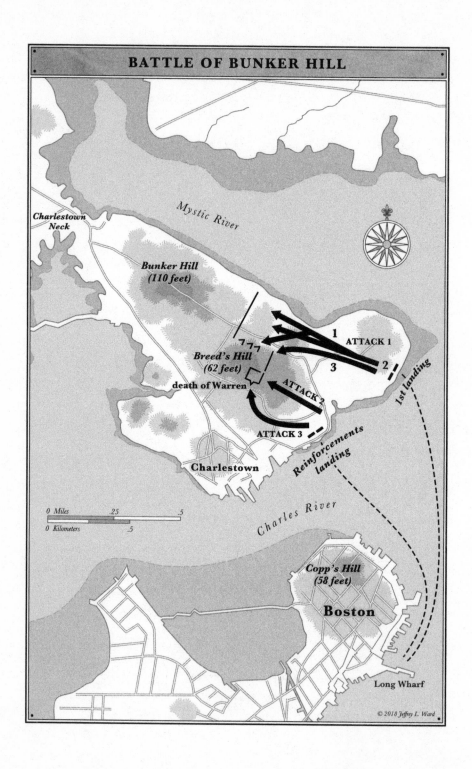

Charlestown
Neck

Mystic River

Bunker Hill
(110 feet)

1 ATTACK 1

3

2

Breed's Hill
(62 feet)

death of Warren

ATTACK 2

ATTACK 3

Charlestown

1st landing

*Reinforcements
landing*

0 Miles · .25 · .5
0 Kilometers · .5

Charles River

Copp's Hill
(58 feet)

Boston

Long Wharf

© 2018 Jeffrey L. Ward

FOUNDING MARTYR

"The dead, the dead, the dead—*our* dead . . . we see, and ages yet may see, on monuments and gravestones, singly or in masses, to thousands or tens of thousands, the significant word **Unknown**."

—WALT WHITMAN

INTRODUCTION

FOR MANY AMERICANS, 1776 WAS THE SEMINAL YEAR IN THE nation's history—the year the founding fathers signed the Declaration of Independence, initiating one of the greatest revolutions in the modern world. The Boston Massacre, the Boston Tea Party, Paul Revere's epic midnight ride, and the Battle of Bunker Hill loom large as monumental incidents that launched the country's birth, discussed in countless history books. But most of those books fail to mention the role of Dr. Joseph Warren, the revolutionary pillar of that watershed epoch. The complexities behind the resistance movement that led to the American Revolution run deeper than previously realized given that Warren has been largely forgotten. He was killed fighting in the Battle of Bunker Hill in 1775, his body mutilated by British troops. His martyrdom and multiple reburials in the eighteenth and nineteenth centuries have helped obscure his legacy and his many contributions to the cause of American independence.

By the second half of the eighteenth century, imperial strife had been brewing in the colonies for decades. Between 1760 and 1775, Massachusetts was a hotbed of political agitation, social unrest, and economic turmoil. Boston and its surrounding areas were a hub of revolutionary activity. There a small cabal of British subjects—deemed traitors to the Crown—with no organized military or popular support, scant finances, and little hope of success, began an insurrection against the mother country—the greatest military power in the world. Samuel Adams, the most recognizable of these original patriots, is often called "The Father of the American Revolution," but Adams did not foment Boston's revolutionary storm single-handedly. The initial group of radical insurgents was also spearheaded by Dr. Warren, who helped to shape the ideas, policies, and events that catapulted thirteen colonies toward independence. These patriots were, one might say, the "founding grandfathers," as their actions preceded those of Washington, Franklin, Jefferson, and others who rallied to the cause later. In this sense, many of the men we now credit with forming the United States were actually latecomers to the independence movement.

Dr. Joseph Warren entered the political scene at the outset of resistance to British imperial policies in the mid-1760s. He came to form and lead numerous clubs, societies, and organizations that made him a ubiquitous and valuable leader. He was a propagandist, polemicist, author, orator, professor, and ultimately a major general, as well as a doctor, a mentor, and a spymaster. He served as president of the Massachusetts Provincial Congress, chairman of the Massachusetts Committee of Safety, leader of the Boston Committee of Correspondence and the North End Caucus, and grand master of Ancient Scottish Rite Masons in North America. Although younger than most of Boston's radical leaders, he was a shrewd organizer whose vigor and diverse abilities helped propel the Whig faction in Massachusetts.

Of late, historians have resurrected the lives of several New England patriots, all close friends and comrades of Warren. Paul Revere's most recent ride to historical stardom has been, in part, due to David Hackett Fischer's groundbreaking biography. John Adams has emerged as one of the preeminent iconic founders, as a result of the seminal works by David McCullough and John Ferling. Adams, the sole participant in tumultuous pre-1776 Boston to live fifty years beyond the signing of the Declaration, later commented in hindsight, "But what do we mean by the American Revolution? Do we mean the American war? The Revolution was effected before the war commenced." The "Revolution" prior to 1776 was one of the most important but overlooked periods in American history, and occurred in the press, the pulpits, the streets, and the port towns and cities throughout the eastern seaboard. Particularly in Boston, the clashing traditions of strict religious doctrine and rule of law collided with collective crowd action and notions of the right to self-government that helped to spark the radical Whig movement.

In Massachusetts before 1776, Joseph Warren was considered one of the most serious threats to British rule not only by Loyalists and Crown officials but also by the soldiers of the king's army. With his radical actions and ideology, he commanded a greater respect and instilled more fear than most of his other patriot colleagues. He was the only Bay Colony Whig statesman in charge of the major political, social, and military organizations who also fought on the battlefield. Unlike other radical leaders in Boston, he never sought safety; nor did he abandon the cause when tensions with the British erupted into violence. On the contrary, he thrust himself to the forefront of the action while some of his Whig associates remained behind the scenes until the danger subsided.

His fellow revolutionaries John Adams, Samuel Adams, Paul Revere, and John Hancock longed to mirror Warren as a patriot statesman. But he was more than just a politician—he was also an icon of military heroism. The newly appointed general George Washington admired and longed to emulate his battlefield heroics, and subsequent generations of American military leaders would feel his influence. Initially his military exploits turned into the stuff of folklore, and many legends were spun about his actions both on and off the battlefields. Eventually his contributions faded from American memory, obscured by the historical inaccuracies surrounding him: the record favored the living, clouding the early unfolding of the revolution.

Although Warren was not without shortcomings, his numerous talents and connections qualified him for many leadership posts. Of all the revolutionaries in Massachusetts, he was the most ubiquitous, and the steadfastness of his commitment to radical ideology was equaled only by that of the political machinist Samuel Adams. Often, and without much supporting evidence, historical accounts describe Warren as a recruit and protégé of Adams, a cog in the vast Whig party machine, just one of several patriot doctors. But Warren was a staunch revolutionary in his own right even before he formed his close relationship with Adams. Both men were Harvard graduates, but Warren was a respected physician, and extremists at both ends of the political spectrum also considered him a gentleman, which helped to further legitimize the Whig movement in Boston.

For centuries, revolutionary history has relegated Warren to a supporting role, secondary to Samuel Adams, when in fact, both men worked together and often complemented each other's strengths. For a time, the doctor was more publicly visible than Adams: he delivered two popular Boston Massacre Orations, and he exerted much influence in the highest and lowest social circles; but he also operated an intricate spy ring that helped launch the Revolution. His clandestine maneuverings worked to counter the complex intelligence system the British had implemented in and around Boston that successfully infiltrated the highest patriot ranks. Warren mastered this dangerous chess game of intrigue and deceit before General Washington's famous spy network, which lost legendary patriot Nathan Hale to the British.

On the night of April 18, 1775, Warren's espionage system induced him to send several riders into the countryside to alert Adams, Hancock, and others about the pending British operation—a bold act popularly mislabeled "Paul Revere's midnight ride." Warren's decisive action set off the "shot heard around the world," resulting in the Battles of Lexington and Concord, where a musket ball grazed his head.

One month before Bunker Hill, he warned Samuel Adams, "We must now prepare for every thing as we are certain that nothing but success in our warlike enterprises can possibly save us from destruction." Warren had become the point man, leading those monumental events in Boston and helping guide the actions of the founding fathers at the First Continental Congress.

Dr. Joseph Warren died as a perceived traitor to King George III in 1775. By contrast, many patriot leaders went on to achieve illustrious careers in the new government of the United States as "Americans." Following Warren's premature death, John and Samuel Adams and John Hancock continued their rise to fame as the Whig leaders of the fledgling nation, while George Washington achieved immortality as the father of his country. Most of these rebel insurgents would die in their beds as old men. Warren was not part of this later triumphalist phase of American history. My purpose in this book is not to undermine the lasting contributions of other leading Whigs but to uncover and underscore Warren's. It is unlikely that any of the men we now esteem as "founders" could have achieved that hallowed appellation had they, like Warren, died a year before the signing of the Declaration.

Warren's accomplishments during his brief life, in the pre-Declaration microcosm of Boston, were nothing short of incredible. His patriot colleagues attended both Continental Congresses, where they gained enduring praise and fame. Dying a young and unlucky martyr before the colonies united, Warren lost his place in the pantheon of founding fathers, even though his actions were instrumental in achieving independence. Just two weeks after his death, George Washington took military command in Boston, demarcating the Warren and Washington epochs.

Although he possessed an esteemed military reputation in 1775, Washington had never commanded an army. His martial exploits to that point had been questionable at best and were fought under the aegis of His Royal Majesty. By contrast, Warren had fought in several battles against Britain as an unpaid volunteer, helping to disprove the colonists' belief that the king's troops were an invincible juggernaut.

Warren, a patriot well known throughout the colonies, reached his apotheosis in the spring of 1775, and his martyrdom deepened the fissure between the colonies and Great Britain. The New England towns were strongholds of revolutionary activity until British forces evacuated Boston in the spring of 1776, which marked the end of an era for both Warren and his native town. Washington went on to lead the Continental Army to achieve a miraculous victory culminating at Yorktown.

Following the Stamp Act crisis in 1765 and up to the Battle of Bunker Hill in 1775, Warren was at the center of almost every major conflict that transpired in the environs of Boston, both prominently and behind the scenes. During those years many of the nation's future founders, other than Samuel Adams, were relatively inactive within the radical movement and largely unknown throughout the colonies. This book reanalyzes the history of that momentous time span to reveal the influence Warren exerted.

Warren's public record is particularly rich in terms of his writings: the seminal Suffolk Resolves (a precursor to the Declaration of Independence), his two important Boston Massacre Orations, and his stream of propaganda that appeared in various newspapers, broadsides, and pamphlets. Many private letters written between Warren and his political comrades, associates, and friends are preserved in public collections. Until now, a good number of them have never made their way into any of the works published on Warren.

A cache of letters, journals, diaries, and various memoirs from generations of Joseph Warren's family also exists, as a valuable resource with a host of personal information. And since Warren was a doctor, his surviving ledgers are important primary historical evidence that fills in gaps within the Warren literature. The numerous ledgers of Boston merchant John Greenleaf document the various supplies Warren purchased over a decade. In researching for this book, deconstructing these ledgers was critical to understanding the doctor's complex practice. Incredibly, within the course of my archival spadework, I was fortunate to locate a small portion of one of Warren's lost medical daybooks and two letters from the 1850s regarding Warren and the missing books, previously concealed in a private collection. Dr. Warren's meticulous patient lists, dates, notes, prescriptions, remedies, fees, and even samples of his handwriting help to underscore the life of a career physician whose public and private lives steadily shifted toward rebellion.

The historiography of the American Revolution has shifted in the previous half century. From the neoprogressives' study of the ideas and radicalism behind the movement for liberty to bottom-up "social history," to the "new cultural history," scholars continue to explore the many spheres surrounding the imperial crisis. The causes of the Revolution cannot be explained by any one particular interpretation—whether it be an intellectual deconstruction of imperial oppression, domestic strife within the colonies, or economic backlash. Rather, the causes span various schools of thought. These evolving trends and debates have helped illuminate the roles of lesser-known individuals and groups including women and slaves—all of whom contributed to our collective past. However, a figure as important as Warren has largely escaped attention.

While the majority of books on Warren focus on his death and martyrdom, this is the first one to fill in the more obscure parts of Warren's personal life—from his family and childhood to his years at Harvard and apprenticing with Dr. James Lloyd—a key period in the formation of his character, his social networks, and ultimately his medical and political career. This book also provides information on Warren's adult years and explores his much-neglected but leading role as a combatant at Bunker Hill, using information drawn from previously unknown or unavailable sources.

Moreover, the period following Bunker Hill is a vital part of the Warren story that until now has remained largely untold: his gruesome death and certain letters written by his fiancée, Mercy Scollay, and by Warren's peers in the Continental Congress before they received word of his demise. This book traces Warren's death, its aftermath, and his remains' eight-decade postmortem journey, which finally ended when they were reburied for the last time in 1856, after images of his skull were taken. It explores the vicissitudes of his multifaceted legacy and outlines his bloodline to his present descendants, which boasts an impressive military succession.

I researched and examined a vast array of primary sources, including medical ledgers, private and public letters, newspapers, broadsides, journals, diaries, probate records, Harvard archives, Freemasonry documents, inventory lists, cemetery accounts, church files, photographs, maps, prints, and other materials that long slumbered in the archives of historical societies and libraries. While tunneling into such documentation and searching for new evidence, I branched out to investigate Warren's political comrades, schoolmates, patients, family, friends, and others. Learning eighteenth-century history, vocabulary, traditions, medicine, culture, and the topography—especially in New England—was a necessary and vital component of doing the research. I used not only documents but also relics, as resources, and slowly Warren's nebulous world came into focus. These materials from the colonial, antebellum, and postbellum periods helped me uncover the story of his life and death while highlighting his role in the rebellion and his influence on American independence.

By connecting the existing evidence with my own studies—and the expertise of scholars and academics from a variety of fields—I have attempted to weave a more complete Warren tapestry that elucidates a time, a place, and a cast of characters different from some persistent misinformation in the literature. Grounded in primary source documents, this is the first completely nonfiction book written about Dr. Joseph Warren in almost sixty years. It is intended for readers both within and beyond the academic community in an effort to make history more popular, not popular history.

A fiercely independent thinker, Warren—the son of a Roxbury, Massachusetts, farmer—rose to the heights of power in the Whig faction and helped to foment the war that culminated in an independent America. Years later, invoking that critical period, the statesman Daniel Webster asserted that "it was a thinking community that achieved our revolution before a battle had been fought." Warren was a high-ranking Whig member of that ideological rebellion who also fought in the initial military phase of the Revolution, a rare combination of statesman and warrior. More than just a political theoretician, this hands-on doctor led by example. His effective arsenal of voice, pen, and sword was unrivaled by any other patriot. Had he lived, in all likelihood his name would be remembered among those of the original founders. This is his untold story.

1

NO TURNING BACK

"The mistress we court is LIBERTY;
and it is better to die than not to obtain her."
—JOSEPH WARREN TO SAMUEL ADAMS, JUNE 15, 1774

THE FATEFUL DAY HAD COME. ON THE MORNING OF JUNE 17, 1775, just days after his thirty-fourth birthday and appointment to the rank of major general, Dr. Joseph Warren, away from his family and closest political allies, lay motionless inside Hastings House in Cambridge, Massachusetts. Suffering from one of the debilitating headaches that had plagued him for years, he listened as the steady fire of cannonade rumbled in Charlestown, a few miles away. It had not rained for weeks, and the sun was already scorching. Following one of the mildest New England winters on record, events in and around Boston had reached a boiling point. The stage was set for a grim conflict that would culminate in a scene of devastation. Weeks earlier the doctor had presciently written, "No business but that of war is either done or thought of in this colony."

More than three hundred miles away in Philadelphia, a group of patriot delegates from Massachusetts, including the cousins Samuel and John Adams and the wealthy merchant John Hancock, were attending the Second Continental Congress, which had been in session since May 10. Unsanctioned by the king, this nascent extralegal governing body anxiously awaited news from Warren's dispatchers about the explosive situation in the Bay Colony, where the Whig movement had been resisting Crown policies for over ten years. When Warren sent his trusted messengers, including his close friend and patriot associate Paul Revere, to the congress with information, it was shared and discussed by scores of men with opinions and beliefs as diverse as the colonies from which they hailed. But by the time a response reached the doctor, many days, often weeks, would elapse. Because time was of the essence, Warren had to take decisive action at his discretion. At the peak of his power, he was effectively alone in directing the events unfolding in the Bay Colony.

At this moment Warren was unquestionably the de facto patriot leader in the epicenter of the American rebellion. The United States did not exist in 1775. The colonists were still British subjects under Crown rule, more than a year away from the day John Hancock would boldly write his prominent signature atop the famous document penned by Thomas Jefferson. At that point, George Washington—an inactive colonel of the Virginia Regiment since 1758—had yet to achieve his everlasting glory. *Common Sense,* Thomas Paine's seminal political pamphlet, had yet to be published. Weeks earlier, on May 5, the internationally famed statesman Benjamin Franklin had returned to the colonies after living in Britain for over a decade.

Warren, meanwhile, was one of the most prominent physicians in Massachusetts, a refined and educated gentleman revolutionary blessed with a charismatic personality, good looks, and a keen political acumen. Described as "elegant in his personal appearance . . . and devoted as much to classical studies as professional learning," he was an admired and trusted patriot insider making influential political decisions. And given his deep Yankee lineage, which dated back to the mid-seventeenth century, the doctor had numerous social and familial relationships connecting him to politically diverse groups throughout a Bay Colony that had ruptured into bitterly opposed factions. Paradoxically, for a time, he seemed almost destined to take a leading role on the side of government loyal to the king, given his intimate ties to the most powerful Tory families in Massachusetts—in fact, his medical practice had flourished because of Tory patronage. But he had chosen the path of most resistance, becoming a tireless patriot fighting in what he referred to as the "present struggle for the liberties of America."

As tensions mounted between the king's troops and the Bay Colony populace, strong resentments fueled incidents that directly involved the omnipresent doctor. In fact, Warren's central role in the Boston Massacre, the Boston Tea Party, the Battles of Lexington and Concord, and the Battle of Bunker Hill led one of His Majesty's commanders stationed in the colonies to refer to him as "the famous Dr. Warren, the greatest incendiary in all America." Although he could display the restraint and tact of a consummate statesman in volatile political situations, Warren was also prone to outbursts of rage, spewing venom from his lips, his quill, and his fists. At times, his extreme Whig ideology called for death over submission to the Crown.

With Warren spearheading the patriot resistance and thousands of angry British soldiers spread throughout Boston, Warren's home on Hanover Street was no longer safe for him. Concerned for the safety of his family, he secretly arranged to relocate them to Worcester, a town more than thirty miles away, where they would stay under the care and protection of his friend Dr. Elijah Dix. He insisted that their identities remain anonymous, lest any vengeful mercenary should discover their whereabouts. For close to a decade, Warren's actions had frustrated the British both behind the scenes and in the public eye. But in that first half of 1775, he would help ravage the Crown, draining its purse and crippling the king's forces. By dispatching midnight riders into the countryside on the evening of April 18, 1775, he effectively set off the revolutionary war's first battles, at Lexington and Concord.

Considerably younger than most of his compatriots, and with even more to risk, Warren had refused to leave the environs of Boston, possessing what many called "uncommon firmness in situations of danger." Despite having to care for his family and his medical patients and despite being on the verge of financial ruin, he remained on the front lines, surrounded by danger, and under constant threat of arrest and execution. But once Britain imposed sanctions aimed at punishing the colonists for the Boston Tea Party, Warren began to shift his efforts from resistance to open and armed rebellion. Now ready to attain independence at any cost, Warren wrote to Samuel Adams, "The mistress we court is LIBERTY; and it is better to die than not to obtain her."

As chairman of the Massachusetts Committee of Safety—a provisional body of government in charge of military matters—Warren attended a council of war in Hastings House in Cambridge on June 16, 1775. There, as the patriots of New England prepared for an open battle, he helped devise strategies. While he served as the main leader of the radical Whig faction in Boston, the blurred Rubicon between the two sides was finally crossed.

Before Bunker Hill, Warren's compatriots knew that he intended to fight in the explosive engagement. Despite all their efforts to dissuade him, he remained determined to participate: "The ardor of dear Doctor Warren could not be restrained by the entreaty of his brethren of the Congress." Upon discovering his nomination to the rank of general in the fledgling Provincial Army, one colleague would later confess, "I was sorry when I heard of this appointment; because I thought, a man so much better qualified to act in other capacities than most are, ought not to be exposed in this way, unless in case of necessity. But his zeal hurried him on." News of Warren's fervor stretched beyond his political and military circles to his friends, neighbors, patients, and enemies. And although he was a valuable Whig leader, doctor, and statesman, Warren had decided to cast his fate with that of his countrymen on the most dangerous part of the battlefield—the redoubt on Breed's Hill.

The realization of a separate, even independent America, free from what Whigs viewed as oppressive British imperialist policies, would have been much compromised if the king's troops had plowed to victory that afternoon of June 17. Warren understood that he needed to rally the provincials if the Whig cause of liberty were to endure. So when he received word that British "regulars were landing," though thoroughly exhausted and not having slept for days, he rushed from bed armed with a book of prayers, intelligence reports, and pistols concealed on his waist. The guns were no extravagance: Warren was by now rumored to be a wanted man. The king's troops stationed in the Bay Colony had lambasted him with death threats, even attempting to assault him physically, for he "was well known to their officers, and he could not walk in the streets without being exposed to their insults or sneers."

Wasting no time, Warren exited Hastings House near Harvard Yard. Procuring a horse along the way, he galloped toward Charlestown to fight as "the roar of cannons, mortars, and musquetry" raged around him. The fighting, which had commenced earlier that morning, continued as the king's forces fired upon the provincials throughout the day. Although days earlier appointed the rank of major general by the Massachusetts Committee of Safety, Warren, upon his arrival, declined repeated exhortations from Gen. Israel Putnam to take over his command.

Almost twenty-five years older than Warren, "Old Put" was a short man with a stout build and "a remarkable head of white bushy hair." He had arrived in Boston in August 1774 and stayed with Warren, and the two men had become fast friends. They could not have been more different in demeanor or appearance. A legendary and battle-tested veteran, Putnam had fought heroically for Britain against the French during the Seven Years' War. Without being "adept either at politics or religious canting," the gruff veteran frontiersman seemed "totally unfit for everything but fighting." Just a day earlier the old warrior had stirred the patriots' martial zeal, promising they would "fill hell to-morrow, so full of the redcoats, that the devils will break their shins over them." Like Warren's political comrades, Putnam lamented seeing the doctor so eager and willing to place himself at the center of such a deadly situation. Veteran leaders on both sides knew that the next time their forces clashed, there would be no mercy. Warren had fought the British at Lexington and Concord and in two subsequent skirmishes, and for months he had "spent part of every day in military exercises," but he did not possess the military expertise of the other patriot officers.

What Warren lacked in knowledge of battle tactics, he compensated for with sheer nerve and courage. When the king's troops had scorned the provincials as cowards, an enraged Warren declared, "These fellows say we won't fight: by heavens, I hope I shall die up to my knees in blood!" Believing he was more valuable leading his compatriots on the fields of action than hiding safely behind a desk and a military title, he was eager to get into the thick of action.

Death was no stranger to Warren. He had experienced it up close over the years—first as a boy, later as a doctor and husband, and more recently at Lexington and Concord. He knew well the horror associated with battle, aware that by sunset many bodies would litter the Charlestown peninsula. According to one account, he had decided to place himself "where wounds were to be made, rather than where they were to be healed." He armed himself with his pistols, a musket, and a sword, refusing to leave anything to chance, knowing that a long-distance shooting match could quickly turn into a vicious hand-to-hand brawl. Then, amid incessant British bombardments, he navigated his way up the grassy slope toward Breed's Hill, where patriots had hastily constructed an earthen redoubt and lightly fortified lines earlier that morning.

The officer in charge of the redoubt was Col. William Prescott, who had seen action both in King George's War and in the French and Indian War. He had all the look of a stern and calculating veteran. Like Warren, he had promised to fight to the death if necessary, declaring, "I will never be taken alive. The tories [Crown sympathizers] will never have the satisfaction of seeing me hanged." Some fifteen years older than Warren, the seasoned warrior immediately attempted to subordinate his command, as Putnam had done, but again the doctor refused. Warren assured Prescott that he was there not to interfere or tout his "unofficial" military status but to fight as a volunteer soldier against his country's enemies. But many provincials, especially Prescott, were ready to follow any order or command issued by General Warren—not only the highest-ranking military officer on that field but also the top political and civilian figure present. Surrounded by his compatriots, this was where Warren would make his stand.

To many colonists, armed rebellion remained an unspeakable option in 1775. Most delegates at the Second Continental Congress opposed such a drastic measure, preferring to petition George III in the hopes of reaching an amicable resolution. To take up arms against one's country was high treason, punishable by death. That blistering June afternoon the sharp clap of artillery fire marked the death knell of American loyalty to Britain. The man who had spent most of his adult years saving lives now readied himself to kill as many of the king's soldiers as he could—fellow British subjects, some of whom were his Masonic brethren, patients, business associates, and even friends.

Now leading his patriot brothers, risking everything, a fully armed Joseph Warren stood at Breed's Hill on the precipice of what descended into a bloody civil war and ultimately a global conflict that would last more than eight years. Not only would the clash inflict mass death, torture, disease, famine, rape, and civilian casualties, but the struggle also displaced tens of thousands of the king's loyal subjects, and sowed the seeds of destruction for the Native-American populace, while shattering the hopes of so many African-American slaves, whose dreams of independence remained shackled in the nightmares of human bondage. By day's end on June 17, the Bunker Hill engagement would see more savage fighting and human carnage than any other battle of the American Revolutionary War, presaging the horrors of the prisoner-of-war camps and ships where so many captured soldiers came to wish their end had indeed come on a battlefield. And as the sun set behind Boston's Back Bay, with it forever sank the hopes of any peaceful reconciliation between the colonies and Great Britain. The war had begun.

2

CHILDHOOD HAMLET

"High Waye Towards Roxburie"

JOSEPH WARREN'S RISE FROM THE SON OF A HUMBLE ROXBURY farmer into a powerful gentleman revolutionary has remained buried beneath centuries of historical neglect. Once referred to as the "Lost Town" by many early Bay Colony settlers, Boston—a peninsula surrounded by water on three sides—had, within several decades, overcome its initial tribulations and grown into the most important town in British North America. Cotton Mather, the infamous New England Puritan minister, had at the beginning of the 1700s called Boston "the metropolis of the whole English America."

Settled in 1630, Warren's hometown of Roxbury lay two miles south of Boston and housed six hundred residents across ten thousand acres. Some of the earliest accounts describe Roxbury as a "faire and handsome countrey-towne; being well watered with coole and pleasant springs issuing forth the rocky-hills." As a young boy, Warren would have been able to see, from the top of one of its many hills and peaks, the landscape laid out before him in a sprawling vista, connecting his hometown to the bustling town of Boston. Lush gardens bounded by a harvest of fruit trees and "fruitfull fields" enhanced the town's landscape, while rich natural resources of timber, water, and stone helped pad their coffers. The massive indigenous puddingstone conglomerate rocks were identifiable by distinctly rounded pebbles and remain, to this day, the last relics of the vanished eighteenth-century village. Along these large and numerous pebble-stone streets stood homes, stores, meetinghouses, taverns, and inns, built from stone, lime, wood, and brick. Constables patrolled the town's quiet streets to maintain order after the nine o'clock bells signaled inhabitants to return home. Numerous farms, gardens, orchards, and meadows lent the quaint New England town a rustic and bucolic atmosphere. Much of Boston's ice supply came from Roxbury's vast array of brooks, streams, ponds, and lakes, and the town's large wooded areas also provided much material for shipbuilding, home construction, and barrel furniture making.

Roxbury connected peninsular Boston to the mainland via a mile-long, forty-yard-wide isthmus called Boston Neck, which stood above numerous marshes and mud flats. In the early eighteenth century, long before Back Bay and South Boston were filled in, Boston was virtually an island, like Manhattan. The Neck, a land bridge stretching across the harbor at the town's south end, was the only connection to the mainland. To reach Boston by foot or cart, travelers had to pass through Roxbury to cross the Neck.

Rows of majestic elm trees lined the neck's sides, as well as several houses and barns, including a "Wind-Mill." During high tide and storms, the Neck was often submerged, making the passage treacherous and occasionally deadly. A narrow wooden gate, which some called the Fortification Gates, kept out undesirables and dangerous wild animals.

The only other regular entry to Boston was from the north via the Charlestown ferry. Both points of access loomed ominously, as the Neck featured a large hangman's gallows where many public executions had occurred over the years. West of the center of Charlestown on the road headed to the ferry, a large iron cage had been placed, which at one time held the decomposing skeleton of a slave who had poisoned his owner—reminders that the "city upon a hill" had a draconian side, rife with slavery, violence, and harsh punishments under the strict rule of law.

Violence was a familiar part of New England culture. Executions had a long and vivid history in the Bay Colony—and Boston's many newspapers published accounts of departed souls executed at the Tyburn gallows in London. Boston's own pillories, stocks, gallows, whipping posts, and branding irons were well worn, stained by the blood and tears of thieves, murderers, Sabbath-breakers, runaway slaves, and practitioners of bestiality, whose punishments particularly animated the crowd. The punishments inflicted were excruciating, including ear cropping, branding, and being "severely pelted by the populace." Slaves were often put to death. Often during such ghastly spectacles only the toll of church bells could drown "the screams of the culprit and the uproar of the mob."

Slavery in New England was less rampant than in the South and comprised only part of an economy that revolved primarily around rum, molasses, and sugar, but the slave trade was still booming. Advertisements announcing the sale of slaves appeared regularly in Massachusetts newspapers, while other notices offered the enslaved free of charge: "A likely, healthy Negro child, a week old, to be given away." Boston in particular "was preeminent as the port of departure for slave ships," as chattel slavery dated back to the late 1630s. Thus, it should come as no surprise that the "peculiar institution" pervaded the Warren household. The family owned two slaves, "One old Negro Man Servt and young Negro Girl."

Built in 1720, the Warrens' three-story Roxbury home stood on Braintree road and was described as beautiful with "many fine fruit trees round it." The property sprawled across acres of pastures, orchards, fields, swamplands, and salt marshes. (Used for salt hay, salt marsh acreage was deemed more valuable than that of pasturage or woodland.) It had a large wooden barn, which the family referred to as the "great barn," and a smaller barn, a "cyder millhouse," as well as a large well and several outhouses. Scores of apple trees stretched atop land that had a rich soil "in a very high state of cultivation."

Warren's father, Joseph Warren, had married Mary Stevens—who, at twenty-seven, was more than fifteen years younger than her husband—in the spring of 1740 and they began their new life together in their picturesque house. They soon expanded the property by purchasing sixteen acres of land from Mary's father, Capt. Samuel Stevens. And just over a year later, on June 11, 1741, they welcomed the first of their four sons, Joseph Warren.

Raised on the farm, where the lessons of industry and honest labor were taught by example and preached almost as much as the Bible, the future revolutionary came from a hard-working household. His father was a town selectman (a member of the local government board) and farmer who grew Warren russet apples, one of the United States' oldest apple varieties, dating as far back as 1649. First cultivated by Warren's American ancestors, the namesake apples are indigenous to Roxbury. At the height of the apple harvest in October, young Warren helped gather his father's russets, sold them at the market, and packed the rest in straw to preserve in their cellar. Later those apples were used for cooking or made into applesauce, apple butter, and barrels of hard cider, which many preferred to water due to the risk of cholera and typhoid. (Warren and his younger brothers typically drank milk and "small beer," a beverage made with malt that had a souplike texture; it was essentially water that contained small amounts of alcohol, which made it safer to drink.) Besides apples, eggs and milk were sold at the market, as were dairy and cheese.

Warren's humble beginnings forced him to work long, hard hours of intense manual labor. As a boy, he assisted his father with farm chores. Given the frigid New England temperatures, Warren would have been tasked with keeping firewood stockpiled for the house. He also passed many days hunting in the woods and fishing in the

120-acre pond near his home. The port of Boston was another spot where Warren could catch a variety of fish, oysters, clams, turtles, and other delicacies.

Within the densely wooded areas of Roxbury, Warren went after small game like rabbits and birds and preserved his catches by salting, smoking, and drying them; if the hunting went poorly, the various animals on the farm could provide extra sustenance. Butchering usually commenced in late fall, when the cold weather would prevent the large quantities of meat from rotting. Much work was involved in the killing of a large animal, since every part served a purpose—from pigs, for example, the family obtained sausage, lard for piecrusts, and headcheese. Chickens and turkeys were immediately roasted or made into pies.

In the warmer months, the Warrens kept a large garden where they grew a variety of vegetables and herbs, some for medicinal purposes. What they could not grow was available for purchase at locales like the "Sign of the Wheat-Sheaff" in Boston, where John Townley sold everything from "Dutch lettice" and "speckled dwarf French beans" to "white mustard" and "purple broccoli." Spices were expensive and therefore usually tucked away under lock and key. The Warrens did most cooking in pots, kettles, and skillets over the large open fireplace in the kitchen, which helped keep the house warm during the unforgiving winter. When the chill was extreme, Warren and his family would have slept together in close quarters since all fireplaces were usually extinguished at bedtime to prevent house fires and conserve firewood.

In towns outside Boston like Roxbury, industrious farmers like Warren's father sold their goods at the markets held every Thursday. Citizens of Boston would occasionally rush to the Neck at sunrise to buy the freshest products at the best prices directly from the farmers. More often, Warren and his father would have crossed the Neck and traveled the Old Boston Post Road, passing the whipping posts and stocks into the town center, where farmers converged to barter and sell their products in the cash-strapped economy, battling competition from "hucksters." Not only farmers but numerous shops, warehouses, and private houses persisted in buying, selling, and trading goods even during extreme weather. During the snowy winters, farmers used sleds to transport their wares. For many families like the Warrens, income from the market was a necessity.

Years after Warren's death, the rabid Tory Peter Oliver condescendingly recollected that Warren as a child had been a "bare legged milk boy to furnish the Boston market." The barb, aimed at the family's lesser economic status, also suggested the family could not afford to clothe him properly. But although far from Boston's wealthiest man, the patriarch of the Warren household never had to worry about the constable coming to haul him off "to his majesty's gaol in Boston" for failing to pay his debts. A proud, God-fearing farmer, Warren senior would likely have been categorized as part of the "middling sort": farmers, laborers, and artisans who enjoyed a station in life above the lower rungs of society, but far below men of high standing possessed of real wealth and power.

Still, Joseph Warren was schooled to adapt, survive, and thrive outside the classroom prior to his formal education. Learning to work these markets with his father shaped his character, instilling in him skills that would ultimately prove valuable to the rebellion.

Joseph and his family made occasional trips to what is now Foxborough, Massachusetts, to visit his mother's relatives. Closer to home, Warren would often venture into the busy port of Boston, where he commenced his lifelong love affair with the seaside town. There in the harbor with "every ship, sloop, schooner, and brigantine" huddled together among the wharfs, shipyards, distilleries, brothels, taverns, and warehouses, the curious boy would explore the shipping center. With no sidewalks, Boston's winding, narrow streets were crowded with horses and other beasts of burden, carts, coaches, chaises, and carriages.

Boston was more cosmopolitan than most of its surrounding New England towns. Up and down the labyrinthine thoroughfares, Warren and his father would have been greeted by rows of colorful wooden trade signs and the acrid scents of the day's catch, as well as fermenting ales and breads, wafting along the salt air. In scores of taverns huddled beneath Boston's spires, one could find solace in both spirits and spiritualism. The thick smells of wood-burning fires, tobacco smoked in clay pipes, and ripe New England soil drenched this town by the sea in an amalgam of indigenous odors.

In addition to the occasional processions and military musters that took place in Boston, days of prayer and fasting were held—fundamental parts of the town's evolving culture. Bells tolled and cannons fired when Bostonians rejoiced in monarchical celebrations, and violent processions such as Pope's Day (or Guy Fawkes Day, as it was called in England) wreaked havoc every November 5. With a population upward of fifteen thousand, the commercial town gave young Warren firsthand exposure to the day's various social, political, and economic happenings.

On the way home from the bustling seaport, the Warrens would traverse the meandering lanes of Marlborough and Orange Streets on the "High Waye Towards Roxburie." The dark roads and alleys of Boston were illuminated by torches that blazed along the wharves, offering ships a welcome beacon as they approached from the sea, along with the occasional displays of "bonfires, squibs, [and] rockets" that sometimes lit the town's roads and alleys. Though felled trees, heavy snow, and inclement weather could seriously damage the travel routes, the roads in Roxbury were well maintained as repairs were often paid by a town-imposed tax, or a public lottery like the one the town held in 1759 to raise funds "for paving the Publick High-Way from Boston line to the foot of the Meeting-House Hill in Roxbury," where in 1740 an enormous bear had been killed. At night, when Joseph returned to the farm, the Warrens' quaint home was cast aglow by a roaring fire, tallow and beeswax candles, lamps fueled by "Refin'd Sperma Ceti" oil, and perhaps even an inexpensive and primitive "rush light" derived from the rush stalks from nearby ponds and lakes.

Young Joseph Warren saw much on the bustling streets of Boston, but he also had learning opportunities back home. In Roxbury, the popular Grey Hound Tavern on Washington Street served as the community's social hub. Although towns similar in size to Roxbury had more than one tavern, Roxbury natives patronized the Grey Hound to discuss politics and current events, gossip, eat, drink, and shop. The owner, John Greaton, sold writing paper, tobacco, and newspapers to tavern patrons. In an area in the rear of the structure, near the necessary house, patrons could have engaged in dogfights, cockfights, boxing bouts, and wrestling matches. Visitors could join in the revelry of dancing, music, and gambling or play card and board games. The Grey Hound—and taverns in general—also hosted lectures, club meetings, subscription balls, art exhibits, slave and estate auctions, and even the sale of lottery tickets. Every Thursday in May 1764, Mr. Greaton's tavern was where the "constables and collectors of Taxes for the County of Suffolk . . . receive the Money due to the county." The tavern had even exhibited a catamount in 1741.

If all of that failed to entice a passerby, the Grey Hound was "a favorite resort for sleighing parties in the winter where good cheer was afforded for man and beast," since taverns also served as beacons for weary travelers in search of lodging and provided stables to accommodate horses. By the mid-eighteenth century, taverns like the Grey Hound had become important sociopolitical centers of discourse and learning. In Boston, when courts were in session or when other local events transpired, an amalgam of social classes converged in the taverns. Taverns offered basic mail services and books and pamphlets to read, and people could post advertisements and notices on its walls announcing upcoming sales, rewards for lost or stolen items— including runaway slaves, servants, and animals—and general news and events. In the fall of 1756, "a small trotting horse" had "strayed from Mrs. Warren's pasture," and Mary Warren posted a three-dollar reward for its safe return.

In addition to the meetinghouses, these community hubs regularly exposed Warren to the political events of the day. More importantly, he came to see how crucial taverns were as gathering places where events could be organized for people from all walks of life. Ultimately, Warren helped transform many New England taverns into the nerve centers for rebellion and revolutionary activity.

One issue that was on the lips of taverngoers during Warren's youth was New England's changing economic conditions. As a boy, Warren would have witnessed how politics and government could personally strike at family. The economic strife afflicting Massachusetts contributed to the bitter political rivalries that eventually led to the patriot revolt. The chronic shortage of specie made debt an increasing problem for many cash-strapped farmers and artisans, who sank under the weight of an elite merchant class. In the late 1730s, a group of men had sought to revive the economy by creating a Land Bank, to issue paper money backed by land instead of scarce coin. The Land Bank garnered much support but was opposed by the powerful and wealthy, who sought to continue their own dominance over the economy. Among the opponents were many merchants as well as Massachusetts royal governor Jonathon Belcher, who reached out to Parliament for assistance in dissolving the Land Bank "scheme," "conspiracy," and "dangerous affair." Sworn affidavits claimed that upward of twenty thousand men from the country were planning to join more than one thousand men in Boston in an uprising against merchants. (The scenario would ultimately play out years later, on April 19, 1775, but against the king's troops.) In response, arrest warrants were issued against several men "concerned in a design and combination with a number of evil-minded persons to come into the town of Boston in a tumultuous manner, tending to the disturbance and disquiet of the Government and affright and terror of His Majesty's good subjects, and against the King's peace and dignity."

The governor issued a proclamation warning government-appointed officials, justices of the peace, members of the House, and militia leaders "not to sign or give encouragement to passing of said notes" and promised to dismiss anyone who disobeyed. One of the first to resign his Crown-appointed commission, in November 1740, was a principal founder of the Land Bank—Samuel Adams's father, Deacon Adams. While hundreds of men and their respective families became mired in Land Bank debt, having to pay off their devalued notes, two of those most afflicted were the Deacon and Dr. Samuel

Stevens, Mary Warren's father. In order to pay off the Land Bank debt he had incurred, Stevens was forced to sell "several rights of land in Winchester, and in several other towns," in addition to "several yoke of oxen . . . a number of cows and heifers, and five or six horses." For the distressed Stevens, the controversy would rage for decades, taking a toll on his finances and his family. Hounded by numerous suits, he and other Land Bank partners, debtors, and sheriffs saw the consequences pass down to some of their children.

While Mary Warren likely never became directly involved in the suits, the Land Bank controversy struck a personal chord within the Warren family. Given the magnitude and residual issues of the problem, many came to harbor bitter resentment against Parliament's intervention, which had sealed the Land Bank's fate. Mary's father, Samuel Stevens, was no exception. For more than twenty years, his numerous pleas for help to the court underscored his desperation and disgust: "Petition of Samuel Stevens . . . complaining of the cruel exactions made upon him for the Land-Bank notes, by which he is in danger of being utterly ruined, and praying for relief." The controversy had such long, deleterious effects on Warren's kinfolk that young Joseph, like Samuel Adams and many others, came to question Parliament's long reach into the colonists' local affairs and pockets. The class lines being drawn were mirrored by a surging political divisiveness. The rifts that would eventually rend Britain's overseas empire started to form deep within New England's bedrock—in particular, in Warren's backyard.

Beyond the Land Bank dispute, Warren and his family were no strangers to fights against oppression and discord. Several generations earlier, in the late seventeenth century, Warren's great-grandfather, Robert Calef, a merchant and clothier, had taken an unpopular stand against the witch hysteria plaguing Salem, ultimately publishing a book, *More Wonders of the Invisible World*. Since the religious Mather family was so powerful in Massachusetts, no publisher would dare print Calef's "heresy," forcing him to seek publication in England. But Calef's work helped stymie Cotton Mather's attempts to launch a sequel to the barbaric Salem witch hunts in Boston. Reverend Mather was so incensed with Calef that he spearheaded efforts to have him arrested: Increase Mather—Harvard's president and Cotton's father—was so enraged that he burned a copy of Calef's book in the college yard. That Calef had taken on one of the colony's most influential families was a testament to Joseph Warren's courage and moral principles— traits that Mary Warren helped instill in her firstborn son.

Warren's father, the pious, well-respected selectman and industrious farmer, insisted his four sons—he had no daughters—receive the best possible education in political thought, literature, and religious fervor. All were afforded the opportunity to attend school. Joseph probably learned to play the fiddle or violin, as was the custom for many young men during the colonial period; cultural refinement in music and dancing was second only to religious instruction.

The senior Warren had "studied the scriptures with great zeal, and impressed upon his children a deep love and veneration for the Bible." For close to two decades, he served as precinct treasurer of the First Church in Roxbury, and in 1736 he was part of the church committee that formulated a proposal to build a new meetinghouse. Upon completion of the new church in the summer of 1741, just after the birth of his son Joseph, he purchased one of the more expensive pews for just over thirty pounds and within close proximity to the more costly pew just acquired by his new father-in-law, Capt. Samuel Stevens.

Meanwhile, outside church walls and pews, an intense religious revival, the First Great Awakening, was raging along the eastern seaboard. In the 1730s and '40s, preachers like Jonathan Edwards and George Whitefield scorched the environs of Boston with their fire and brimstone sermonizing. Edwards, influenced by the writings of the Enlightenment philosopher John Locke, modified the principles of Calvinist doctrine, which claimed that God predestined the salvation of people regardless of their actions in life. Whitefield stressed the need for personal piety against the rationalism that he believed had corrupted Congregationalism in New England. With a view of God less austere, he preached about an individual's direct relationship to God and thereby instilled a new sense of hope in his audiences.

This evangelical revivalism helped restructure the institutional hierarchy of Calvinist denominations. Thousands flocked to hear these charismatic messengers of God preach from outdoor pulpits, where class structure and expensive pews were absent. These skilled orators evoked impassioned responses from their spiritually hungry audiences, creating a more personal religious experience for many worshippers. Since religion was the central cultural force of the time, such intense emotional notions helped test the limits of imperial authority and became ingrained within an inherently insurgent New England civilization, contributing significantly to the political and social reforms that took place in the 1760s and '70s.

The print culture in the colonies was expanding broadly, so during the Great Awakening, writings and sermons from itinerant preachers, such as Edwards's *A Faithful Narrative*, were published, as well as numerous works from the colonial clergy, helping to shape public discourse. Some of Boston's church elders became not only powerful spiritual leaders but also influential patriots. Joseph Warren's future pastor, Dr. Samuel Cooper, would become a strong advocate and supporter of the Whig agenda. In 1740, Whitefield had preached to thousands of New Englanders at Reverend William Cooper's Congregationalist church. (Samuel Cooper succeded his father's pulpit in 1746.) Following the American Revolution, one Tory pejoratively referred to some of Boston's clergymen as the "black regiment" because of their radical patriot leanings.

The patriarch of the Warren household was by all accounts an extremely pious man, even by strict Puritan standards. Some of the volumes in his library included Philip Doddridge's *Rise and Progress of Religion in the Soul of Man* and Samuel Willard's *Body of Divinity*, two particularly religious books, as well as "other good divinity books." Over the years, he had accumulated an extensive collection, even spending upward of ten pounds on Latin books for his eldest son Joseph. Books in colonial America were also an expression of one's financial and intellectual wealth—the larger the library, the greater the social standing within the community. In the evening, Joseph Warren would often sit and listen to his father recite the word of God, inheriting the "Old Puritan hatred of injustice in any form." Mary Warren's family also adhered to "the diligent study of the scriptures," which "were rigidly practiced and enforced." Warren's devotion to the scriptures stayed with him throughout his brief life, as he was "said to have possessed a knowledge of their contents that was unsurpassed." Both his parents' "principles were Calvinistic," and Joseph Warren inculcated in him a "strong hatred of oppression."

Warren's father's influence extended past Bible study. According to one Warren descendant and family biographer, the father—he was about forty-five when his son was born—once told Joseph, "I would rather a son of mine dead than a coward," a statement that might have influenced him to fight at Bunker Hill. Warren was said to have "told a younger brother that the recollection of that conversation, particularly the last sentiment in it expressed by his long departed father, thrilled in his memory and incited him to action." Over the years, Warren never strayed far from his humble roots; nor did he ever forget the valuable lessons he learned from his father. Although he would become one of Boston's elite sons, he would never become an elitist.

3

THE HARVARD YEARS

"Being Possessed of a Genius which promised Distinction."
—PETER OLIVER
(CIRCA 1781, IN REFERENCE TO WARREN)

IN THE STRATIFIED SOCIETY OF EIGHTEENTH-CENTURY PURITAN New England, a young boy who aspired to become a respected gentleman scholar would need a formal college education. Harvard College was well over a century old by the time Joseph Warren was eligible to attend the oldest institution of learning in all of British North America, and it was one of the few places where a young man with a modest family background could, through hard work and determination, elbow his way out of mediocrity. Realizing their eldest son's potential, both of Warren's parents sought to give him that opportunity.

Warren's parents had always been strong advocates of education, and in 1751, when he was around ten, they sent him to Roxbury Latin School, which stood less than a quarter mile from the family property—close enough for a young Warren to hear the school's "good handsome bell" resonate every day throughout his childhood. Several years before he attended, the tiny one-room schoolhouse, where lottery drawings occasionally took place, had fallen into disrepair, then been rebuilt.

Modeled after the grammar schools of Elizabethan England, Roxbury Latin prided itself on providing a high level of scholastic instruction in the humanities and religion. (Literacy rates were actually higher in Boston than in Britain.) Such education had been built into the school at its creation; religion in Massachusetts played an integral role in every aspect of colonial life, and schools were no exception. Beginning in 1642, in the battle against Satan's plot to deceive men by keeping them "from the knowledge of the Scriptures," Massachusetts required towns to establish schools to teach boys to read and write in order to learn the laws of God and country. And so in 1645, under a charter granted by Charles I of England, the Roxbury school was founded by the Rev. John Eliot, a pious man with "a cheerfull spirit . . . apt to teach . . . the knowledge of God in Christ." The school's charter explains that "the inhabitants of Roxburie out of their religious care of posteritie have taken into consideration how necessarie the education of their children in literature wil[l] be, to fitt them for publicke service both in Church and Commonwealth in succeeding ages."

Warren attended Roxbury Latin for four years, preparing for college. He surely knew it was a rare opportunity, and that expectations regarding his success were high. He was determined not to disappoint, assisting the schoolmaster with small repairs and necessary chores like carting wood without complaint, particularly when punishing snowstorms blanketed the town.

Roxbury Latin was a feeder institution to Harvard, and it prepped and drilled its students accordingly. One of Warren's assigned texts was the 1720 *English and Latine Exercises for School Boys*, on how to write and speak Latin. William Cushing, a future U.S. Supreme Court justice, instructed Warren. Other teachers would later become Revolutionary Whigs or Loyalist Tories, exposing Joseph from an early age to a diverse group of educated men. That and the school's strict religious instruction prepared him for the day he would apply to the college.

Four years at Roxbury Latin made him well versed in religion, the classics, and the rules of grammar.

Admission to Harvard required a series of tests, mostly oral. Examination dates were posted in the local newspapers. After Warren's graduation from Roxbury Latin in 1755, the formal announcement appeared in the June 30 issue of the *Boston Gazette*: "Notice is hereby given to all who desire an admission into Harvard-College this year, That the president and tutors have determin'd to attend the business of examination on the eighteenth and nineteenth of July next."

In July, the normally placid town of Cambridge was bustling with preparations for Harvard's annual commencement ceremonies; among those graduating was John Adams. Given the Bay Colony's dearth of social holidays, commencement was one of its largest celebratory events. Reverent town elders decried the festivities as a wild bacchanalia, but throngs from all over New England attended, usually overindulging in gambling, eating, dancing, drinking, and other revelries. Various pious stewards railed against "the prophaness of some of the public disputes on . . . Commencement Day," as the Puritan society of New England considered such celebrations anathema. Yet this institutional rite of passage was also a revered tradition that recognized the next group of young men set to fill leadership roles within the community.

Approximately two hundred families lived in Cambridge, an old-fashioned town described by one of Warren's schoolmates as "mountainous, yet fruitful . . . [with] two ponds in town; one of them above three miles in circumference, and famous for the abundance of fish that are catched in it," along with "the longest row of elm trees in New England, set in exact order, and leading directly toward the meeting-house." One farm of around seventy-five acres boasted a fine apple orchard, much mowing land, numerous stone fences, and "a handsome well-finished house . . . fit for a gentleman." When the ponds froze over during the winter, students would skate and even dine on the ice.

To take part in the admissions exams, Warren likely made the five-mile trip from Roxbury to Harvard on horseback. Realizing the importance of appearance, particularly for the son of a farmer, he arrived outfitted in his finest cotton and silk garments, a wig, a pair of leather shoes, and knee breeches. We can imagine the nervous youth making his way into the hushed and shadowy exam room. On July 18 he presented himself to the faculty to be "examined before the tutors," who tested his ability to write and translate Greek and Latin authors, as well as his knowledge of the "rules of grammar."

The following day Warren stood before Harvard's imposing president, Edward Holyoke. Dressed in his black robe and his long curly white peruke, the aging sage in the Jacobean chair possibly gripped the circular oak pommels that he had personally made and affixed to his "bizarre throne." Although quite portly, he was also described as having "a noble commanding presence." For almost two decades, he presided over the entrance exams, testing hundreds of aspiring scholars, who promptly returned the favor by nicknaming him "Guts." He would have scrutinized Warren to see whether he "hath a good moral character." He did—he passed all the exams, obtained his copy of the College Laws from the steward, and presented it to Holyoke "to have his admittatur signed."

Upon his return to Roxbury, Warren must have felt as John Adams had four years earlier: "I was as light when I came home, as I had been heavy when I went." Undoubtedly, Warren's proud parents rejoiced upon hearing the good news. The embittered Tory, Chief Justice Peter Oliver, later declared of Warren, "Being possessed of a genius which promised distinction, either in virtue or vice, his friends educated him at the college in Cambridge, to take his chance of being a curse or a blessing to his country." Unknown to the young scholar, his experiences at Harvard would not only shape his own life but also alter the destiny of a fledgling nation.

Joseph Warren began his first term at Harvard in mid-August 1755: at fourteen, he was one of the youngest boys in his freshman class. In socioeconomic standing, he ranked thirty-first in the class of forty-five entering freshmen. Highly stratified, like eighteenth-century colonial society generally, Harvard's system placed a premium on wealth and prestige and ranked freshmen accordingly. (At the top of the freshman ranks that year was the son of Connecticut governor Jonathan Trumbull.) For a farm boy on the bottom tier, the prospect of moving up based on merit was unlikely. A student's ranking centered primarily on the standing of his parents and little else.

A student could move up in rank if new information came to light. On June 10, 1755, Harvard staff noted that "Pollocks place in his class changed" as "we had not then been inform'd of the state and condition of his family, He coming to us from a distant province. . . . But being now satisfied . . . he ought to have a place in his class, superior to what we then assigned him."

Conversely, a student could move down—the more common practice. If a student fell from the good graces of the faculty for poor behavior, his rank was lowered. Sometime before Warren entered, Jedediah Foster had been fined and demoted four places for "contriving and abetting the firing of squibs in the college yard" while celebrating Pope's Day. One of Warren's classmates, Benjamin Hobbs, was downgraded eight spots on the freshman list of 1756 for "throwing bricks" inside "the door of the Hebrew School."

Those at the top of Harvard's system enjoyed access to the finest privileges the school had to offer, including the best accommodations and food. After ranking of the entering freshmen was completed, disappointed young men who believed their low ranking unjust naturally felt resentful. Given Warren's upbringing, the ranking system likely weighed upon his sense of fairness.

Ranked near the bottom of the social scale and younger than almost all his classmates, Warren was a prime target of hazing from upperclassmen. At the start of the term, the nervous freshmen "cubs" were taken to the school's Long Chamber to listen to their older fellows dictate the College Customs, a list of expected submissive behaviors—and were threatened with harsh punishments if they failed to obey.

In this "system of freshman servitude," every senior scholar subjected the new students to a variety of mistreatments and chores. The "cubs" had to run errands and make obsequious gestures toward their superiors. A typical freshman would attach himself to a senior student and serve him exclusively, in exchange for protection against the abuses of others. And like all the students, they had to perform compulsory maintenance work on Harvard's surrounding grounds.

Between studying, performing physical labor, and placating the whims of their elder classmen, adjusting freshmen had little time for diversion. Their schoolday began at six in the morning, when Holyoke delivered the usual soporific prayers in Holden Chapel. Warren must have felt at home listening to Harvard's president, as he had when his father had preached in his childhood home. Warren would then take breakfast from the Buttery hatch, usually bread, a warm beverage, and milk or beer, consuming it in the yard or in his chamber. Harvard tutors lived at the college and lectured between eight and noon. When students were not in classes, they spent time at the "play place," located where College Yard now lies.

After lectures, dinner was served in the Commons Hall, between one and three in the afternoon. It usually consisted of roasted or boiled meats, puddings, and "a cue of beer." According to one Harvard historian, the school had "a reputation for poor food that clung to it for more than two centuries," leading to a number of school "food rebellions" over the years. For Warren, this aspect of college life was challenging since Mary Warren was an excellent cook, particularly known for her savory pies. Every time Warren visited the family farm, his mother likely loaded him with extra victuals that she had prepared.

Harvard in the mid-1700s was a small college consisting of four brick buildings, a chapel, and fewer than ten faculty members. The Commons Hall, in the center of the first floor, had "the buttery in the front right-hand corner, with the kitchen behind it." Modeled on the Commons Hall at Cambridge University in England, the hall at Harvard, although considerably smaller, stood four stories and featured high ceilings, intricate woodwork, large windows, and a stone-paved floor. Large oil paintings of the King and Queen of England looked down on their subjects—a constant reminder of royal suzerainty. Students often complained about "the chilling dampness that reigns through the room."

The space served not only as a dining hall but also as a lecture room and chapel. Each table accommodated ten students, who sat with their class according to social rank. The elite sat first and received the best food portions. Tutors, graduate students, and wealthy undergraduates paid double tuition for the privilege of sitting at a "high table," where they supervised meal activities. Warren sat "at the lower table," where fellow students served as the four waiters. Students' names were written on a placard "in a large German text, in a handsome style, and placed in a conspicuous part of the College Buttery." Warren, like all the freshmen, "paid the steward a shilling to have his name posted in the buttery. . . . His order in the list of names on the 'buttery table' [bulletin board] . . . determined the student's precedence through college, and even in the catalogue of graduates."

Regardless of class rank, all students were subject to Harvard's imperfections and even its seedy aspects. Harvard in the eighteenth century was much different from the institution today. Lacking many basic amenities, the school was far from sanitary. Students brought their own knives and forks to Common Hall, cleaning them and their mouths using the tablecloth at the end of the meal. Cider was consumed from "a common can passed from mouth to mouth." Meals were served on pewter plates (which later, along with much of the lead in Boston, would be melted and used for ammunition by the Continental Army). Students ate wearing mittens and, by meal's end, the stone floor was usually strewn with remnants of the repast. Leftovers got taken outside and tossed into "a vast pigstye" at the rear of the hall, where pigs and rats fought over them. Cleaned but "once a quarter," the hall was by most accounts quite unsanitary.

Students supplemented meals by hunting and fishing. In the spring of 1758, one of Warren's friends wrote of their food-seeking forays, "Went a gunning after Robins . . . went fishing with 13 of my Class mates . . . catch'd 3 cods besides dog fish skates and Sculpins." Even with this supplementation, however, Warren accumulated a debt for his victuals, owing close to one hundred pounds for "dyat from May 1757 to July 6 1759"—a debt that remained unpaid for decades.

Students were allowed two hours of personal recreation, followed by study time in their chambers. Then came supper, a much lighter evening meal consisting usually of leftover meats made into a pie and served with bread. At sunset, candles illuminated Holden Chapel's interior, and President Holyoke commenced the evening prayers. The butler rang the evening bells, marking the moment when students were to "retire to their chambers, and not unnecessarily leave them." Warren and his classmates would often meet in their chambers to study, argue about politics, discuss the war with France, and share gossip.

Many scholars, instead of changing into a "gown" to retire, filled their nights with extracurricular activities. Even in Puritan Bay Colony society, Harvard's elite students dabbled in vices, consuming massive amounts of alcohol. Beer and certain wines were staples, but the alcoholic punch concoctions made by the students in college yard, like "flip" and "negus," became particularly troublesome to the college faculty. Evidently consumption of punch was so uncontrollable that the year of Warren's graduation, the board of overseers gave up and recommended repealing "the law prohibiting the drink of punch." Students would travel to other towns to acquire libations, as noted in the diary of Warren's friend Samuel Gardner: "My chum went to Newton to get cyder," but there were "no bottles to be had."

Another favored nighttime activity was gambling, which the faculty deemed a serious offense. Fines and physical punishments were meted out for initial infractions followed by more stringent sanctions for repeat offenders: "If any resident graduate shall play at cards or dice . . . he shall not be allowed to continue any longer at the college." During Warren's first year, the day after Christmas, President Holyoke and the tutors compiled a list of "scholars . . . guilty of playing at cards" whom they summarily punished. Seventy-eight students, representing every class, received fines. Warren played no part in the gambling, nor was he fined or punished, but fourteen of his classmates were.

Beyond their dormitories, students pursued illicit pleasures. Whoring seems to have been a favorite pastime with students who covertly dabbled as part-time degenerates. Various taverns in Cambridge were "marts of luxury, intemperance, and ruin" where one could drink, gamble, and enjoy the company of loose women. At a tavern along the road to Charlestown, women offered themselves to anyone willing to pay for the service. Some students likely made their way to other seedy haunts where they could choose from an array of prostitutes. Nor was it unheard of for women of ill fame to provide fleeting trysts in the Harvard dorm rooms.

Students rarely missed the opportunity to leave campus to view the public executions and torturous punishments sanctioned by the court—all part of a culture deeply rooted in violence. Within weeks of Warren's enrollment at Harvard in September 1755, two slaves, Mark and Phillis, were executed in Cambridge for killing their master with poison. Mark was hanged, his corpse tarred and "brought down to Charlestown Common, and hanged in Chains on a Gibbet erected there for that purpose," where it remained for the next two decades. Phillis was burned alive at a stake near the gallows. The gruesome executions were "attended by the greatest number of spectators ever known on such an Occasion." A Boston man made the journey to witness the spectacle, noting the event in his diary simply as "Mark hanged and Phillis burnt."

During Warren's sophomore year, in the spring of 1757, a man was publicly put to death in Cambridge for a murder he had committed the year before. Benjamin Edes and John Gill (Warren's future patriot comrades) printed broadsides for the execution titled *The Last Words and Dying Speech of John Harrington* and sold them next to the prison. Near the gallows in Cambridge stood Porter's Tavern, where patrons flocked on execution days for additional entertainment. Public exhibits of barbarity were sensationalized and showcased, and many students and townsfolk, including Warren, viewed the morbid spectacles. Cambridge came to be known both for education and for violence, as satirized in verse: "Cambridge is a famous town, Both for wit and knowledge, Some they whip and some they hang, And some they send to College."

Some youths were known to run through Harvard Yard making "indecent tumultuous noises" of "hollowing" and "Huzzas," even hurling "brickbats through tutors' windows." Other students raced horses right on Harvard Common, in one instance precipitating a riot. In 1760 John Adams, just a few years after his own graduation, worried about the evils of tavern life and "the trifling, nasty vicious crew, that frequent them," declaring "young people are tempted to waste their time and money, and to acquire habits of intemperence and idleness that we often see reduce many of them to beggary, and vice and lead some of them at last to prisons and the gallows."

On campus, transgressions ranged from tardiness and absence to "blasphemy, fornication, robbery, forgery," or "any other very atrocious crime." These infractions were punishable financially or in extreme cases by expulsion. A student who failed to pay a fine was "admonished, degraded, suspended or rusticated, according" to the "nature and degree of the offense." Harvard's president, professors, and tutors could mete out justice in the form of "boxing," the successor punishment to whipping, which consisted of striking the offender on the side of the head as he knelt. A student deemed guilty by the faculty was also required to make a public confession in the chapel.

Throughout his years at Harvard, Warren's only noted infractions were absences beyond the allotted time allowed under the rules, for which he was fined. He was either clever at eluding school authorities or more focused on his studies and his family obligations in Roxbury. Harvard officials recorded some antics: on the last day of the school quarter, Warren and his fellow scholars celebrated by repeatedly "tossing [one] another in a blanket." The faculty promptly put an end to it, warning that any scholar "guilty of, or any way accessory to" such action would face stiff punishment.

A few sources, however, portrayed Warren as an audacious prankster. According to one newspaper, "Some of his college exploits are related, in an old book printed in 1778, with apparent glee by the writer." The colorful stories indicate college mischiefs typical of the mid-eighteenth century: "All the shaving cups, and other pieces of crockery-ware adorned by handles were frequently gathered together by Warren, tied in a bunch, and hanged over the door of the principal professor's room in such a manner that when that personage sought egress the suspended articles would come clattering to the ground, disturbing and alarming, with the horrid din, the whole college population." Supposedly when Warren was not nailing his roommates' shoes to the floorboards, he was placing frogs in his friends' pockets. And on more than one occasion, the young scholar "would get out of the building at forbidden hours, by tying the sheets, in the dormitories, together, and thus making a rope by which he could (with his companions) get through a window and reach the ground unharmed. The Chambermaid was bribed to say nothing about the knots and wrinkles in the linen under her charge."

Fifty years after the fact, one Harvard alumnus recounted an even more daring episode. A group of students locked themselves in a room on a top floor, for actions that they wished to keep secret from a disapproving Warren. Warren climbed to the roof nearby, slid down an old wooden rainspout, and climbed into the room through an open window. As he got to his feet, the rotted spout crashed several stories to the ground below. He stoically remarked to his astonished classmates that the collapsed spout had been useful. Evidently in 1807, the story's author retold the event with so much fervor, animation, and detail that the listener who wrote it down had little doubt as to its veracity. While the tale's authenticity remains in question, it suggests Warren's daring personality.

MOST OF WARREN'S ENTERING FRESHMEN CLASSMATES WERE AWAY from home for the first time in their lives and looked forward to any opportunity to return home. Students received four different vacations during the school year. The first came four weeks immediately after the July commencement, followed by "a fortnight from and after every third Wednesday in October." In the third week of October 1755, Warren returned home to Roxbury for two weeks.

Both he and his family would have looked forward to the extended reunion. Not only did they miss each other, but Warren could alleviate the daunting workload that their aging patriarch was shouldering. Warren must have experienced some level of guilt at not being able to help with the strenuous farm chores while he was in Cambridge. October was a busy time on the farm as the apple harvest reached its zenith.

Given the standard rootstock, rich soil, and underdeveloped pruning methods, the russet apple trees in Warren's orchard would have reached thirty feet in height and fifteen feet in width upon maturity. Apples tend to grow in clusters near the top of the tree, surrounded by dark green foliage. The height of the trees and the relative lack of branch strength made apple picking a hazardous affair.

So it was that on the morning of Wednesday, October 22, Joseph Warren, Sr., age fifty-nine, ascended a ladder to gather apples, as he had done so often throughout his life. He lost his footing and plummeted to his death.

ROXBURY,
October 25, 1755

On Wednesday last, a sorrowful accident happened here. As Mr. Joseph Warren, of this town, was gathering apples from a tree, standing upon a ladder a considerable distance from the ground he fell thence, broke his neck, and expired in a few minutes. He was esteemed a man of good understanding, industrious, upright, honest, and faithful; a serious exemplary Christian; a useful member of society. He was generally respected among us, and his death is universally lamented.

Given that Harvard was in recess, Warren was almost certainly at home, helping his father as he had in every other harvest. Warren would have agonized over the loss, lamenting that he had left the farm to pursue his studies, possibly even blaming himself for his father's death. This was his first experience with the tragic passing of a loved one, and it would have far-reaching consequences; his youngest brother, John, not yet three, was said to have witnessed "the sight of his father's body borne home to the house," which "made an impression upon his mind" that "was never effaced."

The senior Warren was laid to rest in the Old Burying-Ground—known to elders as the Eliot Burying-Ground, after the Rev. John Eliot—toward the back of the cemetery, surrounded by many of the town's fine subjects. The probate record referred to the deceased Warren as a gentleman, indicating his elevated social standing in the community. Joseph Warren, outfitted in traditional black mourning garb and white gloves, stood in the graveyard with Mary Warren, his three younger brothers, and others who gathered to pay their respects.

During this period, funerals in New England bordered on the extravagant, such that the family of the deceased often grieved twice: once for the loss of their loved one, and again for its effect on their finances. For young Warren and his family, the incident was a financial catastrophe. The family had to pay not only the costs associated with a burial—a coffin, coach, and horses—but also for mourning apparel, including white gloves for all the pallbearers, and likely for mourning rings as "presents." The cost of burying the elder Warren was an exorbitant forty pounds—the equivalent of approximately eight hundred days' pay for a typical journeyman laborer, or just under what Warren would later be paid for a year of teaching at Roxbury Latin in 1760. (Samuel Adams regarded such funeral customs as "a sensless and impoverishing fashion" that "proved ruinous to many families in this community.")

The senior Warren had died intestate, and the probate judge of Suffolk County, Thomas Hutchinson, ordered that an appraisal be taken of the estate. With Mary now facing a hefty Harvard tuition bill in addition to the funerary expenses, the Warrens' tenuous economic situation became a veritable disaster.

Money troubles followed Warren back to Harvard, where day-to-day expenses were numerous. To better acclimate to their new surroundings, students could purchase "wines and other liquors, tea, coffee, chocolate, sugar, bisket, pens, ink and paper, and other suitable articles" from the school commissary, known as the Buttery. The butler, who ran the Buttery, collected money from the students and kept track of their punishments, fines, and absences. Harvard students paid out of pocket for being shaved by a barber, having firewood carted, and hiring a slave to assist with tasks. Throughout the deep freeze of winter, students had to pay in order to keep the fires burning to warm their frigid chambers. Warren also needed books for his courses, like *Hebrew Gramar*, which the school supplied to every entering freshman. It was written by one of Warren's first Harvard instructors, Judah Monis, who taught Hebrew to the scholars so they could interpret the Old Testament.

All these daunting responsibilities and worries following his father's death thrust fourteen-year-old Joseph into his first leadership role, as family patriarch—a heavy burden for any boy. He likely considered returning to school overwhelming and infeasible. But newly widowed Mary Warren, now left to care for the farm and her young boys, insisted that he pursue his education. With a heavy heart, he obeyed.

Back at school, the land itself seemed to reflect Warren's emotional tumult. On November 18, 1755, a large earthquake struck about forty miles from Boston, near Cape Ann. President Holyoke's son, Dr. Edward Augustus Holyoke of Salem, recorded the terrifying event in his diary: "About 4h. 15m. we were awakened by a greater earthquake than has ever been known in this country. . . . I thought of nothing less than being buried instantly in the ruins of the house." The quake caused much destruction, particularly near the wharves in Boston, razing hundreds of chimneys and damaging roofs, church spires, brick buildings, and scores of stones fences. To many, it must have seemed apocalyptic. Numerous sermons and poems immediately claimed that it was God's cautionary reminder to the sinners of New England to repent: "It is because we broke thy Laws, that thou didst shake the earth."

A week later one of Warren's professors, the astronomer John Winthrop, delivered a lecture about the earthquake in Harvard's chapel, explaining that a mixture of heat and chemical vapors had caused the ferocious propulsions from within the earth's core. Warren surely pondered the issue from both a scientific and a religious standpoint. Over the next several months a debate over the earthquake, between Winthrop and Pastor Thomas Prince of the Old South Church, raged in the newspapers. Warren was being exposed, for the first time, to a world beyond Puritan beliefs—one where science, not just religion, could explain certain phenomena.

Warren and his schoolmates became very fond of Winthrop, who was himself a lifelong friend of Benjamin Franklin. On clear nights, when the stars illuminated the skies above Cambridge, Warren and his classmates would sometimes gaze through Winthrop's telescope from the rooftop of Harvard Hall, letting their imaginations drift toward the heavens.

Years earlier the English astronomer Edward Halley had predicted that a comet would appear in the sky around 1759. That year his prediction caused a great stir at the college, where students and faculty were constantly looking out for Halley's comet.

On April 4 Winthrop ascended the roof of Harvard Hall and spotted the celestial body there in the heavens, just as Halley had predicted. Over the next few days, Warren and his friends shared in the thrill. Comet-seeking became the rage, and the search to catch another glimpse continued for months. In a period infused with Puritan stringency, bereft of lavish indulgences and technological advancements, the occurrence of a natural phenomenon—whose date had been predicted—was met with a sense of pure wonderment. Since colonial Massachusetts was fraught with superstitions, fears of witchcraft, and other mysticisms, some believed the comet to be an omen. One Bostonian later claimed, "The people of New England at that time pretty generally believed in hobgoblins and spirits, that is the children at least did." Doubtless the event was a marvel to behold.

Unfortunately, his father's passing would not be Warren's only encounter with death that year. His uncle Ebenezer died several months later, and his friend and classmate Benjamin Johnson drowned in the Charles River at Cambridge the following summer. Warren and his classmates would have donned their "academical vests" and marched with other students and faculty in a funeral procession for one of their own. It would have been a time of extreme personal sadness and loss, but with his family and academic responsibilities weighing heavily on his shoulders, Joseph immersed himself in his studies.

WARREN WOULD CALL CAMBRIDGE HIS HOME FOR MOST OF THE next four years. Eventually, he would adapt to his surroundings and thrive in Harvard's social oasis. At the college, his room was located in "the fourth quarter, first district," of Massachusetts Hall, located near the west entrance to Harvard Yard. Built several decades earlier, the Georgian-style brick building had thirty-two chambers and sixty-four small private studies for students. Warren's meager accommodations included a lone shelf, a wooden bench, and a bed. He had partially furnished his room with a "great" chair and small mirror from his Roxbury house. Many students' rooms were loaded with personal possessions, as one mid-eighteenth century Harvard inventory revealed: "tables, chairs, and featherbeds; pictures and looking-glasses; Spectators, Tatlers, Gentleman's Magazines, and books of plays; pipes and tobacco, rum and other spirits . . . corkscrews, glasses, beakers, punch bowls, chafing dishes, and tea sets; clothing, wigs and crisping irons; and one Bible." Such items were indicative of the wealth and social standing of the scholars training to become men of consequence.

Harvard's rigid system of hierarchy put less privileged students at a disadvantage that often followed them throughout their lives. Lower-ranked students rarely rose to societal prominence. But while Warren's place in the Harvard ranking system would never change, his social standing among his peers rose dramatically as he became aligned with some of the school's top-ranked students.

The custom at Harvard was for lower-ranked scholars to room together. According to college records, when Warren was a freshman in June 1756, he roomed alone; then a few months later in September, he was placed in the "cellars in the fourth district" with Josiah Bridge (ranked twenty-eighth out of thirty-seven freshmen in his class of 1758). His rudimentary accommodations in the cellar had scant items—not even any of the usual shelves or benches.

Following his stay in the "cellar," Warren would room in some of the school's finest accommodations. Perhaps most telling of his social rise, Nathaniel Ames—a student two years behind Warren at Harvard—recorded in his diary in 1758, "Cato a play acted at Warrens Cham," meaning the chambers belonging to Warren. But his roommates from 1757 through 1759 were Abiel Leonard and Samuel Cotton, who ranked eighth and sixth, respectively, in Harvard's class system. This hints at how swiftly and seamlessly the underclassman had risen to a level on par with first-rate scholars, since Samuel Cotton "served as a Scholar of the House" and Leonard "held Gibbs and Hollis scholarships."

The play that Ames referred to was Addison's *Cato*, which personified the ideals of honor and republican virtue—standards for aspiring gentlemen scholars to emulate and live by. In addition to *Cato*, Harvard students performed a variety of other plays in their chambers, such as *The Roman Father* and *The Orphan*.

During his Harvard days, Warren began developing his oratorical skills. In 1756 the faculty decided to "raise the standard of elocution" and voted that President Holyoke "select some ingenious dialogue" of a "Latin author and . . . appoint as many students as there are persons in such dialogue, each to personate a particular character . . . and prepare himself to deliver it in the Chapel in an oratorical manner." Warren, by performing Latin dialogues in Harvard's Chapel and acting out theatrical performances in his chamber, was honing skills that he would put to use in the riveting Boston Massacre Orations and other dramatic speeches in the years to come.

Also during his stay at Harvard, Warren expanded his social ties, making important and lasting connections. He met many scholars who would become Loyalists and Whigs, even leaders of both political factions. Through Nathaniel Ames, Warren would have met Daniel Oliver, the oldest son of Massachusetts Superior Court's chief justice, Peter Oliver. His classmate John Greenough was a cousin of the Loyalist merchant Richard Clark, through whom he met Matthew Merriman, who would later donate money to the Whig cause. Warren befriended Sam Otis, the staunch Whig, future quartermaster of the Continental Army, and the youngest brother of the incendiary James Otis, Jr. Warren became intimate with fellow student John Avery, who would later become a member of the Loyal Nine—a pivotal patriot organization during the imperial crisis. Finally, Warren formed a relationship with his roommate, Abiel Leonard, whose father, a reverend, had been born in Plymouth and raised in a household passionately devoted to Scripture, like Warren's own.

In 1759, when Warren and his classmates were seniors, most colonists were proud British subjects under the rule of King George II. Britain continued to assert her scientific and military preponderance throughout the world, waging a war with France over imperial expansion. Massachusetts had sent many of her sons into battle, engendering a martial spirit and culture in the community among young men. During the cold seasons of the Seven Years' War, many students proudly wore surtouts, heavy frock coats fashioned after those worn by cavalry officers. In June of that year the royal governor had pronounced a provincial fast because of the Canada expedition.

It seemed only natural for Warren and some of his classmates to ask the school's administration for permission to form a military company at Harvard. The long-awaited response finally came that spring. Since "many of the undergraduates have preferr'd a Petition to Us, for Liberty to Exercise Themselves in the Use of the Fire-Lock," the faculty voted to "hereby grant them the liberty they have asked." But even before the faculty gave permission, the "scholars formed themselves into a company, chose their officers," and thus founded what would later become the Marti-Mercurian Band. As the founders of Harvard's militia unit, Joseph Warren and his fellow students would meet, drill, march, and "explode . . . vollies in the field of exercise." Though Warren had used firearms when hunting game, this was his first exposure to the rudiments of formal military drill—lessons that he would later take to the battlefield.

In February 1759, an outbreak of measles in Cambridge proved so pervasive that Harvard's faculty shut down the college for three weeks. Widespread disease meant death for many of those infected and terror for those who feared potential contraction. The unfortunate souls who were struck broke out in a terrible skin rash. Symptoms included conjunctivitis, sore throat, and fever. President Holyoke's stepdaughter, "Miss Betty Epes aged 22 years," died from the sickness. Smallpox, dysentery, tuberculosis, and cholera were among the other potentially fatal diseases in the long list of maladies afflicting the population.

The arrival of spring that year brought a different wave—one of great excitement. Harvard seniors would soon graduate, and their anticipation, like summer temperatures, soared. During their final "quarter," students swam in the Charles River. Back at Harvard, Warren's divinity professor, Dr. Wigglesworth, "gave our class his farewell discourse and a very good one it was." When the term ended on June 29, Jonathan Trumbull, the highest-ranked senior, delivered a "very handsomely . . . finely performed" valedictory oration in Latin.

Commencement, held on Wednesday, July 18, 1759, took place in the old First Parish Church at the corner of Harvard Yard. Heavy rain the day before made the college grounds muddy. The seniors awoke at four, in a dark, still, muggy New England morning. After taking breakfast, the young men began preparing for graduation.

During the ceremony the "cloudy but excessive hot" weather made everyone in attendance quite uncomfortable since they were dressed in layers of finery. Students were outfitted in dark-colored gowns, which could cost upward of fifteen pounds for materials, including silk.

Additionally, graduates had to pay for their degrees and for presents for their tutor and for Harvard's president.

Finally, the seniors stood ready to receive recognition from the college faculty. Mary Warren and Joseph's three younger brothers arrived from Roxbury to witness the graduation ceremonies. Mary had sacrificed much to allow her firstborn son to complete his studies and was undoubtedly quite proud. Joseph "was highly distinguished as a scholar" and "had an honourable part in the performances" at commencement. Royal Governor Thomas Pownall, whom John Adams referred to as "the most constitutional and national Governor . . . who ever represented the crown in this province," made an appearance, accompanied by his council and military escort as well as members of the General Court.

Afterward students would have enjoyed a lavish dinner feast, replete with alcohol and a variety of desserts. Making the ceremony even more celebratory, the faculty decreed in 1759 that "it shall be no offense if any scholar shall, at Commencement, make and entertain guests at his chamber with punch." The following day, Warren and his "chums" attended the "Grand Dance in the Hall." The dance would have likely commenced with the hierarchical and ceremonial minuet, followed by the more democratic country dances, jigs, and hornpipes.

That same day, Warren and his fellow graduates went to visit their classmate Samuel Gardner, who had taken ill and was unable to attend the gala. Given that they had all grown close over the last four years, the graduating class of 1759 decided that none of their mates should miss the fanfare, so they brought the celebration to their ailing friend.

Once the festivities subsided and commencement ceremonies drew to a close, the town of Cambridge fell into its usual midsummer slumber. And as the new entrance exams were being held to determine the next class of college freshmen, Joseph Warren, now eighteen, packed up his Harvard memories along with his clothes, his books, and his few other possessions, and made his way home to Roxbury to begin his new life.

4

SPECKLED MONSTER

"fair faced young Gentleman"
—JOHN ADAMS TO ABIGAIL SMITH (LATER HIS WIFE),
APRIL 13, 1764

AT THE HEIGHT OF THE NEW ENGLAND SUMMER, THE WARREN farm's lush landscapes, green vegetation, and fragrant blossoms welcomed the return of the new patriarch. Joseph Warren knew his family had sacrificed in recent years, and he arrived home ready to honor his obligations. Mary Warren, with little assistance, had shouldered the rigors of running the farm, tended to the household chores, and raised her boys, all while trying to meet the financial costs of her eldest son's college education. And as the balmy weather gave way to the autumn chill, the new apple harvest brought painful memories of the tragic death of their father four years earlier. The three younger Warren brothers missed the strong male presence that had helped mold their eldest brother. Joseph tried to fill that void as he helped with the heavy workload demanded by farm life.

But before long, the fences surrounding the farm came to symbolize constraint. The Roxbury homestead, however welcoming, seemed a world away from Harvard. Joseph, despite his low social ranking, had befriended the scions of some of New England's most prominent families. Harvard had opened for him a new existence, with possibilities that ensured that his postgraduation days in the countryside would feel limited.

In the spring of 1760, Warren took a position as master of Roxbury Latin School. It seemed a perfect fit for an alumnus and son of Roxbury, and teaching was a somewhat common first job for Harvard graduates; John Adams had accepted a similar position upon his own graduation a few years earlier. On April 11 the administration hired Warren to teach "for one quarter of a year at ye rate of fortey three pounds nine schillings and fourpence a year." Warren paid a portion of his income to his mother in partial compensation for his Harvard tuition. He likely taught arithmetic, reading, Greek, Latin grammar, and writing to his new pupils, while trying to strengthen their moral character.

Warren's Harvard classmates had spread across the town upon graduation, and so, in the summer and fall of 1760, Warren began spending more time in Boston, where he gravitated to the world of Freemasonry. Masonic organizations had reached American shores not long after 1700 and in the ensuing decades had grown popular. Members of these charitable fraternal organizations championed integrity, honor, and compassion. For Warren, Masonry offered an opportunity to meet men of power and influence, as well as a chance to continue his own moral self-development.

The Lodge of St. Andrew had been chartered in Boston in November 1756, and Warren was determined to become a member. Members of the rival and more prestigious St. John's Lodge in Boston were mostly wealthy merchants. St. Andrew's, in comparsion, was mostly composed of younger striving craftsmen, with the exception of John Hancock, who rarely attended. Given Warren's status and age at the time, joining St. Andrew's was the more logical choice. In June 1760, the lodge celebrated its annual feast in honor of St. John the Baptist at the Grey Hound Tavern in Roxbury. (Masons traditionally celebrated two annual feasts—St. John the Baptist on June 24, and St. John the Evangelist on December 27.) Warren was likely present, and by the following year he was "received as an entered apprentice" and then was fully "admitted to membership" on November 26, 1761. Warren's Harvard background would have made him an attractive candidate, and as a member of the lodge, he joined old friends from school and made many new ones, including Paul Revere, Thomas Crafts, Dr. Samuel Danforth, Jr., and John Hancock. The gift of fraternization that had served him so well at Harvard continued in Boston society.

Warren remained in Roxbury during his yearlong stint as master of Roxbury Latin, but from at least 1761 through 1762, he lived in Boston on Cornhill (now Washington) Street between Dock Square and School Street.

A number of factors likely pushed Warren toward a career in medicine, including his father's premature death and the influence of his mother's father, Dr. Samuel Stevens, and Harvard's Professor Winthrop. No major medical schools had yet been founded in the colonies, so not long after graduation, he began studies at Harvard in pursuit of his master of arts degree in medicine.

In colonial America, "the term of two years' study only was then required to qualify a student for the practice of medicine," so Warren carried out his studies independently and largely outside Harvard's confines. One of the many books he used was the 1664 work *A Description of the Body of Man: Being a Practical Anatomy*. Every Harvard degree candidate had to choose a question to address either in the negative or in the affirmative, and the one Warren chose was "Do all diseases arise from obstructions?" Much debate surrounded this question, since in the eighteenth century the true nature and causes of disease were unknown. Warren's dissertation attempted to prove that obstructions were only one source of disease. All candidates were expected to present themselves at the college no later than July 14, 1762, and a week later at commencement, some of the dissertations were partially delivered before the faculty.

To learn the craft of doctoring, Warren had to undertake a period of apprenticeship with an established physician. Those from well-off families typically went to study in Europe, but Warren lacked the resources to go there, so he apprenticed under a physician in the colonies. Still, his talent and Harvard connections meant he would not lack for a prestigious mentor.

Even before receiving his master of arts degree from Harvard, Warren had started his apprenticeship under the auspices of Dr. James Lloyd, one of Boston's most famous and pioneering physicians. Born to a wealthy merchant Anglican family, Lloyd was cultured, socially connected, and highly accomplished, with deep financial resources. He had received a first-rate medical education, studying in Boston for five years under the esteemed physician Dr. John Clark before traveling to London, where he trained under the acclaimed surgeons William Cheselden and Samuel Sharp. Lloyd had the fortunate "opportunity of studying all the elementary branches of his profession under the first masters," who were pioneers in their profession.

When Lloyd returned to the colonies in 1752, he brought with him a superior medical knowledge and honed technical skills. Such cutting-edge training was of great value, as medicine during the colonial period was anything but advanced. Boston's newspapers were fraught with advertisements touting cures for "swelling ulcers," "the bloody flux," and everything from "the itch or any other breaking out" to "that most tremendous disorder called a cancer." Shops sold an assortment of patent drugs and medicines such as "Hooper's Female Pills" and the ever-popular "Turlington's Balsam of Life," which reputedly cured "many thousands . . . when all other medicines had failed." Other treatments such as bleeding, cathartics, purges, and elixirs were prescribed for any variety of maladies.

In Europe, however, great strides were being made in the field of medicine, and Lloyd was au courant with these innovations. Throughout the 1750s, he helped transform the practice of medicine in Boston. Well versed in everything from surgery and obstetrics to the creation of prescriptions and remedies, he championed smallpox inoculations and provided obstetrical care for pregnant women based upon the teachings of the Scotsman Dr. William Smellie, whose lectures he had attended in London.

Lloyd's status was enhanced by the lavish house and sprawling gardens he had built at the head of Queen Street in Boston. He loved hosting, and the elaborate landscaping and opulent interior welcomed many guests to his various functions and dinners. An avid horticulturalist, he had an affinity for gardening that enhanced his ability to mix the numerous remedies he prescribed. His growing clientele included some of the most powerful names in the Bay Colony and Great Britain, such as Gen. William Howe and Lord Hugh Percy, both of whom would temporarily live with Lloyd. Known as a generous man, he personally extended loans and credit to friends, patients, family, and business associates, to the staggering amount of more than three thousand pounds.

Warren had chosen his mentor wisely. When he began his medical training with Lloyd and became acquainted with Lloyd's vast social network, he was suddenly immersed within the highest realms of Boston society, a world beyond medicine. Warren lived with Lloyd during at least part of his apprenticeship, learning how to conduct himself as a gentleman physician. The colonists' definition of a gentleman differed from traditional British notions. Without a distinguished birthright, colonists could never be on par with the British aristocracy, no matter their education or fortune. Already aware that those subjects in England looked down on them as second-class citizens, the colonists felt relegated to subservience. Various rules developed among the colonists had created a similarly hierarchical social structure. To be a gentleman in the colonies denoted not noble birth but a level of wealth, education, gentility, and refinement. Warren's father had been referenced as a gentleman, and Joseph certainly aspired to mirror his father in this regard.

In addition to learning how to run a successful practice, Warren soon mastered the nuances of a bedside manner and social interaction with Boston's elite. Living under Lloyd's roof, Warren had to comport himself as an extension of his mentor's household. Ensconced in an opulent lifestyle, he learned proper etiquette and how to entertain, acquiring his own taste for luxury in the process. Even Warren's appearance transformed, as he began to dress in the exquisite, high-end fashions of the day—donning the finest silks and the most expensive patterned fabrics. Lloyd transformed Warren from an educated farm boy into a skilled and respected town physician.

AS JOSEPH WARREN DOVE INTO HIS APPRENTICESHIP, EVENTS WERE unfolding in Boston and London that further divided the two cities. Beginning in 1760, Boston was ravaged by social strife, economic hardship, and political upheaval. During the French and Indian War, military expenditures had kept merchants, builders, and manufacturers afloat, but as the war drew to a close, Massachusetts's economy started sinking. The Bay Colony had sent more than its fair share of men to fight, and now in Boston "there was a disproportionate number of women compared to other cities; they included a very large number of widows." Those soldiers lucky enough to return home found few jobs, and the widows and children of their fallen comrades swelled the ranks of the poor. As the prices of food and firewood rose, the standard of living for the working class declined. Hundreds of destitute souls, homeless and unemployed, flooded the town from neighboring areas, looking for relief. Advertisements like the one announcing "several likely children, of both sexes and different ages [were] to be bound out into good families, either in town or country, by the overseers of the poor," appeared in local papers with greater frequency.

Adding to the woes, outbreaks of smallpox occurred around the town. Then on March 20, 1760, a destructive fire "suppos'd to be greater than any that has been known in these American colonies" consumed Boston. The blaze spread southeast from the center of town; the flames could be seen more than thirty miles away. Several days after the inferno, in Natasket, almost nine miles from Boston, "several shingles, letters, and other papers, partly burnt, were found upon the hills ther[e], which were blown tither by the violence of the wind at the time of the fire." Close to four hundred buildings burned, including homes, warehouses, shops, stores, and ships, leaving many people with nothing.

Bostonians sought solace in the fact that "notwithstanding the continuance and rage of the fire, the explosion at the South Battery, and the falling of the walls and chimnies, Divine Providence has so mercifully ordered it, that not one life has been lost, and only a few wounded." Other colonies pooled their resources and collected more than fifteen hundred pounds for their northern brothers and sisters, who remained thankful. They steadfastly rebuilt their town of ashes, widening streets and building more durable structures of brick and stone.

Meanwhile political dissension was beginning to flare. Political power in Massachusetts operated through a top-down-bottom-up structure. The Boston Town Meeting was the "basic participatory institution in the political system of colonial Massachusetts," dealing with local problems and electing local officials and representatives to the General Court's lower house.

Massachusetts's initial charter had established the province as a self-governing private corporation. It was revoked in 1691, and the following year a new, revised charter increased the governor's power, allowing Britain to exert greater political and military control over what was now a royal colony. No longer elected to office, the governor was now appointed directly by the Crown and assumed total command over the military. The General Court—the bicameral legislative body consisting of the upper house, the Council, and the assembly or House of Representatives—was responsible for passing laws, levying taxes, setting punishments and fines, and appointing officers. Freeholders—white men of property—elected members of the assembly, who in turn chose the Council members. While the governor could veto any act of the General Court and negate any Council member appointed by the assembly, members of the assembly determined the salaries of the governor and the treasurer. But the governor, able to summon, adjourn, or dissolve the General Court and answerable only to the king, held more power over the legislature than any other citizen of Massachusetts.

Massachusetts governor Thomas Pownall supported greater financial support from Parliament to help cover colonial war expenditures, a stance that won him much support from the population. But on June 3, 1760, Pownall left Boston; never again would a royal governor enjoy such popularity.

At first all was well with his replacement, Sir Francis Bernard. Arriving in Boston on August 2, 1760, Bernard received a warm welcome from the colonists. He had previously served as the royal governor of New Jersey, where he had enjoyed relatively harmonious relations with the legislature. In October of that year, King George II passed away in England, "in the 34th year of his reign." Bernard proclaimed that a funeral sermon was to be preached and that all attendees must appear in traditional mourning apparel.

George III, grandson of the late king, ascended the throne at only twenty-two, just slightly older than Joseph Warren. Many colonists held celebrations and cheered for their new monarch. John Hancock, in England at the time, attended the lavish coronation ceremony. In honor of the coronation, at Bernard's suggestion, Harvard printed *Pietas et Gratulatio,* a collection of Latin and English compositions, written by "gentlemen, who are now members of said college, or have taken a degree there within seven years." We cannot know if Warren contributed to the collection, since several verses remain anonymous, but many of his Harvard associates, future patients, and future political comrades wrote odes, poems, elegies, and orations. Copies were sent to London and presented to the young monarch and the royal family.

This era of good feeling did not last long. The Seven Years' War (called the French and Indian War in the Americas) had embroiled Europe in battles around the globe, and its end in 1763 helped establish Britain as the preponderant power in North America, particularly with the acquisition of Canada and French territory east of the Mississippi. But the long conflict burdened King George's vast, new empire with an enormous war debt of more than 120 million pounds.

In the war's aftermath, Britain began to restrict westward expansion, establish new taxes, and limit the power of the provincial legislatures, causing a miasma of discontent to descend upon Boston. An opposition formed within the Massachusetts House of Representatives and the Boston Town Meeting. Those supporting the policies of royal administration were called the court or government party and consisted of Tories, Friends of Government, or (later) Loyalists; they tended to cluster in the Council (upper house). The opposition, clustered in the House of Representatives (lower house), was called the popular or country party and comprised the Sons of Liberty, patriots, and Whigs.

Exacerbating this factional division, Governor Bernard favored decidedly pro-Crown positions. The Bay Colony soon became embroiled in a heated dispute. Bernard's two predecessors, governors William Shirley and Thomas Pownall, had promised James Otis, Sr., the speaker of the Massachusetts House of Representatives, a seat on the Superior Court of Judicature. Some had promised that if Otis were "not appointed a justice of the Superior Court [Otis Jr.] would set the province in a flame even if he perished in the attempt." But when Chief Justice Samuel Sewall died in 1760, Bernard appointed the lieutenant governor, Thomas Hutchinson, to the position. Hutchinson and his family wielded tremendous power in the Bay Colony, and his appointment prompted cries of nepotism across the town. John Adams would later write of the Hutchinsons, "Is not this amazing ascendency of one family, foundation sufficient on which to erect a tyranny? Is it not enough to excite Jealousies among the people?"

Otis's son was James Otis, Jr., a lawyer and advocate general. Indignant over the snub to his father and outraged about a patronage system that threatened to foster tyranny, James Jr. began to publicly oppose Bernard and some of the Crown's administrative policies, in particular, the writs of assistance.

Originally issued in 1751, these writs allowed customs officials to conduct arbitrary searches of homes and businesses to mitigate the smuggling so rampant in port cities throughout the colonies. The writs were set to expire six months following the death of George II, but instead new writs were issued with the strict intent of enforcement. The holder of a writ could not be held responsible for any damage caused during a search and also could transfer it to another individual. Many colonists became alarmed. In 1761 the younger Otis masterfully argued that the writs were illegal and violated the inherent rights of British subjects—a stance widely popular among Boston's merchants and the businessmen he represented. Years later John Adams vividly recollected that in a courtroom, "Otis was a flame of fire! . . . Then and there was the first scene of the first act of opposition to the arbitrary claims of Great Britain. Then and there the child Independence was born."

In 1761 Otis won a seat in the lower house of the General Court, whereupon one future outspoken Tory astutely predicted that "out of this election will arise a damn'd Faction, which will shake the province to its foundation." Indeed, two years later, town elections swept many radical candidates into office, to the dismay of some "Friends of Government." But even many Tories were initially opposed to parliamentary intervention, which threatened their autonomy and the system of self-government to which Massachusetts colonists had long been accustomed. Some of the earliest leaders of the incipient country party—James Otis, Jr., Samuel Adams, Oxenbridge Thacher, and Royall Tyler—argued against the power of Parliament to impose various taxes, claiming that it "annihilates our Charter Right to govern and tax ourselves."

Joseph Warren was familiar with both sides of the political debate. His teachers at Roxbury Latin and Harvard would become both Whigs and Tories, and his mentor Lloyd was a firm Loyalist. Despite their political differences, Warren and Lloyd remained close friends and associates. That Warren's political beliefs differed from those of his mentor demonstrated his maturity and his commitment to principle.

By the late spring of 1763, having completed his medical apprenticeship with Lloyd, Warren opened his own practice in Boston. The services he provided ranged from treating "venereal disease" to "reducing fractures and dislocations." He ran a full-service apothecary shop and also sold nonmedical "sundries" like "figgs," Madeira wine, and "wraping paper." Unlike many Boston physicians, he provided obstetrical care to pregnant women, as did his mentor Lloyd and many female midwives.

Beginning in 1764, Warren purchased a variety of items from Boston merchant John Greenleaf, indicating a bustling and diverse practice. His shelves were stocked with patent medicines like Turlington's Balsam of Life, and he colored and flavored medicines in both powder and liquid forms. Warren would use the leather he purchased to cover his containers and also as a plaster to apply medicinal ointments on the skin. Making the medicines necessary to treat his patients was a labor-intensive process. One can imagine Warren sitting by the hearth and mixing and measuring ingredients such as aloe, Peruvian bark, oil of absinthe, white sugar, cinnamon water, gum guaic, lavender, niter, red sanders, calumel, opium, anis seed, and "Ung Egypt." Unguentum Egyptian ointment is made with verdigris, honey, and vinegar and used for "cleansing and deterging ulcers, and keeping down fungous flesh." Opium was expensive but commonly administered as a cough suppressant and to treat diarrhea and pain symptoms. He used calamine to soothe skin irritations, chalk to ease heartburn, and cinchona bark to combat fevers. He used Lisbon wine as a medicinal as well as an ingredient in the "Lisbon Diet Drink."

His lab would have included a balance (scale) to measure solids, graduated glass cylinders for measuring liquids, vials and syringes of all sizes (including a "penis syringe" to battle sexual diseases), a "mortar" and pestle, an amputation saw and knife, forceps, styptics to stop bleeding, delftware and "stone" drug jars, pill tiles, lancets for bloodletting, "surgeons needles," glyster pipes to administer enemas, and implements for tooth extractions such as a dental chisel and tooth key. When he moved to Hanover Street in 1770, he set up an anatomical

room where he kept, among other objects, several wired skulls. Warren's wide array of medical services spoke to his training, his ability to
handle a diverse caseload, and his desire to succeed.

In addition to seeing patients at his fledgling practice, Warren made
house calls. Some of his earliest clients were relatives, merchants, ship
captains, tradesmen, convicts, widows, slaves, and laborers. Early on
he attended the family of John Wheatley, a Boston tailor and businessman who owned Phillis Wheatley, an enslaved woman who later
became the colonies' first published African-American female poet.
For a time, Warren took meals with the family, treating them for various illnesses. When the smallpox hit Boston in the winter of 1764, he
administered their inoculations.

Fear of smallpox was never far from the colonists' minds. A densely
populated port town like Boston was particularly vulnerable to the
highly contagious pox since ships from various parts of the world
docked at its wharves. Advertisements in Boston newspapers announcing slave sales or wet nurse services made sure to mention whether the
featured individual already "had the small pox," thus making them
immune to future outbreaks, to the relief of potential buyers.

When the new scourge struck in January 1764, "the coldest time of
the whole year," the selectmen of Boston alerted the public that thirteen
families in the North End had been infected. All dwellings of infected
persons were to be immediately "smoked and cleaned" to prevent the
spread of the disease. Any infected family was to alert the town selectmen and then "hang out on a pole at least six feet in length, a red cloth
not under one yard long, and half a yard wide, from the most public
part of the infected house" as a quarantine warning. Failure to comply
resulted in an exorbitant fine of fifty pounds, and if the offender failed
to pay, they were subject to a brutal whipping of up to thirty stripes.

During that initial outbreak, ten of the first twelve infected people
died. A draft was composed to dig ten graves and to place the deceased's body "immediately into a tarred sheet and coffin." The selectmen ordered that the gravedigger bury the bodies only at specific
hours; another man was to travel ahead to announce to people on

the street that a smallpox corpse was being carted to the graveyard. At that time it was believed that the disease was spread by breathing infected air.

Many fled the town in panic, waiting for the epidemic to run its course. Wealthier citizens had the luxury of traveling to their country estates. Merchants and shopkeepers moved their goods to the country and advertised the sale of their wares from the town outskirts. Others, like Paul Revere, stayed in the town. When one of his children contracted the disease, he and his family remained under house quarantine, with a guard posted outside their home.

As the hated pox descended upon Boston, the General Court decided to hold its session in Cambridge instead of Boston, lest members contract the disease. This move would prove disastrous to Harvard. On January 24, "in the middle of a very tempestuous night, a severe cold of snow attended with high wind" enveloped the college town, which was nearly vacant because the students were away. A fire lit earlier that night to warm members of the court overheated the flue and sparked "a beam under the hearth in the library." It went undetected until the flames soared. The high winds spread the fire rapidly, while the frozen water pumps sat useless. In the end, Warren's alma mater suffered "the most ruinous loss it ever met with since its foundation . . . perhaps irreparable . . . Harvard-Hall the first of our buildings, and the repository of our most valuable treasures, the public library and Philosophical apparatus . . . which for many years had been growing, and were now judged to be the best furnished in America, are annihilated." This irreplaceable loss to the beacon of learning was in some ways more devastating than the Boston fire four years earlier. It marked the ominous beginnings of a "most ruinous" winter.

Smallpox, known as "the speckled monster," was a scourge that could ignite more than dread alone. The practice of inoculating against smallpox had been debated for decades and was still controversial. When the pox hit Boston in 1721, the Rev. Cotton Mather and Dr. Zabdiel Boylston had championed inoculation, to the outrage of an angered and naïve populace who believed "Heaven's vengeance" was imminent. Many saw the pox as God's divine intervention, not to be challenged, and inoculation as pure heresy. The issue was so explosive that Mather's house was firebombed with an attached message that read, "Cotton Mather, You Dog, Dam you, I'll inoculate you with this, with a Pox to you."

That fear and suspicion had not fully abated by the 1764 outbreak. Though many people had come to believe in the efficacy of inoculation, in early February the town selectmen "moved for an absolute law to be made to prevent inoculation in any instance until the distemper was in 30 families at once." Heated arguments to the contrary peppered Boston newspapers, asserting that "when our lives are threatened with a pestilence, have we not the same liberty to save them as when they are endanger'd by the violent assault of an enemy? . . . The disease was never known to be so mortal as it has been this time." But as the "speckled monster" continued to spread, the selectmen finally called for "inoculating hospitals to be taken at the outskirts of the town." Soon two inoculation hospitals were opened at isolated locations, Point Shirley and the nearby island fort of Castle William.

While hundreds fled to the countryside, Joseph Warren remained in Boston treating patients, battling the outbreak in his first public test as a physician. As a Lloyd protégé, he was able to capitalize on his mentor's standing to put himself on the front lines of the outbreak. Toward the end of February, Warren and several other doctors, including Lloyd, set up facilities in Castle William, where they would administer inoculations and care for infected patients.

The doctors at Castle William were responsible for furnishing their own supplies, and since Warren had been in business for only a few months, he needed money to keep himself stocked with necessities. Lloyd came to his rescue, loaning him twenty-four pounds in cash and providing several feather beds, blankets, and at least one pillow. Lloyd also paid Richard Draper "for advertisement" in the newspaper announcing that services for inoculations were available for a fee.

Warren would "reside at Castle William day and night." Less experienced than most of his colleagues, he was thrust into a world of malaise. The castle's forty-eight rooms held almost five hundred infected patients, many of them writhing in pain, with soaring fevers and nasty pustule eruptions. The stench of human waste and the foul pungent odor associated with the pox must have made Warren's work almost unbearable. Perhaps worse than the morbid physical aspect was the psychological toll of not knowing if the inoculations would ultimately prevent death. Warren did what he could to make his space sanitary and his patients safe and comfortable. He purchased goods and hired laborers to wash and change out the barracks, unload wood, and empty slop buckets. Though he had little himself, he loaned money to fellow doctors and provided services for them on account. Through it all, he continued to make house calls, visiting and treating patients for ailments other than the pox.

In April 1764, John Adams and his brother departed their hometown of Braintree and set out for Boston to receive their inoculations from Warren and Dr. Nathaniel Perkins, a senior colleague. Upon their arrival, Adams reported in a letter to his wife,

> *Dr. Perkins demanded my left Arm and Dr. Warren my Brothers. They took their Launcetts and with their Points divided the skin for about a Quarter of an inch and just suffering the Blood to appear, buried a Thread about (half) a Quarter of an Inch long in the Channell. A little Lint was then laid over the scratch and a Piece of Ragg pressed on, and then a Bandage bound over all. . . . Warren is a pretty, tall, Genteel, fair faced young Gentleman. Not quite so much assurance in his address, as Perkins (perhaps because Perkins was present) Yet shewing fully that he knows the Utility thereof, and that he will soon, practice it in full Perfection.*

From this encounter began a friendship that would last for the rest of Warren's life. More than eighty years later, Adams's son, John Quincy, fondly reminisced about "Warren a dear friend of my father, and a beloved Physician to me."

During the smallpox epidemic, Dr. Warren inoculated hundreds of petrified but ultimately grateful individuals, none of whom died. To indigent citizens who could not afford the procedure, Warren did his best to provide it free of charge, a notably generous effort considering he had just started his practice and still owed Lloyd a considerable sum of money. The average recovery period was six to eight weeks, and when his patients healed, Warren provided them a certificate "setting forth that such person is so cleaned and freed from infection, as not to endanger others." He made new friendships, and as his practice grew, so did the public trust in his work. One historian later wrote that "in the year 1764, when the small pox spread through Boston, and vast numbers were inoculated, he was among the physicians who were most eminent in the profession." The selectmen took notice of the doctors' efforts and in May "voted unanimously, that the thanks of the town be and hereby are given those gentlemen physicians, who in this season of difficulty and distres have generously inoculated and carried through the small-pox, [to a] considerable number of the inhabitants."

All told, approximately five thousand people received inoculations during the epidemic, and less than one percent succumbed to the disease—numbers previously thought unimaginable. In late August it was announced that "the town is now clear of that distemper, and the intercourse between town and country restored."

The people in and around Boston who survived that winter's hardships and frigid temperatures were wiser and battle-tested, as evidenced by faces pitted with pox scars. The community had pulled together and bonded to confront a shared peril. Warren emerged as a new leader, one who helped the poor, the weak, and the vulnerable during the deadly crisis—a man "in whom the people in the environs of Boston and Cambridge placed their highest confidence."

That summer—ironically, on the evening of July 4—a severe thunderstorm unlike any in recent memory illuminated the sky. "The whole heavens seem'd to be in a continued Blaze" wrote one observer, "like small globes of fire sparkling and discharging themselves in the air." In retrospect, it seems a portentous sign, as the dark pending storm clouds of imperial crisis fast approached Boston Harbor.

5

NEW BEGINNINGS

"Now first in business in this town."
—DR. THOMAS YOUNG REFERRING TO
DR. WARREN'S MEDICAL PRACTICE

DURING THE GRUELING MONTHS WHEN JOSEPH WARREN WAS AD-
ministering smallpox inoculations, he had fallen in love. He courted
the young woman, and on September 6 the *Boston Gazette* announced
that "Doct. Joseph Warren, one of the Physicians of this Town[, was
married] to Miss Betsy Hooton." At eighteen, Elizabeth Hooton was
deemed one of the more attractive and wealthy young ladies in Boston. Her ailing father, Richard, a successful merchant and member
of St. John's Masonic Lodge, had died just a few months before at
only thirty-seven and had bequeathed the lion's share of his estate to
her. For centuries, many historians have speculated that Warren chose
Elizabeth as his bride primarily for pecuniary gain, but in the fall of
1764, after growing his practice during the smallpox epidemic, he was
no longer in dire financial straits, and in any case if financial security
were his goal, with his new prominence he could have married someone with even loftier status.

The ceremony took place in the Congregational Church on Brattle Street in Boston, where both Warren and his wife were faithful members. It was performed by the Rev. Samuel Cooper—a Harvard graduate and son of a fiery Boston minister—who accepted a Portuguese coin from Warren in payment. After the couple exchanged their vows, the custom was to hold a jubilant wedding frolick with much dancing and feasting to celebrate.

During the previous decades, Reverend Cooper had tended to the spiritual needs of Boston's wealthiest congregation. His friends included burgeoning radicals like James Otis, Jr., the Adamses, and John Hancock. While Cooper publicly refrained from political speeches, privately he rebuked the Crown's repressive policies and blamed it "for encouraging the Soldiery to murder us." He declared that "all arts have been employ'd to terrify, cajol, divide, and mislead us." Cooper's study of Scripture, and his embrace of the fundamental principles of natural law, contributed to his belief that "men are born equal and free; that no man has a natural claim of dominion over his neighbors" and that "such a society have a right freely to determine by whom and in what manner their own affairs shall be administered."

Many of Warren's fellow parishioners came to be closely aligned with Cooper both socially and professionally. Later some Loyalists outside the church would see the parish as a rebel stronghold whose congregation hid beneath the religious cloak of their deceitful minister, who was "sowing sedition and conspiracy among parishoners." The Loyalist Peter Oliver said of Cooper that "no man could, with a better grace, utter the word of God from his mouth and at the same time keep a two edged dagger concealed in his hand" and "mix privately, with the rabble, in their nightly seditious associations." John Adams would later declare that Samuel Cooper had been among the most ardent patriots.

Warren's connection to Cooper and the Congregational church was an early step toward radical politics. Warren already knew some of the other parishioners as fellow Masons, and though he continued to have good relations with Tories such as Thomas Hutchinson and Lloyd, his social life came increasingly to be dominated by radical organizations. That Warren's wife came from an Anglican family might have also helped him make connections among Boston's Anglican elite. For about fifty pounds, he purchased a pew in the church opposite the southern door, allowing him to depart discreetly if a medical emergency demanded his immediate attention.

Days after his wedding, Warren was back in Roxbury visiting family with his new bride. During that crisp and colorful New England autumn, he continued to help his family run the farm, loaning them money and paying for items such as hemp seed as they readied themselves for the harvest. Bostonians and their neighboring townsfolk, putting a year of intense sufferings behind them, once again settled into their familiar routines, preparing for winter.

Three thousand miles away, in an attempt to fill Britain's vacant postwar coffers, the king's ministry turned its gaze toward the colonies. British prime minister George Grenville had already established new taxes and duties in England to raise revenue. He believed colonial taxes were too low. Furthermore, as he was aware, rampant smuggling infected port towns like Boston, and some colonial customs deputies were less than zealous in performing their duties, while others were corrupt and open to bribery. A British standing army approximately eight thousand strong had been left behind after the Seven Years' War to protect the colonists and also British interests in North America. Therefore, Grenville reasoned, the colonists should help cover expenses made in their own defense.

In April 1764, Parliament passed the Sugar Act, which imposed taxes on molasses and sugar, restrictions on lumber exports, and duties on Madeira, indigo, and coffee. Additionally, duties doubled on goods that passed through England en route to the colonies. Although the act actually reduced duties on molasses, enforcement would no longer be lax as in years past, as Britain abandoned its unofficial policy of salutary neglect regarding trade laws. The provision that targeted smuggling forced those accused of violating trade laws to post bond and stand trial in a vice admiralty court with no jury in Nova Scotia—for many colonists, a shocking rebuke to due process.

When news of the act arrived in North America, colonists reacted immediately. In May, the Boston Town Meeting wrote to Boston's representatives in the General Court asserting that the "new taxations upon us . . . annihilates our Charter Right to govern and tax ourselves.—It strikes at our British privileges. . . . If taxes are laid upon us in any shape without ever having a legal representative where they are laid, are we not reduced from the character of free subjects to the miserable state of tributary slaves?" This missive also provided advice and recommendations for Boston's representatives.

On September 29, 1764, John Rowe, a friend and patient of Joseph Warren, noted in his journal: "The Black Act takes place this day." Born in England, Rowe was a successful Boston merchant and owned much property, including the wharf named after him. He was connected to many wealthy and powerful New Englanders who also viewed the new measures as onerous and unjust, especially in light of British wartime gains made with the help of colonial militia. Unlike the Crown, colonial militia units had not gained much materially from the victory. In light of the Sugar Act, the British standing army now seemed more like a threat to enforce acts of tyranny than a defender of fellow subjects of the king. With the subsequent passage of the Quartering Act in May 1765, the colonies faced the additional burden of housing and feeding British regulars at public expense.

Most of the people Britain taxed without consent were dependent and powerless—servants, women, children, and those without property. Being taxed without representation thus cast white, propertied Bostonian men into the basement of Britain's social structure, which galled them. Colonists also argued that they were being denied the basic British right of a trial by jury, since accused smugglers had to face a juryless court. Parliament exacerbated the tense situation by subsequently passing the Currency Act in 1764, prohibiting paper money in the colonies, of which they had issued a large amount during the late war. Once again, as with the Land Bank controversy, New Englanders claimed Parliament was overstepping the accepted boundaries of imperial authority, especially since the colonists had no direct representative in Parliament. Grenville, determined to enforce the new laws, had the power to nullify any act passed by the colonial assemblies contrary to the new measures. To the colonists, this set a dangerous precedent.

Resentful colonists began to broadly question the shift in policy surrounding imperial control. James Otis, Jr., in his pamphlet *Rights of the British Colonies Asserted and Proved*, wrote that the Sugar Act "set people a thinking, in six months, more than they had done in their whole lives before." A disconnect was growing between the rationale of royal officials and the evolving ideology of many colonists. Imposing taxes and tightening laws on a populace unaccustomed to such intense regulation was anathema to many, especially in the Boston area. New Englanders had suffered particularly hard over the past years. Many Massachusetts men had fought during the war, only to return to the host of difficulties saturating the colony. Britain's latest acts not only threatened the colonists' tenuous economic situation but also laid bare the financial desperation felt on both sides of the Atlantic.

Every November 5, Bostonians celebrated Pope's Day, an anti-Catholic commemoration of the failed Gunpowder Plot of 1605, which had intended to depose the Protestant king James I. Mobs from the North and South ends of Boston paraded in the streets with blackened faces and effigies of the pope, the devil, and various despised imperial leaders. After sunset the two throngs would converge in a violent face-off as men, drunk and out of control, beat each other with clubs and barrel staves. Many broken bones, shattered teeth, and bruises later, the victorious side seized all the effigies and burned them in a spectacular bonfire.

In 1764, the Pope's Day rioting became so unruly that a young boy was killed when his head was crushed under a carriage wheel. Bedlam ensued, and it was reported that thousands flocked to the scene. The experienced and battle-hardened British General Thomas Gage, commander in chief of the North American forces, after hearing of the tumult later wrote to London in dismay: "During these commotions in North-America, I have never been more at a loss how to act."

Several men were indicted for inciting the rioting, including the hatter Samuel Richardson. Warren wrote a doctor's note to the judges on Richardson's behalf, saying he suffered from "nerves much disordered with frequent twitchings and partial convulsions attended with a delirium." Upon reading Warren's diagnosis, the court discharged the hatter. News that Warren had come to Richardson's defense spread through Boston's grapevine. Whether the diagnosis was accurate or exaggerated, some saw in the note a strengthening connection between Warren the doctor and Warren the patriot, the implication being that he had used his status as a doctor to the advantage not only of the lower classes but also of the nascent Whig faction.

The story was consistent with Warren's cautious but growing resistance to British authority. Several weeks prior to the Pope's Day melee, Warren's maternal grandmother, Mary Stevens, fell ill. For nearly a month, he paid numerous visits to her home in Roxbury, tending to her until she died in early November. In the wake of the Sugar Act, as a movement to boycott British products and imports gained steam, Warren refrained from purchasing any English goods for the burial, hoping that "this laudable example will be universally followed" until "the whole Province will adopt it." Such asceticism was not only lauded in Puritan society but was also a social, political, and economic statement against the latest measures of imperial authority. Warren and his family were among the first to boycott and resist the Crown in this way. His motives likely mixed the political and the personal; for Warren, the parliamentary meddling embodied by the Sugar Act surely recalled the Crown interventions decades earlier in the Land Bank debacle, which had prompted so much suffering in his family.

By this time Warren's medical practice had grown to encompass all levels of Boston society. His patients included the Tory upper crust, like the Hutchinsons, the Hallowells, and the Olivers; the lowest classes, including prisoners and slaves; and the middling sort, artisans and mechanics such as William Dawes, Benjamin Burt, and Paul Revere. Finally, Warren's clients also included the core members of the radical movement—Samuel and John Adams, James Otis, Jr., John Hancock, and the Whig printers Benjamin Edes and John Gill. The breadth of his professional connections allowed him to move comfortably not only at Harvard but in Masonic lodges, taverns, and almshouses.

Among these circles and organizations, Warren built a devoted and loyal following of patients. He shared their most intimate experiences— the joy of a family upon the birth of a child, or their collective grief after the death of a loved one. He had evolved into a skilled physician. In the descriptions of services in his ledger, one entry noted "reducing [resetting] her shoulder"—a procedure that would have required a great deal of expertise to perform properly. The ledger is replete with instances of "opening tumor[s,]" fingers and hands, extracting teeth, bloodletting, syringing ears, administering enemas, and performing various other procedures. He experimented with new treatments and prescriptions and consulted with other doctors to advance his skills.

Within just a few years, Warren established one of the largest medical practices in Boston. In 1769 Thomas Young, another popular Boston doctor and a political colleague of Warren's, claimed that Warren's medical practice was "now first in business in this town." Frequently, Warren accepted payment for his services in the form of flour, beer, shoes, and other sundry items. Although plagued with financial hardships during his life, he would at times cancel the fees his poorer patients owed him, like those of the merchant John Morley: "The remainder given in consideration of his misfortune."

By establishing himself as a caring and talented physician, Warren gained much credibility among his fellow townsmen. His practice treated Whig and Tory without prejudice, which helped him to enter the political fray as a respected member of the entire community.

6

ACTS OF VIOLENCE

"Independence was their object."
—PETER OLIVER
(CIRCA 1781, IN REFERENCE TO
WARREN AND TOP RADICAL LEADERS)

WINTER IN BOSTON WAS A BLESSING AND A CHALLENGE. ICE WAS plentiful, as was clean drinking water, but frigid temperatures made walking about town near impossible, particularly with heavy snowfalls. For Joseph Warren, making necessary house calls proved difficult. Crossing rivers and lakes shortened his traveling routes but could be deadly when the ice proved too weak. Since people preferred to remain indoors, safe from the elements, taverns often brimmed with patrons looking to engage in current affairs, seeking cheer from one another and warmth from burning spirits, hot food, and crackling fireplaces.

Seen from the neighboring towns of Roxbury and Charlestown, Boston was a spectacular sight in wintry conditions. Freezing temperatures engulfed the colonial town as the frozen harbor glistened, and icicles decorated the buildings. Streets and rooftops were powdered a pristine white, and the smoke billowing from every chimney brushed a charcoal haze across the sky. Strong winds howled and docked ships creaked, echoing throughout the town. When temperatures dipped to extreme lows for extended periods, life could become unendurable, as staying warm proved futile. Such weather made writing difficult, whether it was Warren recording information in his medical ledgers or Boston merchant John Rowe penning entries in his diary. Even indoor temperatures were so frigid that often, Rowe noted, "the ink freezes as I write."

The weather in January 1765—"the coldest of any for 12 years past together," as Rowe noted in his diary—was so frigid that Boston's harbor froze. Coming on the heels of smallpox and the fires, this problem proved especially painful. Ports to the south like New York City and Philadelphia had already overtaken Boston in size, volume, and economic importance; now Boston's solidified harbor only added to its merchants' economic woes. Moreover, the once abundant credit that Britain had extended to colonial merchants during the Seven Years' War was greatly reduced in peacetime, furthering economic anxiety.

A string of bankruptcies exacerbated the postwar depression in Boston, but none was more catastrophic than that of Nathaniel Wheelwright. One of the town's top merchants, Wheelwright had been extended large amounts of credit during the war: James Lloyd, for one, had loaned him the staggering sum of 1,150 pounds. Wheelwright in turn extended lines of credit to many Bostonians. Wheelwright and his father were rumored, during the French and Indian War, to have behaved traitorously with the French. In 1764, Wheelwright was caught smuggling wine, giving rise to rumors of his financial distress. Additionally, he had been duped into a con artist's scheme involving promises of a buried treasure. In January 1765, the bottom fell out. Wheelwright stopped honoring his debts that month, and it was soon discovered that he owed more money than he was worth, rendering his notes of credit to others worthless. Wheelwright had woven his debt so thoroughly into Boston's financial system that his insolvency set off a shock wave, toppling many other merchants, including John Scollay, a close friend and a patient of Warren's. Action was taken against Wheelwright, who fled Boston that August.

That summer many people suffered the effects of the financial meltdown, and Warren was no exception. According to James Otis, those affected were filled with "horror and dread." Although Warren's list of patients was growing, so was the amount of their outstanding debt. His early ledger book lists the numerous sundry items that he accepted as forms of payment, and lines on pages where he normally entered cash received remained blank. To exacerbate matters, his mother Mary claimed bankruptcy, but was able to take advantage under the new bankruptcy law that set more lenient terms for settling with creditors. Joseph and his brother Samuel took loans from Samuel Bowes and John Hancock in July and October 1765 respectively and as collateral deeded them all 150 acres of the family farm, including "all the edifices and buildings thereon standing."

It was in these straitened circumstances that the Warrens welcomed their first child into the world—a girl, Elizabeth, whom they baptized in Brattle Street Church. Warren also became closer to his wife's family and was chosen as godfather to one of Elizabeth's cousins. Even as his own family grew, Warren tried to shoulder the numerous financial burdens plaguing those around him. During this period he continued to lend money to family, patients, and friends—particularly his mother. To raise additional funds, late that July, he and Elizabeth sold a piece of land in "the Westerly part of Boston," likely inherited from her father, to shopkeeper Andrew Campbell for sixteen pounds.

In March 1765, as numerous bankruptcies threatened Boston's fragile economy, Parliament passed the Stamp Act in order to raise revenue to relieve the mounting debts that the Crown incurred from the French and Indian War, and to help pay for the costs of administering the colonies and keeping British troops on the colonies' western frontiers. The tax affected every level of colonial society, particularly people in cities. Playing cards, dice, and all printed papers were subject to tax, including legal documents, almanacs, mortgages, land deeds, attorney's licenses, newspapers, and even diplomas. Many colonists regarded the tax as odious and burdensome, and worried about the precedent it would establish. For the first time, Britain was directly taxing them. (The Stamp Act was not a duty on shipping but a direct tax on items purchased in the colonies.) If Parliament could impose taxes directly without approval by the colonial legislatures, this new power could become virtually limitless, as Samuel Adams argued.

In late May, word reached the colonists that the tax would take effect on November 1. That June the Massachusetts Assembly sent a circular letter to all the colonial assemblies, inviting them to a congress to be held in New York that October "to unite in a Petition to his Majesty and the Parliament, for relief under the insupportable Grievance of the Stamp Act." Twenty-seven members from nine colonies met at this extralegal body and composed a strong but respectful statement professing loyalty to the king but also declaring that as British subjects, they could not be taxed without their consent.

The passage of the Stamp Act exacerbated radicals' resentments over what they believed to be the unfair patronage system—resentments that dated back to the time when Governor Bernard passed over James Otis, Sr., for a court seat in favor of Thomas Hutchinson. Since then, Bernard had sided with Crown interests over colonial ones, and now his demand for colonial compliance with the Stamp Act only intensified radical ire. Ironically, Lieutenant Governor Hutchinson, increasingly unpopular with many New Englanders, was privately against the Stamp Act. Publicly, however, he fully intended to enforce it and his brother-in-law, Andrew Oliver, was appointed the stamp master for Massachusetts. To many Whigs, this appointment only served to underscore the Tory nepotism so rampant in Boston politics. Hutchinson had opposed the Land Bank and supported the issuance of the new writs of assistance in 1761. Soon, he and his cronies became the chief targets of patriot retribution.

Hatred for the Stamp Act catalyzed colonists' actions against the Crown and united Boston's elite, middle, and lower classes in protest.

To protest the act, a group of mostly tradesmen formed a secret radical political club known as the Loyal Nine, able to organize, direct,
and control crowd action. The club's organizers were friends, Masonic
brothers, and patients of Joseph Warren, including John Avery, a Harvard classmate, known within the group as "mob secretary." Thomas
Chase, Benjamin Edes, and Thomas Crafts were Warren's patients,
and Crafts and Chase were fellow members of St. Andrew's Masonic
Lodge. The Loyal Nine were just one of the many conduits connecting
Warren to powerful patriot cells.

The group courted Ebenezer Mackintosh and Henry Swift—the
leaders, respectively, of the South and North End mobs who battled
every Pope's Day—to form a muscular force. Using this mob as its
instrument, the Loyal Nine conducted a campaign of violent outbursts
and intimidation tactics to respond to the imperial measures. On the
early morning of August 14, 1765, a great old elm tree at Orange and
Essex streets in Boston was hung with an effigy of the newly appointed
stamp master, Andrew Oliver. The ancient tree was so immense that
its branches "seem'd to touch the skies." Hung from another branch
was a jackboot with a green sole stuffed with an emerging devil (meant
to represent despised prime ministers Lord Bute and George Grenville) holding a copy of the Stamp Act. A sign hung on the tree promised vengeance on anyone who tampered with the effigies. Instructions
for the decoration almost certainly came from the Loyal Nine and a
handful of other Whig leaders.

Throughout the day, thousands converged on the ancient and
immense elm, which would soon be dubbed "Liberty Tree." When
Sheriff Stephen Greenleaf, the brother of Warren's medical supplier,
tried to disperse the crowd, mob threats drove him away. That day,
Warren was in the area tending to patients, but with thousands of
angry Bostonians on the march, it would have been nearly impossible
for him to miss the action. At sunset the crowd carried the effigies to
Oliver's dock and tore down a building under construction that was
rumored to be the new stamp office. Then they beheaded the effigies
and burned them in a bonfire on Fort Hill. The throng then marched

to Andrew Oliver's house, where it broke his windows and furniture, drank his wine, and destroyed his garden fencing. Greenleaf made a second attempt to break up the crowd, this time with Lieutenant Governor Hutchinson, but a hail of stones lobbed by the angry mob forced him once again to flee. Oliver publicly declared his intent to resign as stamp master, and fearing for his safety, Governor Bernard fled to Castle William.

Over the next weeks, the vandalism and destruction surged. On August 26, the mobs began a campaign of intimidation and terror by visiting Charles Paxton, the surveyor of customs for the port of Boston. From there, they split into two gangs: one broke into the home of William Story, the deputy register of the vice admiralty court, and ransacked his papers and destroyed personal items. The other group set its sights on Benjamin Hallowell, the comptroller of customs (and another of Warren's patients and friends). Hallowell's home, the greatest in town according to many, was a distasteful symbol of the extravagance enjoyed by a handful of elite men as Boston's working class suffered. The mob broke the windows and furniture, tore down the doors, looted most of the books, papers, and money, and absconded with a lion's share of wine from the cellar.

Finally, at the end of the night the mobs converged on Thomas Hutchinson's home—an extravagant three-story brick Palladian built by his grandfather. To many angry Bostonians, Hutchinson had become the most potent symbol of their economic woes, one of the most visible Crown figures, and the personification of patronage. Armed with axes, rioters burst into the mansion "with the rage of devils [screaming] damn him he is upstairs we'll have him." They annihilated the property, destroying furniture, breaking windows, and slashing paintings. They tore up the grounds and cut trees down. They even began to take apart the roof before abandoning the property early that morning, taking with them Hutchinson's money, clothing, and other personal possessions. One chronicler recalled that the mob left "nothing remaining but the bare walls and floors."

The subsequent arrest of Ebenezer Mackintosh as the suspected ringleader made clear that the Loyal Nine had been the organizing force behind the Stamp Act riots and the link bridging the radical leaders with the mobs. Thomas Gage wrote that "merchants in general, Assembly Men, Magistrates . . . have been united in this Plan of Riots, and without the Influence and Instigation of these the inferior People would have been quiet. . . . The Sailors who are the only people who may be properly Stiled Mob, are entirely at the Command of the Merchants who employ them."

There is no evidence that Warren participated in the riots or helped plan the destructive behavior, but he did travel back and forth from Boston to Roxbury that day, seeing at least four patients. He had already publicly protested the Crown and counted many of the principal resistance leaders as friends, classmates, patients, and Masonic brethren. Likely, these protests galvanized him into more public political activity.

The Stamp Act riots, among the worst in Boston's history, had spiraled out of control and shocked many inhabitants. Aside from the physical damage and the loss of money and property, the sheer psychological terror left the victims feeling violated and petrified. In a town of fifteen thousand souls, a majority of Bostonians likely knew the perpetrators. The following day a meeting held in Boston unanimously condemned the riots and announced that the town selectmen and magistrates would be empowered "to suppress the like disorders for the future." Cadets and several militia companies staffed a night watch "to prevent any such further proceedings." The riots had made a strong statement against imperial policies, but wanton destruction had to cease immediately.

In the short term, the peace held. Law and order were restored. Even that year's annual Pope's Day festivities were peaceful, as mob leaders Mackintosh and Swift wore military habits and appeared without their traditional clubs and barrel staves. The *Boston Post-Boy* noted that "the town remained the whole night in better Order than it had ever been on this occasion."

But the efficacy of mob action had not been lost on the radical leaders, who would turn crowd action into a staple of the radical arsenal. The mobs followed orders, like restrictions on rioting on certain nights during the week. They instilled terror by adorning Tories, their houses, and their buildings with mixtures of human and animal wastes, and by perpetrating outright physical violence, such as beatings with cudgels and cutlasses, "running the gauntlet," riding the "wooden horse," and tarring and feathering. By anointing Mackintosh the prince of paupers, the more well-heeled plotters gained plausible deniability and a layer of insulation. Henry Bass, a member of the Loyal Nine and a cousin of Samuel Adams, wrote in a private letter that "[we] are not a little pleas'd to hear that McIntosh has the Credit of the whole Affair," meaning the Stamp Act riots. Citing the effectiveness of the crowd action, Bass and the Loyal Nine were determined to continue their protests, noting, "We endeavor to keep up the spirit which I think is as great as ever."

The heightened political turmoil spurred Joseph Warren back into the Masonic world, as he rejoined St. Andrew's Lodge a week after Pope's Day. His involvement with politics was on the rise. On October 7, 1765, a month before the Stamp Act was to take effect, he published an article under the pseudonym "B.W." in the *Boston Gazette*, the patriot newspaper owned by his friends and patients Benjamin Edes and John Gill. Here he explained the dangers lurking behind the act and identified those who stood to profit from its revenue. Declaring the stamps a "grievous and unconstitutional Tax," he invoked the argument put forth by Whig leaders "that no man shall be taxed but with his own consent." Since the colony was still paying the provincial debt from the French and Indian War, how, Warren asked, "will it be possible under the circumstances, to endure this tax," which would then "drain the province of the little cash left among us?" In addition, he claimed, the revenue collected would be "perverted to enrich a set of corrupt individuals . . . to make certain Officers among us independent of the People." In closing he urged, "Awake my countrymen, and by a regular and legal opposition defeat the designs of those who enslave us and our posterity. . . . Ages remote, mortals yet unborn, will bless your generous efforts, and revere the memory of the saviours of their country."

For the moment, Warren advocated a nonviolent and legal path of resistance to the injustices. But his opinion evolved rapidly, growing more insistent on the urgency of the colonists' situation and the need for them to make a commensurate response.

At that time the colonies behaved more like independent provinces, and colonists often knew more about events transpiring in Britain than in the other colonies. But the Stamp Act Congress that met in New York in October 1765 attempted to unify the colonies to act in concert against British measures. A few months later Warren, in one of his earliest surviving personal letters, wrote to his friend and former Harvard classmate Edmund Dana—then in England studying medicine—about the Stamp Act:

> *Never has there been a time, since the first settlement of America, in which the people had so much reason as to be alarmed as the present. The whole continent is inflamed to the highest degree. . . . The strange project of levying a stamp duty . . . has roused their jealousy and resentment. They can conceive of no liberty when they have lost the power of taxing themselves, and when all controversies between the Crown and the people are to be determined by the opinion of one dependent man . . . some particular families have been able to acquire a very large share of property, from which must arise a kind of aristocracy: that is, the power and authority of some persons or families is exercised in proportion to the decrease of the independence and property of the people in general. . . . The colonies, until now, were ever at variance, and foolishly jealous of each other. They are now . . . united for their common defense against what they believe to be oppression.*

Warren went on to maintain that the colonists still regarded "His Majesty's integrity and goodness of heart" rather than the "conduct of his late minister." In 1766 the colonists directed their anger and opposition at the ministers and the administration, not at the king himself.

Even so, the ministry in London was shocked at the outcry from the colonists. George III dismissed George Grenville as prime minister over a dispute unrelated to the colonies and replaced him with the Earl of Rockingham, a onetime opponent of the Stamp Act who was connected to many London merchants affected by the burgeoning colonial boycotts. The new prime minister convinced the king and Parliament to repeal the Stamp Act, which they did on March 18, 1766. But lest Britain appear weak—or worse, encourage the colonists to think that their acts of intimidation had been effective—Parliament took care to frame the repeal in terms that discounted the influence of the resistance. Since the boycotts inspired by the act had affected British trade, the ministry concluded that the act had ultimately stood in opposition to Britain's commercial interests. To reaffirm Britain's hegemony, Parliament passed the Declaratory Act, which affirmed its "full power and authority to make laws and statutes of sufficient force and validity to bind the colonies and people of America, subjects of the crown of Great Britain, in all cases whatsoever."

Still, the Whigs had won a major victory, against an unstable, revolving ministry in London. According to John Adams, the act's rescindment "hushed into silence almost every popular clamour and composed every wave of popular disorder into a smooth and peaceful calm." Britain explicitly denied that the colonists' violent outcry had been effective, but patriots came to view their radical "protests" as quite an effective tool paving the way for future mobbish behavior. The radicals would have to strike just the right balance. They were careful not to celebrate the more destructive mob behavior of August 26, but they still needed to promote crowd action that was more effective than that of August 14, 1765.

At the time of the Stamp Act, Warren defined "liberty" as a right to self-government and colonial home rule. This view found favor with a majority of patriot Whigs in America, who believed that a corrupt ministry was conspiring to eradicate the inherent liberty they possessed as British subjects. Patriots despied Crown figureheads in the colonies, like Bernard, for their willingness to enforce policies viewed as destructive to loyal British subjects.

Warren was quickly becoming one of the more radical of the patriots. In his 1766 letter to Edmund Dana about the Stamp Act, he asserted that some colonists believed that the Crown "designed by this act to force the colonies into a rebellion . . . and, by military power, to reduce them to servitude." He introduced the idea of revolution, warning that, "when the rage of the people is raised by oppression to such a height," it would "break out in rebellion." The eminent historian Bernard Bailyn has called "such a supposition . . . perhaps excessive," and in 1766 Warren's outlook was indeed extreme when compared to the Whig mainstream. And as events progressed, Warren's views grew more extreme.

The royal administration in America and Britain thought the radical Whigs were conspiring against the Crown—a "power-hungry cabal that professed loyalty to England while assiduously working to destroy the bonds of authority and force a rupture between England and her colonies," as Bailyn described them. But Warren, along with Samuel Adams and a handful of other fervently radical Whigs, fixed upon separation as the goal, long before the majority of colonists even considered it.

Peter Oliver, brother of Andrew Oliver, subsequently named Warren as the central figure in recruiting a potential candidate into the radical faction:

> Independence, it is true, was declared in Congress in 1776, but it was settled in Boston, in 1768, by [Samuel] Adams and his Junto. I have authority for this assertion . . . a gentleman who was tampered with by . . . Warren, who was a most active Man among the faction. Warren was in Hopes to take this Gentleman into their number, and . . . He told him that "Independence was their Object; that it was supposed that great Britain would resent it and would lay the Town of Boston in

ashes, from their Ships; that an Estimate had accordingly been made
of the Value of the Estates in Town; and that they had determined to
pay the Losses of their friends from the Estates of the Loyalists in the
Country." The gentleman had refused to join with them, but Warren
replied, that they would pursue their Scheme. This scheme was not
divulged to the People, for . . . I believe, they would, then, have been
shocked at the Proposal.

Oliver has Warren plotting for independence just two years after his letter to Dana. Some might argue the account to be exaggerated, but in light of the figure he would become, it suggests he played a significant role in the faction years before the explosive massacre and the Tea Party.

Undoubtedly, support for independence was an extreme position at the time, considering that a majority of colonists were unwilling to take such a step even years later in 1776. For Warren and other intelligentsia of Enlightenment philosophy, the Hobbesian notion of a top-down system of absolute monarchical rule had been replaced with the ideas of natural rights to life, liberty, and property championed by John Locke and John-Jacques Rousseau. Sovereignty originated from below and manifested in virtuous and accountable men, such as Addison's Cato. Years later John Adams explained in a letter to Thomas Jefferson, "The Revolution was in the minds of the people, and this was effected, from 1760 to 1775."

In that era, one of the most important figures in fomenting rebellion was Samuel Adams, cousin to two future presidents and an iconic brewer/maltster. Nearly a generation older than Warren, Adams had graduated from Harvard in 1743. A notably miserable businessman, he found his calling in politics, writing essays against early Crown impositions on colonial self-rule. Adams, known for his piety and intellect, was chosen as a tax collector by the town of Boston and then a representative to the legislature. The Massachusetts assembly then chose him as its clerk, providing a regular salary. He came to wide prominence for his public opposition to the Stamp and Sugar Acts.

By the time of Warren's radicalization, Adams was one of the most important and powerful revolutionary leaders.

Samuel Adams would not become one of Dr. Warren's patients until 1768, but their relationship began a few years earlier. In the mid-1760s, Warren and more than three dozen New England men of consequence joined forces to bail Adams out from under the debts that had plagued him for years. Adams had been a poor tax collector and ended up on the hook for more than one thousand pounds in uncollected money. One Son of Liberty declared that if Adams's "fortune was equal to his [political] abilities . . . He would be certainly one of the richest men in America." Collectively, the patriot group raised the sum for him. A good number of the "subscribers towards Mr. Adams's debt" were Warren's friends, patients, and Whig colleagues. The wealthy John Hancock gave the most, at just over 266 pounds, but Dr. Warren's total donation of over thirteen pounds was higher than that of many others. Considering that Warren was dealing with his own financial turmoil in the wake of the Wheelwright collapse, his donation represented a considerable sum.

Most scholars and historians regard Warren as having been Adams's political protégé, but the balance of power between the two men was more complicated. Samuel Adams did offer Warren guidance and a model for political participation. Though Adams was nearly twenty years Warren's senior and far more politically experienced, theirs was not a mentor relationship such as Warren had shared with Lloyd. Both men were sons of selectmen who had earned master's degrees from Harvard and were considered gentlemen in their community. When Warren entered the faction, he had already adopted a radical political ideology, and he was connected to important figures in the Harvard and Masonic communities. The doctor had much to offer Adams, both financially and politically. In addition to giving Adams money to help pay off his debts, Warren had Tory connections—with the Hutchinsons and Olivers—that made him an attractive representative of the radical agenda. While most Crown supporters saw Adams as the Machiavellian brain behind the rebellion, many also viewed him as a vengeful political charlatan and freeloader who too readily accepted charity from friends and other Whigs. Since money was one of the determining factors of social status, as a successful physician, Warren garnered a certain level of respect from leading British officials that they never afforded to Adams, who had been a failure as a businessman.

And when Warren threw himself into politics, he did so with the same intensity of purpose that had helped him rise through the ranks at Harvard and establish the most successful medical practice in Boston. Within a few years, he would either lead or be a member of the various patriot organizations that formed the radical faction in Massachusetts.

Meeting above the print shop of Benjamin Edes and John Gill, Warren and other patriots would gather to draw up the radical agenda aimed at opposing recent British policies and to write polemical arguments for the *Boston Gazette*. John Adams later described it as "a curious employment, cooking up paragraphs, articles, occurrences, &c.—working the political engine!" Referring to the *Gazette*, Governor Francis Bernard wrote, "If the Devil himself were of one party, [Whig] as he virtually is, there could not have been got together a greater Collection of impudent virulent and seditious Lies, perversions of truth and misrepresentations than are to be found in this publication."

In June 1766, Warren authored a series of articles for the *Gazette* under the pseudonym "Paskalos." Governor Bernard had just vetoed James Otis, Jr.'s, bid to become speaker of the House, and Warren mounted an unprecedented attack. The governor, he claimed, had prepared two sets of letters in anticipation of the possible repeal of the Stamp Act, designed to protect him in case of either outcome. Referring to him as wicked and duplicitous, a coward and a beggar, Warren accused Bernard of sacrificing "the happiness of this province to your foolish passions." Once again acknowledging King George's sovereignty, Warren wrote that "our present most gracious King, is truly the Father of his people," and he also held his friend Lieutenant

Governor Hutchinson in "esteem" and "honor." But with Bernard, Warren warned, "I will no longer refrain my pen, but will freely lash your vices and follies (which you know are many and great) unless you immediately desist from your barbarous attempt to spread dissension and ruin through this my native country."

Some believed this article chastizing the governor was excessively disrespectful and caustic. One week later Warren responded to them, not straying from his initial sentiments. He would withdraw his accusations, he said, only if Bernard were "in a state of insanity." Otherwise Warren was "determined to give loose to my pen, and will be restrained by nothing but the Sacred laws of truth and justice." In closing, the doctor claimed that he was "governed by no party" and had "no interest to serve," suggesting an unwillingness to reveal how intimately involved with the radical machines he had become. The following week, once again writing in the *Gazette*, he advised Bernard, a "worthless treacherous man," to "depart from this province in as honorable a manner as you can." Warren's scathing attacks struck the perfect chord with most angry colonists. His highly charged diatribes would reverberate throughout the colonies and Britain.

Despite his political work, Warren remained devoted to his growing medical clientele. The two practices soon began to reinforce each other in ways that would draw him deeper into the radical movement. In August 1766, Warren traveled to Connecticut, where he investigated the alleged healing properties of certain waters in Stafford Springs.

Ironically, this journey was the farthest he would ever travel from the Boston area. In a geographic sense, the patriot doctor was more "Yankee" than most of his radical comrades. Eighteenth-century Massachusetts was a world with close kinship ties. Whether by social, educational, or religious affiliations, many Bay Colony natives shared a communal spirit, being "closely related by blood and marriage, intensely suspicious of strangers, and firmly set in their ancestral ways." Warren, a fourth-generation American, with extensive family, a wide array of clients, and an intricate network of friends and associates, was embedded squarely in that world. The Whig faction would benefit from networks such as his.

Back home, the string of 1765 bankruptcies—particularly Wheelwright's—continued to gall many Bostonians. Settling Wheelwright's complex estate would take years, and in 1767 Lieutenant Governor Hutchinson appointed Warren the estate's administrator.

It was an odd appointment considering Warren, who was not a lawyer and had little apparent fiduciary experience, and was of no relation to Wheelwright, was experiencing financial challenges. Hutchinson had known the Warren family for many years, having overseen the settlement of Warren's father's estate after he died intestate. Warren knew Hutchinson's son from Harvard, and even in these increasingly heated times, he continued to serve as physician to Hutchinson and members of his family. Hutchinson was probably attempting to help Warren with some patronage while trying to lure him away from the Whig faction.

Notices appeared in several newspapers announcing that "all persons indebted to the estate of Nathaniel Wheelwright, Esq; deceased, are desired to make immediate payment, as the creditors have requested the administrator to sue for every debt which is not paid before the next court. No further notice is to be expected, but the desire of the creditors will be complied with, By Joseph Warren, administrator of said estate." Within weeks it was reported that the trial before the superior court "lasted four days, and we hear, the jury, bro't in their Verdict in favor of the Administrator," Joseph Warren. Warren remained involved as the Wheelwright administrator, dealing with cases surrounding the estate, for several more years. And although he continued to maintain and cultivate relationships with staunch Crown supporters, he drew ever closer to the nucleus of Whig radicalism.

7

UNSHEATH THY QUILL

"The greatest perade perhaps ever seen
in the Harbour of Boston."
—DEACON JOHN TUDOR

AS JOSEPH WARREN'S WEALTH AND SOCIAL STANDING CONTINUED
to increase, so did the size of his family. His son, also named Joseph
Warren, was baptized in the Brattle Street church on September 13,
1767. It was a joyous moment for Joseph and Elizabeth, as well as for
Mary Warren, who gazed proudly upon the grandchild who would
carry on her late husband's name. At a time when infant mortality
was rampant, the Warrens were blessed with two healthy children. But
there were sorrows, too; Warren's maternal grandfather, Dr. Samuel
Stevens, passed away in February 1769, a loss that weighed heavily on
Warren, who'd come to view Stevens as a father figure after his own
father's death twelve years earlier.

Thanks to the will of Warren's departed father-in-law, Richard
Hooton, the growing family was able to feel more comfortable. Elizabeth inherited the majority of her father's estate, and between 1765
and 1767 Joseph received notes and cash payments totaling close to

a thousand pounds from the will's executor. Elizabeth also inherited half the wharf that bore her maiden name, valued at approximately 266 pounds. Finally the Warrens received some property and sundry items from the estate: furniture, coffee, and several pieces of jewelry.

Warren's rigorous work ethic remained constant no matter what extra money was coming in. His practice grew steadily, as did his diverse clientele within the New England community.

In the world of Freemasonry, St. Andrew's Lodge had been involved in a long-standing feud with the rival St. John's Lodge, the original home of Freemasonry in Boston. Warren helped spearhead efforts to reconcile with St. John's for a "happy coalition," and when the grand master of St. John's, Jeremiah Gridley, passed away, Warren and his St. Andrew's brethren attended the funeral. John Rowe claimed the funeral had the largest number of mourners in the history of the Bay Colony to that point.

The community took note of Warren's growing reputation. When a controversy erupted in 1767, he was asked to lend his expertise. Miles Whitworth and Thomas Young, both physicians, had been treating the same patient, a Mrs. Davis, who eventually died. Although Whitworth had originally been attending Davis, Young had been called in to provide additional treatment and consultation. But when Davis's condition deteriorated under Young's care, Whitworth was notified. Young's treatments, he found, involved bleeding the patient. Infuriated, he blamed her death on Young and reached out to his medical peers to weigh in.

Warren, under the pseudonym "Philo Physic," wrote a series of newspaper articles that fanned the flames of controversy. Like the majority of eighteenth-century physicians, he practiced bloodletting, but his letters and medical journals reveal that he believed in a more judicious use of the procedure, on a case-by-case basis. He sided against Young, claiming, "There is nothing in this account that can in the least justify blood-letting, and no judicious physician would prescribe it in such a circumstance." Dr. Young, under the pseudonym Misophlauros, fired back at Warren, leading to an acrimonious exchange in the press. Young threatened to sue over the loss of his reputation, to which Warren replied, "I would just hint to you, that before you can expect to recover damages for the loss of reputation, you must prove that you had a reputation to lose."

By 1767, at only twenty-six, Warren had already been in business for several years, with one of the fastest-growing medical practices in the Boston area. His newspaper articles showcased his acerbic wit and his impressive technical knowledge of his craft—he had that rare mixture of working-class farmer and gentleman scholar that would catapult him to the top echelons of colonial Boston. But it was also notable—and noticed by many who knew Warren's identity—that he had sided with Whitworth, a Tory, even though Young shared Warren's political sympathies. It showed *Gazette* readers, and indeed the Boston community at large, that he could be fair and impartial.

In September 1767, news reached the colonies of a bill pending in Parliament "for granting certain duties . . . and for preventing the clandestine running of goods." (The Declaratory Act in 1766 had asserted that the British government maintained absolute legislative authority over the colonies.) The Townshend Acts, as the bill was known, was named after Charles Townshend, the chancellor of the exchequer. It imposed customs duties on imported paper, paint, glass, silk, and tea from Britain, to pay for royal administration in the colonies. Its enforcement program brought renewed attention to the writs of assistance, the hated court orders allowing customs officials to conduct arbitrary searches for contraband in public and private places.

These new duties were "external" taxes on imports, in contrast to the Stamp Act's direct taxes, but they found no greater favor with the colonists. John Rowe declared them "an imposition on America . . . as dangerous as the Stamp Act." Almost immediately, Bostonians rallied against the Townshend Acts and agreed to refuse to purchase goods imported from Britain. That way they could not only avoid the tax but also hurt influential merchants across the Atlantic. Dated October 28, 1767, the nonimportation agreement garnered more than 650 signatures, including those of Warren and many of his associates, friends, patients, and neighbors, among them more than fifty women.

In February 1768, in an effort to crystallize public opinion against the duties, Samuel Adams composed a circular letter denouncing the Townshend Acts and calling for intercolonial communication and unity. The letter was sent to the other colonial legislatures. Thereupon British secretary of state Lord Hillsborough—who called it "an open opposition to and denial of the authority of Parliament"—instructed Governor Bernard to dissolve the Massachusetts House unless it rescinded Adams's letter, and he sent the same message to royal governors throughout the colonies. Hillsborough then alerted Gen. Thomas Gage, the commander in chief of all British forces in North America, that additional troops might soon be needed in Boston. Parliament exacerbated tensions by proposing that the ringleaders behind the circular letter be tried in Britain for treason.

Fully aware that disregarding Crown orders would only hasten British wrath, the Massachusetts House, in a bold and seminal move, voted 92 to 17 against rescinding Adams's letter. Paul Revere memorialized the iconic vote, making a "Sons of Liberty Bowl" that read "To the memory of the glorious ninety-two . . . who . . . from a strict regard to conscience, and the liberties of their constituents, on the 30 of June 1768, voted not to rescind." The seventeen who sided with the Crown were viewed as "so mean spirited to vote away their blessings as Englishmen, namely their rights, liberty and properties." Their names were conspicuously posted on Liberty Tree.

The House vote prompted Governor Bernard to dismiss the Massachusetts General Court, forcing Warren and the other radicals to coalesce and conduct their "business" in the town meetings. Realizing the threat the town meetings would present to royal authority, Thomas Hutchinson wrote to Lord Hillsborough in Britain declaring that the "associations and assemblies, pretending to be legal and constitutional, assuming powers that belong only to established authority, prove more fatal to this authority than mobs, riots, or the most tumultuous disorders"—an incredible statement considering what the mobs had done to Hutchinson's home and property during the Stamp Act riots. Crown officials agreed, deeming town meetings held for political purposes illegal.

Though many Boston Tories considered town meeting participants a "herd of fools and knaves," Warren recognized their significance, not only serving on several town committees but also urging his less radical friends to join the proceedings. Years later John Adams wrote, "I was solicited to go to the town-meetings, and harangue there. My friend, Dr. Warren, most frequently urged me to do this." Warren served on several town meeting committees. He wrote to John Dickinson, thanking him for his *Letter from a Pennsylvania Farmer*, which acknowledged Parliament's authority to regulate colonial trade and manufacturing but deemed unconstitutional any bill enacted by Parliament for the sole purpose of raising revenue.

Warren also wrote multiple letters to the Londoner John Wilkes, the bête noir of the king's ministry. In 1763 Wilkes had become an icon to many radicals, including Warren, after penning essay number 45 for his inflammatory publication *The North Briton*. The essay ridiculed the king's ministry and faulted George III for peace terms too favorable to France following the Seven Years' War. Criticism of the king was forbidden. The article was declared "a seditious and treasonable libel," and the king ordered Wilkes's immediate arrest, setting in motion a series of events that would lead to his exile, eventual return, and his jailing in 1768. To protest his imprisonment, thousands of his supporters flocked to St. George's Fields near the King's Bench Prison in South London, where Wilkes was serving his sentence. On May 10, the angry crowd began to throw rocks at the soldiers, whereupon the king's troops fired upon them, killing approximately ten and injuring more than a dozen. News of the tragedy, dubbed the "St. George's Fields Massacre," sailed across the Atlantic to the outraged and dismayed colonists just as British troops were preparing to descend on Boston Harbor. Warren would come to emulate Wilkes and his sharp tongue and quill, calling him "the man in whose fortunes he and his posterity are interested." Warren wrote letters to Wilkes as part of a five-man committee on June 6, 1768, and October 5, 1768. On April 13, 1769, Warren took "the Liberty of writing him singly."

When Governor Bernard began to quash the Boston Town Meetings, Warren looked to Wilkes's diatribes to inspire his own response. And as Wilkes had done with his essay number 45, Warren would take his attack on Bernard too far. As the court and country parties battled for control in the Massachusetts General Court, Bernard, hoping to exclude subversives like James Otis, Jr., vetoed radical Whig councilors and then wrote to Lord Shelburne in Britain justifying his decision. When that letter found its way back to the General Court, Warren accused Bernard of misrepresenting the province and slandering a number of its inhabitants to the British administration. In the *Boston Gazette*, under the pseudonym "A True Patriot," he wrote of the governor, "men totally abandoned to wickedness, can never merit our regard, be their station ever so high. If such men are by God appointed, the devil may be the Lord's anointed."

Bernard considered the article libelous and referred it to both houses in the Massachusetts legislature, who found that it was "mischievous in its tendency" and a "false, scandalous and impudent libel on your Excellency." But the Whig-leaning lower House concluded that since no name was specifically mentioned, it would "take no further notice of it," stating, "The liberty of the press is a great bulwark of the liberty of the people." Bernard looked to the Council to prosecute the printers of the *Gazette*, but the body refused. Angered, the governor dissolved the General Court the next day.

The following week Warren penned another article for the *Gazette*, rejoicing in this victory over Bernard. He was satisfied

> *to find all orders of unplaced independent men, firmly determined, as far as in them lies, to support their own rights, and the Liberty of the press. . . . This province has been most barbarously traduced; and now*

groan under the weight of those misfortunes which have been hereby
brought upon it; we have detected some of the authors; we will zealously
endeavor to deprive them of the power of injuring us hereafter.

Here Warren was extending his target beyond the governor, en-
deavoring to take the radical cause to each colonist, vowing—as he
had to Wilkes—that "the iron rod of oppression" shall be broken.

It is remarkable, given his strong public invective in the *Gazette*, that
Warren was able for so long to continue his delicate social balancing
act and keep the respect and admiration of both Whigs and Tories. It
suggests that Warren had found a way to be many things to different
people. Ever since his apprenticeship under the Tory James Lloyd, he
had grown his medical practice thanks to the subscription of many
Tory patients. Shunning or harassing Tories in the early days would
have been financial suicide. And so a mutual respect existed between
Warren and the Tories in his social circles, persisting even into the
early years of political discord. Therefore in June 1768, when John
Hancock's sloop *Liberty* was seized for customs violations, Warren was
seen as the ideal candidate to mediate between the hostile parties.

Hancock, having inherited his uncle's fortune in 1764, was one of
the wealthiest men in Boston. As a merchant, smuggler, and patriot
supporter, he drew intense scrutiny from the customs commissioners.
For years, Boston's merchants had bribed Crown officials to turn a
blind eye to their illicit cargoes, but the passage of the Townshend Acts
brought a crackdown on smuggling.

Prior to the confiscation of the *Liberty*, Warren warned Benjamin
Hallowell, comptroller of customs and also his patient, that if Hancock's vessel were confiscated, it would stoke "a great uproar" of which
Warren "could not be answerable for the consequences." After the
sloop's seizure, just as Warren had warned, an infuriated radical mob
assaulted several customs inspectors and vandalized their homes. The
mob even burned one of their victims' boats. Only after appeals from
Warren and other radical Whig leaders did the throngs disperse.

The terrified customs commissioners fled to Castle William, aboard the king's ship-of-war *Romney*, and desperately tried to negotiate a temporary compromise. Considering Warren "a person of credit," they arranged for a meeting between him and Commissioner Hallowell. Warren proposed that if the *Liberty* were returned to the wharf, he would quell the mobs and ensure that Hancock posted bond. The commissioners agreed, but radical leaders meeting at Hancock's house would make no concessions, and Warren told Hallowell that the offer had been rescinded.

A town meeting was called later that month to protest the sloop's seizure, and Warren served on every committee, in various capacities, urging armed resistance against the Townshend duties and devising resolves and petitions. As chairman of the committee responsible for instructing members of the General Court, he declared that the "invaluable rights and liberties" of the colonists would be protected "at the utmost hazard of our lives and fortunes."

Prodded by the radical leaders, the patriot mobs continued their depredations against customs officials. Alarmed, the Crown dispatched more than two thousand soldiers to Boston. Radical leaders gathered at their homes to devise strategies to resist the landing of Crown forces, to be voted on at the next town meeting. They petitioned Governor Bernard to reconvene the General Court, and when he refused, they called on Massachusetts to form an extralegal provincial convention.

In late September, delegates from towns across Massachusetts gathered at the provincial convention to discuss what steps might be taken against the Crown. Calling the convention was an important step toward resistance to imperial authority, but once the delegates assembled, they lacked unanimity. Several top Whig leaders held positions more moderate than Joseph Warren and Samuel Adams. And many areas in the Bay Colony were not ready for unity and mobilization.

On October 1, British troops entered the town of Boston, including the 14th and 29th Regiments, a detachment of the 59th Infantry Regiment, and the Royal Regiment of Artillery. (Two more regiments arrived in subsequent months.) Their arrival brought the convention to an abrupt end. To many inhabitants, their town appeared to be under siege. It was a visible manifestation of imperial dominance. "We see Boston surrounded with aboute 14 ships, or vessells of war," wrote John Tudor, a North End deacon. "The greatest perade perhaps ever seen in the Harbour of Boston. . . . All the troops landed under cover of the cannon of the ships of war . . . with muskets charged, bayonets fixed (perhaps expecting to have met with resestance as the Soldiers afterwards told the inhabitants)." John Mein, the Tory publisher of the conservative *Boston Chronicle*, who had attacked John Gill of the *Boston Gazette* in the street with a club in early 1768, and who would later be forced from the colony after radical mobs nearly lynched him, happily reported that the convention's members, fearing arrest, "broke up and rushed out of town like a herd of scalded hogs." Thomas Hutchinson reported that "the red-coats make a formidable appearance and there is a profound silence among the Sons of Liberty."

To prevent desertions, Gage had instructed Lt. Col. William Dalrymple, in charge of the two regiments from Halifax, to tell his troops that "the king will reward his officers and soldiers with the estates of the rebels." Evidently in 1768, both Gage (who had arrived in Boston in mid-October) and Warren anticipated a full-scale conflict that would end with the victor confiscating the other's property. With stationed British soldiers numbering roughly the same as white Bostonian men, the colonists felt threatened and overpowered. Warren, aware of the dangers, burned his private papers but remained in the town, conducting business and treating his patients.

With around four thousand redcoats now stationed in Boston, Warren realized that some of them were fellow Masons. Shrewdly, he extended his Masonic embrace toward them. In November 1768 he provided use of the Green Dragon Tavern to the regimental lodges in the 29th and 64th Regiments. And when he and his fellow St. Andrew's brothers sought to appoint a grand master for a new lodge of ancients from the Grand Lodge of Scotland, they requested the assistance of various Masonic British officers then occupying the town. The officers complied, due to "favorable consideration in which the young and popular Warren was held by the military men of that day," and granted the petition. On May 13, 1769, Warren was appointed the Scottish Rite "grand master of Masons in Boston, New England, and within one hundred miles of the same."

The new Massachusetts Grand Lodge of St. Andrew was organized in a ceremony at the Green Dragon on December 27, 1769. Warren was installed as grand master, and two British officers served as senior and junior grand wardens, an arrangement that testified yet again to Warren's ability to move gracefully in conflicting worlds.

Still, the arrangement could not reduce the sheer number of British troops stationed in the town. Their very presence, and the question of where to quarter them, divided Massachusetts along political lines. One observer claimed that even as Castle William remained empty, "the Barraks provided by the Province at a great expense . . . caus'd so many disputes aboute quartering the troops in the town." Warren and the radicals claimed that quartering a standing army in a time of peace without the legislature's consent violated the colony's charter and sought their removal.

Day-to-day relations between troops and colonists were uneasy at best. Many British already held the colonists in low esteem: they were, after all, an inferior lot, thousands of miles from civilized and superior Great Britain—an opinion the troops shared openly and loudly. One of the king's troops wrote a letter to a local newspaper, declaring that the inhabitants of Boston reveled in "debauchery and licentiousness . . . the men are all hypocrites, and the women [whores]; so that the Yankey War, contrary to all others, will produce more births than burials." Some of the troops believed war with the patriots to be inevitable. British contempt for the civilian population festered, as patriot views of the British deteriorated in turn.

If locals regarded the British soldiers' treatment of the colonists as savage, they found punishments inflicted on these same soldiers by their superiors—the British officer class—far more brutal. One soldier from the 14th Regiment, Richard Ames, deserted but was caught and subsequently court-martialed. Sentenced to death, he was shot on the common and buried where he fell. Other soldiers were severely whipped for infractions. Some of the punishments were meted out by West Indian–born blacks serving as company drummers within the 29th Regiment, which further inflamed New Englanders by upsetting the racial hierarchy.

Boston newspaper accounts derided the brutality. The *Boston News-Letter* reported that one soldier was sentenced to "only eight hundred Lashes," of which 380 were administered before he "was then carried off to the hospital to all appearance a dead man." Another soldier received lashes under orders of his "humane officer" until "seemingly *insensible* of the strokes as would have been a statue of marble." When colonists referred to British soldiers as "bloodybacks," it was not simply because of their scarlet-colored uniforms. New Englanders were no strangers to harsh punishments, but if the British officers could inflict such draconian measures on their own men, they reasoned, what might they inflict on the colonists?

Some opportunistic Boston locals and merchants still rented out space to British officers—a practice many found odious—but a majority of Bostonians believed that the presence of armed troops indicated the Crown's plan to implement a regime of oppression, encroaching on liberties to which the colonists were entitled as British subjects. "It is well known indeed," Samuel Adams declared, "that from their first landing, their behavior was to a great degree insolent. . . . [They] really believed, that we were a country of rebels and that they were sent here to subdue us." Many idle soldiers, underpaid and bored, turned to cheap spirits, and inebriated, they became an endemic problem. Reports surfaced of "Disturbances . . . and some tumults . . . occasioned by the insults and outrages of the drunken soldiery, in which colonists and soldiers were wounded." Underpaid soldiers competed with Boston men for the few part-time work opportunities available, and they sexually targeted local women.

Tensions between Bostonians and the British were about to explode. New violent attacks, reminiscent of the 1765 Stamp Act Riots, erupted on the streets with alarming frequency. Threats, intimidation tactics, and other coercive measures stunned communities at home and overseas. The day after the troops arrived in Boston, a British captain declared that John Rowe was a "damn incendiary and I shall see you hanged in your shoes." That same year an off-duty British officer challenged Warren to a fight. The doctor refused the challenge, and the officer grabbed Warren, who struck his assailant and knocked him down. Before long, Warren noticed even more patients who were casualties of confrontations with Tories.

In March 1769, a town committee of which Warren was a member petitioned the king to remove all troops, but the plea fell on deaf ears across the Atlantic, where troop deployments to the town of rebellion were regarded as necessary. Government ministers in Britain ultimately decided, rather than remove the troops, to permanently recall the hated Governor Bernard and receive from him a first-hand report on the deteriorating situation.

And so on August 1, 1769, exactly nine years to the day after his arrival, Francis Bernard departed the Bay Colony, carrying a copy of the request for his removal from office, for which the Massachusetts House had voted unanimously. Across the town, bonfires blazed, bells tolled, and cannons boomed to celebrate that "the king had been graciously pleased to recall a very bad governor." Warren's relentless attacks on Bernard in the press had helped channel the public's resentment directly at the outgoing governor.

With Bernard removed, the radical leadership turned to his successor in the Tory hot seat. Thomas Hutchinson surrounded himself with family and friends to build a political team of loyal allies, arousing patriot outrage at a system primed for tyranny. And as Warren and his comrades were aware, Governor Bernard (as well as General Gage, Admiral Hood, and the Customs Commissioners) had sent numerous disparaging letters to George III that "grossly misrepresented" them. At a town meeting in Faneuil Hall on October 4, 1769, Warren, James Otis, Jr., Samuel and John Adams, and several other patriot leaders were chosen for a committee to "vindicate the character of the town, from the false and injurious representations contained in the letters." That meeting unanimously agreed that merchants who were still importing goods from Great Britain—among them, the two sons of Governor Hutchinson—would be listed on the town records for all "posterity" to know "who not only deserted, but opposed their country." The merchants' names had appeared in several Boston newspapers the previous August, when they had been publicly castigated as traitors to "be looked upon with an eye of contempt." This October meeting marked a critical turning point for Warren, as his relationship with Hutchinson began to sour, hampering his popularity and influence in Tory circles but increasing his power and relevance among Whigs.

IN THE EARLY MORNING HOURS OF SEPTEMBER 5, 1769, A LARGE comet with a long tail streamed above Boston—perhaps a premonition of the terrible events that would unfold later in the day. James Otis, Jr., entered the British Coffee House, where the Long Wharf intersected King Street, and there had a heated exchange with customs commissioner John Robinson over comments Otis had made, which had appeared in the *Boston Gazette* the previous day. He had called the commissioners "blockheads." He had specifically targeted Robinson, claiming that if he "misrepresents me, I have a natural right if I can get no other satisfaction to break his head."

At the coffee house, the pair chose to resolve their grievances with blows, and as Otis led the way out of the room, Robinson grabbed him by the nose. The two men attacked each other with canes, and several of Robinson's friends beat Otis with a medley of weapons. As was reported soon afterward, "The general cry was Kill him! Kill him!" (The *Boston Gazette* would later exaggerate the incident as an assassination attempt.) Several others, including a man who suffered a fractured wrist during the melee, managed to stop the fight.

But Otis had sustained an open wound, which spilled large amounts of blood across his face and made him almost unrecognizable. Warren was immediately summoned and tended to the wound as best he could. Then, outraged, he stormed into the coffee house to openly challenge one of the assailants.

The following day, thousands of indignant Bostonians converged on Faneuil Hall, where one of the accused attackers, William Brown, had been taken. Even before his attack on Otis, the radicals had despised Brown; he was one of the seventeen House representatives who had voted to rescind Samuel Adams's circular protesting the Townshend Acts. Brown was released by justices of the peace Samuel Pemberton and Richard Dana, two of Warren's friends and patients, but relentless mobs followed, threatened, and harassed him. He was spared further harm only by divine providence, when the tail end of a hurricane struck Boston and torrential rains emptied the streets.

James Otis would suffer from periods of great instability after the attack. His injury ended his tenure as a legitimate Whig leader, relegating him to little more than a figurehead. His behavior became wild: "Otis got into a mad Freak . . . and broke a great many windows in the town house." The following month he "behaved very madly, firing guns out of his window." On the advice of Warren and other physicians, Otis retired to the "country for the recovery of his health." He was too valuable for radicals to shelve, but they could not allow such crazed volatility to go unchecked, particularly with mobs, whose ire he influenced, on the loose.

A few weeks after the Otis affair, as an angry crowd (attempting to serve a warrant for the theft of firewood) confronted soldiers marching back from the guardhouse on Boston Neck, a soldier was struck by a thrown object. His gun discharged and hit a blacksmith's forge. That blacksmith, Obadiah Whiston, then punched a British soldier in the face, which nearly precipitated a riot. Within days, on October 28, an infuriated crowd stripped, tarred, and feathered George Gailer, a sailor and suspected customs informer, who had served aboard the *Liberty* when the customs service used that ship to patrol against smugglers. His tormentors then carted him through town for several hours as a warning to other potential informers, "that people might see the doleful Condition he was in."

The mob had achieved its intended effect: to instill "much terror . . . among the inhabitants." With both sides lashing out at each other, and tensions continuing to escalate, it was only a matter of time before Boston's powder keg would erupt into deadly violence.

8

FROM RED FIELDS TO CRIMSON COBBLESTONES

*"OUR STREETS WERE STAINED WITH
THE BLOOD OF OUR BRETHREN."*
—JOSEPH WARREN, 1772

IN JANUARY 1770, IN NEW YORK CITY, SAILORS, WATERFRONT workers, and other townsfolk clashed with armed British soldiers over the posting of anti–Sons of Liberty handbills throughout the city. No one died in the scuffle that was later aggrandized and termed the Battle of Golden Hill, although some were injured. But within weeks, scrapes between colonists, Tories, and redcoats in the streets of Boston would turn deadly.

The arrival of British regiments in Boston had cued Warren to begin preparing for war. Ironically, a song traditionally attributed to Warren called "The New Massachusetts Liberty Song," set to the tune of "The British Grenadiers," was performed at Concert Hall on February 13, 1770, just weeks prior to the grenadiers of the 29th killing colonists on King Street. Announced as "a new song composed by a Son of Liberty," the ballad was a variant of John Dickinson's "The Liberty Song" that he had written in 1768. Even if all of Europe were to attack, Warren wrote, Americans stood ready to fight in defense of their "land where freedom reigns." Warren also attempted to muster a spirit of American pride, bravery, and unity, while raising opposition to the dangerous new encroachments upon the colonists' freedom.

As the Whigs continued to fight the importation of British manufactured goods, Boston merchants' loyalties came under increasing scrutiny. The nonimportation agreements expired on January 1, 1770, whereupon several merchants who had suffered temporary insolvency were quick to resume importing English goods. A surplus of merchandise had been collecting dust, and many customers were eager for the latest offerings of English refinement, so these merchants moved quickly to accommodate demand.

In response, the radical faction published in the *Boston Gazette* a list of recalcitrant merchants who dared defy the expiring compact, deeming it "highly proper that the public should know who they are." Anxious to establish new nonimportation covenants, the radicals needed public support. Several importers cast as traitors soon found the patriot calling card on their shop windows—a smearing of tar and feathers and a smattering of "Hillsborough paint," (human and animal feces). Signs displaying a pointed hand with the word IMPORTER began to appear in front of such stores.

On February 22, in Boston's North End, a demonstration began in front of a shop owned by Theophilus Lillie. For several past weeks on Thursdays, when schools didn't have afternoon sessions, boys set up picket lines outside the shops of importers. Ebenezer Richardson, a despised Customs service employee and outspoken Tory who lived nearby, tried to have the IMPORTER sign in front of Lillie's shop removed. When he failed, he resorted to shouting insults at a crowd of mostly angry young boys who began throwing debris at him. A rowdy mob followed Richardson home, and after briefly exchanging threats with the crowd, he hastened into his house.

But the mob refused to disperse. Instead, it grew in both strength and anger, and the protesters broke a number of Richardson's windows. Trapped in his home, with his wife and daughter, and terrified by the swelling fury pressing at his door, Richardson fired a musket into the throng. Multiple slugs hit a young man and a boy.

The gunshots drew wild howls from the incensed crowd. The mob might have torn apart Richardson's house had not William Molineux, a fervent radical leader and champion of the nonimportation agreement, managed to quell tensions and haul Richardson and an accomplice before a justice of the peace.

Warren, summoned to treat both victims, dressed the injuries of nineteen-year-old Samuel Gore after he "cut slugs" from his thighs, determining that "in all probability he will lose the use of the right fore finger."

Gore would survive intact, but the boy, Christopher Seider, just ten years old, had received graver wounds and died eight hours after being hit. Warren performed the autopsy: "his body was opened . . . and in it were found 11 . . . slugs . . . one of which pierced his breast . . . and passing clear thro' the right lobe of the lungs, lodged in his back." With young children of his own, Warren must have felt anger at such a senseless death. He later testified before a coroner's jury, which officially declared that Seider had been "wilfully and feloniously shot by Ebenezer Richardson." Richardson was subsequently found guilty and sentenced, only to be later pardoned by the Crown in March 1772, at Governor Hutchinson's urging.

Suspicions of a likely pardon fanned the flames of colonial resentment since the royal judges, having already advised acquittal, delayed passing sentence on Richardson, thus preventing him from being hanged weeks after the trial. The radicals believed the administrative system unfair and corrupt. Warren was particularly incensed and likely authored the scathing account of the murder in the *Boston Gazette*.

Warren helped organize Seider's funeral, using his influence to rally thousands of Bostonians to attend. The quarter-mile-long procession was, as even Thomas Hutchinson conceded, "the largest perhaps ever known in America." Those in attendance bore "the evident marks of true sorrow" on their faces. Even for Warren, a physician inured to the reality of death, performing the autopsy of a child shot in the street was a shock, and the funeral was no less haunting. The *Boston Gazette* reported, "The little corpse was set down under the Tree of Liberty, from whence the Procession began. About five hundred school boys preceded; and a very numerous train of citizens followed . . . at least two thousand of all ranks, amidst a crowd of spectators."

In this atmosphere, the week after Seider's murder, several confrontations erupted between British troops and Bostonians. Samuel Adams continued to object to the soldiers' presence, insisting that they were "stationed in our very bowels" and could possibly be ordered to "fire on an unarm'd populace." Months earlier, in October 1769, British Colonel William Dalrymple had expressed concern to General Gage that "government here is in the hands of the multitude, and I am sure something very unpleasant is at hand."

Indeed it was. On the frigid evening of March 5, Private Hugh White struck a young barber's apprentice who had been taunting another soldier, and a mob of colonists began to form in front of the customs house on King Street. Church bells rang, often a signal for a fire, and alarmed Bostonians began flooding into the streets. As the crowd grew hostile, Capt. Thomas Preston, after receiving several summonses, sent Corporal Wemms and a squad to assist the customs house guards. Preston arrived soon after as the crowd was pressing in.

Taking defensive measures, he formed the soldiers into a semicircle. As the angry throng swelled, chaos increased. Cries echoed that night throughout Boston's shadowy moonlit streets, as John Adams wrote: "The people shouting, huzzaing, and making the mob whistle, as they call it . . . is a most hideous shriek."

Soon the disgruntled mob escalated from insults and taunts to throwing oyster shells, rocks, chunks of ice, and snow at the small group of redcoats. The soldiers retaliated by firing into the crowd. Three men were killed instantly, two died soon afterward from their wounds, and several others were injured. While some of the rioters dispersed, many stayed to help the victims sprawled across the cobblestone street. Again Warren was called in to treat the wounded and perform autopsies on the dead. An illuminated moon hovered above Boston, casting an ominous glow upon the horrific scene on King Street, the snow-covered cobblestones now stained with blood.

A town meeting was called for the following day, and Warren was one member who served on a committee urging Hutchinson to remove the troops from Boston before more violence erupted. That evening, Warren and the other committeemen urged the established militia leadership to lead a citizens' guard through the streets in an attempt to prevent further bloodshed. In the event of any problem, on the citizens' guard's command, all Boston men bearing arms were to turn out to the streets. Given the fury of many Bostonians in the wake of what came to be called the Boston Massacre, the fact that British soldiers were able to walk the streets at all was a testament to the radical leaders' control over the populace and militia leaders.

But Warren and the radical leaders could not contain the tempest forever, nor ultimately guarantee anyone's safety. The British understood that they were at risk of inciting a full-scale riot. And so Colonel Dalrymple began removing his troops from Boston. Over the next few weeks, the 14th and 29th Regiments were moved to barracks at Castle William. An atmosphere of fear and mistrust permeated even previously genial gatherings; Warren's St. Andrew's Lodge had met just three days prior to the Boston Massacre, but the British troops would never again attend. Relations between the brethren had been shattered. Political allegiances now trumped fraternal associations.

On March 8, a funeral procession of almost twelve thousand strong marched somberly to bury the dead. "It is supposed," the *Boston Gazette* reported, "that there must have been a greater number of people from town and country at the funeral of those who were massacred by the soldiers, than ever were together on this continent on any occasion." The display of numbers was not lost on Governor Hutchinson, who professed the end of British government rule, which was now at the mercy of the people. In the *Gazette*, Warren and the radicals connected the Boston Massacre to the St. George's Fields slaughter in London two years earlier, when British soldiers had fired on a crowd protesting the imprisonment of John Wilkes.

Thereafter Warren and two friends and patients, James Bowdoin (future governor of Massachusetts) and Samuel Pemberton, were appointed to a committee to prepare a narrative of the events. Although Bowdoin was the principle author of the report, Warren's appointment to the committee was a significant promotion within the radical Whig ranks. After justices of the peace collected close to a hundred depositions from eyewitnesses, the committee produced the incendiary propaganda pamphlet *A Short Narrative of the Horrid Massacre in Boston*, meant to blame the British for the bloodshed, exonerate Boston's inhabitants, and turn the victims into martyrs. At least a quarter of the deponents were patients, friends, or political associates of Warren. The *Narrative* traced events back to the Stamp Act, listing all the injustices the colonists had endured. It claimed that the king's loyal subjects had been "treated as enemies and rebels, by an invasion of the town by sea and land." With British troops saturating the port town, the soldiers persisted in "endangering a great number of peaceable inhabitants" with their incessantly egregious behavior.

Paul Revere crafted a commemorative engraving, and copies of the *Narrative* were printed by the patriots Edes and Gill and distributed. After copies were leaked across the Atlantic, London declared the pamphlet "the most important one ever bro't from America." As it spread throughout Great Britain, so too did Warren's reputation as a leading Whig.

The British soldiers directly involved in the Massacre were to stand trial. The governor threatened to hold them in England, so the Whigs needed to prove that justice under the law was still possible in the Bay Colony. John Adams was told that no attorney wanted to represent the soldiers—that is, to defend the "bloody butchery" committed by the "bloodybacks." But the soldiers had to have a capable defense team to receive a fair trial, so Adams agreed to represent them. The radical Josiah Quincy, Jr., agreed to join the defense after he was "advised and urged to undertake it by an Adams [Samuel], a Hancock, a Molineux, a Cushing, a Henshaw, a Pemberton, a Warren, a Cooper, and a Phillips." In addition to choosing half the prosecution, the radical leadership also in effect chose the soldiers' defense attorneys.

Over the next several months, the need for a fair and impartial trial became ever more urgent. In the wake of the Massacre, mobs took revenge with violent acts of intimidation and humiliation. Owen Richards, a Tory customs officer who lived in Boston's North End, testified that he was "tarred and feathered in 1770 on account of a seizure he made" on board the schooner *Martin*. John Rowe recorded the event in his diary: "There was a very great hallooing in the street and a mob of upwards a thousand—it seems they had got an informer." About one month later, on June 19, a riotous crowd took Patrick McMasters from his shop for failing to comply with the nonimportation agreement. The mob dragged him through town in a cart that held buckets of tar and feathers. Terrified, McMasters "Sunk down Speechless" and fainted. He was brought to an apothecary who administered smelling salts and awakened him whereupon the procession began once more. But instead of giving him a coat of tar and feathers, the crowd, after beating and abusing him, brought him to Roxbury, where he was warned never to return to Boston.

The Boston Massacre trial was delayed until October 1770, in hopes that the initial anger of the colonists would subside and the British troops would be removed from the town. Upon hearing news of the delay, Warren, on a committee of town leaders, stormed into the Superior Court's chambers with a large crowd to disrupt the proceedings. Rumors purported that Warren tried to intimidate the judges. Thomas Hutchinson likely implicated Warren as one of the ringleaders when he referred to "the designs of particular persons to bring a revolution and to attain independency."

Warren by this time was a powerful force within the Whig party. Between his connections to almost every sector of Boston's population through his work as a doctor, and his recent acquisition of Hooton's wharf, he was familiar not just to Boston's upper class but also to "a motley rabble of saucy boys, Negroes and mulattoes, Irish teagues and outlandish Jack Tars"—as John Adams referred to the mob on March 5. In fact, for all his sophistication, Warren was not far removed from the rabble himself, having interacted closely with lower classes in his youth. He had the trust and support of many at the bottom of the Puritan social barrel, the "infernal" group who had been wreaking havoc in Boston's streets for several years.

When the trial finally was held, Adams and Quincy successfully defended their clients, and all but two of the soldiers involved in the Massacre were acquitted. The two were found guilty of manslaughter, branded, and returned to their regiments. If there were ever a time for tensions to explode into riots, it was now.

And indeed many Bostonians were indignant over the soldiers' acquittals. But just at the moment when further bloodshed seemed inevitable, a surprising calm came over the colony. On the same day as the Boston Massacre, Parliament had begun to repeal parts of the Townshend Act, and as the news filtered across the Atlantic, many colonists yearned to return to the peaceful relations they had shared with Britain prior to 1765. The general mood turned conciliatory, and with the most pernicious duties now lifted, the opposition's radical ideology appeared extreme and unnecessary. According to Hutchinson, John Hancock "intended to quit all active concern in public affairs, and to attend to his private business." Even John Adams, content in his own "retirement," professed, "Farewell, politicks."

Warren and Samuel Adams had, after all, accomplished many of their initial goals. Francis Bernard and the British troops were gone, and the Stamp Act had been rescinded. Parliament had repealed all the Townshend duties except one—only the tax on tea was upheld (since the bulk of the Act revenue came from the duties on tea) to emphasize parliamentary supremacy. The radicals had little to point to as sufficient reason to promote rebellion, let alone independence. After months of fomenting riots, they suddenly found themselves in the unfamiliar position of losing momentum.

For Warren, though, the bloody event of March 5 did not end with the soldiers' trial. For years afterward, he continued to treat

Christopher Monk, making visits to "dress" the wound, until Monk eventually died from complications of the injury in 1780, the massacre's sixth victim.

And so Warren fought to ensure that the radical wing retained some power in the Boston Town Meeting. In 1770, Warren along with several others assisted Josiah Quincy, Jr., in preparing instructions for Boston's representatives to the legislature. The instructions admonished the colonists to continue to develop "the more martial virtues," should they have to "hazard all" for their liberties, even as they simultaneously called for a "firm and lasting union of the colonies." Warren worked hard to keep the injustices once perpetrated by the Crown front and center in colonists' minds.

A year after the massacre, Warren was part of another committee that sponsored an annual oration to commemorate the event and maximize possibilities to foment opposition to the Crown. James Lovell, Warren's friend, was chosen as the first official speaker. Weeks earlier, on the first anniversary of Christopher Seider's murder, Bostonians had been urged "to revive the memory" of the martyred boy.

Warren understood the importance not only of written but of visual propaganda. Given the popularity of Revere's Boston Massacre engraving, the Whig leadership once again leaned on him to capture public attention. With Warren's support and likely urging, Revere made and displayed a harrowing exhibition from his home on Fish Street in Boston's North End on the first anniversary of the massacre. The drawings, hung from Revere's three windows, depicted Seider's lamented ghost, the murderous Boston Massacre soldiers, and a woman symbolizing America who was pointing to the tragedy. Written on the Seider display were the words: "Seiders pale ghost freshbleeding stands / And vengeance for his death demands." Lanterns were hung to illuminate the transparent scenes from behind, making the display particularly harrowing. Thousands turned out to behold the ghoulish but dramatic spectacle, marveling for hours as the tolling of church bells solemnized the memory of the victims and their grieving community.

The following year, in 1772, the Whig leadership turned to Warren to deliver the Massacre's anniversary address. It would be the first true test of his spoken words' effectiveness as much as it would be an honor. He understood the importance of the occasion and agreed. He had been developing his speaking skills for years, ever since delivering Latin orations as a student at Harvard. His ability to deliver fiery radical arguments without alienating his Tory friends had not gone unnoticed in the Whig camp. Samuel Adams was a shrewd propagandist, but the Tories viewed him as a contemptuous zealot, and with his neurological issues, particularly a noticeable hand tremor, possibly affecting his speech, he lacked the "pillar of strength" image that patriots wanted to convey under growing public scrutiny. For this they needed the youthful and admired doctor, who had earned "the esteem and regard of the polite and learned" and was "greatly beloved by those who tread the humble walks of life."

The anniversary came at a bittersweet time for Joseph and his wife: their third child, Mary, had recently died. Elizabeth would then give birth to another girl, whom they would name after Mary and baptize in Brattle Street Church a few weeks later, on March 22.

On the March 5 anniversary, a blizzard buried Boston under almost a foot and a half of snow. But more than four thousand people—more than a quarter of the town's population—defied the blustery weather and gathered in the Old South Meeting House to hear Warren speak. At half past noon, the meetinghouse was so crowded that "it was with much difficulty the orator reached the pulpit."

Ascending the black-shrouded podium, Dr. Warren looked out over the familiar audience and began. A natural at the pulpit, with a passion for Scripture, he had missed his calling as a preacher. He now aimed to reignite the flames of passion in his patriot brethren and stir them to action in the name of liberty.

With great fervor, Warren invoked the "mighty revolutions" of the past, citing historical precedents from ancient Rome, declaring that the "public happiness depends on a virtuous and unshaken attachment to a free constitution." Parliamentary sovereignty remained the foundation of the uncodified British constitution. Unless a British subject was "governed by no laws but those to which he either in person or by his representative hath given his consent . . . the constitution must be destroyed." Warren went on to list the abuses that the colonists had suffered under the acts of Parliament "for taxing America, and the standing army sent in at a time of peace for the enforcement of obedience to acts which upon fair examination appeared to be unjust and unconstitutional."

Even with the acts repealed and the army out of the town, Warren claimed that a precedent had been set, as he warned of new encroachments upon citizens' liberty: "for if they may be taxed without their consent even the smallest trifle, they may also without their consent be deprived of everything they possess." After appealing to their pockets, their logic, and their reason, he aimed for the audience's emotions. His rising voice, suffused with feeling, declared that "the true fatal fifth of March 1770, can never be forgotten—the horrors of that dreadful night are but too deeply impressed on our hearts—our streets were stained with blood of our brethren." Warren had seen firsthand the tragic aftermath of the massacre, not simply as a patriot but as the doctor who tended the dead and wounded victims. His eyes had been "tormented with the sight of the mangled bodies of the dead."

His ultimate goal in his speech was to declare the ideology of the Whigs publicly yet not overtly. Although he and some of his patriot colleagues had whispered about independence, that radical position could hardly be announced to the anniversary crowd—it would be tantamount to treason. Allegiance to Great Britain had to be maintained while, at the same time, insisting that a relationship between the colonies and the mother country was becoming impossible.

So Warren reminded the colonists that every measure they had taken had been answered with nothing but scorn and violence. The time for another kind of action was at hand: "If we complain our complaints are treated with contempt; if we assert our rights, that assertion is deemed insolence; if we humbly submit the matter to the impartial decision of reason the SWORD is judged the most proper argument to silence our murmurs!—But, this cannot long be the case." The British treasured the notion of liberty, he said, and they were aware "that all who have once possessed her charms had rather die than suffer her to be torn from their embraces." He urged his countrymen to "use every method in your power to secure your rights" and "with united zeal and fortitude oppose the torrent of oppression."

It was a bold gambit: a call for a united defense of colonial liberties at a time when little "oppression" was occurring. Warren concluded by declaring, "May our land be a land of liberty, the seat of virtue, the asylum of the oppressed, a name and a praise in the whole earth, until the last shock of time shall bury the empires of the world in one common undistinguished ruin!" It was a call for an America set apart.

Warren's speech cost him favor among Tories, but it had its desired effect on his fellow patriots, causing his popularity to soar. He almost instantly became the face of the radical Whig party. The *Boston Gazette* reported that he "received the unanimous applause of his audience." Even Thomas Hutchinson proclaimed that "the fervor, which is the most essential part of such compositions, could not fail in its effect on the minds of the great concourse of people present." One of Warren's descendants would later claim that his oration "had so great an effect on the people they were determined to resort to arms if their petitions were unsuccessful." In thirty-five minutes of impassioned dialogue, Dr. Joseph Warren had helped resurrect the radical movement from political slumber.

9

A TIME TO MOURN

"What then when virtue's brightest lamps expire."
—JOSEPH WARREN, 1773

THE POSTWAR DOWNTURN THAT STRUCK BOSTON HARD IN THE MID-1760s was exacerbated by the subsequent political struggles that led to the nonimportation covenants. But for all of Warren's financial struggles, he and Elizabeth were fortunate enough to have received a sizeable inheritance from Richard Hooton. Warren's financial blessings also included the lucrative position of almshouse physician, which he held between 1769 and 1772. In his first year at the post, he made 730 visits to almshouse patients, earning close to two hundred pounds, and over the next two years, he made more than twice that amount. By this time his practice was among the largest and most reputable in the Boston area, and he began to accept medical apprentices, which helped with the heavy patient workload.

Warren's lifestyle soon reflected his rising fortunes. In the fall of 1770, he rented a home from Joseph Green's widow on Hanover Street, blocks from the site of the Boston Massacre. The elderly widow,

Anna Green, remained in the household, retaining the front two chambers for herself, "her maid and negro man," while Warren and his family moved into the rest of the stately home. Throughout his stay Warren maintained the property and even had the house "glazed," for which the Greens reimbursed him. Warren had also agreed to rent some of the home's furniture and several months earlier had purchased property from the Green family in the form of "a Negro Boy." Although most of Warren's descendants would be outspoken abolitionists, his own parents had owned at least two slaves and subscribed to the institution of human bondage while championing the cause of liberty—a hypocrisy that plagued many colonial leaders. While no surviving documentation has been found regarding Warren's thoughts on slavery, no slaves are listed among his property in his probate will.

Men of Warren's high social position and influence were generally great landowners, not renters. With his growing wealth, Warren must have been keen to join the ranks of propertied men. In July 1770 he and Elizabeth purchased an estate with several outbuildings and a vast expanse of property in West Boston for eight hundred pounds, with money borrowed from Warren's compatriot and friend James Bowdoin.

Almost immediately Warren hired carpenters, painters, and builders to expand and repair the property. The tradesman William Crafts (the older brother of Thomas Crafts, a member of the Loyal Nine) performed most of the work on Warren's West Boston and Roxbury properties, and he also worked on Warren's Brattle Street pew, repairing "2 elbow pieces, 1 draw, and 2 crickets." The doctor spared no expense in remodeling; the property would have rivaled Boston's finest estates. When the house was completed, it featured a "great entry," two kitchens—with two stove chimneys and ovens—a large cellar and porch, and an attic with at least twelve dormers. A "summer house"—a gazebo surrounded by a garden—and a factory house were also built and repaired. To the rear of the main structure stood a water pump, and surrounding the house was a decorative fence.

Warren hired a painter to paint the property and bought a number of household items including lamps, dressers, hogsheads, and tables. The house was whitewashed, and the rooms within were painted popular mid-eighteenth-century colors such as lead, "blew," and olive. Warren ordered an incredible amount of materials for repairs, including a thousand shingles for the roof and several thousand feet of plank for new floors, staircases, and walls, and he had new doors and windows installed.

Such an elaborate project reveals Warren's desire to live in one of the finest gentry houses in Boston, one that would reflect his social status as a leading gentleman. Most of the construction work, repairs, and painting would take years to complete; some would not be finished until the beginning of 1775, just as the Whig rebellion was boiling over into revolution. Due to the political upheaval, neither Warren nor his family would ever live in the home he had custom-designed for them.

While their estate was being renovated, the Warrens continued renting. But their home was an opulent setting, partly due to the furniture that they rented from the Greens, and partly due to their own items of extreme luxury. The interior was well equipped for entertaining, richly fitted out with extravagant furnishings of a kind found only in the grandest of estates: fine ceramics, Chinese porcelains, top-of-the-line utensils, and even a monteith—an elegant and luxurious silver piece used to chill wineglasses. The house was well stocked with alcohol. Punch, Lisbon wine, Madeira, and port were just some of the libations Warren would have served to his guests. At a time when carpets were so expensive that they were often hung from walls rather than placed on floors, the Warrens owned at least four—two Wilton carpets valued at an exorbitant eighty pounds, and another pair decoratively painted for prominent display. The windows were adorned with silk curtains, which were incredibly expensive, as were the costly feather beds, and the mahogany and maple bedsteads. Numerous mirrors and tapestries also decked the walls.

Between 1772 and 1774, Warren ordered and purchased a tall-case, eight-day mahogany clock from Benjamin Willard in Roxbury. Depicted above the clock's brass face was a seafaring background and lighthouse with a sailing ship crossing an ocean, rhythmically keeping pace with the pendulum. The maxim "Ut Hora Sic Vita Transit" was engraved around the scene, which translates to "Life Flies as the Hour Passes." Clocks, particularly eight-day clocks, were expensive finery available to only the wealthiest members of society. Not only did the clock's price tag indicate economic status, but owning such an item signified a high social position within the community since it suggested that one's time was important enough to be tracked precisely.

Among the several paintings hanging on the walls were the couple's portraits—Warren's by John Singleton Copley, and Elizabeth's by Copley's half-brother Henry Pelham. The Copley portrait is the first known image ever created of Warren and as such bears closer study for a look at him in the prime of his career. That Warren could command a portrait by Copley was itself evidence of his elevated social rank. Fetching high fees and often booked up to a year in advance, the "Tory Painter," as patriots often called Copley, had painted some of "the best works a colonial American artist had ever produced." His extensive body of work would comprise more than 350 portraits, including many of Warren's political associates, patients, and friends. For years Warren was close to Copley and his family; in 1772, he would deliver Copley's son.

A portrait of such high quality required much intimate sitting time, with the artist carefully studying his subject. Copley captured, in neoclassical style, a young, robust, genteel, and determined Dr. Warren. Years later, after Warren's death, frontispieces, paintings, engravings, and sketches would depict him as the war general he became, wearing epaulettes and holding a musket or sword.

But the Copley portrait captures Warren the professional, the physician who helped cure the sick. He sits relaxed on a Queen Anne side chair, legs spread apart, his pose informal with the buttons on his alabaster silk waistcoat undone, allowing the ruffle to protrude. He leans somewhat forward, engaging his audience to come closer. His left arm covers anatomical sketches and a leather book—perhaps a medical journal or daybook—while his right hand rests upon his knee. The sketches, the most obvious emblem of Warren's profession, are of two skulls: one whole and one that's been sawed apart. The drawings are ironic considering Warren's ultimate fate, and subsequent burials are reminiscent of a *memento mori*. His professional standing as a doctor is also represented by his black broadcloth coat, partly draped over his right arm. His white silk stockings fastened with silver knee buckles, the embroidered buttons, ruffled cuffs, white silk-lined coat, and white wig further signify the doctor's high social status. His hands appear gracile and gentle—serving him well when delivering a baby—yet firm and steady enough for the grisly amputations he would perform without anesthesia. This doctor had already saved many lives.

As in all of Copley's paintings of this era, his subject's sealed lips hint of the strict, old-world Puritan culture marked by sumptuary laws. But the pomposity, haughtiness, and stern demeanor evident in portraits of Warren's peers are absent here. Warren's deep slate blue eyes betray his naturally warm and friendly disposition. His glance is somewhat askew as he gazes slightly to his left, casting a shadow over part of his face. He is ensconced in mystery, surrounded by lush fabrics of matching colors. Copley used these symbols—from the draped tablecloth and background curtain to the chair on which he sits—to suggest the doctor's lofty taste and bestow on him an air of dignity. The outside view to the left is barely visible but resembles a bucolic scene of a rolling grass hill beneath a blue sky, with perhaps the bustling seaport of Boston in the far background. The base of the pillar to his right is a classical symbol of strength and stability. Warren's face bears no visible marks or pox scars. It appears smooth and clean-shaven, as was the custom for civilized men of the day. In an era when full-immersion bathing was generally limited to a few times a year, the doctor is always described as looking clean and well polished.

His fair skin was much-desired for the period, as many colonists purposely concealed themselves from the sun, and women sometimes wore flour-based cosmetics to produce a pure white complexion. Like his peers, Warren spoke with a heavy nasal twang similar to modern dialects indigenous to the Northeast. When John Adams described him as "a pretty, tall, genteel, fair faced young gentleman," Warren was still just twenty-three years old. Considerably taller than the average person of the time, he stood just above six feet, and he exuded a rare charm, complemented by his good looks, which were acknowledged when "the ladies pronounced him handsome."

Since having one's portrait painted was a formal occasion, subjects were often dressed in their finest clothing and highest-end accessories. In colonial America, wearing a wig was traditional, though not compulsory, among people of significance and wealth. In addition to lending an air of formality, wigs were worn as a fashion and social statement, since less than 5 percent of the population could afford such a luxurious accoutrement. Peruke shops, usually located near taverns, offered clients an array of services including wig maintenance, immersion bathing, and shaving. In such shops in Boston, Warren could mingle with well-to-do patrons for political discourse. In the Copley portrait, his pigeon-winged wig, which sits above his prominent forehead, is dusted a grayish-white color, likely from perfumed flour, dressed with a mixture of cinnamon, cloves, and fat. Curled at the sides, with the hair on top drawn back into a queue, the wig is typically smaller and simpler than the perukes of earlier generations. Even the material of Warren's wig was indicative of social standing, as human hair made for the finest sort, whereas wigs made of horse mane, yak, and goat were worn by lesser ranks.

If the portrait announced Warren's ascent to the ranks of the well-heeled, even more indicative of his elite status was his carriage and chaise. Simply owning such items made a social statement, but Warren decided to have the carriage painted vermilion. The single most expensive color, vermilion was also in high fashion overseas, among Britain's wealthiest subjects. When the ostentatious carriage rumbled through Boston's narrow streets, it never failed to draw attention.

Warren also showcased his new station in life through his wardrobe and accessories. From Nathaniel Abraham's shop, "At the Sign of the Golden Key, in Ann-Street," he purchased the finest linens, satins, and silks, as well as high-end accessories like "button moulds" and

"Cotton Hose." In addition to the standard black customarily worn by doctors, bright colors and ornate accessories filled the doctor's highly fashionable closet. His wardrobe cost about as much as that of the much wealthier John Hancock.

Unlike Samuel Adams—a bluenosed relic who fervently embraced the Puritan anachronisms of the previous century—Warren's taste for the finer things was anything but the puritan aesthetic. A generation younger than Adams, he had been exposed to the latest London fashions at Dr. Lloyd's genteel estate. Long gone were Warren's halcyon days as a "bare legged milk boy" helping his father on the farm, and he seemed determined to put great distance between himself and the young man who had arrived at Harvard with so little. He was a man of many contradictions: his pious devotion to Scripture stood at odds with his exorbitant expenditures and luxurious lifestyle, which his Puritan ancestors, who had imposed the sumptuary laws against such extravagance, would surely have frowned on.

As the Whig party stagnated in the early 1770s, Warren felt decisive measures had to be taken. To shore up support for the radical agenda, he helped formalize aspects of the North End Caucus, which one contemporary described as an organization whose "regulations were drawn up by Dr. Warren" and consisted of "mechanics" and "whigs" who "never did anything important without consulting him." Based in Boston's North End neighborhood, the caucus, whose membership included Warren's radical co-conspirators Samuel Adams, William Molineux, and Dr. Thomas Young, became powerful. In 1772 it met just prior to the town meetings in March and May, when representatives to the General Court were chosen. Caucus members "agreed who should be in town offices, in general court, in the provincial congress, from Boston. . . . The most prominent characters of this *caucus* . . . were guided by the prudence and skillful management of Dr. Warren . . . a man calculated to carry on any secret business."

Aware that the colonies had to act in unison if the resistance movement were to make forward strides, Warren and Samuel Adams also organized a means of intercolonial communication: they formed the Boston Committee of Correspondence to open lines of dialogue with Massachusetts towns. At the Boston Town Meeting of November 2, 1772, attendees voted unanimously to create the committee and to proclaim "the rights of the colonists, and of this province," in a pamphlet titled *The Votes and Proceedings of the Town of Boston*. Samuel Adams chaired it, and Warren was appointed to a subcommittee to write the "Infringements and Violations of Rights" section—an indictment of the British administration that outlined several grievances later worked into the Declaration of Independence.

The committee's formation gave rise to many others in the Bay Colony and, by the next year, in other colonies. A steady flow of news, information, and ideas circulated among the colony-level committees, ultimately facilitating the presentation of a united colonial front in dealings with the mother country.

Warren's first biographer, Richard Frothingham, sought to "attest how large a credit is due for the inauguration of committees of correspondence . . . to Samuel Adams, and Joseph Warren." Warren continued his ascent within the Whig apparatus. Indeed, their contribution cannot be overstated, particularly as other Whig leaders continued to retreat after the partial repeal of the Townshend Acts, curbing their active participation even in the Sons of Liberty. John Hancock and Thomas Cushing (another radical Boston merchant) both refused to even serve on the Committee of Correspondence. John Adams continued to relish his "retirement," professing, "Above all things, I must avoid politicks, political clubbs, town meetings, General Court &c. &c. &c." After a supposed breakdown, Adams had moved his family back to Braintree, where they all lived for more than a year and a half, before returning to Boston in 1772. Warren maintained a close relationship with, and a great respect for, John Adams, but also regarded him politically as "rather a cautious man."

Governor Hutchinson, for his part, was increasingly concerned over the activities of the radical Whigs led by Samuel Adams and Warren. In a letter of December 8, 1772, he claimed that throughout Boston the "doctrine of independence upon the Parliament and the mischiefs of it every day increase." Efforts to catalyze the resistance against British authority, he thought, were gaining traction. One month later, in a speech to the Assembly, he declared, "I know of no line that can be drawn between the supreme authority of Parliament and the total independence of the colonies." He had always been a champion of parliamentary supremacy, but his efforts to subdue the increasing radical whispers of independence had little effect.

By this time, Warren and his family were living in a large brick dwelling at the "Head of Wing's-Lane, near the Flesh and Fish Markets," rented from the prominent Boston merchant Peter Chardon. This house contained a large cellar as well as a warehouse and stable where Warren could house his horses and his newly painted vermilion carriage. The Chardon house was close to the property he had been renting from the Green family, making it convenient for his patients. It was also a more expensive rental: Warren was paying Chardon an extra 13 pounds per year. He lived in the Chardon property from at least November 1774 through April 1775, leaving on the morning of the nineteenth to join his patriot brothers in battle.

He had also expanded his role in the world of Freemasonry: a year earlier he had received a commission "appointing him Grand Master of Masons for the Continent of America," strengthening his Masonic power and social reach. In this capacity, he granted charters for several new Ancient Grand Lodges throughout New England, but opposed efforts made by British officers to induct new members into their traveling Masonic lodges as political tensions heightened. As the grand master of St. Andrews, Warren celebrated the festival of St. John the Baptist with his brethren, marching "in procession from Concert Hall to Christ Church." They then "proceeded to Masons' Hall, where an elegant entertainment was provided . . . dedicated to the purposes of benevolence and social festivity." Warren's commitment to the lodge is evident from the fact that during his years as grand master, between 1769 and 1775, he missed only three meetings.

AT HOME, ALL WAS PACIFIC. ALTHOUGH THE WARRENS HAD LOST their daughter Mary, Elizabeth had given birth to two more children—a son, Richard, and their fourth and final child, a daughter also named Mary. Many of Warren's friends and associates had lost children of their own, experiencing similar anguish. Warren was becoming closer to his compatriots like Paul Revere, John Hancock, and Samuel and John Adams. Even though John Adams had distanced himself politically from Warren's radical faction, he remained a close personal friend of Warren. When Joseph and Elizabeth celebrated the birth of their child, John presented them with a silver porringer handle with the initials J A to J W engraved on the handle.

Warren and Elizabeth's solid union was sustained by their genuine affection for each other. As a token, she had woven a bracelet made from his hair and had a goldsmith encase it within an ornate setting. Such fashionable jewelry pieces showcased one's love for a spouse, close family member, or child. Enjoying their high social position with property in the town and country, outfitted with the latest and richest fashions, jewelry, and transportation, the Warrens were living a grand life. But when Elizabeth was taken ill in the spring of 1773, that life came crashing down.

The couple had been married for over eight years, and their youngest child was barely a year old. Elizabeth's illness must have seemed grave enough to prompt a reassessment of the family's future, as on April 10, 1773, she and Warren, of their "free will and Accord," signed over her entire inheritance of Hooton's Wharf, along with "half of the Shops and Warehouses thereon," to Warren's brother Ebenezer. The property was to be for the sole use and benefit of their respective families and heirs. With Elizabeth gravely ill, the couple realized that their children would likely spend much time at the ancestral compound in Roxbury and were trying to help their extended family financially. Such generosity suggests the strong bond that existed between the Warren family, but it also underscores practical concerns: perhaps fearful of his growing Whig reputation, Warren may have thought it prudent to remove the property from his name in case the British should ever arrest him as a traitor and attempt to seize his assets.

Undoubtedly, Warren applied all his medical knowledge and skill to try to save Elizabeth. But she died at twenty-six on April 27.

Three days later she was buried. With his four children, family, friends, and associates present at the ceremony, Dr. Warren laid his "dearest friend" to rest. Grief-stricken, he wrote a poem in her honor, which appeared in the *Boston Gazette* under her death notice, opening a rare window into Warren's most intimate thoughts regarding his beloved Elizabeth:

If fading Lilies, when they droop and die

Rob'd of each charm that pleas'd the gazing Eye,

With sad Regret the grieving Mind inspire,
What then when virtue's brightest Lamps expire?

Warren acknowledged Elizabeth's support throughout their marriage, and her caring and nurturing disposition:

Good sense and modesty with Virtue crown'd
A sober Mind when Fortune smil'd or frown'd
So keen a feeling for a Friend distress'd
She could not bear to see a Worm oppress'd.

Relying more than ever on his deep religious convictions, he continued to attend services at Reverend Cooper's Brattle Street Church. As a lasting memento of his love for Elizabeth, he ordered a gold mourning ring, in neoclassical style, depicting a funeral urn under a weeping willow covered by glass and surrounded by sixteen precious stones (likely diamonds). Elizabeth's name, the date of her death, and her age were inscribed in Latin around the side of the ring. Black enamel around the outer gold band was a feature distinguishing mourning rings from fashionable rings. Mourning jewelry was quite popular in the eighteenth century and also an item of extreme luxury. One with so many precious stones hints at Warren's elevated financial status but also his love for his beloved wife. Warren's mourning ring, along with the woven bracelet Elizabeth had made from Warren's hair, became cherished family heirlooms worn by the couple's direct descendants for many generations.

Premature deaths were a grim reality facing colonists in an era fraught with disease, epidemics, folk remedies, and lack of modern medicine. While such tragedies were a familiar part of everyday life for most colonists, familiarity never desensitized them to the pangs of loss, despite the austere images conveyed in stoic portraits. To cope with the death of a spouse, those who were left behind often remarried quickly. An assault on modern notions of acceptable grieving periods, colonists often wasted little time before their next conjugal union. Some remarried out of convenience and necessity, while others fell in love again.

Warren, now thirty-one and a widower with four young children, had little time to grieve, let alone search for new love. He was busy running one of the busiest medical practices in Boston while helping to spearhead the radical faction's fight against British oppression. Constantly engaged in his work, and with at least one slave and several medical apprentices living in his household, he reached out to his mother for assistance with his children, and she immediately complied. Two of Warren's brothers, Samuel and Ebenezer, were still in Roxbury and helped care for their nieces and nephews. Warren always found solace in his church, and when the meetinghouse was rebuilt and the Reverend Cooper preached his first sermon there on July 25, 1773, Warren and his children were doubtless in attendance.

In the days after Elizabeth's death, Warren kept himself occupied with work. His Masonic duties were likely a welcome distraction. The doctor attended a lodge meeting "upon an especial occasion" just a week after his wife had passed away.

The lodge drew many men from all stations of life with whom Warren was able to identify, and since Masonry was a hotbed of resistance to British authority, the lodge served as a well from which Warren could draw patriot recruits. Members of this charitable and fraternal organization became closely aligned both socially and politically. Warren and Paul Revere, for example, were fellow Masons as well as political associates and friends. Warren, rungs above Revere on the social ladder, belonged to the Whig party elite, yet unlike many other patriot leaders, he related easily to the Boston mechanic. Both men had lost their fathers when they were teenagers. Both had experienced the death of a child, and their wives had died within the same week. Revere would become one of Warren's most trusted political allies and even named a son Joseph Warren Revere.

Revere was a tradesmen and thus not part of Boston's elite. Warren was his lifeline to the upper echelon of the Whig leadership. The doctor cultivated Revere's talents and expanded his connections, all to the benefit of the patriot movement. The two men would soon be bound together in one of the most famous acts of resistance in the battle for control between Britain and the colonies.

10

A BITTER CREW

"Our Warren's there."

—"THE RALLYING SONG OF THE TEA PARTY"

THE ESTABLISHMENT OF THE COMMITTEES OF CORRESPONDENCE connected the colonies more closely than ever before. And within Massachusetts, the Boston committee increased its political influence by taking from the town meeting the responsibility for writing instructions for Boston's representatives to the General Court. On April 9, 1773, Warren was appointed a member of the committee to prepare the instructions, making recommendations and outlining the political agenda. He was the only person appointed to every instructions committee between 1769 and 1774, and through his drafts he had a significant and growing influence over broader state politics. According to Warren's second biographer, John Cary, "Committees all over Massachusetts adopted the policies and plans outlined by Warren and Adams in the Boston committee, and, through instructions to the towns' representatives in the General court, made them colonial policy. . . . The importance of the Boston instructions was indicated by the close relationship between them and the business transacted in the following sessions of the General Court."

In the late 1760s, around the time of the Townshend Acts protests, Thomas Hutchinson and Lieutenant Governor Andrew Oliver had written a series of letters to the Crown. Now, in June 1773, Samuel Adams, with Warren's assistance, pushed for their publication, insisting that they showed that Hutchinson and Oliver had exaggerated events and demonized the colonists' actions. The letters were published, turning the two most powerful Tories in Massachusetts into villains throughout the colonies. Governor Hutchinson claimed the letters had been taken out of context and merely underscored the supremacy of Parliament while accurately describing Boston's political developments in those years, but his pleas had little impact, as incensed colonists took to the streets and burned effigies of both men. In any case, since Warren had become closely and publicly aligned with Adams at the top of the radical faction, Hutchinson and other Crown supporters had little doubt concerning his role in the publication of the letters. Warren also likely urged Revere to create a political cartoon casting a diabolical and traitorous Hutchinson as the newest Crown villain.

By this time, the rift between Warren and his Tory network was nearly complete. Warren would soon claim that Thomas Hutchinson had betrayed his native countrymen in a "most vile and treacherous manner." The patriot doctor now had little tolerance for most Tories, even if they were his former patients. By early 1774, he was no longer treating Boston's elite Tory families—the Hutchinsons, the Olivers, the Clarks, or the Hallowells. Exactly who decided to terminate these professional relationships is unknown. But with the proliferation of Warren's radical political ideology and a growing Tory backlash against Crown resistance, both the patriot doctor and his Tory clientele may have come to feel ill at ease about continuing such an intimate relationship.

On May 10, 1773, Parliament passed the Tea Act, which granted the nearly bankrupt British East India Company a monopoly on the exportation of dutied tea to the colonies. Over the years, Warren had warned about such new encroachments by British authority; now they were becoming a reality. Objecting to the act's obvious restriction of free trade, colonists were also concerned that Britain would control the importation of more goods into the colonies. To many merchants, the prospect of other monopolies raised the frightening specter of a plot to seize colonial rights.

Resistance to the monopoly on the tea in Boston was centered in the North End Caucus, whose members, spearheaded by Warren, secretly voted and pledged with "their lives and fortunes" that the "tea shipped by the east-India Company shall not be landed." The Crown had assigned five agents to sell the tea, three of whom happened to be former patients of Dr. Warren—Governor Hutchinson's two sons, Elisha and Thomas Jr., and the merchant Richard Clarke, the father-in-law of the painter John Singleton Copley. The North End Caucus appointed Warren, along with Drs. Benjamin Church and Thomas Young, to a committee to draft a resolution aimed at the tea consignees. An anonymous letter was sent to Clarke, demanding that he appear at Liberty Tree on November 3 to resign his commission. The consignees met and consulted with each other and determined it was in their best interests not to appear before the disgruntled mob gathering at Liberty Tree.

Instead, they met at Clarke's warehouse. Perhaps they hoped he held some sway with the Whigs, given Copley's associations with their top leaders, many of whom he had painted over the past decade. When they failed to appear at Liberty Tree, Warren, accompanied by the patriot incendiary William Molineux, Dr. Church, and a furious mob of 300 people, went to Clarke's warehouse to deliver an ultimatum—resign the commissions or be considered enemies of the country. When the commissioners refused to resign, Molineux incited the crowd, which rushed the building and laid siege to the warehouse, ripping the doors off the hinges, and fighting the agents and merchants to a standoff.

Two days later, on Pope's Day, the Tory engraver Henry Pelham (half-brother of John Copley), well aware of the attack on Clarke's warehouse, noted that the mobs were at it again. He decried the "shouting of an undis[c]iplined Rabble . . . and the infernall yell of those who are fighting for the possessions of the devill. . . . I have been several days attentively observing the movements of our Son's of Liberty, which was once (like the word tyrant) an honorable distinction." Almost two weeks later, on the evening of November 17, a furious mob descended on Clarke's house, shouting obscenities and breaking windows.

When Warren realized that the agents would not relinquish their commissions, he and his colleagues decided on a more destructive plan of action. The first cargo of duties tea arrived in Boston Harbor on board the *Dartmouth* on November 28. The ship landed and unloaded all its goods except for tea. By British law, the vessel had twenty days, till midnight on December 16, to unload all its cargo and pay the duties; if it did not do so, the Crown could seize and sell the unloaded cargo. The radical leaders would have to convince the consignees or Governor Hutchinson to return the tea. If they did not, any acts of retribution would be committed directly on Crown property. The Whigs placed the ships under a group watch to ensure the tea would not be landed. Warren was one of the Whig leaders who "attended constantly" at the series of tea meetings held in November and December.

On December 11, a committee headed by Warren visited the well-connected merchant John Rowe, attempting to gather as much information as possible prior to the tea being landed and unloaded. The committee inquired about Captain Bruce and his ship, the *Eleanor*— partly owned by Rowe—which was carrying approximately 112 chests of tea. (Francis Rotch, the owner of the two other ships carrying the tea, was one of Warren's erstwhile patients.)

On every second Thursday of the month, the St. Andrew's Lodge held its meeting at the Green Dragon Tavern, where Warren's North End Caucus sometimes met. On December 16 (the second Thursday of the month), Warren and four other Masonic brothers attended a meeting of St. Andrew's at the Green Dragon, but the "lodge closed on account of the few members in attendance." Instead, the day's action was centered on the Old South Meeting House, where thousands thronged throughout the day to deliberate what to do about the tea. In the evening, Warren joined the assembled radical leaders, and was one of the "chief Speakers," to await a response from Francis Rotch, who had applied to Governor Hutchinson for a pass that would allow him to return the tea. Hutchinson refused his request. When Rotch returned to Old South and delivered the news, Samuel Adams announced to the crowd that nothing more could be done at that point.

Within fifteen minutes from the frigid and rain-soaked streets came a sudden "hideous yelling . . . imitating the powaws of Indians and others the whistle of a boatswain, which was answered by some few in the house; on which numbers hastened out as fast as possible." As the meeting dissolved, patriots disguised as Mohawk Indians, their faces blackened, some armed with clubs and cutlasses, hastened toward Griffin's Wharf. There they boarded three docked vessels—the *Eleanor*, the *Dartmouth*, and the brig *Beaver*—which collectively held more than 340 chests of the East India tea. Warren remained in Old South until only approximately fifty to one hundred people were left.

That night the "bitter brew"—worth over nine thousand pounds—was dumped into Boston Harbor. The entire affair, according to Henry Bromfield, an elegant and eminent Boston merchant, "was conducted with the greatest dispatch, regularity and management, so as to evidence that there were people of sence and of more discernment" directing the mobbish participants. When it came to organized crowd action, little happened spontaneously. Such a large-scale incident involving scores of patriot actors was most certainly planned and controlled by the top Whig leaders, including Warren.

Warren's exact role in this incident remains unclear. Naturally, anyone who participated in the event knew they risked arrest by British authorities, underscoring the need for disguise. Most historians assert that Warren was not a participant in the Boston Tea Party, or they claim that the existing evidence is inconclusive. While Warren most likely did not physically dump chests of tea into the harbor, he was almost certainly one of the event's main orchestrators. After all, he had been involved in almost every aspect of opposing the Tea Act since the news of its passage had arrived months earlier. And along with Samuel Adams, Thomas Young, and Josiah Quincy, Warren was present in the Old South Meeting House just prior to the commencement of the destruction of the tea—which provided these leaders with a solid alibi to avoid arrest. Given the proximity of Griffin's Wharf to the Old South, Warren was highly unlikely to go anywhere else upon leaving.

Additionally, as an owner of Hooton's Wharf and many of the buildings situated there, Warren would have been familiar with the seafaring trades, the maritime culture, and the waterfront populace. Likely he had an extensive network of contacts in this important sector of Boston's economic life, providing him with additional knowledge regarding the tea issues.

Decades after the event, however, a popular street ballad surfaced, likely written by Boston Freemasons to memorialize the event, placing Warren at the center of the Boston Tea Party. "The Rallying Song of the Tea Party" reads in part:

> *Rally Mohawks! Bring out your axes*
> *And tell King George we'll pay no taxes*
> *On his foreign tea!* . . .
> *Then rally, boys, and hasten on*
> *To meet our chiefs at the Green Dragon.*
> *Our Warren's there and bold Revere,*
> *With hands to do, and words to cheer,*
> *For Liberty and laws!*
> *Our country's "braves" and firm defenders*
> *Shall ne'er be left by true North-Enders*
> *Fighting freedom's cause!*

The nineteenth-century song connects both Warren and Revere with the Boston Tea Party. It acknowledges the doctor's leadership of the participants within the walls of the Green Dragon Tavern. The ballad refers to Warren as a Mohawk chief who encouraged his "braves" to unite in "fighting freedom's cause." Warren was also considered one of the "True North-Enders." While no evidence supports the ballad's claims that Warren was an active participant in dumping the tea, his more important involvement in the weeks leading up to the incident cannot be refuted.

The radical leadership, including Warren, took great care to plan the event, even meeting with John Rowe. The Tea Party proceeded in an orderly fashion without violence or injury, and no damage, other than the tea destruction itself, occurred to the actual vessels or to any of the other property thereon. The patriot leaders successfully kept the mob in check and focused on the specific task at hand, avoiding a wild melee. John Adams declared that the event was "so bold, so daring, so firm, intrepid and inflexible, and it must have so important Consequences, and so lasting, that I cant but consider it as an Epocha in History." His diary suggests that leading patriots—especially Warren—were well aware of how monumental their actions were.

Following the Tea Party, Paul Revere was dispatched to alert Philadelphia and New York about the events. Less than two weeks after the destruction of the tea, Warren and Revere celebrated the Feast of St. John the Evangelist with more than forty fellow Masons and several of the men involved in the Tea Party. Then a month after the orderly Tea Party, on the icy evening of January 25, 1774, the fifty-year-old British customs official John Malcolm, highly unpopular among patriots, was tarred, feathered, and severely beaten in a most brutal attack. After hours of torture, the mob dumped him by his house nearly frozen and almost dead. Tories and even many moderate patriots viewed the incident as "an outrageous violence."

When news of the destruction of the tea reached London, Parliament had to take a stand. The outraged prime minister, Lord North, wasted no time in pushing the Coercive Acts through Parliament between March and June of 1774, to punish Boston's unruly colonists and, he hoped, break their resistance. These laws later came to be known as the "Intolerable Acts": the Boston Port Act (March), the Massachusetts Government Act (May), the Administration of Justice Act (May), and the Quartering Act (June).

Their cumulative effect was to shift greater control over Boston politics to London, while punishing Bostonians for their rebellion. The Government Act specified that within the General Court, Council members would no longer be elected by the lower house but would instead be appointed in London by a writ of mandamus. Furthermore, town meetings could be held only once a year unless specifically approved by the governor. The Boston Port Act closed the port of Boston and transferred the seat of colonial government to Salem, as a temporary measure until Bostonians paid back the cost of the destroyed tea.

Bostonians learned of the Port Act's passage two weeks before it was to go into effect. Warren wrote, "We have this day received information, that a Bill . . . for blocking up the harbor of Boston until the tea, lately destroyed at one of the wharves in this town, be paid for." On behalf of the Boston Committee of Correspondence, he invited eight other towns to Fanueil Hall "that we may together consult what is proper to be done in this critical state of our public affairs." On June 1, the Port Act went "into operation amid the tolling of bells, fasting and prayer, [and] the exhibition of mourning emblems." Even in Philadelphia bells rang and Virginia held a day of fasting and prayer in a show of patriot solidarity.

Warren's growing influence as a leader amongst the radicals in the country party was also evident from his appointment to head a committee to draft a Solemn League and Covenant, which called for an end to all commerce with the mother country. It established a set of stringent boycotts to cease all import and export trade with Britain and the West Indies, such that no person could "buy, purchase or consume" items arriving from Britain in any port. The effectiveness of the boycott would depend on the cooperation of the rest of Massachusetts and the other colonies. On June 5, Warren presented his Solemn League and Covenant that his subcommittee had drafted to the Boston Committee of Correspondence, and it was adopted and soon distributed throughout Massachusetts. Yet the town meeting didn't get a chance to discuss Warren's covenant until late June.

In the June 17 Boston town meeting, Warren managed to stave off a challenge to the existence of the Boston Committee of Correspondence. But the real opposition came at the June 27 to 28 town meeting where attendance was so high that the meeting had to move to Old South. A motion was made to censure and abolish the Boston Committee of Correspondence, which failed on June 28. With less than unanimous support, several towns and many individuals believed Warren's covenant too extreme. But the town voted to support the committee and its work. With this Whig victory, the government party (Tories) could mount no future opposition in the town meeting.

British General Thomas Gage had recently replaced Thomas Hutchinson as the new royal governor in May 1774, signaling the dawn of military rule in Boston. Many Tory Bostonians saw Gage's arrival as an overdue blessing: subjected to wanton mob tyranny, they viewed the patriots as the aggressive oppressors. A few months earlier in March 1774, Andrew Oliver, the lieutenant governor of Massachusetts, had passed away; most Crown supporters believed that the publication of Oliver's letters had hastened his death. Then at the funeral, his family and other mourners who attended were insulted and abused by a hostile, insensitive whig mob. The deceased's brother, the maligned chief justice Peter Oliver, was forced to miss the entire burial, fearing certain attack from what Thomas Hutchinson described as the "rude and brutal behavior of the rabble." All this only intensified the friction, mistrust, and distaste between patriots and Tories.

Upon General Gage's arrival, Tories "generally expected and hoped, that he [Gage] had Orders to send to England several Persons, who had been declared by his Majesty's Law Servants to have been guilty of high Treason." Considering Warren's outspoken resistance to Crown authority, many Boston Loyalists were likely eager to see him removed from the province and brought to justice in London. With Hutchinson gone and Boston now moored by British economic and military anchors, radical leaders found themselves particularly vulnerable. But even as arrest now loomed as a real threat, Warren and Adams continued to mobilize against oppressive Crown policies.

WARREN'S ACTIVITIES IN THE PUBLIC SPHERE HAD TEMPORARILY halted any romantic pursuits. However, in 1774 he became involved with Mercy Scollay, whom he had known for years. Mercy's father, John Scollay, was a wealthy merchant who went bankrupt in the Wheelwright collapse of 1765, but he had honored his debt, earning great respect within the community. He eventually rebuilt his fortune and became a Boston selectman, fire marshal, and staunch patriot.

Mercy's mother, also named Mercy, was the sister of Warren's friend and medical supplier John Greenleaf, and like Warren, the Scollay family maintained a strong relationship with the Reverend Dr. Samuel Cooper. In the spring of 1774, Mercy made several visits to Warren's medical practice as a patient, which initiated a personal relationship.

Raised as a gentleman's daughter, she had learned to read and write, recite Scripture, sew, and embroider. Although Mercy had been ensconced in opulence and groomed to rub elbows with members of Boston's high society, her family had, like Warren's, experienced difficult financial upheavals. As a daughter of John Scollay, and living in a pro-Whig household, Mercy was well versed in Boston politics. Her attraction to Joseph Warren likely went beyond his appearance or personality to his staunch Whig politics and his leadership in championing the colonists' God-given liberties. Warren's charm and personal magnetism were traits that helped endear him to people both socially and professionally (and now romantically).

Much of the surviving writing in Mercy's hand dates from 1776 and beyond, with the exception of a remarkable letter sent to overseas cousins on June 1, 1774, the day the Port Act took effect. Like strong-willed New England female patriots Abigail Adams and Mercy Otis Warren, who were married to top echelon Whig leaders and refused to conform to their inherited docile societal roles, Mercy was an outspoken and dedicated advocate for the cause of American liberty. In her letter, she outlined the situation in Boston and revealed herself to be an ardent patriot supporter whose "heart bleeds for the calamity of my nation land!" She refused to remain silent during "the commencement of commercial distress in America!" explaining the "ministerial cruelty and oppression from Britain!—our harbor is block'd by the fleet of our mother country, shut up by those who ought to be the most indulgent to our trade but alas are now trying (by the iron rod of power) to sink us." With the port completely shut down and business paralyzed, Mercy believed that "the ruin of this once flourishing Metropolis" was imminent. George III, she declared, "has staind his reign with plots for their destruction! . . . while the greedy rapaciousness of an unprincipled soldiery, are making their ravages in our seaport Towns." Once a "land flowing with milk and honey . . . and I (Mercy) trust in God at some future period it will again be the case."

To blame the king himself was an incredibly bold and treasonous position to take in the spring of 1774. But Mercy took solace in the knowledge that the colonists could subsist on their natural resources and talents: "Thank Heaven! We can supply ourselves with necessary's at home—if we put our hands to the spindle" and "if our sea coasts are invaded by lawless power, we must return to the back countrys and like our forefathers, live on the vegetable world." Skilled in sewing and embroidery, she was ready to use her abilities to help strengthen home manufacturing in support of the nonconsumption agreements. Many of her friends and family members were adversely effected by the port's closure, and in a brief verse included in her letter, she lamented "poor Boston" as a "Deserted village":

But now the sound of population fail
No chearfull murmurs fluctuate in the gale
No busy steps the grass grown footway tread
For all the bloomy fluid of life is fled.

She vowed to continue the fight for liberty: "I feel invigorated when I think we suffer in the cause of freedom." Patriots, she wrote, would always "stand their ground and firmly maintain their rights and privileges against arbitrary power and oppression." In closing, she hoped that her overseas family might "never feel the pangs that . . . fill the breast of your Affectionate, tho melancholy and dejected cousin." Joseph Warren could hardly have found a woman whose political sentiments better matched his own.

When the Port Act was debated in Parliament in March 1774, its members understood that great numbers of troops would be needed to enforce the act and maintain order in Boston. "If we sent over a small number of men," one member argued, "the Boston militia would immediately cut them to pieces. . . . If we sent over a larger number, six or 7,000, the Americans would debauch them." On June 14 and 15, the Fourth King's Own Regiment and the 43rd arrived at Boston's Long Wharf, and over the next few months more British troops were transferred there from Quebec, Halifax, New York, and New Jersey. General Gage proudly declared that among Loyalists "there is now an open opposition to the [radical] faction, carried on with a warmth and spirit unknown before . . . and I hope it will not be very long before it produces very salutary effects." Gage's hopes were quickly doused by the further inflammatory actions of zealous patriots. He concluded that when dealing with the radicals, "lenient measures, and the cautious and legal exertion of the coercive powers of government have served only to render them more daring and licentious."

Since Governor Gage had the authority to block Boston's town meetings, Warren proposed holding a county convention in order to plan opposition to the Coercive Acts. On June 6, Warren demanded that a Continental Congress be held to unite the colonies against Great Britain. "I am for dying rather than betray the rights of America," he wrote, warning that "the event of this struggle insures happiness and freedom or miserable slavery to this continent. . . . Act then like men. Appoint a general Congress from the several colonies."

That same month Warren was appointed to a donations committee meant to help relieve the hardships many families now suffered as a result of the Port Act. The closure of the port meant that everyday necessities such as firewood had to be transported overland, which cost more time and money. With Boston isolated and its economy crippled, the radicals desperately needed support and unity from other colonies that they had been seeking for years.

They were not disappointed. Lord North and many in Parliament had assumed the other colonies would seize the opportunity of Boston's closed port to take over its trading ventures, but instead they banded together in an impressive display of solidarity, sending grain, rice, flour, and other necessary supplies to the besieged town. Warren, writing letters on behalf of the Committee of Donations to other towns and colonies in appreciation of the contributions they were sending, met Israel Putnam, a beloved veteran of the French and Indian War. "The celebrated Colonel Putnam is now in my house," Warren wrote Samuel Adams, "having arrived . . . with a generous donation of sheep." The two men undoubtedly discussed the developing political situation, beginning a brief but close friendship.

Warren's efforts against the Crown had helped push colonial sentiments in favor of Boston's plight. What was happening in Boston, people in other colonies reasoned, could happen to them, as their fundamental liberties—their inherited constitutional and natural rights as British subjects—were under assault. Even those who disapproved of the tea destruction stood behind Boston, including George Washington who, in a letter of June 1774, declared that "the cause of Boston . . . is now and ever will be considerd [sic] as the cause of America . . . and that we shall not suffer ourselves to be sacrificed by piecemeal."

Soon, approximately four thousand British soldiers arrived in Boston's closed port. London ordered General Gage to gather evidence about the Tea Party and to prosecute its leaders. He instructed magistrates to arrest anyone who signed his name or requested a signature on the Solemn League and Covenant, Warren's boycott document. Lord Dartmouth, who had replaced Lord Hillsborough as secretary of state for the colonies, hoped these orders would help to "prevent those unwarrantable assemblings of the people for factious purposes, which had been the source of so much mischief."

But as the eminent historian Gordon S. Wood has asserted, "many colonists had little reason to feel part of His Majesty's realm or to respect royalty," simply because "the crown was too far away to make its presence felt." In fact, in 1740 Massachusetts had been called "a kind of commonwealth where the King is hardly a stadtholder." Such sentiments were especially resonant for Joseph Warren, a fourth-generation American who had become increasingly radical over the years. Through his growing social and political connections, he was able to influence popular sentiments now coalescing against the king. As many in the Bay Colony questioned the monarchy, independence, once a radical prospect, was becoming more of a reality than ever before.

Warren's own rhetoric escalated as he challenged the colonists either to act "like men" or "expect the derision of schoolboys and the execrations of posterity." According to Warren, if the colonists refused to stand with the radicals and enforce the Solemn League and Covenant, they were cowards, relegating themselves to a deserved everlasting ignominy. Some viewed the Solemn League and Covenant as too extreme and many protested, especially with the threat of arrest looming over any and every person who put their name to it. And yet the boycott went beyond economic pressure, as Warren hoped to exact a social cost on potential violators. "All trade, commerce, and dealings whatever" would cease with anyone who violated the compact.

The initial opposition to his boycott was discouraging: Warren was pushing hard and the majority of people were unwilling to go that far. On June 15, he wrote to Samuel Adams, who was in Salem attending the General Court. (General Gage had moved the meeting place of the General Court to Salem as instructed in the Coercive Acts.) Warren maintained that "the mistress we court is LIBERTY; and it is better to die than not to obtain her. . . . You will undoubtedly do all in your power to effect the relief of this town, and to expedite a general congress; but we must not suffer the town of Boston to render themselves contemptible, either by their want of fortitude, honesty, or foresight, in the eyes of this and other colonies." Although he held no official post, Warren again called for a congress of all the colonies, instructing "the Father of the Revolution" not to showcase political extremism, which would risk other colonies' ostracizing Boston as an overzealous radical stronghold. (Samuel Adams and his cousin John would follow this advice throughout their future participation in the Continental Congresses.) At the General Court in Salem, a committee led by Samuel Adams and other top patriot leaders pushed for a united congress of colonies, deeming it "highly expedient and necessary . . . to deliberate and determine upon wise and proper measures to be by them recommended to all colonies, for the recovery and establishment of their just rights and liberties, civil and religious."

Upon Samuel Adams's return from Salem, he went to Warren's home to inform his gathered radical comrades that the House had appointed five delegates to attend a continental congress at Philadelphia's Carpenter's Hall starting on September 1, 1774. The unity the radical Whigs had sought for years was finally to be fulfilled within a few months. Now they had a chance to persuade the rest of America to unite in the cause of freedom and ultimately independence.

Ultimately, four men were sent to represent Massachusetts, including Samuel and John Adams. (Originally five delegates were chosen, but James Bowdoin was too ill to make the journey.) Warren would stay in Boston to lead the Whigs, remaining with his four young children and his ailing patients in need of care. (Whether Warren was ever considered a delegate candidate—his young age a likely determining factor against sending him—will never be known with certainty, but the fact that he remained behind as one of the top radicals in Boston's political arena spoke to the growing confidence the Whig leadership placed in him.) That year, even as he was directing Whig policy throughout the Bay Colony, Warren was treating some twenty-five to fifty new patients every month. His practice continued to grow despite the absence of Loyalist clients. His house had become not only a meeting place for important political business but also home to numerous apprentices. And he was also busy courting Mercy Scollay. Warren's private and professional life was perhaps even more consuming than his political life. His professional success benefited the Whigs on numerous fronts. He imparted his political philosophies to his patients and medical students, just as he would often part with his finances to advance the rebellion.

Warren likely helped pay for a new set of clothes and shoes for Samuel Adams to wear at the Continental Congress, to exude the appearance of a sophisticated statesman rather than a shabby-looking leader of crass rabble-rousers. On August 10, the two Adamses and the other two Massachusetts delegates left Boston in a horse-drawn coach accompanied by several armed servants. Before their departure, they gathered at Coolidge's Tavern in Watertown where their friends and associates—including Warren—bade them farewell. With two of his closest associates on the three-hundred-plus-mile journey south, Warren remained in Boston at the forefront of the military, economic, and political firestorm, becoming the de facto leader of the Whig party in Massachusetts.

11

RESOLVED

"Our Liberty must be preserved; it is far dearer than life."
—JOSEPH WARREN, 1775

WHILE BRITAIN'S POLITICAL TIDAL WAVE CRASHED INTO BOSTON'S desolate and defenseless port, Joseph Warren continued to organize resistance to Crown policies. Boston, surrounded by British ships of war and thousands of soldiers, was under occupation. Several Boston clergymen recommended a day of fasting and prayer due to the town's abysmal situation. Even Harvard's annual commencement celebration was dampened since the prevailing tension "prevents it being kept Publick as usual."

In September 1774, the British executed one of their own soldiers—twenty-one-year-old Valentine Duckett—on Boston Common for desertion. For patriots, the spectacle was yet another example of British cruelty.

Before sunrise on the morning of September 1, General Gage had ordered more than 250 British troops from various regiments into

East Cambridge to confiscate a store of gunpowder from the arsenal "belonging to the Province." The maneuver—intended to prevent patriots from seizing the ammunition—set off an alarm through the countryside. Exaggerated reports of wanton British destruction brought hundreds of armed militias from neighboring towns pouring into Cambridge. Finding that the troops had already removed the powder and returned to Boston, the incensed patriots redirected their anger toward the Tories whom General Gage had appointed to the Mandamus Council under the Coercive Acts. Descending upon the Loyalist area that later came to be called "Tory Row" near Harvard College, patriot throngs demanded that the appointees resign.

The next morning, Warren received a message imploring him "to take some step in order to prevent the people from coming to immediate acts of violence, as incredible numbers were in arms and lined the roads from Sudbury to Cambridge." Warren summoned members of the Committee of Correspondence to accompany him to Cambridge and on the way they crossed paths with Lieutenant Governor Thomas Oliver, who was en route to Boston to ask Gage not to send British troops to deal with the rabble, in the hopes of avoiding bloodshed. Warren agreed. Thousands of armed patriots were gathered, and Warren claimed that if the soldiers were dispatched to the scene, "I doubt whether a man would have been saved of their whole number."

Warren, and several other patriot leaders, managed to restore peace and order, though his success was double-edged. Nobody could deny his kinetic leadership, and yet for Crown Loyalists, Warren's increasing power over the patriot "rabble" gave them all the more reason to fear and despise him.

Although Tory elites momentarily breathed a sigh of collective relief that the threat had passed, another incident—perhaps a deadly one—might occur at any time. Along with other frightened Loyalists, Thomas Oliver immediately sought to move his family and his possessions out of Cambridge to Boston, where the king's troops would protect them. Over the next several weeks Oliver's family and neighbors followed. General Gage strategically placed cannons near the Boston Neck and doubled the guards by the entrance, in case country militias decided to attack the British forces in the town. Warren objected to the maneuver; Boston's port was already shut, and this move now blocked the town by land. He appealed to Gage, explaining that "it is natural for the People to be soured by Oppression . . . when their Exertions for the Preservation of their Rights are construed into Treason and Rebellion." He reminded Gage that the inhabitants of Boston were already suffering and that these latest actions would prove ruinous if he continued "upon shutting up the Avenues to the Town, and reducing the Inhabitants by Distress and Famine, to a disgraceful and slavish Submission."

With his patriot comrades out of town, Warren had exhausted the available options for the relief of his community. He lamented the idea of a war with mother Britain—nobody wanted to spill blood unnecessarily. He had described General Gage in a letter to Josiah Quincy as "honest" and "upright" and averring that Gage was sincerely "desirous of accommodating the difference between Great Britain and her colonies in a just and honorable way." But Warren was also a realist, and his instincts as a politician helped guide his actions. The Crown did not appear to be backing down. So while publicly professing loyalty to the king, he remained on the defensive and prepared for armed conflict and even separation.

Warren broached the idea of separation in a letter to Sam Adams, informing him of the unfolding situation in Massachusetts. "Our all is at stake," he wrote.

> *We must give up our rights, and boast no more of freedom, or we must oppose immediately. Our enemies press so close that we cannot rest upon our arms. If this province is saved, it must be by adopting measures immediately efficacious. I have mentioned, in my letters to you, the most mild plan that can be adopted; viz non-importation and non-exportation . . . but it may not be amiss to try how far some further*

*steps for securing our rights might (if absolutely necessary) be approved
by our brethren on the continent. I firmly believe, that the utmost cau-
tion and prudence is necessary to gain the consent of the province to
wait a few months longer for their deliverance, as they think the cord
by which they were bound to the King of Britain has been, by his act,
cut in sunder.*

Meanwhile Warren had been working on a document that would
signal the transformation of the resistance movement into a rebellion.
The Coercive Acts had nullified parts of Massachusetts's charter, giving the royal governor unprecedented control and inhibiting democratic government by the people. A county convention had been called
in response, to include representatives from Suffolk County. (Massachusetts counties had started holding conventions with Berkshire holding the first on July 6, in Stockbridge; the trend moved east across
the province.) On August 16, Warren had informed Samuel Adams
that "the selectmen and committee of correspondence met, and chose
five members to attend the county congress at Stoughton to-morrow."
That following day, as head of the appointed Suffolk delegation, Warren arrived at Doty's Tavern in Stoughton (now Canton) "in a stylish berlin, drawn by four horses, with a coachman in livery on the
box and footman on the rumble." The location in Suffolk County had
been suggested by Samuel Adams so that the meeting could operate at
a safe enough distance from garrisoned Boston.

At this first convention, the delegates discussed and passed resolutions for resisting the Coercive Acts, but since many towns had not
appointed delegates, another convention was called, to be held in Dedham on the morning of September 6. On August 26, various town
delegates met and chose Warren to be the chairman of that Suffolk
convention—in yet another instance of Warren's increasing influence.
Aware that the convention would "have very important consequences,"
Warren helped hone a set of resolutions drawn up in response to the
Coercive Acts. When the convention met at the house of Mr. Richard

Woodward in Dedham on September 6, a committee was appointed, led by Warren, to finalize the document. The convention adjourned and agreed to meet three days later in Milton at the home of Daniel Vose. Later that day Warren returned to Boston, where he tended to patients and put the finishing touches on the document that would be known as the Suffolk Resolves. On September 9, scores of patriots representing nineteen districts and towns assembled in Milton, where Warren read the resolves aloud to the cheers and approbation of the delegates, who voted unanimously in favor.

According to Warren biographer John Cary, the Suffolk Resolves "so closely parallels Warren's stated views, and in some cases his very wording, that it seems likely he was its principle author." Warren's other main biographer, Richard Frothingham, also asserted that Warren drafted the resolves. At a minimum they were profoundly shaped by his influence. Arguably the Suffolk Resolves were Warren's single most important and influential piece of writing. An insurrectionary document, it instructed colonists to reject the acts of Parliament and to prepare to defend themselves against the violent onslaught that Britain would likely unleash because of their disobedience. The document professed loyalty to the king but seemingly to pacify the more centrist and conservative Whigs. With Boston's streets "thronged with military executioners" and its "harbors crowded with ships of war," the "encroachments of liberty" were omnipresent. Citing the "unrelenting severity" of Britain's use of power, and the "gross infractions of those rights to which we [the colonists] are justly entitled," the resolves asserted that "no obedience is due from this province" to any of the late acts of Parliament. Instead the acts were to be "rejected as the attempts of a wicked administration to enslave America." One key resolve was a broad boycott, and Warren outlined his plan to "withhold all commercial intercourse with Great-Britain . . . and abstain from the consumption of British merchandise and manufacturers." The colonists had to "defend and preserve those civil and religious rights and liberties, for which many . . . fought, bled and died." The

Suffolk Resolves' response to the Quebec Act demonstrated New England society's lack of religious freedom. Considering Warren was the document's main author, those views likely mirrored his own views regarding religious tolerance.

The resolves also called on the Bay Colony inhabitants to raise colonial militias. Warren urged them to "use their utmost diligence to acquaint themselves with the art of war as soon as possible." Lest anyone think the people of New England were too extreme, Warren professed that "we are determined to act merely upon the defensive." But the prevailing logic dictated that if the colonies united to reject Parliament's measures, Britain would eventually have to resort to violent measures to impose its will. Even if the Crown retreated to its prewar policies in an attempt to preserve harmony between itself and the colonies, such placation would ensure that the colonies no longer obeyed mother Britain. In the resolves, Warren made certain to mention that Suffolk County would "pay all due respect and submission to such measures as may be recommended" by the Continental Congress—for that body would decide what mode of action America would pursue. Once the country convention approved the resolves, Paul Revere was dispatched to ferry them to Philadelphia.

At the First Continental Congress, the diverse group of delegates from New Hampshire to South Carolina assembled under one roof for the first time, carting with them all their prejudices, mistrust, and preconceived notions about one another. As John Adams astutely observed,

> *The colonies had grown up under constitutions of governments so different, there was so great a variety of religions, they were composed of so many different nations, their customs, manners, and habits had so little resemblance, and their intercourse had been so rare, and their knowledge of each other so imperfect, that to unite them in the same principles in theory and the same system of action, was certainly a very difficult enterprise.*

As Warren had advised in his letter to Samuel Adams, the Bay Colony delegates needed to take measured steps to gain the support of the other colonial representatives. Many viewed Massachusetts as a hotbed of political extremism, headed by radical insurgents. Samuel Adams had explained to Warren that "a certain degree of jealousy [existed] in the minds of some, that we aim at a total independency, not only of the mother country, but of the colonies, too; and that, as we are a hardy and brave people, we shall in time overrun them all."

On September 16, Paul Revere arrived in Philadelphia with the Suffolk Resolves, and the following day the document was presented to the Continental Congress, whose members applauded as it was read aloud. They approved and adopted all of Warren's proposals unanimously—remarkable under the circumstances. At one moment, the local Massachusetts boycott against British goods had become a unified colonial boycott. With several strokes of his quill, Warren's opus had unified the colonies in a critical first step toward solidarity. John Adams recorded the monumental event in his diary the same day: "This was one of the happiest days of my life. . . . This day convinced me that America will support the Massachusetts or perish with her."

On September 2, the day of the "powder Alarm," General Gage had issued a proclamation declaring that he would not convene the General Court that was scheduled to meet in the Salem Court House on October 5, 1774. Warren and the other Massachusetts radical leaders, anticipating Gage's action, had already planned to form an extralegal congress to provide an interim government for the Bay Colony outside the governor's control and to prepare for a "defensive" war. On September 22, Warren was chosen to represent Boston at the Massachusetts Provincial Congress—his first official office. Delegates from across the colony gathered for the congress assembled in Concord on October 11. Days later the *Massachusetts Gazette* published the news that five resolves had arrived from the Continental Congress in Philadelphia—supporting their brethren to the north—of which the first read, "Resolved, That this congress approve of the opposition made by the inhabitants of the Massachusetts Bay to the execution by force, in such case all America ought to support them in their opposition."

On October 14, in Philadelphia, the Continental Congress adopted a declaration of rights and grievances and sent an address across the Atlantic to muster support against the Coercive Acts. In an effort to punish Britain economically, the Congress formulated a plan of united commercial resistance—the "Continental Association"—hoping it would convince Parliament to repeal the acts. Committees of Inspection were formed throughout the colonies to enforce the boycott against Britain, hoping the tactic would prove more effective than in years past. When the Congress dissolved on October 26, 1774, it agreed that if Parliament failed to resolve the colonies' grievances, it would meet again on May 10, 1775.

Loyalists condemned the Continental Congress and its actions, and even many of the assembled delegates favored accommodation with the mother country. Uncertainty and fear gripped both sides of the political divide. Warren commented on the bleak situation in Boston: "The treatment which the inhabitants receive from the soldiery makes us think that they regard us as enemies rather than fellow subjects." Fights between the inhabitants and British troops continued to occur, with the potential to ignite a full-scale conflict at any time.

But just as tensions reached a fever pitch, the radical leadership in Boston suffered challenging losses. Within just a few months, Warren lost three of his closest allies. Josiah Quincy, Jr., whose health was in rapid decline, departed for London to plead the Whig case to members of Parliament. Dr. Thomas Young, fearing for his family's safety, packed up and moved with them to Rhode Island. And in an even greater blow, William Molineux died on October 22, 1774. Warren had treated him for his severe fever the day before he died. For years the Whig merchant had helped lead public demonstrations and mob actions targeting Loyalists and Crown officials. An immensely popular figure in the lower rungs of Boston society, Molineux was one of Warren's close comrades, and his tremendous zeal for "the Liberties of America" had gained him the respect and loyalty of the patriot rank-and-file. His death came as a relief to many Tories, some of whom claimed that he had committed suicide using Warren's laudanum, due to embezzlement and financial issues. Chief Justice Peter Oliver, with the rabble's jeers and taunts during his brother's funeral still ringing in his ears, was of the opinion that Molineux was "a most infamous disturber of the peace, and urged on the mobs to commit their mad and desperate schemes." Even the moderate Whig merchant John Rowe referred to Molineux as "the first leader of dirty matters." The popular Warren was Molineux's natural successor as leader of the Boston working class, and he immediately stepped in to fill that role.

That fall, in a letter to Josiah Quincy in London, Warren wrote,

> It is the united voice of America to preserve her freedom, or lose their lives in defense of it. Their resolutions are not the effects of inconsiderate rashness, but the sound result of sober enquiry and deliberation. I am convinced that the true spirit of Liberty was never universally diffused through all ranks and orders of people, in any country on the face of the earth as it is now through all North America.

This time, Warren believed, the British had no intention of backing down from their increasingly stringent policies against the colonies: "The plan which has been so long concerted, to deprive America of her rights, seems now to be executing, and that the ministry have chosen the town of Boston as their first victim." Convinced that Britain was intent on total colonial subjugation, Warren reiterated his preference for a nonviolent push to independence: "If the late Acts of Parliament are not to be repealed, the wisest step for both countries is fairly to separate, and not spend their blood and treasure in destroying each other."

Across the Atlantic, though, George III saw violence as inevitable. "The New England governments are in a state of rebellion," he declared in November 1774. "Blows must decide whether they are to be subject to this country or independent." Both leaders knew that armed conflict was on the horizon; the question that remained was whether American independence would rise up in a brilliant dawn or set beneath a bleak shadow.

Warren remained omnipresent in New England, "constantly busied in helping forward the political machines in all parts of this province." At the first Massachusetts Provincial Congress, he became an instrumental force. On October 27, the Congress appointed a Committee of Safety—an executive body designed to handle all military matters— and the following day Warren was one of nine members elected to the committee. He dutifully attended every meeting from November 2, 1774, to January 25, 1775. Initially John Hancock was chosen as chairman, but Warren soon became the body's de facto leader; it would play a crucial role in the near-term political affairs of Massachusetts and then the united colonies. Warren also continued to lead in Boston and became increasingly active in the Boston Committee of Correspondence and the Boston Town Meetings. Warren was part of every important political organization in the Bay Colony.

At the same time Warren's medical practice continued to grow, as his patriot clientele swelled. His patients' needs called him out around the clock: he spent Christmas Day 1774 tending to at least a dozen patients, delivering one woman's baby. His circumstances were not easy, considering that he was a widower with four children, but his relationship with Mercy Scollay brought an air of happiness and normalcy to a brokenhearted household. As an ardent patriot, she supported his public actions while caring for him and his four children, to whom she became very attached.

Warren's expanding influence as a radical insurgent was a constant source of worry to those closest to him. Their fears were warranted, as he remained under the constant scrutiny of the British lion: the Crown deemed most of the political organizations he was connected to illegal, and his actions treasonous. He was ever more in danger of arrest. For his part, General Gage, commander of the British troops in America, realized he had to dismantle the growing patriot hydra from the top down. On January 18, 1775, he recommended to Lord Dartmouth in London that the most "obnoxious" of the radical "leaders" be "seized." Lord Dartmouth replied, "It is the opinion of the King's Servants, in which His Majesty concurs, that the first and essential step to be taken towards re-establishing Government, would be to arrest and imprison the principal actors and abettors of the Provincial Congress whose proceedings appear in every light to be acts of treason and rebellion."

But General Gage was aware of Warren's activities, thanks to Dr. Benjamin Church, a high-ranking Whig and Warren confidant, who had secretly flipped sides, becoming a spy in Gage's employ in early 1775. He gave the British commander additional verification that Warren was a strong catalyst fueling the rebel movement. "Friends of Warren," wrote James Spear Loring, "were then constantly expecting that some attempt would be made to seize him by the regulars."

Exacerbating matters, the street altercations between soldiers and colonists continued. Several days after Gage's letter to Lord Dartmouth, "an affray happened between the officers and the town house watch" that, according to John Rowe, caused "great uneasiness in town." Within days of the scuffle, Warren was chosen as a delegate to the Second Massachusetts Provincial Congress, which convened at Cambridge on February 1, 1775. He was appointed to the most important committees, where he handled fiscal and military matters, including appropriating funds for the Massachusetts delegates to the Second Continental Congress. He also encouraged the making of saltpeter to increase the patriots' seriously depleted stockpile of ammunition.

On February 10, Warren, who was in Boston at the time, received word that Gage was sending troops to "disperse the Congress" in Cambridge. He told Samuel Adams that he was "sorry I was not with my friends; and although my affairs would not allow of it, I went down to the ferry in a chaise with Dr. Church, both determined to share with our brethren in any dangers they might be engaged in." Church accompanied Warren, but as a spy for General Gage, he knew the rumor to be incorrect. Warren's lack of regard for his own safety often placed him in dangerous situations, but that was typical of his behavior. He soon realized the importance of having a reliable intelligence system to avoid such false alarms in the future.

Warren began to correspond with radical leaders from other states, trying to win their support for the policies he was directing. On February 20, he predicted to the patriot Arthur Lee that "the event, which I confess I think is near at hand, will confound our enemies, and rejoice those who wish well to us. . . . I am of the opinion, that, if once General Gage should lead his troops into the country, with design to enforce the late Acts of Parliament, Great Britain may take her leave, at least of the New-England colonies, and, if I mistake not, of all America." The gears of war, he understood, had been set in motion.

During the next four days Warren was present for every meeting of the Massachusetts Committee of Safety, spearheading efforts to organize the colony's military affairs.

THE ANNUAL ORATION COMMEMORATING THE BOSTON MASSACRE was scheduled for Monday, March 6 (since the actual anniversary fell on a Sunday), at the Old South Meeting House amid threats and rumors of violence. Word circulated throughout Boston that any man who spoke at the oration would be killed: "Many men who would otherwise have been desirous to speak on the anniversary of the massacre, now thought it most prudent to keep quiet." Warren, on the other hand, volunteered to deliver the speech. It was an audacious decision. He was by now a notorious figure, his incendiary actions well known to the entire British army in the Bay Colony. To the dismay of his family and colleagues, British soldiers promised to assassinate him and "took every opportunity of calling him a rebel, and telling him . . . that he would meet the fate of a rebel, that of being hung." One day when Warren was crossing the Neck—past the spot where the executions took place—some nearby British soldiers yelled to him, "Go on, Warren, you will soon come to the gallows."

On March 5, Samuel Adams declared, "To-morrow an oration is

to be delivered by Dr. Warren. It was thought best to have an experienced officer in the political field on this occasion, as we may possibly be attacked in our trenches." Perhaps more than anyone, Adams was aware of the danger awaiting Warren. Would the soldiers make good on the death threats against him? In this volatile situation, neither side knew what to expect.

On the morning of March 6, Warren, armed with a pair of pistols, set out to treat patients. Throughout the day, several thousand Bostonians and British soldiers gathered at the Old South Meeting House and awaited his arrival for the oration. When he finally arrived, it took the form of a provocation: "A single horse chair stopped at the apothecary's opposite the meeting," reported *Rivington's New York Gazette*, "from which descended the orator [Warren] . . . and, entering the shop, was followed by a servant with a bundle, in which were the Ciceronian toga. . . . Having robed himself, he proceeded across the street to the meeting." The mere act of delivering the annual oration was tantamount to a capital crime, but doing so in costume was perceived by the incensed soldiers as a deliberate act of mockery to the sovereignty of Great Britain.

Old South that day was a microcosm of the town of Boston, with soldiers dispersed among the local populace. Hostile, armed redcoats packed the meetinghouse and surrounded the pulpit, intent on disrupting and intimidating Warren from the outset: "The aisles of the meeting-house, the steps to the pulpit, even the pulpit itself, were occupied by the British." Warren entered Old South prepared to deliver yet another fiery annual oration.

Standing at the pulpit, surrounded by the enemy, he stared them down. He was aware, he began, "of the obligation I am under to obey the calls of my country at all times." He would never shirk his duty, he said, even in the face of danger, as "that personal freedom is the right of every man." Dispensing with the muted lexicon of past orations, he delivered an emotional diatribe that tore into the British ministry. "The madness of an avaricious minister of state," he proclaimed, "has . . . brought upon the stage, discord, envy, hatred, and revenge, with civil war close in their rear." The erstwhile harmonious relationship between the colonies and the mother country had been shattered as "the hearts of Britons and Americans . . . now burn with jealousy and rage." The colonists' fears of standing armies had been validated, he argued, by the "army sent over to enforce submission to certain acts of the British parliament." The result was "the many injuries offered to the town"—none more horrific than the Boston Massacre.

Amid the staccato hissing of the British officers, Warren's incendiary rhetoric elevated in tone and pitch as he evoked "the baleful images of terror" from the night when King Street was "bespattered" with the "brains" of innocent Bostonians. Now, five years later, his earlier warnings of further encroachments upon American liberties had proven true. "Our streets are again filled with armed men," he noted. "Our harbor is crowded with ships of war." Leading to the climax, Warren declared, "Our Liberty must be preserved; it is far dearer than life. . . . We cannot suffer even BRITONS to ravish it from us." Surrounded by British soldiers after weeks of assassination threats, Warren claimed, "It is the hand of Britain that inflicts the wound. The arms of George our rightful king have been employed to shed that blood."

Warren called for the people of Boston to support "the wise measures recommended by the honourable, the continental congress," which he had devised in his Suffolk Resolves. But "if these pacific measures are ineffectual," he urged, "and it appears that the only way to safety is, thro' fields of blood, I know you will not turn your faces from your foes; but will undauntedly press forward, until tyranny is trodden under your foot . . . and you have fixed . . . LIBERTY . . . on the American throne." In closing, he appealed to the massive crowd: "Our Country is in danger, but not to be despaired of. Our enemies are numerous and powerful—but we have many friends, determine TO BE FREE, and Heaven and Earth will aid the RESOLUTION. On you depend the fortunes of America. You are to decide the important question, on which rest the happiness and liberty of millions yet un-born. Act worthy of yourselves."

Warren's impassioned words, resounding for more than forty-five minutes within the walls of the meetinghouse, would soon resonate throughout the colonies. As one Bostonian marveled many years later, "It has always been a wonder to me, that the war did not commence on that day." A British soldier wrote that "this day . . . a most seditious, inflammatory harangue . . . was delivered by Dr. Warren, a notorious Whig . . . it was known for some days that this was to be delivered; accordingly a great number of officers assembled at it." The soldier expressed his desire to "have the pleasure before long" of seeing War-ren dead "by the hands of the hangman."

Warren had authored an article that appeared in the *Boston Evening Post* that same day in which he argued that "the Americans would be compelled by the great law of nature to strike a decisive blow; and . . . publish a manifesto to the world showing the necessity of dissolving their connection with a nation whose ministers were aiming at their ruin." The echoes of the words Thomas Jefferson would use over a year later in the Declaration of Independence—the "great law of na-ture" and "the necessity of dissolving their connection"—are striking. Warren set the tone for a separate American nation, independent from Great Britain, and over the next several months, he would set those words into action.

War with mother Britain was not a foregone conclusion in the win-ter of 1775, but Warren's March Massacre Oration did little to assuage tensions. In response to the oration, a Loyalist physician from Salem, Dr. Thomas Bolton, delivered a parody of the speech from the British Coffee-House balcony. In addition to lambasting the top Whig lead-ers, Bolton publicly accused Warren, "a man who by his greate skill in Chemistry, could turn water into milk, and sell it for six coppers the quart," of supplying the laudanum for Molineux's suicide. That same month a group of British soldiers attacked the home of John Han-cock, breaking his windows and destroying his fence. A few days after the Hancock incident, a group of redcoats and royal officers stripped, tarred, and feathered a man, then hauled him through the streets with a paper tied around his neck reading, "American liberty or democracy exemplified in a villain who attempted to entice one of the soldiers of his Majesty's 47th regiment to desert and take up arms with rebels against his king and country." Soldiers garrisoned in the Puritan town behaved in ways that pious Bostonians considered indecent, using profane language, becoming inebriated, and continually violating the Sabbath. On Sundays, soldiers "sported themselves in Scateing [skating] for several hours in open View of one of our Meeting Houses," while packs of soldiers incessantly played the tune "Yankee Doodle" outside church windows.

Assassination rumors continued to spread through the spring of 1775. Samuel Adams and John Hancock were unquestionably marked as enemies of the king, but Warren's continued public presence as the frontline Whig commander vaulted him to the top of the Crown's most despised list, making him a prime target of the soldiers. One British officer claimed that had Warren made any disparaging remarks against the king during his 1775 Massacre Oration, the soldiers would have run their swords through not only Warren but also "Hancock, Adams and hundreds more."

Warren knew his life was increasingly in peril. In February, he secretly began arranging to send his children and Mercy Scollay to the countryside. His trusted friend and colleague Dr. Elijah Dix had agreed to sell him a house and at least twenty acres of land in Worcester. Warren implored Dix that if his possessions "should arrive before any of my family I must beg you would take care of them, as the chests and trunks will contain things of the greatest value to me. Pray keep this matter secret."

In April, Gage made plans to send troops into the New England countryside—which Warren believed would likely trigger the "bloodshed" he had long warned of. He wrote again to Dix, urging him to arrange for transport of his possessions from the Roxbury homestead out to Worcester. He also informed Dix that his children, accompanied by Mercy Scollay, would arrive within the week. The doctor himself would remain in Boston. Those possessions Warren was unable to send out to Roxbury, Milton, and Worcester, he began sending to the house of Mercy Scollay's parents for safekeeping.

At some point, just prior to the Battles of Lexington and Concord on April 19, Joseph Warren said his goodbyes to Mercy and his four children as he loaded them onto his carriage, then watched as they rode off toward Worcester. It was the last time he would ever see them.

12

JOSEPH WARREN'S RIDE

"seeming to thirst for BLOOD."

—NARRATIVES OF THE EXCURSION OF
THE KING'S TROOPS: APRIL 19, 1775

FOR YEARS, JOSEPH WARREN HAD ANTICIPATED THAT A TRULY EX-
plosive event between the troops and the colonists would thrust them
toward war. For more than a decade, the Whig faction in Boston had
resisted unjust and oppressive Crown policies and actions. Bostonians
in particular had suffered for more than nine months under the Coercive Acts, which Britain seemed intent on enforcing. Now Warren,
with numerous medical apprentices able to handle his caseload, and
his family and most of his personal possessions away, focused his efforts on the current situation with Britain. As head of the Committee
of Safety, he was responsible for organizing and arming the provincial
militias, and more than ever he depended on a growing spy network
to guide his moves.

In early 1775, as British troops occupied Boston and its surrounding countryside, many Bostonians of diverse social ranks served in
various intelligence roles and capacities. They joined in well-organized

associations and volunteer groups, made individual observations, and received information from friends and relatives, and passed it along. Warren helped direct these intelligence gatherers. His overlapping involvement with Freemasons, the Sons of Liberty, the North End Caucus, the Boston Committee of Correspondence, the Massachusetts Committee of Safety, and the Massachusetts Provincial Congress placed him in a unique position, for no other Whig leader belonged to so many groups. These radical Whig organizations—whose members were mechanics, merchants, artisans, lawyers, masons, printers, laborers, seamen, and other doctors—stood on the front lines of the resistance. Paul Revere revealed that in late 1774 and early 1775,

> *I was one of upwards of thirty, chiefly mechanics, who formed ourselves into a committee for the purpose of watching the movements of the British soldiers, and gaining every intelligence of the movements of the Tories. We held our meetings at the Green Dragon Tavern. . . . We were so careful that our meetings should be kept secret, that every time we met, every person swore upon the Bible that he would not discover any of our transactions but to Messrs Hancock, Adams, Doctors Warren, Church and one or two more.*

Most of the Whig leaders were away from Boston for extended periods in 1774–75—attending the Continental Congress or seeing to personal matters or fearing possible arrest—so Warren became the de facto spymaster, receiving and acting on the intelligence reports. Indeed his office became an espionage center where patriot spies from all levels of society filtered their vital intelligence. Information was transmitted from almost every corner of Boston's streets. For instance, a British officer had deliberately leaked information about the pending British mission into the countryside to a gunsmith, who passed it along to a member of the Committee of Safety, Col. Josiah Waters, who reported it immediately to Dr. Warren. Intelligence about the secretive mission was also passed to Paul Revere from, among others, an anonymous stable boy and William Dawes, a Boston tanner who was one of Warren's patients and a trusted Son of Liberty. Revere, in turn, promptly passed these reports up the patriot ranks to Warren.

James Lovell, the schoolmaster who was the first Boston Massacre orator in 1771, was another of Warren's informants. (After Warren's death, British soldiers discovered his letters containing sensitive information in Warren's coat, and he would be arrested and jailed.) Dr. Samuel Mather—Harvard graduate, minister of the Second Church of Boston, and son of Cotton Mather—was also secretly sending Warren information, an especially noteworthy connection as Mather was married to Thomas Hutchinson's sister. Warren evaluated all this information, used it to develop patriot plans, and sent it when pertinent along lines of communication that he had helped establish to patriot colleagues throughout the colonies.

The British also had an effective intelligence system. Soldiers dressed in civilian clothing tried to glean as much information as they could from wharves along the waterfront, local urban haunts, and country taverns and inns. James Lovell's father, John, was a staunch Loyalist and informant for General Gage. Operating as spies for opposing sides, this family was not the last to be torn asunder by differing loyalties. And thanks to the paid services of Dr. Benjamin Church, Gage was privy to most of the intimate secrets of the radical leadership.

Although both sides employed spies and suffered intelligence leaks, the radical spy system under Warren ultimately proved more effective. In April 1775 his office was inundated with information regarding a mission Gage was planning. "Gen Warren had directed a number of men to keep watch on the motions of the British, and to let him know when there was any appearance of an attack," wrote one of Warren's descendants. "These men discovered this plan of theirs, and immediately gave Warren information of it." Warren's men had learned that Gage intended to send troops to Concord to seize or destroy stores of patriot cannon and other artillery ordnance that Warren and the Committee of Safety and supplies had sent there.

It was the event Warren had been expecting: British troops were about to march into Lexington and Concord. Knowing that the patriots could hardly afford to lose more munitions, Warren seized the opportunity to strike a decisive blow that very night. He summoned Revere to his home and ordered him to "immediately set off for Lexington, where Messrs Hancock and Adams were, and acquaint them of the movement." Adams and Hancock were staying at the parsonage of the Rev. Jonas Clark, from which they planned to travel to Philadelphia for the Second Continental Congress that would convene the next month.

Even as Warren was instructing his messengers, British Lt. Col. Francis Smith marched twenty-one companies of light infantry and grenadiers into the New England countryside under a brightly lit moon, with orders to destroy and seize patriot munitions in Concord. Having to wade through the marshes in Cambridge slowed the march, giving Revere and the other messengers extra time. Through a highly organized communication system, Revere had established a prearranged signal to alert compatriots across the river in Charlestown of the British route of departure from Boston. When he received orders from Warren, he put his signal in place—two lanterns lit in the belfry of Boston's Old North Church, which indicated that the redcoats were coming by sea. Undetected, Revere boated across the Charles River, and when he arrived in Cambridge, he mounted a waiting horse and sped off into the countryside.

In addition to sending out Revere, Warren also sent William Dawes—who left via Boston Neck. Warren urgently instructed his riders to warn Hancock and Adams of the British arrival and to alert the countryside militias of the pending danger from a force that was described by patriots after the incident as "seeming to thirst for BLOOD," intent on "plundering and burning . . . houses and other buildings . . . driving into the street women in child-bed" and "killing old men in their houses unarmed." According to the Massachusetts Provincial Congress, the decision to muster the province's military forces was to be made by a vote of the Committee of Safety, not by one patriot. While Warren instructed both Dawes and Revere to warn

Adams and Hancock about the British expedition, Revere, operating under Warren's instructions, also alerted the militia officers he knew along the way.

WARREN SPENT THE REMAINDER OF THE NIGHT TENDING TO HIS personal affairs: destroying sensitive documents that could be considered treasonous, reviewing his patient caseload, and leaving last-minute instructions for his apprentices, friends, and associates in Boston. While the start of the war on that morning was not a foregone conclusion, Warren knew that a violent engagement loomed on the horizon. As his messengers alerted the colonists about the approaching forces, pealing bells began to echo throughout the New England hamlets. In Boston later that morning, Warren learned that just before dawn British soldiers under Colonel Smith had killed nine militiamen in Lexington. The British, the patriots claimed, had fired without provocation and had drawn first blood on the colonists. Now the news was being rushed to every New England town. Gathering only the most important of his few remaining possessions and instructing his student William Eustis to look after his patients, Warren mounted his horse and left his home, never to return. He rode to the Charlestown ferry, where he crossed the Charles River. In Charlestown he met with local patriot leaders and tried to gather more information about what had ensued. One local saw Warren "riding hastily out of town" and asked him if reports of New Englanders killed in Lexington were accurate: "He assured me it was. He rode on." Passing through Cambridge, Warren hastened west to Menotomy (now Arlington), where the most vicious fighting of the day would occur. Revere's mission as a patriot messenger on April 19 has overshadowed the fact that Warren not only sent the silversmith, but he also willingly rode into the battle that morning and fought in the most dangerous portion of the conflict.

That morning, with the roar of gunfire from the Lexington green at their backs, Adams and Hancock—in fear of "sudden arrest, if not assassination"—had already fled several miles in a chaise to the Second Continental Congress. Adams had explained to Hancock, his younger and rasher counterpart who wanted to remain in Lexington in case of a clash, that as leaders of civilian government their job was to remain out of battle in order to keep the government running. Warren, on the other hand, who had now become the highest civilian leader remaining, hastened to rendezvous with the militia. Soon after the shots at Lexington, Colonel Smith's troops caught up with Maj. John Pitcairn's companies and departed for nearby Concord to seize the patriots' hidden cannon. Major Pitcairn had earlier declared, "I assure you, I have so despicable an opinion of the people of this country that I would not hesitate to march with the Marines I have with me to any part of the country, and do whatever I was inclined. I am satisfied they will never attack Regular troops." Pitcairn had grossly underestimated his opponents' resolve.

On Gage's orders, Smith sent his troops into the town of Concord on a seek-and-destroy mission, which led to a skirmish on North Bridge and casualties on both sides. As word of the fighting spread, militia companies from nearby towns descended upon the theatre of action, whereupon British troops made a hasty exodus from Concord around noon. But with more and more patriot militiamen pouring in from the surrounding countryside, the British march back to Boston turned into a veritable death crawl. Hundreds upon hundreds of camouflaged militiamen fired upon the exposed and defenseless retreating British columns. One British lieutenant lamented the fiasco in his diary:

> We were fired on from houses and behind trees, and before we had gone ¹/₂ a mile we were fired on from all sides, but mostly from the rear, where people had hid themselves in houses 'till we had passed and then fired; the country was an amazing strong one, full of hills, woods, stone walls, &c., which the rebels did not fail to take advantage of, for they were all lined with people who kept an incessant fire upon us, as we did too upon them but with not the same advantage, for they were so

*concealed there was hardly any seeing them; in this way we marched
between 9 and 10 miles, their numbers increasing from all parts, while
ours was reducing by deaths, wounds and fatigue, and we were totally
surrounded with such an incessant fire as it's impossible to conceive.*

On their return, in Lexington, Smith's troops were fortunate to
meet with Lord Hugh Percy's reinforcements—he arrived from Boston with two field pieces. Percy let the beleaguered soldiers rest and
used his fresh troops to engage the relentless patriot flanks. The con-
tinual firing of his moving cannons helped keep the swarming militia
units at a careful distance.

Warren met with patriot Gen. William Heath at a meeting of the
Committee of Safety at the Black Horse Tavern in Menotomy. He
then followed Heath into battle. That afternoon, in addition to treating the wounded, Warren fought in the heated skirmishes against
King George's Royal Soldiers as they pushed their way toward Boston. In Menotomy the fighting had become particularly intense; there
"from his ardor in pressing on them [Warren] was near being killed. A
musket-ball came so close to him as to take off a lock of his hair which
curled close to his head." For Warren this incident may have inspired
feelings similar to those of George Washington, who had escaped several close calls with death in battle: "I can with truth assure you, I
heard bulletts [*sic*] whistle and believe me there is something charming
in the sound." Perhaps some part of Joseph Warren believed that he
could not die on a battlefield.

The British troops had been marching for nearly twelve hours.
They were outnumbered, their ammunition was running low, and
their casualties were on the rise.

The disastrous expedition finally came to a close when British
troops reached Bunker Hill in Charlestown around sunset. General
Heath ordered the militia to pull back, since Gage's troops now occupied the high ground of Bunker's Hill where he had a good defensive
position for his troops to prevent the militia units from coming over
the neck. Moreover, the flash from the provincials firing their mus-

kets exposed their positions to British cannonade. In describing the fighting of the patriots, one British soldier wrote, "They fought like bears, and I would as soon storm hell as fight them again." The British forces had suffered close to three hundred casualties, almost triple the American casualties.

The following day Warren personally wrote Gage, telling him, "Your Excellency, I believe knows very well the part I have taken in public affairs: I ever scorned disguise." Both men, he suggested, "rely upon the honor and integrity of each other" in allowing people to hasten to their respective sides. Perhaps trying to make a personal appeal to Gage's decency, Warren expressed regret that he had never "broken through the formalities which I thought due to your rank and freely told you all I knew or thought of public affairs" because of the "vileness and treachery of many persons around you, who, I supposed, had gained your entire confidence." Gage never recognized Warren's authority.

The Committee of Safety met over the next few days, and Warren composed a letter to the Massachusetts towns imploring all New Englanders to assist in the formation of a patriot army. Although the language carried his familiar incendiary tones, the situation had never been graver: "The barbarous murders committed on our innocent brethren . . . have made it absolutely necessary that we immediately raise an army to defend our wives and children from the butchering hands of an inhuman soldiery." On April 23, the Second Massachusetts Provincial Congress unanimously resolved that "an army of 30,000 men be immediately raised and established."

As militia units continued to arrive and surround Boston, Gage and his army were under siege, the troops bottled up in Boston. Many Loyalists wanted to enter the peninsula under Gage's protection, while many patriots were just as eager to flee the garrisoned town for the safety of the countryside. For years, Warren's dire rhetoric had warned of the events that had now come to pass.

Following Lexington and Concord, as he had done after the Boston Massacre, Warren and other members of the Committee of Safety launched a propaganda campaign blaming the British for firing the first shots. Depositions collected for the report maintained that the British soldiers had fired first and that "the troops of Britain, unprovoked, shed the blood of . . . the loyal American subjects of the British King" and "committed violence and waste" with a "devastation . . . almost beyond description." Warren swiftly and secretly dispatched the report to London with Captain John Derby on the *Quero*, instructing him to keep it "a profound secret from every person on earth" until he had sailed across the Atlantic. Many in London favorably received the packet, but most important, it arrived almost two weeks before General Gage's version of the events did.

On April 29, the Second Provincial Congress authorized the Committee of Supplies "to purchase every kind of military stores, provisions, and all other supplies" deemed necessary to supply the army in the defense of the colony. For the moment, Gage's forces were contained in Boston, but that stalemate could change at any moment, and the provincial forces needed to be ready for a showdown.

Now guilty of treason against the Crown and unable to return to Boston, Warren remained in Watertown, lodging at several locations—the Marshal Fowle house (now known as the Edmund Fowle House), the tavern of Dorothy Coolidge, and the mansion house of John Hunt. He traveled to Cambridge and Roxbury for public and private matters. He wrote to Mercy in Worcester, expressing his relief that she and the children were safe, and he requested that she ask Dr. Dix to hire another ten to twenty acres of land "as I shall keep several horses and cannot think of being deprived of indulging myself in the Leisure Hours of this one year in the Pleasures of Agriculture."

Warren was lucky to be alive after his close encounter with a musket ball, but British military control of Boston changed his life—and those of many of his countrymen—irrevocably. His medical practice was essentially shut down since so many patriot sympathizers had fled for surrounding countryside. His Boston property and whatever goods remained there were at the disposal of the king's troops (subject to looting and seizure), as were other public and private buildings. During the siege of Boston, the British stripped Old South Meeting House of its furnishings, burned them for fuel, and used it as a riding school for troops. They employed the Brattle Street Church as a British army barracks. Since the battle for Boston and its surrounding towns would likely be protracted, and the future of the town was uncertain, Warren had planned for his new life in the country, looking forward to spending at least the next year farming and being with his family. He had arranged to pay Dr. Dix for the additional expense of bringing more of his goods out to Worcester. On May 13, Warren thanked Dix for all his efforts and discretion. He would attempt to visit Worcester within two weeks, he told Dix, and planned to hire and care for patriot refugees who had been forced to leave Boston and were now desperate for work. Ever since the port was closed, great economic woes had touched every household, and Warren's was no exception. He was so grateful to Dix that he urged his friend, "Any sum of money that you may want for your private use, pray take."

General Gage agreed to let Bostonians leave the town if they surrendered their arms—news that was read in the Provincial Congress on April 30. Many vacated the garrisoned town, leaving behind most of their possessions, as hundreds of Loyalist refugees swarmed past them into Boston. The minister of Boston's New North Church, Andrew Elliot, described the scene: "Much the greater parts of the inhabitants gone . . . the rest following as fast as the Genl [Gage] will give leave.—Grass growing in the public walks and streets of this once populous and flourishing place—Shops and warehouses shut up— business at an end and everyone in anxiety and distress." The once-thriving metropolis had essentially become a military bastion.

On May 2, Warren was elected president of the Second Provincial Congress and assumed the post immediately, pledging to heed the "order, and attend his duty in Congress in the afternoon." Still chairman of the Committee of Safety as well, he was now at the zenith of his power, engaged with every aspect of the colony's political and military affairs. In the meantime, after Lexington and Concord, Col. Benedict Arnold had come from Connecticut to Cambridge, where he approached Warren about seizing the cannon at the British Fort Ticonderoga, in upstate New York. The two men seem to have impressed each other, and Warren helped persuade the Provincial Congress to provide Arnold with "ten horses, two hundred pounds of gunpowder, two hundred pounds of lead balls, and one thousand flints," along with one hundred pounds to help fund the expedition. The mission was ultimately a success, and Warren urged that the cannons "be forwarded this way with all possible expedition, as we have here to contend with an army furnished with as fine a train of artillery as ever was seen in America."

Gage, well equipped with artillery, received additional reinforcements in the form of six hundred marines on May 14. And to Warren's mind, Gage was well motivated to inflict maximum damage on the rebels. In a letter to Joseph Reed the next day, he wrote, "The repeated intelligence I received from the best authority . . . of the inhumanity and wickedness of the villains at Boston who had the ear of General Gage, compelled me to believe that matters would be urged to the last extremity." And yet the next day, in a letter to patriot Arthur Lee, Warren expressed his belief that Gage was not quite ready to fight his way out of Boston. Still, Warren claimed that if Gage did decide to fight, "he will but gratify thousands who impatiently wait to avenge the blood of their murdered countrymen."

On May 19, Artemas Ward was promoted to "general and commander in chief" of the Massachusetts Army—Warren personally delivered his commission. According to John Adams, during Ward's ceremony, Warren "made a harangue in the form of a charge, in the presence of the Assembly, to every officer, upon the delivery of his commission; and he never failed to make the officer, as well as all the Assembly, shudder upon those occasions." By now known for his emotional diatribes, Warren underscored both the duty and the honor associated with the commission. Although a strong advocate of obedience and subordination within military ranks, he realized the importance of mutual camaraderie, respect, and affection between soldiers and their commanding officers, asserting that they will not "obey any person of whom they do not entertain a high opinion." Indeed, Warren was among the youngest and least experienced of most of the men he was commissioning, yet he seems to have occasioned little resentment or bitterness from his military and political comrades. By all accounts, he was much respected, admired, and beloved among patriots.

On May 21, General Gage dispatched four British sloops—two of which were armed—south from Boston Harbor to Grape Island, near the coast of Weymouth, with instructions to procure hay. Gage's besieged army was in need of fresh provisions, including livestock and fodder, of which there was plenty on the harbor islands and farms near the coast. When locals sighted the sloops, many believed an attack was imminent and sought to escape into the countryside. In Roxbury, General John Thomas immediately ordered three companies of provincials to defend the locals. Warren rushed to the scene to fight in the skirmish. From the Weymouth shore, Warren reported that even though the town was too far from Grape Island for "small arms to do execution; nevertheless our people fired frequently." The British returned fire, "but the shots passed over our heads, and did no mischief." In the end, the British made off with "one or two tons of hay," and while there were no patriot casualties, it was said that three British soldiers sustained injuries. The remaining hay was burned to keep it out of British hands. For many locals, Warren's presence demonstrated his devotion to his countrymen, of whom he said, "I love,—I admire."

Within days, Warren participated in another engagement, known as the Battle of Noddle's Island. While the Grape Island incident had been a defensive response to British attempts to gather fodder, the Noddle's Island fight found the colonials on the offense. The Massachusetts Committee of Safety had decided back on May 14 to remove the livestock and fodder from several harbor islands to stymie the flow of provisions needed by Gage's forces. Gage received word of the plan and instructed Vice Adm. Samuel Graves to keep his ships on high alert for patriot activity on the islands. Beginning on May 27, provincial forces led by Cols. John Stark and John Nixon successfully removed livestock from Hog's Island, located across the harbor to the east. When a small detachment of provincials arrived on nearby Noddle's Island and began burning provisions, British ships were immediately dispatched, including the 120-gun schooner HMS *Diana*, to intercept the rebel action. Warren accompanied Gen. Israel Putnam to Chelsea Neck, where the fighting became particularly intense, as the ships fired grapeshot on the provincials. After getting caught in the tide, the *Diana* ran aground, and provincials boarded the abandoned ship, absconded with its four-pound cannon, swivel guns, and other valuables, and set fire to the vessel. Provincials suffered a few wounded militiamen, and while British reports claimed two deaths, rumors that they suffered greater losses abounded.

For Gage, the defeat underscored the need to break the siege of Boston. Supplying his forces with fresh provisions from local land sources was an absolute necessity, as he could not rely solely on supplies coming via sea from other colonies, Nova Scotia, and England. The arrival of the British frigate *Cerberus* brought Gage the reinforcements he needed to break the siege.

After weeks of sailing across the Atlantic, *Cerberus* docked in Boston Harbor ferrying Gens. Howe, Clinton, and Burgoyne and fresh troops on May 25. In Cambridge the following day, Warren wrote to Samuel Adams at the Continental Congress in Philadelphia, "Yesterday arrived the three famous generals." The heavily armed warship was a welcome sight to Gage, who had been desperate for reinforcements, and it reassured the Loyalist population that the Crown was intent on quelling the rebellion.

The period between Lexington and Concord and the Battle of Bunker Hill has been referred to as the "sixty days." Warren was the only patriot leader—both civilian and military—who personally engaged in all four skirmishes and battles within this time frame. Warren not only fought in these battles against the British but also helped advance the rebellion into a revolution. He assisted in organizing a provincial army with militia from Massachusetts, New Hampshire, Connecticut, and Rhode Island, and he communicated effectively with patriots in other colonies, in London, and in Canada. He helped obtain a copper plate to print colony notes. He opened negotiations for an alliance with the six Indian Nations, suggested surgeons for the army, and delegated military commissions. He helped procure arms, ammunition, and food for the soldiers and helped establish a navy, all while performing a host of other duties. As a physician with an eye toward another hostile engagement, Warren also approached his civic and military duties from a medical standpoint, as one of the books he possessed was titled *Diseases incident to Armies*. Warren's brushes with smallpox and other diseases cautioned him to try and prevent potential outbreaks within the provincial camps. In the few remaining weeks of his life, his influence would extend beyond the borders of the Bay Colony.

After Joseph Warren and Gen. Israel Putnam shared in the fight at Noddle's Island, their relationship grew stronger. On June 6 they boarded a phaeton for Charlestown to exchange prisoners with the British. They traveled with several British officers and four wounded marines to the home of Dr. Isaac Foster, who had trained under Dr. James Lloyd at approximately the same time as Warren, where they were met by numerous Crown officers. The exchange "was conducted with the utmost decency and good humor," and "the parties passed an hour or two together very agreeably," likely because the senior British officer knew Putnam from the previous war. Although Gage still refused to recognize Warren in any official capacity, the officers, well aware that Warren was the top patriot leader in Massachusetts, accorded him a respect usually not reserved for a rebel without military experience or official title in the eyes of the Crown.

Within a week, General Gage issued a proclamation declaring that all rebels except Hancock and Adams would be subject to pardon if they submitted to the Crown. Warren's name was not included with the duo, even though his actions were even more treasonous than his colleagues'—particularly since he had personally taken up arms against the British at Lexington and Concord and the recent island skirmishes. Perhaps Gage saw an opportunity to entice Warren to surrender while most of his closest associates were in Philadelphia.

If so, the maneuver failed. The Provincial Congress issued its own declaration pardoning all those "misguided fellow countrymen" and "other public offenders" against the Whig cause. The announcement included its own short list of unpardonables, topped by General Gage.

WARREN'S ROLE IN THE FIGHT FOR NODDLE'S ISLAND APPEARS TO have been nominal, yet he continued to hasten to skirmishes wherever they broke out. Patriot leaders, aware of his value, were dismayed that he took unnecessary risks, while New England provincials were cheered by his mere presence. Whatever his role, it was enough to gain him favor among top patriot military leaders and helped earn him his commission.

On the afternoon of Wednesday, June 14, the Third Provincial Congress made Joseph Warren a major general. The committee planned to "wait on the Hon. Joseph Warren, Esq., . . . and desire his answer to this Congress of his acceptance of said trust." That same day the Second Continental Congress in Philadelphia established the Continental Army for the common defense of the colonies, unifying the loosely banded militia units that comprised the provincial forces of the New England army and the army of New York. The next day, June 15, George Washington was appointed its commanding general; Artemas Ward would be his second-in-command. It was a watershed day in the colonial rebellion, but word took days to travel north from Philadelphia, and news of Washington's army would not arrive in time to reach Warren, who was already rushing toward his fate at Bunker Hill.

13

HILL OF LAMENTATIONS

"My God, I never saw such a carnage of the human race."
—GENERAL ISRAEL PUTNAM, CIRCA 1788

IN LESS THAN TWO MONTHS, GENERAL GAGE'S FORCES—PART OF
the greatest military in the world—had been shamed and outfoxed by
inexperienced and inferior militias. They had left Gage's army with
hundreds of casualties and a lack of fresh provisions, not to mention
bruised egos among the elite officer corps. Surrounded by provincial
soldiers and cut off from supplies on land, Gage needed to break the
siege of Boston. His best options were to move his men into the high
ground north and south of the town, at Charlestown and Dorchester
Heights, respectively, from which he might gain a foothold to press
into the mainland.

Intelligence reports flooded both sides of the Charles River, as
patriot and British military leaders attempted to gain any advantage. The Committee of Safety got intelligence from a "gentleman
of undoubted veracity" that Gage intended to take Bunker Hill and
Dorchester Heights on June 18, so it decided to act quickly. Believing

the number of their forces at Roxbury insufficient to defend Dorchester Heights, they decided to fortify Bunker Hill instead—the highest point on the Charlestown peninsula—the day before the supposed attack. Warren attended the session of the Provincial Congress in Watertown on June 15, where it was "decided that possession of the hill called Bunker's Hill in Charlestown, be securely kept and defended" to counteract the anticipated British assault.

The following evening, after the bells in Watertown struck nine, Warren was summoned from a meeting of the Provincial Congress and received secret dispatches sent from Reverend Mather, who had given them to his teenage daughter Hannah with strict instructions to deliver them only to Dr. Warren. She concealed them beneath her clothing and had sneaked them out of Boston on the ferry earlier that evening. Those very dispatches *may* have contained intelligence alerting Warren of Gage's intended movements.

That same night in Charlestown Heights, Gen. Israel Putnam and Col. William Prescott, accompanied by head of the artillery and chief engineer Col. Richard Gridley, reconnoitered the area. The Charlestown peninsula lies north of Boston and begins from a narrow isthmus called Charlestown Neck, which connected it to Cambridge to the north and provided the only land route on and off the peninsula. Ultimately, the officers decided to fortify Breed's Hill rather than Bunker Hill. Breed's Hill stood approximately forty-five feet shorter than Bunker Hill. Though this made it more vulnerable to attack, it was closer to Boston and thus provided a better vantage point from which provincial commanders could monitor approaching British forces.

At about midnight, with little time to waste, Colonel Prescott led a detachment of provincials to Breed's Hill. Under cover of darkness, they worked through the night digging ditches and constructing earthen walls as quickly and as quietly as possible, for at daybreak their efforts would become visible to the British forces across the Charles River.

Before sunrise on the morning of June 17, as provincials in Charlestown were finishing their fortifications, Warren left Watertown on horseback and proceeded to Hastings House in Cambridge, headquarters of Gen. Artemas Ward and the meeting place for the Committee of Safety. There he attended a war council and reviewed intelligence reports. He had hardly slept for days, and after the council meeting, suffering from one of his chronic headaches, he retired to a room to lie down.

At dawn on June 17, the first pitched battle in the war for American independence began. The British, discovering the patriot fortification on Breed's Hill, launched a steady stream of cannon fire toward the rebel lines on the Charlestown peninsula, from a battery at Copp's Hill in Boston's North End, and from their menacing warships in Boston Harbor. Colonel Prescott recalled some of the initial gruesomeness of this initial volley: "The first man who fell in the Battle of Bunker Hill was killed by a cannon-ball which struck his head. He was so near to me that my clothes were besmeared with his blood and brains which I wiped off in some degree with a handful of fresh earth."

The provincial soldiers—or as Charles Lee, a future patriot major general, described them, "raw lads and old men half armed, with no practice or discipline"—were about to clash with a much superior fighting force in their first deliberate battle. Outnumbered and short of ammunition, the inexperienced provincials were awed by the imposing sights of the British warships and the king's magnificently outfitted troops. One patriot noted that on the morning of the battle, even before the full attack was launched, the British cannonade caused "many of our young country people to desert, apprehending the danger."

Their cannon fire having failed to dislodge the patriots, Crown soldiers in Boston marched in procession down the Long Wharf to the docked vessels waiting to transport them across the Charles. From the Breed's Hill redoubt, the exhausted and parched provincials—their faces stained with terror and earthen residue after hours of digging trenches under a "star-light night," watched in awe as twenty-eight boats carrying the first wave of fully armed British troops made their way toward the tip of the beach front below the hill, where "the Grenadiers & Light Infantry of the Army had Landed & form'd in good order." The royal soldiers, many of whom harbored hatred of the patriots, stood ready to avenge the humiliation they had suffered during the debacles of April and May. Less than a week before the Breed's Hill clash, a captain of the grenadier company of the 5th Regiment of Foot wrote, "I wish the Americans may be brought to a sense of their duty. One good drubbing, which I long to give them, by way of retaliation, might have a good effect."

Upon seeing the uphill terrain and the patriot defenses, however, many disheartened Crown soldiers realized they were about to march into an open slaughter. But there would be no turning back. The king's generals were taking no chances and, on the morning of the June 17 battle, gave orders that "any man who shall quit his rank on any pretence . . . will be executed without mercy."

That afternoon more than two thousand British soldiers assembled against the rebel forces on the Charlestown peninsula. Lt. John Barker of the king's own regiment recorded the event in his diary: "Between 3 and 4 oclock in the afternoon the whole marched to the attack." The grenadiers and light infantry made the first attack, to the east of the redoubt, along the Mystic River, toward the rail fence where patriot Col. John Stark—a veteran of the French and Indian War—had rushed with his New Hampshire forces to prevent a British flank. With thirteen companies under his command, Stark fortified his position as a hail of projectiles rained around them.

When Warren learned that British regulars had arrived at Charlestown, he rose immediately to join the provincial forces. Several friends and colleagues tried to dissuade him from joining in the battle, but he hurried toward the scene. Even from his Harvard days performing military drills as precursor art of the Marti-Mercurians, "Warren for several years was preparing himself by study and observations to take a conspicuous rank in the military arrangements which he knew must ensue." And no commander on the field in Charlestown knew the terrain better than Joseph Warren, who had lived his entire life in the area.

Back at the redoubt, Colonel Prescott had sent a group of provincial marksmen to Charlestown's abandoned buildings with orders to fire at will on the redcoats. In response, the British turned their cannonade upon the town. Admiral Graves—who had lost the *Diana* several weeks earlier—set Charlestown ablaze, making "a most awful, grand and melancholy sight." The steady bombardment tore through buildings and set fire to them, the small fires coalescing into a monstrous blaze that tore rapidly through the town. A great cloud of smoke hung ominously "like a thunder cloud" above the scene of battle.

As the inferno raged, Stark and his men repelled the first British land assault, sending constant fire into the advancing king's forces until they retreated. Afterward Stark would declare, "The dead lay as thick as sheep in a fold." Stunned and angered, the British commanding officers gathered their troops and prepared for another attack.

Greatly outnumbered in men, ammunition, and artillery, the provincial soldiers expressed their relief and appreciation upon seeing Warren enter the redoubt, greeting him with huzzahs and cheers at the outset of action. His narrow escape of death at Lexington and Concord and his fighting at Grape and Noddle's Islands had, in the eyes of many, cloaked him with an aura of invincibility. At Breed's Hill, his presence bolstered morale and almost certainly helped prevent a premature mass retreat by the provincials. Most of these men had admired his leadership for years and were well aware of the risk he was taking by being in the redoubt. Since he had only just been nominated for a military commission, many of the men at Breed's Hill were unaware of Warren's pending status as a general. He had declined command on the field from both Putnam and Prescott, yet Warren was determined to conduct himself in a manner worthy of such a commission.

Warren had arrived at Breed's Hill dressed in his finery, which included a "light colored coat, with a white satin waistcoat laced with silver, and white breeches, with silver loops," and his wig. His elegant, pristine, light-colored clothing stood out next to his comrades' soiled, dark-colored frocks and greatcoats and made him an easy target for enemy fire. Armed with pistols, sword, and musket, he also carried his cherished Bible. It was perhaps his most important weapon that afternoon, for it had fueled his faith and hence his belief in this cause. Like most pious New Englanders, he likely recited Scripture to himself just prior to the attack.

As they had at Lexington and Concord, the provincials shielded themselves behind makeshift trenches and barricades, with orders to hold their fire until the advancing enemy force was within effective striking range. British drum calls beat ominously and grew louder as the king's men, in their regal uniforms, drew closer. With all the confidence of the British Empire at their heels, the royal troops ascended Breed's Hill in succession, waiting to unleash all their fury and might onto what they saw as a hiding rabble of cowards. In and around the redoubt, the anxious provincials waited, their white knuckles gripping their assorted flintlock weapons tightly. They waited, hoping their initial shots would be deadly enough to repel the massive onslaught.

As the facial features of the approaching redcoats became visible—some with the hardened scowl of seasoned war veterans, others with the soft visage of innocence twisted in terror—the waiting rebels fired their weapons. The crackling of gunfire thundered across the battlefield. Muskets spewed billows of clinging smoke, engulfing both attackers and defenders. Warren directed the most accurate marksmen to take aim at the British officers, easily identifiable by their regal uniforms. The provincials discharged one lethal volley after another into the advancing ranks, while Warren "set them an example with his musket," firing repeatedly at the king's exposed men.

"Our first fire was shockingly fatal," a provincial fighting near Warren declared. "The enemy were thrown into confusion and retreated a short distance. Their lines were broken, and it was some minutes before they had conveyed their dead and wounded into their rear." Pacing the lines, encouraging the provincials, and tending to the wounded, Warren readied the men for the next attack. The redcoats continued their march, even as scores of men dropped on the field with each patriot salvo. But the most savage fighting had yet to occur.

After their unsuccessful attempts to crush the rebels, the rattled British forces paused to rest and regroup. They had mounted Breed's Hill during the hottest part of the day under an oppressive sun, dressed in their heavy uniforms, and hauling provisions, blankets, cartridge boxes, and their brown Bess muskets (which alone weighed around ten pounds). For their final charge, the redcoats were directed to discard all unnecessary accoutrements and to attack in columns with bayonets fixed. The British artillery was moved within close range of the redoubt to raze the breastwork and help cover the frontal assault, raining a vicious bombardment of shells on the patriot forces.

Gathering momentum, the British troops pressed up Breed's Hill toward the provincials' earthen fortifications. It was no easy task to break through into the redoubt, which was covered with "trees, stone walls, and rails." One patriot colonel recalled how the British "advanced in open order," and "as fast as the front man was shot down, the next stepped forward into his place; but our men dropt them so fast, they were a long time coming up. It was surprising how they would step over their dead bodies, as though they had been logs of wood." So many corpses lined the hill that many of the surviving combatants in "terrible desperation piled up these dead bodies into a horrid breastwork to fire from," hoping to mount some form of protection and defense.

The hubris and arrogance initially displayed by the king's men had melted away in the heat of battle, replaced by the chilling reality of warfare. One British soldier later admitted that "too great a confidence in ourselves . . . occasioned this dreadful loss." The battle was exacting horrendous losses on the king's soldiers, many of whom were "wounded and dying, exerting their last, feeble remains of strength to crawl out of the line." Scores of New Englanders—experienced veterans, ordinary men, farmers, even free African-Americans—were killing some of Britain's finest officers. His Majesty's regiments were stunned, watching in disbelief as their comrades and commanders were picked off one by one. The patriots—armed with a broad assortment of fowling pieces, coach guns, and pistols—"mowed them down in heaps," until their casualties reached more than a thousand. The stunned British forces were on the verge of another costly and unprecedented defeat.

When the redcoats once again attempted to attack the fortification, General Burgoyne recalled, "now ensued one of the greatest scenes of war that can be conceived." Their scowling commanders shouted at the remaining British troops to press on, "pushing men forward with their swords," while the troops, exposed and with incredible nerve, withstood yet another crushing volley, then finally began to penetrate the fortified lines. The patriots shot their last ammunition, their firearms sputtering to a halting silence that was quickly shattered by the piercing howls of British war cries. Two British marine companies and a detachment of the 47th Regiment raged forward with seventeen-inch bayonets fixed to their smoothbore muskets—some with their swords drawn—as the glint from their steel weapons flickered. General Howe led the right portion of the assault, and Sir Robert Pigot attacked the southern and eastern edges of the redoubt, flanking it from three sides at once.

Redcoats flooded the patriot lines, their battle cries resonating as far as Beacon Hill as they charged through the thick, heavy clouds of black powder smoke, ash, and dirt. They unleashed their fury in brutal hand-to-hand combat, driving "their bayonets into all that opposed them," and almost immediately felling a few dozen men near Warren. Warren himself had been wounded but "fought gallantly" and brandished his sword in desperation, as he was overtaken in the redoubt. A group of provincials surrounded by redcoats, inspired by the doctor, grabbed their empty muskets as cudgels, picked up the swords of the fallen, and rushed the onslaught. Their wails replaced the roar of musket fire as they pushed forward, some throwing stones and then even their fists at the attackers. General Howe, a veteran of many desperate battles, declared that "he never knew nor heard of such a Carnage in so short a time." The patriots, he recalled, fought "more like devils than men." The fighting turned into the most basic and primitive violence as men stabbed and clubbed each other to death. Many of the men fought over their graves, as the battleground soon became a mass burial pit, to the horror of both sides.

SOON THE OVERWHELMED AND EXHAUSTED PROVINCIALS STARTED to retreat. Only a faint breeze drifted along the air, and a dense fog of smoke, ash, and dirt hung heavy, choking the men and rendering the redoubt barely visible. One of the king's men likened the chaotic, densely packed scene to a raging hornet's nest. Desperately, Warren tried to rally the patriots one last time, but his pleas were drowned by the shrieks of dying men. Finally, hours after the initial fighting began, the battle drew to a close.

In a mass exodus, the surviving provincials clamored to get across the Charlestown Neck into Cambridge, their sole route of retreat. Desperate to escape, the battle-weary men ran as fast as they could to avoid death, leaving the hellish scene behind them. John Waller, one of the British officers who escaped the battle unscathed, described the nightmares he had witnessed in the redoubt: "'twas streaming with blood and strew'd with dead and dying men the soldiers stabbing some and dashing out the brains of others." To escape the melee, some had to drop and crawl over the maze of corpses and slither along the dirt that was becoming drenched by the blood from the entrails and scattered limbs of soldiers who had been sliced open and rent apart.

Joseph Warren, wounded but still fighting, "lingered to the last," trying his best to cover his retreating men. He purposely remained behind to ensure that his patriot brothers made it to safety, and he was the last man to leave the redoubt—just as he had been the last patriot leader to evacuate Boston on the day of the Battles of Lexington and Concord. He had made a habit of willingly putting himself in harm's way, but this time he remained at the scene too long.

"After performing many feats of bravery, and exhibiting a coolness and conduct which did honor to the judgement of his country, in appointing him a few days before one of our major generals," Warren was struck just under his left eye by a fatal shot that ripped through his face and exited the back of his head. He dropped near a small locust tree by the rear of the redoubt. As he lay dead on the field, a British soldier stormed up to him in a blood rage and "immediately [stabbed] him through the body" with his bayonet. As Warren had "hoped" for several months earlier, he had indeed died up to his "knees in blood"— but as a British subject.

One provincial close to the action described Warren's death in a letter to John Adams: "His whole soul seemed to be fill'd with the greatness of the cause he was engaged in, and while his Friends were dropping away all around him, gave his orders with a surprising calmness, till having seen the enemy in the breast work he unwillingly left the front and then fell amid heaps of slaughter'd enemies." Peter Oliver, who was not present at the battle, also composed a description of the fateful event: "Major General Warren . . . who commanded in the redoubt, exerted himself to prevent their rushing out at the passage, but all in vain. He was the last man who quitted it; and while his men were running off, he very slowly walked away; and at about 20 or 30 yards distant from the redoubt he dropped." Oliver, who believed that "Warren had a mind susceptible of all duplicity," described the doctor as leading his men and urging them to fight—even when all others had quit the redoubt. Indeed, Warren had sacrificed himself to protect his men, giving his life for the patriot cause.

Although the Whigs had achieved a moral victory, showing they could hold their own against a full onslaught of the king's troops, the resistance movement had suffered a serious blow. Charlestown lay in ruins, and the remaining patriot forces scattered in retreat. His Majesty's forces, though weakened, were not crushed; nor were they forced to evacuate Boston. They had carried the day, and in their possession was perhaps the greatest spoil of war: Warren's body. Provincial Army Capt. John Chester wrote that the British were "in possession of his body and no doubt will rejoice greatly over it.—After they entered our Fort they mangled the wounded in a Most horrid Manner,—by running their Bayonets thro them,—and beating their Heads to pieces with the Britch's of their Guns." Some of the soldiers and officers had understandably turned savage, summarily executing various wounded, defenseless patriots who were trying to crawl away. Of those thirty or so patriots taken prisoner, many would die from their wounds after lingering in the Boston jail.

Following their pyrrhic victory on Breed's Hill, a small group of seething redcoats circled the body of the "murdered worthy . . . Doctr. Warren," adorned in the conspicuous finery so out of place among the other corpses. The doctor's attire was now covered with blood, as was his right hand. Warren had been the hallmark of everything the British soldiers despised, and now they vented their fury upon him. They removed his clothing and looted his personal items, including his cherished Bible, his sword, and the letters containing sensitive information tucked in the fold of his waistcoat. As his body lay sprawled upon the ground, his ashen complexion stained by a stream of blood, His Majesty's soldiers repeatedly bayoneted his corpse in a violent butchering. Lt. James Drew of the Royal Navy, it was later claimed, returned to the redoubt, walked over to Warren's body, and spat in his face before cutting "off his head and commit[ing] every act of violence upon his Body." What was left of Warren remained on the field overnight. "He was buried hastily in trenches, on the morning after the battle," his mutilated corpse tossed unceremoniously into a shallow ditch in a mass grave of slain and murdered patriots.

The sun was setting on the bloodiest day to date in the history of the American colonies. On the battleground, bloating corpses swarmed with flies as the smell of blood, dirt, and carrion smoldered from the scorched earth. The sight of such wanton devastation undid even battle-tested veterans. As the British wounded were brought across the Charles that evening, the Loyalist customs commissioner Henry Hulton described how Boston's "streets were filled with the wounded and the dying; the sight of which, with the lamentations of the women and children over their husbands and fathers, pierced one to the soul.

We were now every moment hearing of some officer, or other of our friends and acquaintance, who had fallen in our defense, and in supporting the honor of our country."

As one officer aptly noted, "The horrors and devastations of war now begin to appear with us in earnest." General Gage, who had participated in some of the most hard-fought battles in England's recent history, later lamented, "The loss we have sustained is greater than we can bear." On the patriot side, General Putnam, perhaps the provincials' most experienced war veteran and fighter that day, later recalled, "My God, I never saw such a carnage of the human race." The battle had set a vicious precedent between the British and the colonists from which there could be no turning back.

The following morning, Sunday, June 18, British troops in Charlestown waited for tents and provisions to be sent over to begin their encampment. The harrowing process of clearing the battlefield had begun. Fully armed British search parties combed the hill for surviving comrades, sifting through the corpses to get at the wounded. Their fleeting hopes that some brothers-in-arms were still breathing, had been taken prisoner, or had deserted shrank with each passing moment as the grave reality of the mounting casualty list began to set in. It took nearly three days to fully remove the wounded and bury the dead British troops "lying in heaps on the ground." The burial detail had to move swiftly lest the bodies burst from the heat or, worse, fall prey to rats, which were already gnawing voraciously at the slain.

When word of Warren's death reached the upper echelons of the British command, it caused confusion at first. Officers dismissed initial reports of his fall as rumor, refusing to believe that the top Whig commander, in charge of the major political, social, and military bodies in Massachusetts, would have risked his life by personally fighting. Arguably the most stunned was General Howe, who believed Warren's death was worth five hundred of the bravest provincial soldiers—almost double the number of royal troops that died in the vicious melee. Reports came out of Boston declaring that "the officers and soldiers triumph very much at the death of Doctor Warren." Warren's disfigured body was dug up for those British leaders who insisted on seeing physical proof of his death. Lt. Walter Laurie, in charge of the burial detail, wrote, "Doctor Warren, president of the Provincial Congress . . . and next to [Samuel] Adams in abilities, I found among the slain, and stuffed the scoundrel with another rebel, into one hole, and there he and his seditious principles may remain."

The horrific acts of violence committed upon Warren's body continued even after the fighting ceased. Finally General Gage forbade his troops to desecrate or unearth patriots buried on the field of battle, promising harsh punishments to offenders. Still, Gage could ill afford to let his patriot adversaries discover the heinous acts committed by his soldiers and officers, which would only feed the fury for independence. He needed to contain the situation. But releasing Warren's butchered remains to his family, friends, and associates would provoke further colonial wrath. A disheartened Gage expressed his disgust in one brief sentence: "I wish this cursed place was burned."

He could offer no courtesy to his erstwhile foe, and so the tattered remains of Joseph Warren's naked corpse remained in a shallow grave on Breed's Hill.

FOUNDING MOURNERS

"He is now gone, and closes an illustrious Life."
—JONATHAN WILLIAMS AUSTIN TO JOHN ADAMS, JULY 7, 1775

IT HAD BEEN ALMOST TWENTY YEARS SINCE GEN. GEORGE WASH-
ington had been involved in a military conflict, let alone a successful
one. As he accepted command of the Continental Army in Philadelphia on June 15, 1775, he admitted to his fellow delegates in Congress
that "I feel great distress, from a consciousness that my abilities and
military experience may not be equal to the extensive and important
Trust. . . . I, this day, declare with the utmost sincerity, I do not think
myself equal to the Command." On June 23, he wrote a letter to his
wife, then bade his congressional brothers farewell and rode off toward
the epicenter of revolution for the past decade—the town of Boston.

Six days after Bunker Hill, news of the battle had not yet reached
the Continental Congress. As Washington set out, he had no idea of
it or that Warren had perished. Receiving word only as he traveled
through New York made him even more desperate to reach the army
at Cambridge.

In the meantime, John Hancock and Samuel and John Adams had all written covert missives to Warren about Washington's nomination and pending arrival, letters Warren would never receive. As president of the Continental Congress, Hancock, with his signature penmanship, entrusted Warren with the delicate task of receiving the new General and making all the necessary arrangements to ensure a smooth transition of power: "His commission is made out and I shall Sign it to morrow. I submit to you the propriety of providing a suitable place for his residence and the mode of his Reception." He asked Warren to make sure that Washington's commission was read aloud "at the head of the whole Forces." The fact that Hancock chose Warren, rather than Gen. Artemas Ward, to handle such important matters underscores the influence Warren commanded in Massachusetts.

Meanwhile, Samuel Adams's letter to Warren was about the Continental Congress's choice of Charles Lee as Washington's second-in-command. Adams said he relied on Warren to assuage any potential prejudices against Lee, an erstwhile British soldier. "If any should be disaffected to his Appointment," Adams wrote, "pray use your utmost endeavor, to reconcile them to it."

Perhaps most telling as to how indispensable Warren had become to the patriot movement was the letter that John Adams wrote to him on June 21. The indefatigable Adams had already met with much opposition in Congress over his radical ideology. "We find a great many bundles of weak nerves," he wrote Warren. "We are obliged to be as delicate and soft and modest and humble as possible." Eager to be home with his Massachusetts brethren, he wrote, "I am almost impatient to be at Cambridge . . . I wish We were nearer to you," and he promised Warren that "we shall maintain a good army for you." Desperate for information, Adams asked Warren to please "pray stir up every man, who has a quill to write me. We want to know the number of your army, a list of your officers, a state of your government, the distresses of Boston, the condition of the enemy, etc." All these letters from Philadelphia asked much of the man they still believed to be alive.

At almost midnight on June 24, an express rider carrying news of the battle and Warren's death galloped into the dark, hushed streets of Philadelphia. It was the eve of the Sabbath, and congressional sessions were never held on Sundays—church would be the order of business in the morning. Upon receiving word of the arriving rider, the slumbering delegates leaped from their beds and hastily dressed to hear the latest report. Stunned at the shocking intelligence, and in disbelief over Warren's death, scores of men gathered near the chambers of the delegates to commiserate and pray for their slain comrades.

Although he had never attended either Congress, Warren was well known to the delegates since they had unanimously adopted his Suffolk Resolves back in September 1774. Slowly they came to realize that the battle on Breed's Hill had been only the beginning: the colonists would continue to face the largest and most powerful military in the world. The Massachusetts delegates, in particular, understood the ramifications of losing Warren, making an abysmal situation appear all the more impossible.

Rumors, conflicting accounts, and wild exaggerations about Warren and Breed's Hill were spreading throughout the colonies. Most thought the initial accounts, placing Warren in the redoubt fighting His Majesty's troops, were utterly ludicrous. Yet Warren was missing. Some said they had seen him escape the redoubt, while others claimed he had been taken prisoner. But still others swore that they had witnessed his death. Word of his death soon circulated among the patriot rank and file.

Whigs throughout British North America mourned Warren, particularly his radical associates and the New England provincials. "He is now gone, and closes an illustrious Life," the Chelmsford militia captain Jonathan Williams Austin wrote to John Adams, whom he studied law under, "with all the Glory those can acquire who bleed and die for the preservation of the Rights of their Country and Mankind." Warren's death was an immeasurable loss to the patriot cause on so many levels. Those who had fought at his side were distraught, especially since he had almost made it out alive. The entire army mourned the tragic loss of the revolutionary leader. Just days after the battle, one patriot soldier wrote that "the greatest loss sustaind is the death of Dr. Warren. A main spoke in the wheel of Politicks at this critical juncture—he is universally lamented in the camp."

James Warren, Warren's successor as president of the Massachusetts Provincial Congress, described his "inexpressible grief" at receiving word of Warren's death and condemned the gruesome actions of the British: "With a savage barbarity never practiced among civilized nations, they fired and have utterly destroyed the town of Charlestown." Of the ensuing bedlam, he wrote, "It is impossible to describe the confusion in this place." But he remained unaware of the extent of brutality committed during the battle, particularly against his comrade Dr. Joseph Warren.

So many different versions of Warren's death were being told that it was difficult to separate fact from fiction. But shocking reports and rumors soon circulated about how Warren's remains were butchered and beheaded, leaving little doubt of the veracity of the redcoat barbarity. Abigail Adams told her husband,

> We learn from one of these [British] deserters that our ever valued friend Warren, dear to us even in death; was [not] treated with any more respect than a common soldier, but the [savage] wretches call'd officers consulted together and agreed to sever his Head from his body, and carry it in triumph to Gage. . . . What Humanity could not obtain, the rights and ceremonies of a Mason demanded. An officer who it seems was one of the Brotherhood requested that as a Mason he might have the body unmangled, and find it a decent interment for it. He obtained his request but upon returning to secure it, he found it already thrown into the Earth, only with the ceremony of being first placed there, with many bodies over him.

Accounts poured in from both the British and the American sides. Incredibly, more than a year after Warren's death, a report still circulated in London that he had survived the battle and was living there. Exaggerated stories told of Warren giving a motivational speech after being shot in the face. Conflicting tales of where he had been hit by the fatal bullet became something of an obsession among those trying to discern if Warren had been retreating or facing the British when he was shot.

Samuel Adams, more than anyone, realized how devastating the doctor's death was to the radical faction. In addition to being Adams's "closest friend," Warren had been his strongest and most talented political ally. "The death of our truly amiable and worthy friend, Dr. Warren, is greatly afflicting," he wrote. "He fell in the glorious struggle for public liberty." Much like Adams, Warren had sacrificed both personally and financially to advocate the Whig agenda. His dedication had freed the other Bay Colony patriot leaders to attend the Continental Congresses, knowing they could leave provincial matters in his capable hands. As one historian wrote, "Warren's death doubled [Samuel] Adams's resolve to continue the struggle." Warren had sacrificed his life for the patriot cause, and his political associates refused to let him die in vain.

John Adams received letters from two different sources attesting to Warren's rumored beheading, and while no record exists of his personal reaction, he was likely devastated. Warren had been Adams's great friend and his family physician, and he had aggressively courted Adams for the radical movement, even when Adams had tried to retire from public life. As a testament to his importance, when Adams's wife wrote him about Bunker Hill on June 18, the day after the battle, she began with Warren's death:

> *The day; perhaps the decisive day is come on which the fate of America depends. My bursting heart must find vent at my pen, I have just heard that our dear friend Dr. Warren is no more but fell gloriously fighting for his country—saying better to die honourably in the field than ignominiously hang upon the gallows. Great is our loss.*

Adams seemed to feel that too much had been asked of Warren. In a letter to James Warren, he wrote,

> *For God's sake my Friend let us be upon our Guard, against too much Admiration of our greatest friends. President of the Congress, Chairman of the Committee of Safety, Major General and Chief Surgeon of the Army, was too much for one Mortal, and This Accumulation of Admiration upon one Gentleman, which among the Hebrews was called Idolatry, has deprived us forever of the Services of one of our best and ablest men. We have not sufficient Number of such men left to be prodigal of their Lives in future.*

The doctor was beginning to transcend mortal status, as one newspaper even referred to the "Godlike Warren" as "thy country's guardian angel."

Many felt Warren would have been destined for even greater things. Thomas Hutchinson, who had known him for years, both personally and professionally, firmly believed that "if he had lived, [Warren] bid as fair as any man to advance himself to the summit of political as well as military affairs and to become the Cromwell of North America." Peter Oliver, former chief justice of the Massachusetts Superior Court, felt that had Warren lived, "Washington" would have "remained in Obscurity."

At the moment of Bunker Hill, however, these Loyalist government officials regarded Warren, of all the patriots, as one of the most dangerous threats to royal authority. They considered Warren a main figure responsible for the mounting hostilities and the outbreak of war. The vicious treatment of his body on the battlefield, which broke all British rules of engagement, speaks to the fear and loathing he inspired among many Britons, from generals to soldiers to civilians. Days after the Bunker Hill slaughter, one Loyalist, distraught that the "respectable . . . virtuous . . . gentlemen, brave British soldiers, should fall by the hands of such despicable wretches" was comforted by the fact that Warren the "rascally patriot . . . happily was killed," as "he commanded and spirited the people . . . to defend the lines."

Some saw Warren's death as his just desert for boundless ambition. John Singleton Copley's half-brother Henry Pelham, the Loyalist who had painted Elizabeth Hooton Warren's portrait and was closely tied to Mercy Scollay, wrote, "I have often passed Doct Warren's grave. I felt a disagreeab[le] sensation, thus to see a townsman an old acquaintance led by unbounded ambition to an untimely death and thus early to realize that ruin which a lust of power and dominion has brought upon himself and partly through his means upon this unhappy country. I would wish to forget his principles to lament his fate."

But even among Britons, Warren's battlefield conduct earned a measure of respect. One member of Parliament proclaimed that "to see an irregular peasantry, commanded by a physician, inferior in number, opposed by every circumstance of cannon and bombs that could terrify timid minds, calmly waiting the attck of the gallant Howe, leading on the best troops in the world," was a vivid testament to Warren's nerve and his critical role on the battlefield that day.

In any case, after months of battles, Bunker Hill finally achieved the break with the Crown that Warren had long sought. George III declared the colonists to be in "open and avowed rebellion, by arraying themselves in a hostile manner, to withstand the execution of the law, and traitorously preparing, ordering and levying war against us." The rebellion had indeed become a war.

WORD OF JOSEPH WARREN'S PARTICIPATION IN THE FIGHTING reached his family shortly after Bunker Hill. Staying with Dr. Dix in Worcester, Warren's children and fiancée were desperate for news, hoping he was somewhere safe or in hiding or had been captured alive. John Warren, the youngest of the four brothers and Joseph's medical protégé, was the first to have received the melancholy and distressing tidings *that my brother was missing. Upon this dreadful intelligence I went immediately to Cambridge, and inquired of almost every person I saw whether they could give any information of him. Some told me he was undoubtedly alive and well, others, that he was wounded; and others, that he fell on the field. . . . I passed several days, every day's information diminishing the probability of his safety.*

At one point while John Warren was seeking news of his brother, a British sentinel stopped him and thrust his bayonet into his torso, leaving him a lifelong scar. Unable to get close enough to Charlestown to confirm his worst fears, John prayed and hoped for the best. But days after the battle, when no concrete reports or signs of General Warren surfaced, his family, friends, and associates began the painful process of accepting his death.

When the rumors of Warren's gruesome end were eventually confirmed, the family was devastated. Further information about the treatment of his body on the battlefield sparked outrage and disgust. As the British occupied Boston and Charlestown, Warren's disfigured body remained buried on Breed's Hill as the family wondered exactly what had transpired and where his corpse had been placed.

Warren's mother, Mary, was heartbroken at the death of her first-born child and resolved to fully support the cause that had taken him. Throughout the siege of Boston, Mary Warren willingly put her estate at the disposal of the Continental Army. The valuable fruit trees on the property, which provided her main income, were cut down for firewood. The family used the farm's provisions to feed soldiers and had temporary shelters built to house those brave enlisted men. They even provided a safe haven for deserters of the British Army. When the siege ended and the conflict moved south, what remained of the Warren property stood in ruins "without a tree or a green shrub around it." The ancestral compound had been stripped of almost everything of value, and Mary Warren was left with virtually nothing. Yet while many patriots sought compensation for their sacrifices, the Warren family refused to make any claims or accept money for the numerous losses they had sustained.

Joseph Warren's children suffered the most, having lost their remaining parent and most of their family's possessions. Warren's death left Mercy Scollay alone and grief-stricken in Worcester with Warren's four orphaned children—Elizabeth, Joseph, Richard, and Mary. On June 30, 1775, John Warren asked the Dix family to continue to look after the children until he could make arrangements to come to Worcester, assuring them that he would fully honor every promise—financial or otherwise—that his brother the general had made. Concerned for his distraught nieces and nephews, he implored the Dix family "to take all possible care to render them comfortable and prevent their being in want of anything necessary."

In years to come, reports would surface that Warren had stormed off to Charlestown swept up in a patriotic rage to martyr himself in battle. While he no doubt had a reckless thirst for danger, the evidence suggests that he had looked forward to a life with Mercy Scollay and his children. He had continued to make payments on the large property in West Boston, and he had made many preparations for life in the countryside during or after a reckoning with British forces. And yet it is hard to argue that he showed much foresight about the far-reaching consequences his death might have. When he fell at Bunker Hill, his affairs were not in order, a lack of planning that would have severe consequences for those he left behind.

Following Warren's death, the wealth and property that he had spent a lifetime amassing quickly dissolved. On September 11, 1776, Warren's erstwhile friend and political colleague James Bowdoin repossessed the mansion estate in West Boston; all the custom construction work and upgrades that Warren had specifically ordered to suit his family's needs now benefited another family who rented the property from Bowdoin. In the weeks leading up to Lexington and Concord, Warren had emptied the Hanover Street home he rented from Peter Chardon, moving his possessions out to Roxbury, Worcester,

Milton, and to Mercy's parents' household in Boston. His medical practice, a business he labored to build for over a decade, was dismantled; his remaining patients sought care from other physicians. The final entry in his medical ledger was dated May 8, 1775, and likely was written by his apprentice William Eustis (a future governor of Massachusetts).

Perhaps the gravest affair left unresolved was Warren's relationship with Mercy Scollay. They had never married, and as a result she had no legal standing over the children. She never received the respect and benefits due her as Warren's widow, and both she and the children suffered.

Mercy continued to care for the children. In August she took Elizabeth and Mary with her in Warren's horse and chaise and traveled to Watertown to try to meet with John Hancock, with Samuel and John Adams, and with other patriot leaders regarding Warren's remains and her rights to keep his children under her guardianship.

To her dismay, upon her arrival, Mercy discovered that many of Warren's possessions had been damaged, lost, sold, or stolen. John Warren, she learned, had sold every featherbed Warren had owned to the Massachusetts government, which was furnishing General Washington's headquarters in Cambridge. The highly cherished Copley painting of Warren was unaccounted for and rumored to be somewhere near Roxbury. All the looking glasses (mirrors) that Warren had carefully shipped out of Boston had been broken and shattered. Mercy was appalled by the seemingly callous treatment of the general's belongings.

Without legal standing as Warren's wife, she was left at the mercy of his family. Relations turned bitter. Both parties wanted the children, and all the grief and confusion surrounding Warren's death added to the painful situation. As Mercy later explained, she was "religiously bound by the promise I made my friend that in case he fell a victim to the rage of power I would be protectress of his offspring." But after meeting with Hancock, Samuel and John Adams, and Dr. Cooper, she discovered that "nothing can be done respecting the children til a judge is appointed and I cannot hold them one moment after the relations claim their right."

Within weeks of Mercy returning to Worcester, Warren's other brother Ebenezer arrived to take the general's two sons back to Roxbury. Mercy pleaded that the boys be allowed to stay with her and their two sisters, "which their Papa had hope for . . . under the care of those he confided in." But Ebenezer insisted that his mother, Mary, was desperate to have the boys with her, "as it was impossible anyone could love them so well as blood relations." At that point, Mercy realized "it was in vain to oppose their measures."

Two months later, unannounced, Ebenezer Warren returned to Worcester to claim Elizabeth and young Mary. Mercy's worst fears had all come to pass. She had lost the love of her life before they were able to marry, and now all the children had been taken from her. Writing to John Hancock, Mercy described the heart-wrenching scene: "My eyes are surcharged with tears as resolution brings to view the dear little creatures clinging round my neck, and begging everybody not to let uncle Eben take them." Mercy, along with her host Mrs. Dix, implored Ebenezer to allow the girls to remain with her—or at least her favorite child—young Mary, barely three years old—to raise as her own. But she had no choice. The removal of the children broke Mercy's heart, and she could not bring herself even to attend Joseph Warren's funeral later that spring.

The British evacuated Boston on March 17, 1776, nine months to the day after the Battle of Bunker Hill. After they departed, John Warren was one of the first to be given permission by General Washington to enter Charlestown. Following his somber tour, he put his deepest thoughts to paper: "This day I visit Charlestown, and a most melancholy heap of ruins it is. . . . When I considered that perhaps . . . I might be standing over the remains of a dear Brother, whose blood had stained these hallowed walks . . . how many endearing Scenes of paternal friendship [were] now past and gone forever."

On April 4, some of those closest to Joseph Warren, including his brothers John and Ebenezer, crossed over to Charlestown to find his body. A few people had seen where Warren had fallen and had a general idea as to the whereabouts of his remains. A sexton began to dig carefully in the vicinity, and a while later "a corpse began to appear" less than three feet underground on Breed's Hill. Warren's remains were located under a "person buried in trousers." His unclothed body was horribly decomposed, but his brothers identified him by the "two artificial teeth" that had been "fastened in with gold wire" prior to his death. Understandably shaken and appalled, the brothers could no longer bear to witness and walked off. Some friends were so revolted by the reports of how his body had been mutilated that they refused to believe those were Warren's remains, but the dental evidence was irrefutable.

The slain general's remains were brought to the statehouse, where they lay in state for several days. On April 8, they were carried on a funeral bier—draped with a pall—by the "Hon. General Ward, Brigadier-General Frye, Dr. Morgan, Col. Gridley, the Hon. Mr. Gill," and Mercy's father John Scollay. A procession of several hundred mourners and a detachment of Continental soldiers moved in somber unison to King's Chapel. "Col. Phiney's regiment marched first," reported the *Virginia Gazette*, "with drums and fifes in mourning; then the Free Masons, the remains, the relations, friends, and town's people." All the usual Masonic ceremonies were performed for the former grand master. Inside King's Chapel, a moving funeral dirge was played. Mary Warren wept. Warren's Masonic brother and friend Perez Morton, said to be one of the most talented writers in Massachusetts, delivered the eulogy. Dr. Samuel Cooper kneeled over the remains of his dear friend and prayed. Warren's children—the oldest barely ten—undoubtedly had tears in their eyes as the large funeral procession arrived at the Old Granary Burial Ground, where their father was laid to rest, nameless, behind the shadows of the Minot family tomb.

EPILOGUE

MERCY SCOLLAY, AFTER THE CHILDREN HAD BEEN TAKEN FROM
her and after Warren's funerary solemnities, suffered "distress [that] . . .
rendered me for a time incapable of writing or feeling any animating
sensations." In a room of the Dix house, she had etched her name
on a glass windowpane with the diamond ring Warren gave her—a
permanent testament to what had once existed between the engaged
couple. It was a touching and ironic gesture. While Warren had been
in Watertown, separated from Mercy and consumed with the business of the Provincial Congress, he had engraved his own name on a
window in the old Marshal Fowle house, just prior to his death on the
battlefield. Grief-stricken, Mercy lamented that without her beloved
fiancé, "the curtain is drop'd, and impenetrable darkness succeeds
the sunshine prospect." In describing her heartbreak, Mercy wrote of
a "pain in my stomach that wasts [sic] my flesh and sinks my almost

exhausted spirits, mama mourns over me and says if I don't get better I shall kill her, for she can't part with me yet."

Mercy expressed her resentment and frustration over losing the four children to John Warren and the rest of his family, declaring she had been "very ungenerously treated [since] she had a prior claim to the children." John replied that he was surprised by her words, considering that the general had never mentioned such an arrangement to him; he also hinted that the children's attachment to her had waned, which deeply hurt Mercy. Against the advice of her friends, Mercy petitioned to see the girls again, even though "it would be a fresh opening [upon] an unhealed wound." The following month they were reunited, and Mercy found the children's "tenderness for me unabated, poor Betsey still cries to come and live with me." Mercy continued to see the children, and over the months she grew closer with the Warrens, particularly Mary: "the old lady is my fast friend and treats me with a tenderness, not inferior to that she bestows on her own children."

Mercy worried that the children were not in school: they should "be educated befitting the noble mind of their heroic parent and I fear his affairs are in too perplexed a state too afford them proper supplies at least for some time." She was stunned by the lack of support coming from his fellow patriots: now that Warren could "no longer be serviceable . . . all his former exertions in the cause of his country seems obliterated from the minds of those who I tho't would be foremost to pay a grateful tribute to his memory . . . to promote any scheme for the benefit of his beloved offspring."

But beginning in 1778, Benedict Arnold—who had quickly bonded with Warren in Cambridge after Lexington and Concord—began to send Mercy money to help with the expenses of raising the children. Arnold could sympathize with the orphans' plight: his own first wife had died just days after Warren's battlefield death, leaving him with young children. Arnold asked that Mercy "take particular care of the education of Betsey, and prevail . . . to have Richd sent to the best School in Boston at my expense." He also wrote that John Hancock had "promised to use his interest to have the children taken care of."

Arnold told Mercy that he would petition Congress to help the children financially, and if Congress failed to act, he promised "a handsome collection by private subscription. At all events, am determined they shall be provided for." Samuel Adams, who admired Mercy's "fidelity to our departed friend [and her] unceasing anxiety for the education and future well-being of his children," insisted that Congress cover the education costs of Warren's eldest son, Joseph. Mercy mused that the general would be pleased with her unyielding devotion: "the departed hero should laugh at me for my romantic attachment to his little ones," as she reminisced about the playful side of her loving relationship with him.

By July 1780, Benedict Arnold—now a secret agent for the British—had given Mercy close to three thousand pounds for the children's boarding, education, and clothing. That same month Mercy wrote to Arnold, "The pains you have taken and the example you have set calls forth my gratitude." A few months later Arnold's treason was uncovered, sending shockwaves throughout the colonies and leaving Mercy and the Warren family in disbelief. That Arnold switched sides adds an interesting dimension to his generosity toward Warren's children. Was it driven by guilt? Or had the Continental Congress's neglect of Warren's orphans nudged him closer to his infamous betrayal? In either case, his largesse amounted to an incredible act of charity for a man accused of putting specie over his beloved comrades and country. It hints at how impressed Arnold had been by Joseph Warren. In the coming years, Arnold would name his favorite horse after the martyred hero.

John Warren followed in his brother's footsteps as a doctor and a soldier, serving as a surgeon in the Continental Army. His mother worried about losing yet another child to the conflict, and on August 6, 1778, she expressed relief at his current safety but also fear of an uncertain future. "I greatly rejoice to hear of your health and temporal prosperity," she wrote. "You inform us of the great host that are coming against us, but I hope that god will scatter them, so that they will not be left to hurt you or us. But my child, eternal things lie with such weight on my mind, I can't help but reminding you of the importance of securing your ever-lasting well-being. . . . In the most calamitous times, oh let us get unto Christ, that ark of safety in these tempestuous days."

John eventually adopted his brother's four orphaned children, welcoming them into his household along with most of General Warren's remaining possessions. By late 1779, Warren's oldest son Joseph was in Chelsea under the tutelage of the Reverend Mr. Phillips Payson, a first-rate scholar. That same year the two younger Warren children, Richard and Mary, stayed with Mercy in her father's home, for which Samuel Adams believed she "deserves the greatest praise for her attention to them. She is exceedingly well qualified for her charge; and her affection for their deceased father prompts her to exert her utmost to inculcate in the minds of these children those principles which may conduce 'to render them worthy of the relation they stood in' to him." Of the elder daughter, Elizabeth, Samuel Adams wrote that "no gentlemans daughter in this town, has more advantages of schoole than she has. . . . She learns music, dancing, writing and arithmetic, and the best needle-work that is taught here." Mercy remained involved in the children's lives, and by the summer of 1780 she felt "satisfied that I have discharged my duty towards the dear little orphans."

Once the children grew up, they took their separate paths. Elizabeth matured into an accomplished young woman and married in September 1785, just over twenty years after her own parents' wedding. She lived on School Street in Boston, had no surviving children, and died in 1804 at thirty-nine. Warren's son Joseph was educated at Harvard and graduated in 1786 at eighteen. For a time, he was an officer at Castle William—the very place his father had administered smallpox inoculations during the 1764 outbreak—where he guarded convicts before the prison was built. Eventually he went to live with his uncle Ebenezer in Foxborough, Massachusetts, where he became a schoolteacher. He was the first of Warren's children to die, passing away at twenty-three on April 2, 1790, in his uncle's house. He was buried in Rock Hill Cemetery in Foxborough and later moved to Forest Hills Cemetery in 1860. Joseph Warren's youngest son, Richard, ventured south to Alexandria, Virginia, where he became involved with a mercantile business. Upon his return to Boston, he died of consumption in the spring of 1797, while staying with his uncle John.

Mary "Polly" Warren, the youngest child and Mercy's favorite, married twice. Her marriage to a Mr. Lyman of Northampton on October 16, 1797, lasted about five years until his death in 1802. None of their children survived. A year later Mary married Judge Richard English Newcomb of Greenfield, who had recently lost his first wife and two young children in a dysentery outbreak. The birth of their only son, Joseph Warren Newcomb, brought them great joy. Gen. Joseph Warren's current direct descendants all trace their roots back to this sole surviving grandchild, whose son married the granddaughter of Gen. Israel Putnam, thereby joining the patriot bloodlines of Bunker Hill fame.

Mercy Scollay never bore biological children. For the rest of her life, she considered Warren's orphans her own. Tragedy had also struck Mercy's family, and the Scollays endured many painful losses. Her father had gone bankrupt in 1765, and her brother James had drowned before the war. Mercy lost other brothers, John Jr. and Daniel, in 1775 and 1784 respectively. Her parents both passed away in the early 1790s. By 1797 Mercy was living in Medfield, Massachusetts, with her youngest sister Mary and her husband.

Mercy had been thirty-four when Warren was killed and she would never marry, remaining Warren's unrecognized widow until her death more than a half-century later.

In one of her last letters, in 1824, she wrote that "my sands are running low, and I may soon be called to quit all earthly scenes." She died during the blustery winter of 1826, at eighty-four, more than fifty years after Bunker Hill. Haunted by thoughts of what might have been had Joseph Warren survived, she referred to herself as one "whose whole life has been subject to corporeal or mental disquiet." The physical pain she endured in her later years never blunted the heartbreak she carried to her grave.

In 1825, just before Mercy's death, General Warren's remains were exhumed from the Minot tomb in the Granary Burying Ground in Boston—where they had rested anonymously for a half century—and were reburied, alongside those of his brother John, in St. Paul's Church, just a short distance from where he and Mercy had once lived. Less than a year later, without much notice, Mercy was laid to rest in the distant Vine Lake Cemetery in Medfield. An urn under a weeping willow—the same mourning scene depicted on the ring Joseph Warren had made when his wife Elizabeth passed away in 1773—was engraved upon Mercy's headstone. Sadly, Joseph Warren and Mercy Scollay remain separated in death as they were in life.

WARREN'S LEGACY

ON THE MORNING OF AUGUST 1, 1855, DR. JOHN COLLINS WARREN, the nephew of Gen. Joseph Warren and son of Dr. John Warren, sat alone in his private library. It was his seventy-seventh birthday. Gazing out the window into Boston's Old Granary Burying Ground, which lay directly below, he was surrounded by his collection of more than six thousand books and various fossil and human specimens. John Collins was an avid and meticulous collector of pathological and anatomical specimens. He insisted that his servants keep the house "very neat and in good order in every part," but some claimed the home's interior was more macabre than the graveyard below. His collection of ephemera was also quite diverse and included a three-hundred-pound bear head, and a favorite box held "the hair of General Washington."

The exterior of his Park Street mansion "took high rank among the Boston residences, and there were few that surpassed or even equaled it in size and pretensions." Large paintings of Gen. Joseph Warren and Dr. John Warren were prominently displayed, greeting the many dignitaries, guests, and patients who visited the home. The residence doubled as a lecture hall and operating facility, where Dr. John Collins Warren trained many of his medical students, instructing them in his "high brusque authoritative tones." The front part of the house looked out over Boston Common, and to the home's rear lay the Old Granary Burial Ground. Just beneath his back window, and "almost touching the wall of Dr. Warren's house," was the Minot tomb, which had housed the remains of his illustrious uncle, Gen. Joseph Warren, for fifty years until Collins had them moved to his tomb at nearby St. Paul's Church in 1825. For years the doctor had glanced out his window upon the various headstones bearing the names of Franklin, Hancock, Revere, and others, serving as a daily reminder of the illustrious patriots of his uncle's era.

For decades, John Collins Warren had diligently preserved the general's legacy. In 1822 he had purchased land on Breed's Hill "with a view of preserving uninjured the few remaining traces of that important event." A year later, twenty-six prominent Boston citizen-activists, including John Collins, founded the Bunker Hill Monument Association for the purpose of erecting a monument in honor of the battle, and within two years the association had purchased the whole battlefield. In 1849 Collins directed the placement of the markers to indicate where the breastworks of the redoubt had stood and the exact spot where General Warren was killed. During the seventy-fifth anniversary celebration, he conferred with Governor Everett about the possibility of reinterring General Warren's remains at the Bunker Hill memorial, but the two men decided that if such a ceremony were to occur, it should take place on the battle's centennial in 1875, with Warren's remains bequeathed "either to the state or to the Bunker Hill Association."

Now Collins was once again planning to move his famous uncle's remains, hopefully for the final time. On August 1, 1855, he wrote in his journal: "Called on the Mayor and the Superintendent of the Cemeteries to open my tomb under St. Paul's to make what dispositions of

Warren's eighteenth-century family home in Roxbury, Massachusetts, sketch from the nineteenth century.

Edward Holyoke, Harvard's ninth president, by John Singleton Copley, ca. 1760.

Warren's medical mentor,
Dr. James Lloyd (1728–1810).
From James Thacher, American Medical
Biography *(Boston, 1828)*

Elizabeth Hooton Warren,
by Henry Pelham.
Museum of Fine Arts, Boston

Contemporary sketch of Warren's
mourning ring for his deceased wife,
Elizabeth Hooton Warren, based on a
sketch and description of the ring from
Providence Evening Press, June 14, 1875.
Illustration by Mark Stutzman

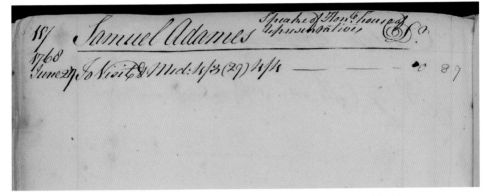

Warren's medical ledger entry for Samuel Adams, 1763–68.
Massachusetts Historical Society

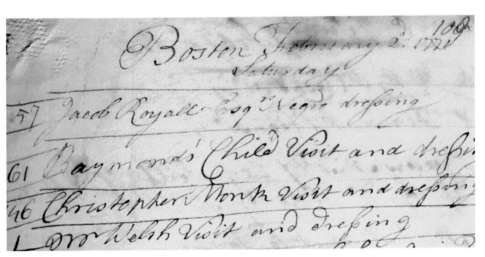

Warren's medical ledger entry for Christopher Monk,
sixth victim of the Boston Massacre, 1771.
From the author's collection

The Killing of Christopher Seider,
woodcut, 1772.
Historical Society of Pennsylvania

"The wicked Statesman,
or the Traitor to his country,
at the Hour of DEATH,"
political cartoon (engraving)
of Thomas Hutchinson by
Paul Revere, ca. October 1773.

Warren's clock.
Scottish Rite Masonic Museum and Library,
Lexington, Mass.

"The Death of Warren" by John Norman, frontispiece to Henry Brackenridge's play *The Battle of Bunkers-Hill*, 1776.
Library of Congress

The Death of General Warren at the Battle of Bunker's Hill, June 17, 1775,
by John Trumbull, 1786–87.
Wadsworth Atheneum, Hartford, Conn.

Bunker Hill Monument,
etching, ca. 1843.

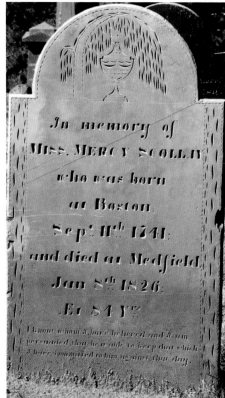

Headstone of Mercy Scollay,
Vine Lake Cemetery,
Medfield, Massachusetts.

Battle of Bunker Hill
Centennial Parade,
Washington Street, 1875.

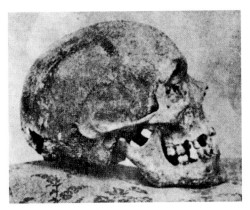

Warren's skull.
Massachusetts Historical Society

Dr. John Collins Warren,
with hand on a random skull, daguerrotype, ca. 1849.

Dr. Joseph Warren, by John Singleton Copley.

Museum of Fine Arts, Boston.
Reproduced with the express permission of Dr. Carolyn M. Matthews, Trustee.

the contents I think proper." He had purchased a new family plot, an eight-foot-deep, five-hundred-square-foot tomb in the 275-acre suburban Forest Hills Cemetery in Roxbury, which he described as "one of the most beautiful objects I had ever seen." He hoped to gather and inter there the remains of various family members scattered in resting places throughout the Boston area. Bridging the gap between life and death, he described the "new tomb which is very nice" as an ancestral compound: "My family and myself have an area large enough for a house and a garden." Rather than reinter General Warren's remains on Breed's Hill, the old doctor had decided to bury his family together.

Unknown to the doctor, this was to be his final birthday—within nine months he would be dead. One contemporary declared that John Collins Warren's "appearance was remarkable, and such as to attract the attention of everyone who came in contact with him." If Joseph Warren's father had been a gentleman farmer, and Joseph himself had brought the family to a new level of social prominence, John Collins Warren was a towering pillar of the free Massachusetts community that his uncle had fought to create. Like his father and his uncle, John Collins had become a doctor; unlike them, he had apprenticed in the glittering capitals of Europe and returned to Boston to begin a long and brilliant career. He had cofounded Massachusetts General Hospital and was one of the first doctors to perform surgery with anesthesia. Now a Boston Brahmin, he could often be seen riding through town in his custom carriage, which prominently displayed the Warren family coat of arms, and carrying fresh fruit to his ailing patients. As one colleague noted, "Whatever place Dr. Warren acquired or maintained in life, no man can say that he did not earn it and keep it by his own fair labor."

On the unseasonably cool morning of August 3, 1855, the remains of Gen. Joseph Warren were removed from the basement vault of St Paul's Cathedral on Tremont Street in Boston. At exactly eleven o'clock, Dr. John Collins Warren, outfitted in his traditional long, fur-collared coat and oversized black top hat, glanced at his gold Swiss pocket watch and, with the assistance of his tall cane, climbed the steps of the church he had helped found. With his own health in fast decline, and his ailing son and successor, Dr. Jonathan Mason Warren, about to depart for an extended voyage to Europe, the old doctor had little time. Accompanied by two of his sons and his son-in-law, William Appleton, Jr., John Collins Warren slowly descended into the underground crypt, where a Mr. Jones, sexton of St. Paul's, stood ready to open the tomb.

The mahogany coffin was removed from the vault, and the draped black cloth was pulled aside, revealing a somewhat faded tin plate that read in engraved black letters, "In this tomb are deposited the earthly remains Of Major-General Joseph Warren, who was killed in the Battle of Bunker Hill on June 17, 1775." Upon opening the coffin, John Collins Warren observed that "the bones were all found in a moist state, disposing to decomposition." The hole created by the ball that struck General Warren in the face was clearly visible, as was a larger orifice to the rear of the head, which Jonathan Mason Warren noted was "becoming enlarged by the crumbling of the margin." After careful examination of the skull, the general's remains were placed in "the vase of pottery marked with the dates of his birth to death," one of four funeral urns that John Collins Warren had special-ordered weeks earlier for the somber occasion. The small group of men then proceeded outside, where a funeral procession of more than twenty people began to march on Tremont Street. But Joseph Warren's remains would not reach their final resting place for another year. One of the most migratory corpses of all the founders, he was finally laid to rest at Forest Hills Cemetery on August 8, 1856.

Warren's postmortem journeys after Bunker Hill, where his body had been mutilated, buried, unearthed, and reburied, were tragic and unbefitting one of the most influential figures in British North America. In the decades before he came to rest at Forest Hills, his remains were shuffled around; at one point they were even believed to have been lost. But the tumultuous journey of Warren's remains pales in comparison to that of his reputation over the next two centuries. Warren's slow descent into obscurity stands in sharp contrast to the time when the popular doctor could be seen hurrying along the winding streets of colonial Boston greeting the "town born."

Almost a decade after the death of John Collins Warren, as the bloodstained curtains closed on the Civil War, a black armband of heartache, shame, guilt, anger, and resentment gripped the fractured nation. After witnessing the war's unimaginable horrors, the quintessential American writer Walt Whitman—who had deep and lasting connections to both the Revolutionary and Civil Wars—declared, "Future years will never know the seething hell . . . the real war will never get in the books." The Bunker Hill clash too had been a bloodbath, where many patriots had been killed, mutilated, and ignominiously shoved into mass burial pits. Whitman's poignant lamentations cried out to American soldiers slain over the past century.

Today Warren's name is unknown to most Americans. After George Washington died in 1799, the phrase "First in war—first in peace—and first in the hearts of his countrymen" was coined to immortalize him, but the same description could easily have been written of Joseph Warren after his death at Bunker Hill.

Perhaps one reason for Warren's obscurity is that his martyrdom quickly overshadowed his many accomplishments. The many contemporary memorials for Warren focused almost exclusively on the battle. John Trumbull's famous painting, *The Death of General Warren at the Battle of Bunker's Hill* (1785–86), portrays a dying and limp Warren in a *Pietà*-like pose in the moment of his apotheosis. Piercing through a cloudy sky, the sun casts a bright aura upon an elegantly robed Warren as fighting rages around him. The painting was engraved, and thousands of copies were sold and distributed. Trumbull's intentions were "to preserve and diffuse the memory of the noblest series of actions . . . to give the present and future sons of oppression and misfortune . . . and even transmit to their descendants . . . those who have been the great actors of those illustrious scenes." Warren was Trumbull's brother's Harvard classmate and friend. Although John Trumbull's depiction of the scene, painted over a decade after the battle was fought, is romanticized and factually inaccurate, the artist successfully immortalized Warren as a martyr who fell while bravely defending the cause of American independence.

Within a year of Warren's death a dramatic play titled *The Battle of Bunkers-Hill,* by Hugh Henry Brackenridge, was performed: it included "a very moving scene on the death of Doctor Warren . . . , near Boston, the morning after the battle at Bunker's-Hill." Additionally, plays by John Daly Burk and John Leacock about Warren and Bunker Hill surfaced in the years following the battle. In 1797, while president of the United States, John Adams attended a showing of Burk's play, *Bunker-Hill: or the Death of General Warren: an Historic Tragedy in Five Acts,* and expressed his dismay at the purely martial depiction of his late comrade, saying, "My friend, Joseph Warren, was a scholar and a gentleman, but your author has made him a bully and a blackguard." Indeed, many who were intimately connected with Warren believed that it was unjust to remember him solely as a martyr at Bunker Hill. Commemorations and odes to Warren continued to appear in newspapers over the ensuing decades.

The question of a memorial monument for Warren was first raised by the Continental Congress in 1777, when at the urging of Samuel Adams, a proposal for the construction of one was adopted. But a decade later, after war had won independence at great cost, a Boston newspaper commented, "We are not in circumstances, (and who can tell when we shall be?) to carry into effect the resolution of Congress, bearing an honorable testimony to the merits and character of General *Joseph Warren,* for erecting a monument to his memory." The war had consumed the states' attention; it wasn't until 1786 that the Battle of Bunker Hill was publicly celebrated in Charlestown, when the town's artillery unit paraded in honor of the sacred day.

In 1794, almost twenty years after Warren was killed in action, the Society of Freemasons in Charlestown, King Solomon's Lodge, finally dedicated a monument in his honor on Breed's Hill. Hundreds marched in the procession "in solemn silence to the Hill, where a circle was formed" around the eighteen-foot Tuscan wood pillar topped by a gilt urn. It was never considered a worthy memorial; one southern visitor who traveled to Charlestown described his "surprise, shame and indignation! The tomb of Warren is a pillar of wood going fast to decay!" Looking out on the riches of Boston and the spirit of its people, "it is impossible not to ask," he wrote, "why have they thus neglected a man, who, living and dead, has done as much honor to Massachusetts as any other citizen she has ever produced?" In 1818 the *Boston Patriot and Daily Chronicle* wrote that "the illustrious WARREN . . . has never been sufficiently appreciated," and that same year the Massachusetts Legislature appointed a committee to consider "erecting a monument of American marble, to perpetuate the memory of the brave GEN. JOSEPH WARREN, on the spot where he fell."

The wooden monument was soon destroyed, possibly in an act of vandalism. But from its remnants, King Solomon's Lodge made a gold-headed cane and presented it to General Lafayette at the fiftieth-anniversary celebration of Bunker Hill in Charlestown. A crowd of more than 100,000 gathered that day, including some 190 veterans of the battle, as the cornerstone for the new marble monument was laid. The event marked a high point of Warren's legacy, as the legendary orator Daniel Webster declared "our own deep sense of the value and importance of the achievements of our ancestors . . . and to foster a constant regard for the principles of the Revolution."

But the raising of the new monument, championed by the Freemasons, soon ran into a wall of opposition, as a great wave of Anti-Masonic feeling swept the young nation in the first half of the nineteenth century. The Anti-Masons were "anxious to take down the monument to the foundation," incensed at the idea of paying tribute to a former grand master of the Scottish Rite Ancient Masons of North America. John Collins Warren regretted the vitriolic "party prejudice" and the "attempts to lessen the fair fame of some of the earliest and best patriots of the revolution."

By then Warren's life had passed into distant history, and even his participation in the Battle at Bunker Hill had come into question. In 1825 John Collins Warren recalled "dining at the Honorable Judge Prescott's, son of Colonel Prescott (of Bunker Hill fame), when a conversation took place on the Bunker Hill battle; and some remarks having been made as to the spot where General Warren was killed, a gentleman sitting next to me, of about my age, born and bred in Boston, said to me, 'I thought it had been established that General Warren was not present at the Battle of Bunker Hill.'" After decades when Warren's sole legacy had been his martyrdom in Charlestown, some of the Boston elite had now reached the conclusion that he wasn't even there.

Almost a half century after his death, Warren's legacy was falling into neglect. One problem faced by those who would keep it alive was the lack of readily available documentation about his life before the battle. By 1830 Mercy Scollay and all his children were dead, and most of his personal and political papers had been burned, destroyed, seized, lost, or stolen. He had burned many himself in 1768, when British troops landed in Boston, and in the nineteenth century more of his papers went up in flames in two house fires. Decades after Warren's death, John Collins Warren revealed that in 1775, "the papers and letters of General Warren left by him on the eve preceding the Battle of Lexington, were dissipated or destroyed so that not a single letter remained." Only two of his medical ledgers remained. Moreover, as the original Whig spymaster, he had shrouded his illegal actions, his writings, his intelligence information, and even his private affairs in secrecy. As early as 1867, Ellis Ames, a well-known Massachusetts lawyer and a close associate of Warren's original biographer Richard Frothingham, acknowledged that even "the handwriting of Warren is very scarce."

In 1835, an early piece on Warren tried to go beyond his battlefield fame to ask, "What did Gen. Warren do to deserve all that has been said about him? Did he do anything more than fight bravely, and get killed on the day of the battle of Bunker hill?" A few years later, another brief account expressed regret that "the materials for the biography of one, in whom we feel so deep an interest are not more abundant. . . . It is chiefly, therefore as the young martyr of Bunker Hill, that he lives, and will forever live in the memory of his countrymen."

Meanwhile, efforts to build the marble monument atop Breed's Hill met with numerous setbacks. A lack of funds compounded construction delays and forced the Bunker Hill Monument Association to sell off almost ten acres of the original land. But the monument was finally completed and dedicated on June 17, 1843, the country's first major Revolutionary War monument. The 221-foot obelisk towered over Charlestown, and tens of thousands celebrated. Once again Daniel Webster was the featured speaker, and John Tyler, the nation's tenth president, was the guest of honor, leading a magnificent procession that included thirteen surviving Bunker Hill veterans. The obelisk and Joseph Warren's portrait were printed upon a large beautiful white satin banner that was displayed on the occasion."

But unlike the 1825 celebration, this one was marred by the divisions over slavery. Abolitionists balked at the hypocrisy of Webster and the pro-slavery president participating in a celebration of liberty. John Quincy Adams refused to join the festivities, noting in his diary that Webster was "a heartless traitor to the cause of human freedom" and that Tyler was nothing more than a "slavemonger." "What a name in the annals of mankind is Bunker Hill! What a day was the 17 of June 1775!" wrote John Quincy Adams, who as a boy had known Dr. Warren personally and had watched the Battle of Bunker Hill with his mother. "What a burlesque on them both is an oration upon them by Daniel Webster, and a pilgrimage of John Tyler, and his Cabinet of slave-drivers."

Still, the efforts on behalf of Warren and his family that had been long before proposed by the Continental Congress made slow progress. In 1846, a special committee in the House of Representatives revisited the proposal, adopted by Congress almost seventy years earlier in 1777, for the "erection of a monument to the memory of Gen. Joseph Warren." Unanimously the committee agreed to allocate five thousand dollars for the project. That year Joseph Warren Newcomb—the general's grandson—had written a letter about the potential statue's placement, and John Collins Warren had suggested it be put "either on Boston Common, or some other public place in Boston." But the monument was never built. Later that same year, Congress passed a bill on behalf of Warren's descendants. Some seventy years earlier, the Continental Congress had voted that Warren's children receive the half-pay of a major general, yet "no such compensation was paid, but instead of it the half pay of colonel was allowed . . . for the difference amounting to about $8,000." The funds have never been disbursed.

Several years later, in 1852, Roxbury contributed a granite block for the Washington Monument with an inscription that read, "The City of Roxbury, Mass.—The Birth-Place of General Joseph Warren." On June 17, 1857, Henry Dexter's statue of Warren, which had been commissioned for the Bunker Hill monument—seven feet of fine Italian marble—was unveiled at the obelisk. Three descendants were living at the time, Joseph Warren Newcomb and his two children, all of whom attended the dedication ceremony and celebration.

During the Civil War, Warren's legacy suffered serious blows from secessionists in the South and even abolitionists in his home state. A South Carolina woman, writing a letter to a newspaper, made reference to the Bunker Hill battle, writing, "Your cowardly northern Yankees ran away headed by Putnam and Joseph Warren; and old Put, having the longest legs, got ahead of Warren, and left him to British bayonets." Even some native Bostonians were replacing founding-generation heroes like Warren with contemporary ones. Wendell Phillips, an abolitionist, "said he did not couple John Brown and Joseph Warren. Both to-day lived in Heaven; but Joseph Warren, of Bunker Hill, was not tall enough to touch the hem of the garment of John Brown, of Harper's Ferry! [claiming] Joseph was only a soldier and nothing more."

General Warren's personal effects generated correspondingly little interest. When the widow of Warren's former medical student, Governor William Eustis, passed away in 1865, her heirs sold their furniture, including a secretery Warren had given to Eustis. The piece had sat in the widow's southwest chamber, and "although urged as the most interesting relic in the sale, it excited no enthusiasm, and was purchased for $18 by a dealer in second-hand furniture."

That same year the first complete biography, *The Life and Times of Dr. Joseph Warren,* was published by historian Richard Frothingham. Given that Warren had perished nearly a century earlier, the press noted it "remarkable that his biographical remains have since heretofore been of the most meager character." At the eighty-fourth-anniversary celebration of the Bunker Hill battle, Frothingham had remarked that

> *the more I study into the character of that man, the larger he seems to grow, the more I see in him a power of those times. He was emphatically one of the great men of that day; there was in him a magnetism, which drew around him wonderfully the affection and confidence of the whole community; not Napoleon the First, I would almost say, on the throne of France, had more influence and moral power than had Joseph Warren in Massachusetts when he fell at Bunker Hill.*

While Frothingham's 1865 book was the most complete to that point, it left many questions concerning Warren's life. Former Massachusetts governor John H. Clifford even called it "more a life of Sam'l Adams" than of General Warren.

A few years prior to the Bunker Hill centennial, Warren's legacy was being subjected to ridicule and erasure. One Philadelphia newspaper derisively commented that "the monument fever has broken out in Boston . . . proposing to to erect a memorial statue or column to General JOSEPH WARREN. . . . There is never any telling where Boston will stop once she gets fairly started." An article in a New York newspaper chided Boston for "putting up statues . . . and the supply of deceased great men . . . seems inexhaustible. Gen. Joseph Warren is now to have this sort of apotheosis; his statue is to be set up in front of his birthplace, on the hundredth anniversary of the battle of Bunker Hill." Even the name of Warren Street in Roxbury was about to be changed. In an incredulous response, the *Boston Daily Advertiser* asked if "such a proposition can be serious . . . which would imply forgetfulness and want of appreciation of a name and service for which every true American heart has been filled with admiration for nearly a century. . . . Few names connected with the American Revolution have been better or wider known than that of General Warren." Even as late as 1873, the "bones of Gen. Joseph Warren, who fell at Bunker's Hill," were still reported to be located in the Granary Burial Ground on Tremont Street, even though they had been removed from that site almost fifty years earlier.

The centennial of Bunker Hill in 1875 ushered in a new sense of hope and reconciliation for a United States that had been anything but united. The site of the first pitched battle of the Revolutionary War now stood as hallowed ground, where hundreds of thousands of proud Americans enjoyed jubilant celebration: "The procession is to be something truly immense—the grandest display, probably, ever seen in this country." For the first time in the postbellum nation, Southern troops marched together with Northern troops, along a ten-mile path passing under a magnificent triumphal arch specially constructed for the momentous occasion. Cheers of exultation echoed through the streets as waving white handkerchiefs saluted the Union and Confederate officers en route to "stand where Bunker Hill once stood." Boston's mayor welcomed Southern soldiers of all ranks, declaring that "the comemoration is no local affair. It must have a national significance, or it can have none."

And on that day of celebration, healing, and reverence, Warren's popularity and legacy reached its zenith. Homes throughout Boston were hung with flags, draperies, flowers, and wreaths while other houses were "prettily festooned with bunting, and a shield [which] bore the name of Warren." Throughout the day, church bells tolled and salutes were fired. Military organizations from all over the country participated in musters and processions throughout greater Boston. Beginning at five in the morning, the "Antiques and Horribles" company marched through Charlestown, headed by "an old English chariot drawn by twenty horses, four abreast-the occupants most fantastically arrayed in suits of mediaeval armor [followed] by fully 2500 people in line." Streets were roped off, and "there were about 700 teams, drawn by nearly 2,000 horses," reported the *Connecticut Courant*. "The number of strangers in the city during the day is estimated . . . between 300,00 and 350,000." In addition to the pomp and fanfare, solemn prayers were conducted in honor of fallen patriot, Confederate, and Union soldiers.

Displayed for the festivities were some of General Warren's treasured possessions: his prayer book, the piece of mourning jewelry he had made when Elizabeth had passed away, and the sword he wielded at Bunker Hill. Many friends and admirers visited the home of Dr. Buckminster Brown, on Bowdoin Street, where they paid their respects to his wife, Sarah Alvord Brown, who was wearing her great-grandfather's mourning ring, and to Warren Putnam Newcomb—the only two living lineal descendants of General Warren.

Before dusk, a magnificent "balloon ascension" was held on the common. At sunset, private and public buildings were illuminated, and a magnificent fireworks display lit up the sky above Boston and Charlestown. Bands performed concerts throughout the town as celebrations continued into the night. The Bunker Hill monument was becoming a beacon for a nation that had been torn apart by fratricide and was slowly limping home again. Gen. Joseph Warren was once again heralded as a patriot hero.

After the centennial celebration in 1875, Joseph Warren's name all but faded from the nation's memory. As an influx of Irish Catholic immigrants settled in Charlestown in the latter part of the nineteenth century, the annual Bunker Hill celebration became more of a celebration of ethnic culture than a remembrance of the battle and Warren's sacrifices. Occassionally a brief flash would spark Warren's dormant legacy. In 1898 a bronze tablet was placed above the entrance to the old American House to designate the site of Warren's Hanover Street residence that he had rented from the Green family, and around this same time statues of Warren were put on display in Roxbury and in Warren, Pennsylvania.

In the twentieth century, Warren essentially disappeared from the broader conversation. The shock and trauma of two world wars made the Revolution appear all the more distant, as the new horrors of modern warfare and genocide trumped the centuries-old memory of atrocities committed by two nations that had since become strong allies. Battle-weary nations turned their gaze to a future where peace, healing, and forgiveness reigned supreme.

During America's bicentennial celebration, patriotic zeal and nostalgia for the revolutionaries swept the country. For a fleeting moment, Warren captured national attention when Ronald Reagan delivered his first inaugural address in January 1981, quoting from the doctor's 1775 Boston Massacre Oration. The nation's fortieth president referred to Dr. Joseph Warren as "a man who might have been one of the greatest among the founding fathers."

Recently, Warren has been experiencing something of a rediscovery. Nathaniel Philbrick's *Bunker Hill* (2013), about the critical battle of 1775, Benjamin L. Carp's *Defiance of the Patriots* (2010), about the Boston Tea Party, and J. L. Bell's *The Road to Concord* (2016) focused on parts of these tumultuous years. All three works are excellent and informative narratives. A few works specifically on Warren have appeared in recent years as well, including the novels *Liberty's Martyr* by Janet Uhlar (2009), and *Following Joe* by Alvin Ureles (2008). Samuel A. Forman's extensively researched *Dr. Joseph Warren* (2011) shifts between nonfiction and fiction and is in various ways more informative than previous works. Additionally, Warren's character has made appearances in a series of comics called *The Dreamer*, where other Warren family members have also been featured. All these publications are praiseworthy in their own right and deserve credit for attempting to rescue Warren from obscurity and to educate the public about one of the most pivotal figures in early American history.

The Broadway musical *Hamilton* (2015) has made people more interested in the Revolution than ever. Perhaps those new voices have helped breathe life back into the revolutionary generation. Small annual commemorations continue to honor Warren in Charlestown on Bunker Hill Day and at Warren's final resting place in Forest Hills Cemetery. On October 22, 2016, the Sixth Masonic District dedicated a new memorial bronze statue to the general at his gravesite. Some of Warren's direct descendants attended the ceremony, where hundreds of Masons and private citizens gathered to pay homage to the revolutionary leader.

Every year tens of thousands of tourists from all over the world visit the Bunker Hill Monument, on the Freedom Trail, where the Dexter statue of General Warren stands majestic. A replica of the first monument erected on Breed's Hill by the Freemasons in 1794 rests at the foot of the obelisk. The Bunker Hill Museum, located across the street from the monument, houses exhibits, dioramas and relics of the seminal battle. On the other side of the Charles River, Warren's portrait by Copley is prominently displayed in the American Wing in the Museum of Fine Arts.

Yet despite the regional memorials and displays, after two centuries Warren remains in the shadow of his founding brothers, forgotten or fictionalized. Glorified as a hero and martyr, Warren's life has been reduced to the events of a single afternoon, his complete story faded into oblivion. Rarely does he receive recognition for writing the pivotal documents that shaped the policies of the colonies on the eve of independence. His broadsides, newspaper articles, pamphlets, resolves, correspondence, political tracts, songs, and orations reveal how he helped steer a course to revolution and ultimately freedom from British tyranny. Few of the voluminous works written about American liberty, the founding fathers, and the United States after 1776 mention Warren. And many written specifically about the events before the signing of the Declaration of Independence misrepresent Warren, present erroneous information, assert improbable speculations, or exclude him altogether.

Uncovering the full scope of Warren's actions and the critical roles he played in the decade prior to Bunker Hill illuminates a human story as much as a political or military biography, for behind the marble facade and the calcified legend rests a complex man who helped lead and propel the colonies to declare independence in 1776. Without Warren, the rebellion in Boston would have faltered and possibly ended in failure. Unequivically one of the most important figures in the movement for independence, Dr. Joseph Warren worked to achieve his vision with his unique arsenal of voice, pen, and sword. He was a founding grandfather of the United States.

Warren's death was not in vain, as he had chosen to dedicate his life to the republican virtues of honor and liberty. Less than a year before Bunker Hill, he had boldly declared to his fellow patriots, "When liberty is the prize, who would shun the warfare? Who would stop to waste a coward thought on life?" Warren lived by those words, and when the time came for the colonies to take a bold stand against Great Britain, he did not hesitate to be in the center of the action. Perhaps the Committee of Safety's battle report eulogized him best, as "a Man whose Memory will be endeared to his Countrymen, and to the worthy in every Part and Age of the World, so long as Virtue and Valor shall be esteemed among Mankind." Although Warren's fate was sealed on the battlefield, June 17, 1775, the values and principles he championed endure, while his story remains a tale of inspiration.

NOTES

xiii **"the dead, the dead, the dead—*our* dead"**: Walt Whitman, *Specimen Days & Collect* (Philadelphia, 1882–83), pp. 79–80. For a half century, Warren was buried in the tomb of the Minot family—unmarked. For some time, the location was unknown even to his descendants.

INTRODUCTION

1 **the founding fathers:** Generally the term "founding father" is reserved for those men who lived beyond 1776 and were involved with the Declaration of Independence, the Constitution, or both. Due to Warren's involvement in so many epic revolutionary events, I believe him to be an exception to this rule.

2 **a hotbed of political agitation:** In the colonial period, according to the eminent historian Gordon Wood, "nowhere were events more spectacular than in Massachusetts." Wood, *American Revolution*, p. 33.

3 **"But what do we mean"**: John Adams to Hezekiah Niles, February 13, 1818, in National Archives.

4 **historical inaccuracies surrounding him:** A book published in 2014

about American Independence and the Revolution mistakenly claims that Joseph Warren was a "Massachusetts Lawyer." Another recently published book refers to Warren as a "noted Presbyterian minister."

4　**a supporting role:** In his seminal work *Revolutionary Politics in Massachusetts*, Richard D. Brown lists the "most important . . . politicians who led opposition to administrative policy" (p. 19). Joseph Warren's name is absent. Although Warren was never a member of either chamber of the General Court, he was unquestionably a leader of the opposition against the Crown.

4　**intricate spy ring:** Warren's spy ring drew on his vast network of connections in Boston and the surrounding towns. Washington would have been informed of Warren's intricate system upon his arrival in July 1775. The AMC series *Turn* is based on Rose, *Washington's Spies*.

5　**"We must now prepare":** Frothingham, *Life and Times*, p. 484.

5　**instrumental in achieving independence:** Warren's Suffolk Resolves were an instrumental part of the First Continental Congress. See Chapter 11.

5　**Washington had never commanded an army:** When Washington accepted his new post as general of the Continental Army, he "crossed the threshold into a new life." Chernow, *Washington*, p. 193.

6　**one of Warren's lost medical daybooks:** These fragments prove that the missing medical ledgers did exist, although their current location, even whether they survived at all, remains unknown.

7　**much-neglected but leading role:** While the title of this book underscores Warren's martyrdom, the book attempts to go beyond the death stereotype that still overshadows awareness of his life.

8　**his bloodline:** To date, every study on Warren that takes up his descendants traces them to his brother, John Warren, not mentioning his own continuous bloodline. Many declare that his line became extinct in the late nineteenth or early twentieth century.

8　**vast array of primary sources:** See Provincial Congresses of Massachusetts, *Journal of Each Provincial Congress*, as well as various records from the Lodge of St. Andrew. Since newspapers were the main source of information in the eighteenth century, I searched through tens of thousands of them for information on Warren.

8　**relics:** Previous studies on Warren have been too quick to dismiss his relics as suspect or inauthentic. These items need further investigation by material culture experts in light of the new Warren research, the technological advances within certain fields of history, and the direct connection to Warren's family.

8　**"it was a thinking community":** Frothingham, *Life and Times*, p. 47.

1
NO TURNING BACK

11   **Hastings House:** Hastings House was the temporary headquarters of General Ward and was also where the Committee of Safety—which Warren served as chairman—met. Just two weeks after Warren's death, Hastings House was where Ward and other patriot officers would entertain General Washington upon his arrival from Philadelphia.

11   **debilitating headaches:** Warren was prone to chronic headaches, from which his brother John would also suffer throughout his life.

11   **it had not rained for weeks:** Between May and the beginning of July 1775, there was no heavy rainfall around Boston, making it a "very dry time." On July 2 "a most refreshing rain" finally fell. See Ames, *Diary of Nathaniel Ames*, ed. Hanson, Vol. 1, pp. 282–83. William Clark recorded in his diary that the weather on June 17 was "serene and warm," and most other accounts say that afternoon was extremely hot.

11   **one of the mildest:** See several entries for winter of 1775 in Tudor, *Deacon Tudor's Diary.*

11   **"No business but that of war":** Frothingham, *Life and Times*, p. 476.

12   **wealthy merchant John Hancock:** While Hancock's wealth was impressive, the Massachusetts tax list of 1771 indicated that Jeremiah Lee was then the wealthiest man in the Bay Colony.

12   **"elegant in his personal appearance":** Austin, *Life of Gerry*, p. 86.

13   **intimate ties:** For a time, beginning in 1769, Warren held the lucrative appointed commission of Boston almshouse physician. He also attempted a large business venture with a British doctor in Boston, "James Latham Surgeon to the Kings or Sixth Regiment of Foot," to establish inoculation hospitals. Ms. N-1732 1756–1857, box 1 of 3, John Collins Warren Papers II.

13   **"present struggle for the liberties":** Frothingham, *Life and Times*, p. 319.

13   **"the famous Dr. Warren":** Francis, Lord Rawdon, to Francis, tenth Earl of Huntington, June 20, 1776, in Commager and Morris, *Spirit of Seventy-Six*, pp. 130–31.

13   **Warren's home on Hanover Street:** The house "was on the west side of Hanover Street next to what used to be Earl's Coffee House." Entry for February 12, 1851, in John Collins Warren Journal, John Collins Warren Papers, "Hezekiah Earl's Coffee House was in Hanover Street, near Court Street, and was the starting place of the Accommodation Stage for Worcester"; Baldwin, "Diary of Christopher C. Baldwin," *Archaeologia Americana* 8, p. 7. The coffee house was established in 1806; the American House stood over Warren's home, and the adjacent Codman's buildings sat atop the coffee house. Drake, *Old Landmarks*, p. 70.

14   **"uncommon firmness":** Austin, *Life of Gerry*, p. 85.

14 **"The mistress we court"**: Frothingham, *Life and Times*, p. 317.

14 **"The ardor of dear Doctor Warren"**: Letter of William Williams, June 20, 1775, in Frothingham, *Life and Times*, p. 510. Warren had opted for a military commission in the provincial army over the post of chief surgeon.

14 **"I was sorry when"**: John Winthrop to John Adams, June 21, 1775, in Collections of the Massachusetts Historical Society, Vol. IV, Fifth Series, Heath papers, Boston, 1878, p. 292–94.

15 **Warren understood that he needed**: Warren and his compatriots believed freedom to be a state of nature, whereas liberty required self-discipline and meant taking responsibility.

15 **"regulars were landing"**: John Chester and Samuel Webb to Joseph Webb, June 19, 1775, in Ford, *Boston in 1775*, p. 10.

15 **pistols concealed**: Loring, *Hundred Boston Orators*, p. 48.

15 **"well known to their officers"**: Warren, *Life of John Collins Warren*, p. 42.

15 **"The roar of cannons, mortars, and musquetry"**: John Burgoyne to Lord Stanley, June 25, 1775, Bunker Hill Exhibit, Massachusetts Historical Society.

15 **"a remarkable head of white"**: Dann, *Revolution Remembered*, p. 106.

15 **"totally unfit for everything"**: French, *First Year*, p. 187.

15 **"fill hell to-morrow"**: Frothingham, *Battle of Bunker Hill*, p. 18.

16 **"spent part of every day"**: Warren, *Life of John Collins Warren*, p. 42.

16 **"These fellows say"**: Frothingham, *Life and Times*, p. 168.

16 **"where wounds were to be made"**: Knapp, *Biographical Sketches of Lawyers*, p. 117.

16 **"I will never be taken alive"**: Frothingham, *Battle of Bunker Hill*, p. 17

17 **there not to interfere**: Just days prior to the battle, Warren had been nominated as a major general by the Massachusetts Committee of Safety, but his commission had yet to be made official by the Provincial Congress.

17 **top political and civilian figure**: Warren arrived at Breed's Hill as "a volunteer in the ranks, which he was soon to command." See Austin, *Life of Gerry*, p. 84. *An Elegiac Poem* (1775) states that Warren "commanded on this occasion."

17 **an unspeakable option**: John Adams estimated that two-thirds of the people in the colonies were pro-revolution whereas one-third were against it. His analysis of the numbers regarding the French Revolution—one-third pro, one-third against, and one-third neutral—is often mistaken for a breakdown of American colonists' views of the revolution.

17 **preferring to petition George III**: The Olive Branch Petition was sent to George III on July 5, 1775. Weeks after Bunker Hill, the Second Continental Congress sent an appeal to the people of Great Britain in an attempt to sway opinion in favor of the colonists. Congress also tried to impose economic sanctions against Britain in an attempt to avoid a full-scale war.

17   **casualties:** The war would claim the lives of almost forty thousand patriot soldiers. Prisoners of war accounted for the lion's share of patriot deaths, followed by disease, and then those who were killed in action.

17   **prisoner-of-war camps and ships:** Ethan Allen asserted that "those who had the misfortune to fall into the enemy's hands . . . were reserved from immediate death to famish and die with hunger: in fine the word 'rebel' was thought by the enemy sufficient to sanctify whatever cruelties they were pleased to inflict, death itself not excepted. . . . It was a common practice with the enemy to convey the dead . . . to be slightly buried, and I have seen whole gangs of tories making derision, and exulting over the dead, saying 'There goes another load of d——d [damned] rebels.'" Dandridge, *American Prisoners,* pp. 60–61; at the start of the American Revolution, approximately 90 percent of the African-American population in New England was enslaved.

2
CHILDHOOD HAMLET

18   **"the metropolis of the whole":** Cotton Mather, *Magnalia Christi Americana* (1702). Massachusetts was initiated in 1620 by the Plymouth colony, on the coast of New Plymouth, and a decade later by the colony of Massachusetts Bay, in and around Boston Harbor.

18   **"faire and handsome countrey-towne":** Shurtleff, *Topographical and Historical,* pp. 40–45.

18   **hills and peaks:** Ibid.

19   **Constables patrolled the town's:** For a time, slaves and indentured servants were not allowed on the streets after nine in the evening. *Boston Post-Boy,* November 11, 1765.

19   **"Wind-Mill":** Bacon, *Washington Street,* p. XVIII.

19   **Fortification Gates:** *Boston Post-Boy,* May 5, 1760; *Boston News-Letter,* April 8, 1762.

19   **many public executions:** One example is in Ormsby, *Last Speech and Dying Words.*

20   **Tyburn gallows in London:** *Boston Post-Boy,* September 7, 1761; *Boston News-Letter,* February 7, 1763; *Boston Evening-Post,* September 4, 1758; *Boston Gazette,* May 8, 1750.

20   **blood and tears:** On brandings, "Patrick Freeman . . . a soldier . . . was convicted of Burglary . . . and accordingly burnt in the hand. One Richard Smith was also convicted of breaking into the Province House . . . and sentenced to be branded upon the forehead with the letter B." *Boston Post-Boy,* April 23, 1770. As for public whippings, "David Smith . . . received 25 stripes at the publick whipping-post," *Boston Post-Boy,* March 17, 1760; and "one John Dow . . . was sentenced to be whip'd 20 stripes," *Boston News-Letter,* March 18, 1762.

20   **ear cropping:** *Boston Gazette,* October 12, 1767.

20 **"severely pelted":** *Boston Evening-Post,* March 18,1772. For an example of ear cropping, see *Boston Gazette,* October 12, 1767.

20 **Slaves were often:** Greene, *Negro in New England,* p. 27 and chap. 6.

20 **"the screams of the culprit":** Winslow, *Diary of Anna Winslow,* p. 111.

20 **"A likely, healthy Negro child":** *Boston Evening-Post,* November 3, 1760.

20 **chattel slavery dated back:** In Boston, slave importation decreased after the French and Indian War.

20 **"One old Negro Man Serv":** Suffolk County Probate Records, Massachusetts Archives in Boston, p. 51:633. Both slaves were valued at just over twenty-six pounds.

20 **"many fine fruit trees":** Brown, *Stories About Warren,* p. 12.

20 **salt marsh acreage:** Salt hay was used as fodder for animals and as garden mulch.

21 **"in a very high state":** *Norfolk Advertiser,* January 27, 1838, p. 2.

21 **married Mary Stevens:** The couple married on May 29, 1740, in Roxbury.

21 **sixteen acres of land:** Suffolk County Probate Records, p. 64:472. When Joseph Warren died in 1755, he owned approximately 150 acres. See *Warren to Bowes,* Suffolk County Probate Records, p. 105:19.

21 **Warren russet apples:** Warren russets are still grown today. Current Warren descendants maintain these trees on their farms in Virginia and Michigan.

21 **At the height of the apple harvest:** Many of the Warrens' trees were cut down for the war effort during the siege of Boston. See Daughters of the Revolution, *Glimpses of Early Roxbury,* p. 26.

21 **preserve in their cellar:** Warren's cellar is mentioned in the real estate appraisal, Suffolk County Probate Records, p. 64:472.

21 **apples, eggs and milk:** Warren's family owned cattle, milk cows, oxen, chickens, sheep, at least one horse, a swine, and a "plough mare." These animals are listed in Warren's inventory, Suffolk County Probate Records, 51:631. In 1750, on average, a bushel of apples sold for 2 shillings 6 pence. For further information on the value of goods sold in the eighteenth century, see John A. Caramia, Jr., "Wages and Prices," *Colonial Williamsburg Interpreter* 17, no. 2 (Summer 1996).

22 **Chickens and turkeys:** Although farming was the mainstay of many locals, tanning and cloth production were an additional means of generating money from animals. One New Englander later described her family's preparations for winter: "Towards Christmas the fat hogs were killed, the pork salted, the hams hung in the wide chimney to cure, and the sausages made. The women began to comb flax and spin linen thread; the men went daily to cut and haul the year's firewood." Emery, *Reminiscences,* p. 9.

22 **"purple broccoli":** *Boston Evening-Post,* March 17, 1760.

22 **passing the whipping posts and stocks:** Oliver, *Origin and Progress,*

p. 126. In the seventeenth and eighteenth centuries, men were flogged or received "stripes" for stealing a loaf of bread or other food items.

23 **"to his majesty's gaol in Boston":** Writ of Attachment on George Robert Twelves Hewes, September 3, 1770, Suffolk County Court, Case no. 89862.

23 **"middling sort":** Farmers were notorious for their crafty and shrewd bartering in market transactions. Years later much of the haggling took place at Peggy Moore's tavern (which predated the large Boylston Market). Situated on the corner of Orange and Essex streets, this tavern became a favorite spot of Roxbury farmers, whose exchanges were "so sharp and keen" that it was nicknamed "Shaving Corner" in reference to the farmers' razor-edged style. See Marlowe, *Coaching Roads*, p. 3; Bacon, *Washington Street*, p. XX.

23 **Foxborough:** Warren's maternal relatives, the Stevenses, owned extensive property in the area that was settled as Foxborough, Massachusetts, in 1778.

23 **"every ship, sloop, schooner":** Entry for August 12–13, 1769, in John Adams, Diary, Adams Family Papers.

23 **Boston's winding, narrow streets:** The increase in number and speed of carriages on the Sabbath eventually became so problematic that the Boston selectmen ordered a speed limit not to exceed that of a "foot pace, on penalty of the sum of ten shillings." Also, during mud season, it was quite difficult to journey through the streets, which were usually heaped with animal excrement. Pedestrians often walked in the middle of the street where it was most level, but in the winter that made for "slippery walking." Rowe, *Diary of John Rowe*, p. 74; John Adams, while attending the First Continental Congress in Philadelphia, noted that the streets were "all equally wide, straight and parallel to each other." Adams, *Diary and Autobiography of Adams*, ed. Butterfield, pp. 2:116, 127, 136.

24 **days of prayer and fasting:** More ascetic practices prevailed in the town when someone "paid their debt to Mother Nature" (that is, when they died) or when humbled and grateful people sought to strengthen their relationship with and praise the Almighty.

24 **"High Waye Towards Roxburie":** Bacon, *Washington Street*, p. XI; *Boston Evening-Post*, January 15, 1753.

24 **"bonfires, squibs, [and] rockets":** *Boston Gazette*, October 18, 1762.

24 **roads in Roxbury:** John Adams, *Autobiography*, part 1, sheet 8 of 53, Adams Family Papers.

24 **"for paving the Publick High-Way":** *Boston Evening-Post*, October 8, 1759; Daughters of the Revolution, *Glimpses of Early Roxbury*, p. 9. An example of bear slaying appears in entry for September 26, 1759, in Ames, "Diary of Nathaniel Ames," p. 1:35

24 **"Refin'd Sperma Ceti":** *Boston Post-Boy*, March 14, 1763. Spermaceti is the wax found inside the cavity of a sperm whale's head. Sperma-Ceti Candles were made at the "Manufactory in Weymouth"; see *Boston Gazette*, April 7, 1760. Also one could purchase "blubber and oyl, by the

barrel"; see *Boston News-Letter,* January 10, 1760. Given the high cost of candles and the laborious efforts expended in making them, most households tried to conserve their use. An event where more than a few candles were burning was considered quite newsworthy. More than four thousand candles were burned at the wedding of George III; see *Boston Post-Boy,* October 26, 1761.

24 **Grey Hound Tavern:** The Grey Hound was popular among Harvard students. Morison, *Three Centuries of Harvard,* pp. 110–11. In 1784, the Grey Hound was replaced by Roxbury's first Fire Engine House. See Daughters of the Revolution, *Glimpses of Early Roxbury,* p. 17.

25 **writing paper, tobacco:** *Boston Evening-Post,* March 19, 1764.

25 **"constables and collectors":** *Boston Evening-Post,* April 30, 1764.

25 **a catamount:** *Boston Gazette,* April 20, 1741. If other animals were shown at the tavern during Warren's childhood, he likely went to view them.

25 **"a favorite resort":** Daughters of the Revolution, *Glimpses of Early Roxbury,* p. 17.

25 **"a small trotting horse":** *Boston News-Letter,* September 2, 1755.

25 **nerve centers for rebellion:** Tavern life was part of what the twentieth-century German philosopher Jürgen Habermas would call the "public sphere."

26 **"scheme," "conspiracy":** Davis, *Papers Relating to the Land Bank,* p. 8.

26 **"concerned in a design":** Ibid., p. 21.

26 **"not to sign":** Ibid., p. 7.

27 **"several rights of land":** *New-England Weekly Journal,* August 25, 1741. The sold items were to be paid for in "manufactory bills." The sale was held "at his dwelling house in Roxbury," and offers some proof to refute Nathaniel Martin's assertion: "A petition of Samuel Stevens of Roxbury, complaining of an unjust prosecution by Nathaniel Martin (Martyn) for the payment of a quantity of notes called manufactory notes, although he had already paid his own quota of said notes, and thereby complied with the true intent of the Act of Parliament." See Davis, *Papers Relating to the Land Bank,* p. 29.

27 **Hounded by numerous suits:** At least two of Stevens's children became embroiled in the Land Bank nightmare; his son Timothy Stevens, the brother of Joseph Warren's mother, was one of them.

27 **"Petition of Samuel Stevens":** Davis, *Papers Relating to the Land Bank,* p. 42.

27 **Robert Calef:** Calef was the maternal grandfather of Dr. Joseph Warren's mother. I have also seen the surname spelled Calif and Caliph.

27 **witch hysteria:** Calef's *More Wonders of the Invisible World* (1697) was written to counter Cotton Mather's defense of the Salem Witch Hunt, *The Wonders of the Invisible World,* which also contained a piece by Increase Mather called *A Further Account of the Tryals of the New-England Witches.* Selectmen were part of a governing board; Puritan society believed that the devil's weapon against spiritual enlightenment was illiteracy. In 1647, the

Old Deluder Satan Act was passed to ensure children were taught to read and write in order to understand both spiritual and secular laws.

28   **opportunity to attend school:** In a society dominated by white males, a plethora of unfair practices put the remaining population at a disadvantage For example, girls were barred from the established educational institutions. If a girl šought learning and knowledge, her family, if inclined to indulge, could provide her with a private tutor or send her to one of the many teachers who taught "writing, arithmetick, and reading" or other skills like "wax-work, filligrea, painting on glass, marking, plain sowing, tent-stitch, and Irish-stitch" from their private homes and rented spaces. *Boston Evening-Post*, May 9, 1763; *Boston Post-Boy*, May 19, 1760; *Boston News-Letter*, May 19, 1763; *Boston Evening-Post*, September 15, 1760; *Boston Gazette*, September 20, 1762; *Boston Post-Boy*, February 15, 1762.

28   **play the fiddle or violin:** This information is based on a private conversation with various musical historians and performers from the Colonial Williamsburg Foundation. For many years, New England's strict Puritan society banned theatrical productions of any sort.

28   **"studied the scriptures":** Warren, *Life of John Collins Warren*, pp. 2–7.

28   **more expensive pews:** Thwing, *First Church in Roxbury*, pp. 80, 136, 146.

28   **First Great Awakening:** Other preachers like Gilbert Tennent and the pastor of Boston's Old South Church, Thomas Prince, also participated in, and supported, the religious movement sweeping through Boston in the 1740s.

29   **charismatic messengers of God:** When Whitefield returned to Cambridge, he vilified Harvard as a den of iniquity. That sparked a hotly contested debate, as Harvard faculty roared back that his "furious zeal" and "slanderous" accusations were "a most wicked and libelous falsehood." Twenty years later, after the school library burned down, Whitefield generously donated books and money, effecting a truce. See Morison, *Three Centuries of Harvard*, p. 87.

29   **Boston's church elders:** Jonathan Edwards, a champion of smallpox inoculation, died soon after receiving his inoculation in 1758, which did little to promote the procedure. At the time of his death, Edwards was serving as the president of Princeton (College of New Jersey).

29   **"other good divinity":** Suffolk County Probate Records, 51:633.

30   **"principles were Calvinistic":** Warren. *Life of John Collins Warren*, pp. 2–7.

30   **"I would rather a son":** Ibid.

30   **"told a younger brother":** Folder 2, 1738–1773, John Collins Warren Papers.

3

THE HARVARD YEARS

31   **tiny one-room schoolhouse:** *Boston Post-Boy*, September 17, 1759.

32   **grammar schools of Elizabethan:** Hale, *Tercentenary History*, p. 17. Mas-

sachusetts had a higher literacy rate than most other colonies given its number of schools and the Puritan fervor that stressed reading the Bible.

32 **"from the knowledge":** The Old Deluder Satan Act, passed in 1647.

32 **"a cheerfull spirit":** Whitehill, *Topographical Boston*, p. 45.

32 **"the inhabitants of Roxburie":** Hale, *Tercentenary History*, p. 1.

32 **assisting the schoolmaster:** Warren wrote about schoolboys carting wood and making repairs to the school in a letter dated December 17, 1761. See Frothingham, *Life and Times*, p. 12.

32 **punishing snowstorms:** Entry for December 24, 1751, in Marsh, *Diary of Thomas Marsh.*

32 **One of Warren's assigned texts:** Warren's signed copy is in the Massachusetts Historical Society. A doggerel verse speculated to have been written by Warren appears after the title page: "Wine will make us red as roses / And our sorrows quite forgett / Come let us fudell all our noses / And drink ourselves quite out of debt."

33 **"Notice is hereby given":** *Boston Gazette,* June 30, 1755.

33 **normally placid town:** Morison, *Three Centuries of Harvard*, p. 120. In 1755 Commencement was held on July 16, 1755. See Faculty Records II 1752–1766, UAIII 5.5.2, p. 34, Harvard University Archives.

33 **"the prophaness of some":** *Boston Gazette*, September 29, 1760.

33 **"mountainous, yet fruitful":** Rev. Joseph Wheeler to Rev. Nathan Stone, February 24, 1767, in *Collections of the Massachusetts Historical Society*, series 1, pp. 10:88–89.

33 **"a handsome well-finished house":** *Boston Evening-Post*, February 11, 1760.

33 **ponds froze over:** Ames, "Diary of Nathaniel Ames," Vol. 1: p. 22.

34 **five-mile trip from Roxbury:** In colonial America, everyday clothes were made of linen. Cotton was more expensive since it was labor intensive. Only with the invention of the cotton gin in 1790 did cotton become less expensive.

34 **a wig:** For evidence that freshmen scholars wore wigs, see entry for June 23, 1758, Ames, "Diary of Nathaniel Ames," Vol. 1: p. 13; as well as Harvard inventory lists of the period. Wigs worn by younger men were almost always dark in color, rarely white or gray. Wigs were displayed on wooden heads in peruke and wigmaker shops—hence the pejorative term "blockhead," a popular insult in the colonies.

34 **"examined before the Tutors":** Entry for July 14, 1759, in Page, *Diary of John Page*; Laws of Harvard College, UAI 15.800, box 5, Corporation Laws and Statutes of Harvard 1655–1989, Harvard University Archives.

34 **Dressed in his black robe:** *Harvard's Ninth President, Edward Holyoke*, by John Singleton Copley, ca. 1760.

34 **"bizarre throne":** *Harvard University Gazette*, October 11, 2001. As noted in the June 30 *Boston Gazette*, the exams stretched over a two-day period. See also entries for July 14, 15, 1757, in Page, *Diary of John Page*.

34 **"hath a good moral character":** Smith, *John Adams*, pp. 1:14, 15, 16, 18. On his deathbed, Holyoke murmured, "If any man wishes to be humbled and mortified, let him become President of Harvard College." Morison, *Three Centuries of Harvard*, p. 99.

34 **"to have his *admittatur* signed":** Morison, *Three Centuries of Harvard*, pp. 103–4.

34 **"I was as light":** McCullough, *John Adams*, p. 34.

34 **"Being Possessed of a Genius":** Oliver, *Origin and Progress*, p. 128.

34 **"he ranked thirty-first":** Faculty Records II 1752–1766, UAIII 5.5.2, pp. 46–47, Harvard University Archives. Of this original list composed on February 27, 1756, several students ended up leaving the college, one was never admitted, and another died suddenly during his freshman year.

35 **ranked freshmen accordingly:** "The freshman class . . . was usually placed . . . within six or nine months after their admission. The official notice of this was given by having their names written in a large German text, in a handsome style, and placed in a conspicuous part of the College Buttery. . . . As soon as the freshmen were apprized of their places, each one took his station according to the new arrangement, at recitation and at Commons and in the Chapel and on all other occasions. . . . The parents were not wholly free from influence; but the scholars were often enraged beyond bounds for their disappointment in their place, and it was some time before a class could be settled down to an acquiescence in their allotment. The highest and the lowest in the class was often ascertained more easily (though not without some difficulty) than the intermediate members of the class, where there was room for uncertainty whose claim was best, and where partiality no doubt was sometimes indulged. But I must add, that although the honor of a place in the class was chiefly ideal, yet there were some substantial advantages. The higher part of the class had generally the most influential friends, and they commonly had the best chambers in the college assigned to them. They had also a right to help themselves first at table at Commons, and . . . generally wherever there was occasional precedence allowed, it was very freely yielded to the higher of the class by those who were below." Clifford K. Shipton, *Sibley's Harvard Graduates*, XIV, 1756–1760, Boston, 1968, p. 533. Also in, *Harvard Alumni Bulletin* XXV (March 17, 1933): 647–48. This statement was made by Warren's classmate, Paine Wingate, ranked ninth out of forty-five.

35 **"Pollocks place":** Faculty Records II 1752–1766, UAIII 5.5.2, p. 33, Harvard University Archives.

35 **"contriving and abetting":** Morison, *Three Centuries of Harvard*, p. 115.

35 **"throwing bricks":** Faculty Records II 1752–1766, UAIII 5.5.2, pp. 92–93, Harvard University Archives.

35 **"cubs":** Ames, "Diary of Nathaniel Ames," Vol. 1: p. 16.

35 **"system of freshman servitude":** Morison, *Three Centuries of Harvard*, p. 105.

36 **obsequious gestures:** For example, "In pulling off your hat to persons

of distinction . . . make a reverence, bowing more or less according to the custom of the better bred, and quality of the person." Washington, *Rules of Civility*, p. 13.

36 **compulsory maintenance work:** See the examples in MSS Room Assignment Records, Harvard College Records; in Ames, "Diary of Nathaniel Ames," Vol. 1: p. 47; and in entry for June 28 1758, in Page, *John Page Diary*.

36 **"play place":** Ames, "Diary of Nathaniel Ames," Vol. 1: p. 18.

36 **"a cue of beer":** Wingate, *Life and Letters of Paine Wingate*, p. 1:58.

36 **"food rebellions":** Batchelder, *Bits of Harvard History*, pp. 84, 135. The "Great Butter Rebellion" of 1766 "took more than a month to quell," involving a number of "violent, illegal, and insulting proceedings."

36 **"the buttery in the front":** Ibid., pp. 86–87.

37 **"the chilling dampness":** Tufts, *Don Quixote*, p. 9.

37 **"high table":** Batchelder, *Bits of Harvard History*, pp. 92–93.

37 **"at the lower table":** Faculty Records II 1752–1766, UAIII 5.5.2, p. 74, Harvard University Archives. Whitney is his fellow freshman Phinehas Whitney. The other three waiters were Taylor, Morriel, and Russel. Waiters, a position modeled after sizars at Cambridge and servitors at Oxford, were responsible for their particular table and for any items stolen or damages incurred.

37 **"in a large German text":** Clifford K. Shipton, *Sibley's Harvard Graduates*, XIV, 1756–1760, Boston, 1968, p. 533. Also in, *Harvard Alumni Bulletin* 35 (March 17, 1933): 647–48. Also of note was the statement "I had some classmates who paid for their Commons and never entered the Hall while they belonged to the College." Shipton, *Sibley's Harvard Graduates*, XIV: p. 534.

37 **"paid the steward a shilling":** Morison, *Three Centuries of Harvard*, p. 27.

37 **"a common can":** Batchelder, *Bits of Harvard History*, 128.

37 **"a vast pigstye":** Batchelder, *Bits of Harvard History*, pp. 96–97. Such pigsties were called trash pits or mittens in the eighteenth century.

37 **"once a quarter":** Ibid.

37 **"Went a gunning after Robins":** Entry for April 20, 1758, in Ames, "Diary of Dr. Nathaniel Ames," Vol. 1: p. 12.

38 **"dyat from May":** *Account of Estate of Zachariah Boardman v. Estate of Joseph Warren, April 6, 1784*, Chamberlain Collection of Autographs, Miscellaneous Papers 5 (1777–1797), p. 949, Boston Public Library.

38 **"retire to their chambers":** "The Laws of Harvard College," *Publications of the Colonial Society of Massachusetts* 31 (n.d.): 349. The butler was also responsible for keeping the school's candle supply stocked.

38 **"flip" and "negus":** Flip was a mix of potent beer, sugar, eggs, and rum or brandy, served heated.

38 **"the law prohibiting":** Morison, *Three Centuries of Harvard*, pp. 101–2.

38 **"My chum went to Newton"**: Entries for March 26 and April 7, in Gardner, "Diary for the Year 1759," p. 6.

38 **"If any resident graduate"**: Laws of Harvard College, UAI 15.800, box 5, Corporation Laws and statutes of Harvard 1655–1989, chap. 4, p. 73, Harvard University Archives. Popular card games were whist, similar to modern bridge, and the fast-paced game of piquet.

38 **"scholars . . . guilty of playing at cards"**: Faculty Records II 1752–1766, UAIII 5.5.2, pp. 44–45, Harvard University Archives. The future roommates were Abiel Leonard and Samuel Cotton.

39 **"marts of luxury"**: Batchelder, *Bits of Harvard History*; *Tavern Overview*, Colonial Williamsburg Foundation. Taverns were usually governed by laws set by local courts. While prostitution was prohibited from taverns, "backdoor" services were usually offered.

39 **fleeting trysts**: Morison, *Three Centuries of Harvard History*, p. 116.

39 **Mark and Phillis**: *A few lines on occasion of the untimely end of Mark and Phillis, who were executed at Cambridge, September 18th for poysoning their master, Capt. John Codman of Charlestown*, broadside (Boston 1755), Printed Ephemera Collection, Library of Congress.

39 **"brought down to Charlestown"**: *Boston Evening-Post*, September 22, 1755.

39 **"attended by the greatest"**: *Boston News-Letter*, September 25, 1755.

39 **"Mark hanged and Phillis burnt"**: Field, *Colonial Tavern*, p. 165.

39 **Benjamin Edes and John Gill**: Harrington, *Last Words and Dying Speech*; *Boston Gazette*, March 31, 1760. Public executions at the infamous Tyburn Gallows in London were often written up in Boston's newspapers. See *Boston Post-Boy*, September 7, 1761.

40 **"Cambridge is a famous town"**: Brooks, *History of Medford*, p. 496.

40 **"indecent tumultuous noises"**: Morison, *Three Centuries of Harvard History*, p. 114.

40 **raced horses**: Ibid., p. 111.

40 **"the trifling, nasty vicious"**: Entry for May 29, 1760, in John Adams, Diary, Adams Family Papers.

40 **"admonished, degraded, suspended"**: Laws of Harvard College, UAI 15.800, box 5, Corporation Laws and statutes of Harvard 1655–1989, chap. 3, p. 45, Harvard University Archives.

40 **"boxing," the successor**: Morison, *Three Centuries of Harvard*, pp. 112–13. "Boxing" was stricken from the College Laws by 1767.

40 **"tossing [one] another"**: Faculty Records II 1752–1766, UAIII 5.5.2, p. 79, Harvard University Archives.

41 **"All the shaving cups"**: Warren was also tasked with capturing a half-dozen owls for a prank. *Norfolk Democrat*, January 30, 1846, p. 1.

41 **Evidently in 1807**: "Joseph Warren," in Sparks, *Library of American Biography*, p. 10:97. The story seems credible for a few reasons. First, many

eighteenth-century New England buildings had rainspouts made of wood. Second, Warren was likely agile and unafraid of heights given his apple-picking forays in trees upward of thirty feet high. And finally, the Harvard alumnus even pointed out the exact window of the college building where the reputed incident had transpired, making the tale more believable, especially in light of the vivid recounting. Warren would have been a sophomore or junior when the incident occurred.

41 **four different vacations:** Laws of Harvard College, UAI 15.800, box 5, Corporation Laws and statutes of Harvard 1655–1989, chap. 3, p. 46, Harvard University Archives. After the October vacation, students received two additional vacation blocks.

42 **"a fortnight from and after":** The third Wednesday in October 1755 fell on the fifteenth. Students often began their "vacancy" the night before the first day of dismissal or very early that morning—in either scenario, Warren would not have been at Harvard the day his father died. In Faculty Records II 1752–1766, UAIII 5.5.2, pp. 38–40, Harvard University Archives, no business is recorded between October 11 and November 6. School records for November 7, 1755, note the names of students and their "punishm't for absence beyond time allow'd." Warren's name does not appear on the list, so it is safe to assume that he returned from Roxbury immediately after the allotted vacation or was granted additional leave from his tutors. A student who lived within ten miles of Cambridge was allowed to be absent four days a month.

42 **apple picking a hazardous affair:** At least two ladders were kept on the Warren property to facilitate apple picking and for use in battling fires. As an example from the town of Boston, see "Extract from the Orders and By-Laws of the Town of Boston. For Keeping Ladders to Each House," *Boston Evening-Post*, May 13, 1754.

42 **"On Wednesday last":** *Boston Gazette*, October 27, 1755.

43 **Given that Harvard was in recess:** Previous accounts have erroneously placed Warren at Harvard, instead of at the family farm, when the accident occurred.

43 **"the sight of his father's body":** Warren, *Life of John Warren*, p. 4.

43 **Eliot Burying-Ground:** The cemetery is located in Roxbury at the corner of present Washington and Eustis streets. More than one hundred years later, the remains of Joseph Warren's father and his grandmother were exhumed by John Seaver, the undertaker of Roxbury, "for the purpose of re-interment. The thigh bone and one of the teeth of the father of Gen Warren are the only portion of the remains preserved entire." *Springfield Republican*, October 25, 1860.

43 **white gloves:** "Mens white glaz'd hand gloves" were advertised for sale in many mid-eighteenth-century Boston newspapers, e.g., *Boston Gazette*, February 25, 1760.

43 **mourning rings:** Nehama, *In Death Lamented*, pp. 22-38. On white gloves being purchased for the pallbearers, see *Boston News-Letter*, November 19, 1764.

43   **an exorbitant forty pounds:** Suffolk County Probate Records, p. 64:470.

43   **"a sensless and impoverishing fashion":** *Boston News-Letter*, February 14, 1740. See the advertisement for "a handsome coach and two good black horses, at any hour, paying fifteen shillings for each funeral." *Boston News-Letter*, November 15, 1764; *Boston Evening-Post*, January 21, 1765, and September 24, 1764.

43   **The senior Warren had died intestate:** Suffolk County Probate Records, Vol. 51, p. 680. An appraisal was usually ordered regardless of whether the deceased had a will. In 1743 the senior Warren and Eleazer Williams had acted as "executors" to the estate of the deceased Dr. Philip Thompson of Roxbury—further evidence of Warren's long friendship with Williams and the high esteem in which many in Roxbury regarded him. *Boston News-Letter*, March 25, 1743.

44   **The butler, who ran the Buttery:** "The Laws of Harvard College," *Publications of the Colonial Society of Massachusetts* 31 (1935): 366.

44   **Harvard students paid out of pocket:** Ebenezer Storer made payments to the college steward, the butler, a barber, a sweeper, and even a glazier. Ebenezer Storer diary, Harvard University Archives. HUG 1808.1000.1

44   *Hebrew Gramar*: Faculty Records II 1752–1766, UAIII 5.5.2, p. 37, Harvard University Archives.

44   **Judah Monis:** HUG 1580.5, Judah Monis, 1683-1764. Judah Monis Collection, 1725-1735, an inventory. Harvard University Archives.

44   **insisted that he pursue his education:** Almost 270 pounds were paid for Joseph Warren's Harvard education: "To the expenses of the eldest Son's education at College which he consents to allow 266:13:4." Suffolk County Probate Records, p. 64:471. For his inheritance, Joseph was to receive "a double share" of the estate, compared to his younger brothers. The three younger siblings were to receive 140 pounds. The traditional practice of primogeniture was observed in the colonies. Most of the senior Warren's clothing was not included in the estate appraisal because it was likely cut up and made into clothing for his children.

44   **With a heavy heart:** Given Warren's deep religious upbringing, he may have aspired to a career in the ministry, as so many other Harvard students did. His father's death may have steered him toward a career in medicine.

44   **a large earthquake:** Ezra D. Hines, "Browne Hill," *Essex Institute Historical Collections* 32 (1896): 222.

44   **"About 4h.15m. we were awakened":** Charles S. Osgood, H. M. Batchelder, *Historical Sketch of Salem, 1626–1879*, Salem, Essex Institute, 1879, p. 41. Joseph Warren's youngest brother, John, served part of his medical apprenticeship with E. A. Holyoke. In 1769, Holyoke donated "a telescope of *twenty-eight feet*" to Harvard. See "Grants and Donations to Harvard College," *American Journal of Education* 9 (1860): 151.

44   **The quake caused much destruction:** Tudor, *Deacon Tudor's Diary*, p. 9. But it caused no fatalities.

45 **"It is because we broke":** Jeremiah Newland, "VERSES Occasioned by the *EARTHQUAKES* in the Month of *November*, 1755, broadside, in Massachusetts Historical Society, Collections Online.

45 **a debate over the earthquake:** *Boston Gazette,* January 26 and 28, February 23, and March 1, 1756; As late as 1761, essays were being published in Boston about the great earthquake of 1755; see *Boston News-Letter,* August 6, 1761.

45 **spotted the celestial body:** Winthrop's observations on Halley's comet were read by Benjamin Franklin before the Royal Society in England.

45 **Warren and his friends shared:** Entries for April 4 and 6 in Gardner, "Diary for the Year 1759," p. 6.

45 **Comet-seeking became the rage:** Nathaniel Ames, Sr., the father of Warren's Harvard friend, "observed a Star of a considerable Magnitude to the South-East, near Sirius, having a thick Haze around it, which I found to be a COMET." *Boston Post-Boy,* January 14, 1760.

45 **"The people of New England":** Greenwood, *Revolutionary Services of Greenwood,* pp. 3–4. *Boston Post-Boy,* March 30, 1761, advertised an essay about "a true and wonderful relation of the appearance of three angels (cloathed in white raiment) to a young man . . . near Boston."

46 **Benjamin Johnson drowned:** *Boston Gazette,* June 28, 1756. I believe Johnson, like some other students over the years, drowned while trying to bathe in the river. These deaths became so problematic that finally in 1800–1801, Harvard built a wood-caged bath along the river for students to use. See *Harvard University Corporation, Record of Early Harvard Buildings, 1710-1969: An Inventory,* UAI 15.10.5, Harvard University Archives.

46 **"academical vests":** *Boston Post-Boy,* June 28, 1773, mentions the drowning of another Harvard student and the wearing of vests during the funeral procession.

46 **Massachusetts Hall:** MSS Room Assignment Records, Vol. 1, "1 district 1756 June Ezra Thompson box 13 folder 28," Harvard College Records. This record makes no mention of a roommate, so perhaps Warren roomed alone. Massachusetts Hall still stands in Harvard Yard.

46 **Warren's meager accommodations:** Suffolk County Probate Records, p. 51:633.

46 **"tables, chairs, and featherbeds":** Morison, *Three Centuries of Harvard,* p. 103.

47 **"cellars in the fourth district":** MSS Room Assignment Records, Harvard College Records.

47 **"Cato a play acted":** Entry for July 3, 1858, in Ames, "Diary of Dr. Nathaniel Ames," p. 1:13. Although another Warren, named John, attended Harvard at the same time, the reference here is indeed to Joseph Warren because John Warren is referred to as "Jun Warren" in 1758 and 1759—a reference to his status as a junior. By contrast, in 1758 and 1759 Joseph Warren was a senior sophister and was referred to either as Warren or as "Warren sen." See also entry for May 4 in Gardner, "Diary for the Year

1759," p. 8. *Cato*, a tragic drama written by Joseph Addison in 1712, championed republican ideals and virtues. It was popular in colonial America and was likely a source of many words and actions of the founding fathers. George Washington attended *Cato* performances, as did Patrick Henry, Nathan Hale, and Dr. Joseph Warren.

47 **who ranked eighth and sixth:** The college housing records indicate the hierarchy by listing Leonard's and Cotton's names above Warren's.

47 **"held Gibbs and Hollis scholarships":** Shipton, *Sibley's Harvard Graduates*, pp. 409, 450.

47 ***The Roman Father* and *The Orphan*:** Entries for June 22, 1758, and April 21, 1759, in Ames, "Diary of Nathaniel Ames," pp. 1:12, 29. In 1750, the Massachusetts General Court had banned theatrical productions and stage plays.

47 **"raise the standard of elocution":** Thayer, *Historical Sketch of Harvard*, p. 32.

48 **Warren expanded his social ties:** Entry for July 3, 1758, in Ames, "Diary of Dr. Nathaniel Ames," p. 1:13; Shipton, *Sibley's Harvard Graduates*, p. 302.

48 **Sam Otis:** Years later Sam Otis would hold the Bible upon which Washington was sworn in as U.S. president at the first inauguration.

48 **Abiel Leonard:** Leonard's friendship with Warren had consequences in the fight for American independence. In early 1776 Thomas Paine's *Common Sense* spurred on the cause of independence, selling many copies within the first year of its publication. Paine's pamphlet has also been credited with inspiring Washington's army, and helping spur reenlistments. Paine claimed that 120,000 copies were sold in the first three months; Oliver, *Origin and Progress*, p. 132; *Essex Journal*, December 8, 1775; Washington, *Writings of George Washington*, p. 4:164.

But weeks before the release of *Common Sense*, Warren's friend and former Harvard roommate Abiel Leonard (now a chaplain), delivered an impassioned speech in his "stentorian voice" at the meetinghouse in Cambridge. The enlistment terms for many Continental Army soldiers were expiring (after several months of service) and Washington feared that many men would depart in droves, leaving the army crippled and ineffective. On that blustery winter day, in a massive snowstorm, standing before Washington, several general officers, and many regiments, Leonard made a "very animating, spirited and learned discourse to the soldiery, upon the necessity of their engaging and continuing in the service of America, and of displaying true valor and courage in the defense of her rights and liberties." Leonard's dramatic sermon had its intended effect: it likely helped prevent a mass exodus. Washington reported that close to six thousand men had reenlisted. Leonard's speech and plea has unfortunately been overlooked or forgotten.

A grateful General Washington immediately realized the magnitude of what happened and wrote a letter to Governor Trumbull of Connecticut (the father of Warren's top-ranked Harvard classmate), praising Leonard:

"He has discovered himself a warm and steady friend to his country. . . . Upon the late desertion of the troops, he gave a sensible and judicious discourse, holding forth the necessity of courage and bravery." Back at Harvard, Leonard and Warren had been close roommates, so Leonard's passion was likely fueled by Warren's untimely tragic death. Leonard was also mutual friends with Rev. Samuel Cooper and Gen. Israel Putnam.

Within two years of delivering his speech, Leonard, who suffered bouts of madness, tried to commit suicide by slitting his own throat. Entry for December 26, 1785, in John Quincy Adams, *Diary,* Adams Family Papers. Leonard had been General Putnam's army chaplain; upon "hearing the news, General Putnam and his surgeon rushed 'post haste to the scene of Horror' and reported, 'The cut is so near his Chin that his tongue is wounded and he cannot speak.'" Leonard clung to life for more than two weeks, then died on August 14, 1777. See Shipton, *Sibley's Harvard Graduates,* p. 455;

48   **engendering a martial spirit:** "Our people have been daily inlisting into the service . . . and this province alone will have upwards of four thousand men in the expedition to Crown-Point." *Boston Gazette,* September 15, 1755.

48   **heavy frock coats:** Entry for June 28, 1759, in Page, *Diary of John Page;* entry for June 28, 1759, in Mascarene, *Diary of Margaret Mascarene,* pp. 97–98.

48   **"many of the undergraduates":** Faculty Records II 1752–1766, UAIII 5.5.2, pp. 97–98, Harvard University Archives.

49   **"scholars formed themselves":** Entry for March 15, in Gardner, "Diary for the Year 1759," p. 5.

49   **"explode . . . vollies in the field":** Faculty Records II 1752–1766, UAIII 5.5.2, pp. 97–98, Harvard University Archives.

49   **"Miss Betty Epes aged 22 years":** Entry for February 11, in Gardner, "Diary for the Year 1759," p. 4; entry for February 12, 1759, in Mascarene, *Diary of Margaret Mascarene.*

49   **their anticipation:** Entries for late June in Mascarene, *Diary of Margaret Mascarene.*

49   **"gave our class his farewell":** Entry for June 21 in Gardner, "Diary for the Year 1759," p. 10.

49   **"very handsomely . . . finely performed":** Shipton, *Sibley's Harvard Graduates,* p. 498.

49   **Commencement, held:** *Boston Evening-Post,* July 23, 1759.

49   **"cloudy but excessive hot":** Entry for July 18 in Gardner, "Diary for the Year 1759," p. 12; entry for July 18, 1759, in Mascarene, *Diary of Margaret Mascarene.*

49   **upward of fifteen pounds:** Entry for June 30, in Page, *Diary of John Page.*

50   **graduates had to pay for their degrees:** Ebenezer Storer, *An account of my quarter bills, charges &c from July 11th 1743 to July 13th 1748 at Harvard College,* HUD 1743.83, Harvard University Archives.

50   **presents for their tutor:** Usually a gift of silver was presented.

50   **Mary had sacrificed much:** Diary entries of Joseph Warren's classmates indicate that the families of students almost always attended commencement ceremonies. Entry for July 17 in Gardner, "Diary for the Year 1759," p. 12; entry for July 19 in Page, *Diary of John Page.*

50   **"was highly distinguished":** "Joseph Warren," in *Rees's Cyclopaedia* (American ed.), 1816, Vol. 37.

50   **"the most constitutional":** John Adams to William Tudor, February 4, 1817, in National Archives.

50   **a lavish dinner feast:** For an example of such a dinner, see Storer, *An account of my quarter bills.*

50   **"it shall be no offense if any scholar":** Thayer, *Historical Sketch of Harvard,* p. 55.

50   **"Grand Dance in the Hall":** Entry for July 19, in Gardner, "Diary for the Year 1759," p. 12. A year later, in 1760, Harvard faculty banned dancing during commencement in the Chapel and in College Hall. See Morison, *Three Centuries of Harvard,* p. 131.

50   **Samuel Gardner:** Entry for July 21, in Gardner, "Diary for the Year 1759," p. 12.

50   **packed up his Harvard memories:** *Boston Evening-Post,* June 11, 1759.

4

SPECKLED MONSTER

52   **"for one quarter of a year":** Frothingham, *Life and Times,* pp. 12–13. Mary Warren's signature appears on the back of a letter Warren wrote to the Roxbury Latin School authorities in December 1761, "acknowledging the receipt of thirteen pounds six shillings and eight pence."; See also, Hale, *Tercentenary History,* p. 68.

52   **The Lodge of St. Andrew:** It received its charter under the authority of the Grand Lodge of Scotland.

53   **"admitted to membership":** Palmer et al., *Lodge of St. Andrew,* p. 268.

53   **he lived in Boston on Cornhill:** Ibid., pp. 241, 243. Previous histories have questioned where Warren lived after his Harvard years.

53   **degree in medicine:** In the early 1770s, Harvard had a secretive club for aspiring physicians known as the Anatomical Society or "Spunkers Club." Just prior to the Revolution, several of Warren's medical students were linked to the Spunkers, including his youngest brother John, William Eustis, and David Townshend. But I have found no evidence to suggest that the club existed during Warren's Harvard years, 1755–62, and none of the scant surviving documentation mentions him. John Cary, Warren's 1961 biographer, posited that the club was formed in the early 1770s at Joseph Warren's suggestion. See Cary, *Joseph Warren,* pp. 31–32; Warren, *Life of John Collins Warren,* pp. 228–29.

53 **"The term of two years' study"**: Warren, *Life of John Collins Warren*, p. 13.

53 *A Description of the Body of Man*: The author was Jacopo Berengario da Carpi.

53 **partially delivered:** Not all the theses were read due to the many other activities of the day. Undergraduate ceremonies were conducted in the morning and graduate degrees were administered in the afternoon. See Young, *Subjects for Master's Degree*, p. 19. Nathaniel Ames was also present that day.

54 **auspices of Dr. James Lloyd:** Warren and his mother had both given Lloyd fifty-pound notes of hand as promissory payments for the medical training. Warren was able to repay them within a few years.

54 **Born to a wealthy:** Lloyd's father, Henry, was a successful Boston merchant who retired to Long Island.

54 **William Cheselden and Samuel Sharp:** "Notice of the Late James Lloyd, M.D.," *New England Journal Medicine and Surgery* 2 (1813): 127–30.

54 **"opportunity of studying all":** Ibid.

54 **"swelling ulcers":** *Boston Evening-Post*, November 19, 1761; *Boston News-Letter*, September 11, 1760; *Boston Post-Boy*, August 30, 1762; *Boston Gazette*, April 5, 1762. The "bloody flux" is dysentery.

54 **"Hooper's Female Pills":** *Boston Evening-Post*, December 17, 1764; *New York Gazette*, May 18, 1761.

55 **Known as a generous man:** James Lloyd, Medical Ledger. Boston Medical Library, Francis A. Countway Library of Medicine. Lloyd was also a slave owner who employed a black carriage driver; *Boston News-Letter*, December 28, 1769.

55 **Warren lived with Lloyd:** In addition to recognizing Warren's potential, Lloyd likely connected with Warren on a personal level. Warren lost his father at the age of fourteen, and Lloyd had lost his mother shortly after his birth. Although Lloyd came from a privileged background, he had tasted the bitterness of being held in low regard, as Warren did in his early days at Harvard. Lloyd was apprenticed to Boston's Dr. Silvester Gardiner, who "did not treat him well," and more like a servant than an apprentice living with him. This incident, along with Lloyd's reputation, and Warren's lifelong friendship with him, allow us to assume that Lloyd was a caring mentor and host to his pupils, particularly Warren. See Barck, *Papers of the Lloyd Family*, p. 1:366.

55 **a bedside manner:** Lloyd's care for his patients went beyond death; in certain instances he had his deceased patients interred from his house in Queen Street. See *Boston News-Letter*, August 1, 1771.

56 **exquisite, high-end fashions:** Although the sole surviving painting of Warren depicts him in black, the traditional color worn by physicians in Europe, other primary source accounts describe him as wearing an array of expensive fabrics, colors, and patterns. See later chapters regarding his clothing purchases, his probate inventory, and the primary source description regarding his apparel at the Bunker Hill battle.

56   **economy started sinking:** Approximately one-third of all Massachusetts's eligible men had served in the conflict. "The military spirit greatly prevails in all Parts in this (Boston area) and the other New-England governments; As soon as advice came . . . that a reinforcement was needful, our people have been daily inlisting into the service. And this Province alone will have upwards of four thousand men in the expedition to Crown-Point." Anderson, *Peoples Army,* pp. 60-61. See also *Boston Gazette,* September 15, 1755. The surrender of Montreal in 1760 effectively ended the fighting in North America.

56   **"there was a disproportionate":** Young, *Liberty Tree,* p. 103.

56   **"several likely children":** *Boston Gazette,* May 9, 1763.

56   **"suppos'd to be greater":** *Newport Mercury,* March 25, 1760, Issue 93, pp. 2, 3.

56   **flames could be seen:** Entry for March 20, 1760, in Ames, "Diary of Nathaniel Ames," p. 1:41.

56   **"several shingles, letters":** *New-York Gazette,* March 31, 1760.

57   **"notwithstanding the continuance":** *Boston Post-Boy,* March 24, 1760.

57   **more than fifteen hundred pounds:** *Boston Gazette,* November 3, 1760.

57   **bicameral legislative body:** The Council and the House together with the governor comprised the General Court.

57   **governor, able to summon:** The Council was also an advisory body to the royal governor. All judgeships and the lieutenant governorship also became Crown-appointed positions.

58   **"in the 34th year of his reign":** *Boston Gazette,* December 29, 1760.

58   *Pietas et Gratulatio:* Contributors included Harvard president Edward Holyoke, John Winthrop, the Reverend Samuel Cooper, Dr. Benjamin Church, Master John Lovell, James Bowdoin, and Samuel Sewall. *Boston News-Letter,* March 19, 1761.

58   **the long conflict burdened:** Stoll, *Samuel Adams,* p. 36.

59   **restrict westward expansion:** The Royal Proclamation of 1763 forbade colonial expansion west of the Appalachian Mountains.

59   **"not appointed a justice":** Galvin, *Three Men of Boston,* p. 23; Brown, *Revolutionary Politics in Massachusetts,* p. 18. Brown claims that some of Otis's contemporaries would later trace the beginnings of Massachusetts's political polarization to his quarrel with Hutchinson.

59   **cries of nepotism:** Oliver's son, Peter Jr., attended Harvard (graduating in 1761), where he was a roommate and close friend of Elisha Hutchinson, son of the future royal governor. Additionally, Thomas Hutchinson, Jr., married Peter Oliver, Jr.'s, cousin, Sarah, which helped forge the bond between two of the most powerful Tory clans in the Commonwealth of Massachusetts. Warren was well acquainted with both families. Shipton, *Sibley's Harvard Graduates,* p. 291.

59   **"Is not this amazing ascendency":** John Adams, *The Works of John Adams, vol 2 (Diary, Notes of Debates, Autobiography),* Boston, 1850, p. 78.

60 **"Otis was a flame of fire!":** John Adams to William Tudor, Sr., March 29, 1817, in National Archives; Miller, *Sam Adams*, p. 34.

60 **"out of this election will":** Timothy Ruggles, a future Tory and political ally of Governor Bernard, made this statement when he heard that Otis had been elected. Rugggle's estate was later confiscated and he was listed in the Massachusetts Banishment Act in 1778 along with Thomas Hutchinson and Peter Oliver. For more on Ruggles, see Nicolson, *"Infamas Govener,"* p. 113.

60 **"annihilates our Charter Right":** Entry for May 24, 1764, in Boston, *Report of the Record Commissioners*, Vol. 16, pp. 120–22, esp. 121.

61 **a full-service apothecary shop:** John Greenleaf, Petty Ledger 1764–67 MSS. 280 Vol. 3, Greenleaf Family Papers, Boston Athenaeum.

61 **stocked with patent medicines:** See various entries in Greenleaf's Account books and Petty Ledgers 1753–1777, Greenleaf Family Papers, Boston Athenaeum. Warren may have obtained supplies from sources other than Greenleaf at times.

61 **aloe, Peruvian bark:** Joseph Warren Estate Inventory, Suffolk County Probate Records, p. 647. Sharon Cotner, an expert in eighteenth-century medical history with over thirty years of experience working at the Pasteur and Galt apothecary shop at the Colonial Williamsburg Foundation, conversations with author. In Warren's medical journal, the term *decoction* (abbreviated *decoct*) indicates a mixture.

61 **a balance (scale) to measure:** See the ledgers of both Warren and Greenleaf for the various items.

62 **several wired skulls:** These skulls were unearthed in 1835, when the town excavated the spot where his home once stood.

62 **Warren made house calls:** Relatives who were patients included his mother Mary and his maternal grandparents.

62 **John Wheatley:** Recent works on Warren have suggested certain improprieties regarding Warren and young women, including a close, possibly romantic relationship, with John Wheatley's daughter Mary. One reason is that Warren referred to Mary as "Miss Polly" in his medical journal. Polly was an endearing nickname often used for girls named Mary. However, Warren called several different patients "Miss Polly" in his medical ledger—see entries for Samuel Wentworth and John Hooton as examples. Warren even referred to his own daughter Mary as "Polly." Another reason offered for the possible impropriety refers to John Wheatley "suddenly" settling his account with Warren prior to his marriage to Elizabeth Hooton. The account was settled two months prior to Warren's marriage and I can see no connection between John Wheatley paying his full balance and Warren's personal romantic life. I point this out, not to sanitize Warren's character, but to demonstrate that he simply entered a name in his ledger and was paid money owed to him. Moreover, it has been claimed that Warren lived with the Wheatleys, which has been offered as additional evidence for a relationship. I dispel this notion in the below

note. The suggestion of a romantic relationship with Wheatley's young daughter seems to be yet another exaggerated suggestion that Warren was involved with young teenage women, from Mary Wheatley to Elizabeth Hooton to Sally Edwards. See later chapters where I argue against such claims.

62 **owned Phillis Wheatley:** In addition to owning slaves, John Wheatley had at least one indentured servant who "Ran-away" from his household. *Boston News-Letter,* August 14, 1766.

62 **Warren took meals:** On page five in his medical ledger, Warren listed a payment to John Wheatley of fourteen pounds "to Cash paid for Board." It has been claimed that Warren lived with the Wheatleys, which I believe is incorrect. This represents a payment for meals and not rent, since boarding referenced meals, whereas lodging or housing pertained to rooming. *Board* literally referred to the board upon which one ate. In *Urban Crucible,* Gary Nash uses the term *board* to refer to meals: "As has been pointed out in the English context, 'to eat at one's employer's board'" (pp. 205, 207). During his college days Warren took several "board" meals off campus, so it would have been a familiar practice to him. Also, he was apprenticing with Dr. Lloyd during this period and likely living with him for a time. In 1761–62, he lived on Cornhill (now Washington) Street, thus making it highly unlikely that he ever lived with the Wheatley family.

62 **"had the small pox":** *Boston Evening-Post,* July 27, 1752; *Boston Evening-Post,* July 7, 1755, and *Boston Gazette,* March 12, 1764, and March 9, 1761.

62 **thirteen families in the North End:** *Boston Gazette,* January 23, 1764.

62 **"hang out on a pole":** *Boston Evening-Post,* June 25, 1764.

62 **"immediately into a tarred sheet":** Boston, *Report of the Record Commissioners,* pp. 22, 27.

63 **Merchants and shopkeepers moved their goods:** *Boston Evening-Post,* March 19, 1764, April 9, 1764, and January 30, 1764.

63 **"the most ruinous loss":** Harvard's magnificence stood in ruins. Citizens of Boston and the surrounding towns immediately rallied to collect funds. Harvard president Edward Holyoke appealed to "several charitable Gentlemen . . . to contribute . . . their valuable books" to the college as long as they "have not the Small-Pox in their Houses or near them." Donations from other colonies and from Great Britain began streaming in. Wealthy Boston merchant Thomas Hancock pledged a substantial 500 pounds sterling to replenish the library—a promise his nephew John helped keep after his uncle died, in what came to be called the "Hancock Donation." "Grants and Donations to Harvard College," *American Journal of Education* 9, edited by Henry Barnard (1860), p. 149; *Boston Evening-Post,* March 12, 1764.

"Many benefactors donated actual books and pamphlets, while others provided funds for the purchase of books and replacement of the apparatus. The donors included American colonists as well as Scottish and British individuals and organizations." Quoted from Harvard's description of the scope and content of the collections in Records of gifts and donations made after the fire, 1764–1778, UAIII 50.27.64, box 2, folder 4, Harvard University Archives. See also *Boston Post-Boy*, January 25, 1768. Harvard publicly thanked John Hancock "for this lasting monument of his bounty and public affection." In 1772 Hancock also donated two carpets, wallpaper, and additional books to Harvard. See "Grants and Donations," p. 151.

63 **The practice of inoculating:** Selectmen would often "sett guards round the infected places admitting no body to goe in or come out," making every effort to stop the spread of the pox and avoid the controversy that long surrounded inoculation. Letter from James Gordon to Capt. William Martin, March 9, 1764, in *Proceedings of the Massachusetts Historical Society*, 1880, p. 389. The inoculation was administered in the hopes that the individual would develop an immunity against the Variola major virus.

63 **Dr. Zabdiel Boylston:** Boylston was an ancestor of John Adams.

64 **"Cotton Mather, You Dog":** Mather, *Diary of Cotton Mather*, p. 658.

64 **"absolute law to be made to prevent inoculation":** *Boston Evening-Post*, February 6, 1764.

64 **"when our lives are threatened":** *Boston Evening-Post*, January 30, 1764.

64 **"inoculating hospitals to be taken":** *Boston Post-Boy* February 27, 1764.

64 **put himself on the front lines:** Entries of January 26, 29, 1764, for patient Benjamin Davis, Warren Medical Journal, Vol. 1. Warren Papers.

64 **set up facilities in Castle William:** While administering inoculations, physicians had to take care to avoid the tragedy that had recently befallen one family in Philadelphia. In preparation for the smallpox inoculation, three children were given "tartar emetic" rather than "cream of tartar . . . which by its excess of quantity and violent operation, soon brought on death." *Boston Evening-Post*, December 13, 1762. Peter Oliver, Jr., resided at Castle William for a month under the guidance of Dr. Gelston, with whom Warren also worked closely. The two young Harvard physicians formed a friendship during their tenure at the Castle, where Warren also helped to instruct Peter Oliver, Jr. In February 1770, Peter Oliver, Jr., married Sarah, the daughter of Thomas Hutchinson. See Hutchinson, *Diary and Letters*, pp. 68–69, 75.

64 **Lloyd came to his rescue:** "2 Feather Beds . . . with a Boulster + 1 Pillow, 3 Blanketts, 2 of which were Small + 1 Large." Lloyd charged Warren almost ten pounds for these items. James Lloyd, M.D., M.M.S., ledger, p. 40, Boston Medical Library, Francis A. Countway Library of Medicine.

64 **paid Richard Draper:** Ibid., p. 41. See *Boston Gazette*, December 6, 1762.

64 **thrust into a world of malaise:** John Adams to Abigail Smith, April 26, 1764, Adams Family Papers.

65 **He purchased goods and hired laborers:** Entries for Dr. Nathaniel Perkins and Dr. Samuel Gelston, Joseph Warren Medical Ledger, p. 15, Warren Papers. Warren used the washing services of Abigail Marshall

and her relatives, in addition to receiving "sundry other articles" between March 18 and December 18, 1764. See Warren Medical Ledger, p. 1:34.

65 **continued to make house calls:** See various entries in Vol. 1 of Warren's Medical Ledger, for visits he made outside the castle during the winter and spring of 1764 during the pox scourge.

65 **"Dr. Perkins demanded my left":** John Adams to Abigail Smith, April 13, 1764, Adams Family Papers. John was so worried about spreading the disease to his family that during his inoculation period he smoked the letters he wrote home.

65 **"Warren is a pretty, tall":** Ibid. This is the earliest surviving physical description of Warren.

65 **"Warren a dear friend of my father":** John Quincy Adams to Joseph Sturge draft letter, March 1846, Adams Family Papers. Ironically, as a result of a fall, Lloyd had one of his broken fingers amputated. See Cary, *Joseph Warren*, pp. 21–22.

66 **average recovery period:** *Boston Evening-Post,* June 25, 1764.

66 **"in the year 1764":** Eliot, *Biographical Dictionary*, p. 471.

66 **"voted unanimously":** *Boston Evening-Post*, May 28, 1764. While Warren provided fourteen free inoculations, Dr. Kast provided them to one hundred needy individuals.

66 **approximately five thousand people:** Although most survived the pox outbreak, the wife of patriot Oxenbridge Thacher succumbed to the disease. See Truax, *Doctors Warren of Boston*, p. 24.

66 **"town is now clear":** *Report of the Record Commissioners of the City of Boston*: Vol. 20, Boston, 1889, p. 76. There is no mention of the smallpox in any of the September 1764 entries of John Rowe's diary, which helps confirm the disease had run its course in Boston.

66 **Warren emerged as a new leader:** Eliot, *Biographical Dictionary*, p. 474.

66 **"The whole heavens seem'd to be":** *Boston Post-Boy,* July 9, 1764.

5

NEW BEGINNINGS

67 **"Doct. Joseph Warren, one of":** Henry Herbert Edes, *Memoir of Dr. Thomas Young, 1731–1777, Publications of the Colonial Society of Massachusetts,* 1906, Vol. 11, p. 8.

67 **bequeathed the lion's share:** *Boston Evening-Post,* June 4, 1764. Elizabeth's father, Richard Hooton, died May 29, 1764. He was initiated into St. John's Lodge on December 26, 1753. The Warren-Hooton wedding announcement appeared in the *Boston Post-Boy* and the *Boston Evening-Post* that same week. Elizabeth received the bulk of of her father's fortune, with the exception of over two hundred pounds sterling that Richard had left to a Miss Elizabeth Debuke, some "sundry Wearing Apparell" for his brother

John Hooton, the will's sole executor, expenses for the funeral, and payment for debts and various other expenses. In 1789, the location of Hooton's wharf was on the end of Fish Street. For Richard Hooton's probate will inventory, see Suffolk County Probate Records, pp. 68:508, 509. See also, *Boston News-Letter*, October 14, 1762.

67 **pecuniary gain:** Various historians have claimed that Warren married Elizabeth for her inheritance. But this hypothesis is belied by his engagement to Mercy Scollay years later, whose father, John Scollay, had experienced severe financial difficulties, resulting in bankruptcy in the mid-1760s. Also, in 1773, Warren and Elizabeth would give his brother Ebenezer much of the inherited property. *Boston Gazette*, September 10, 1764. Mercy also had many siblings, making any potential inheritance little more than a pittance.

68 **Congregational Church on Brattle Street:** Cooper, with his elevated family status, had ranked third in his Harvard class. His father also served as a preacher at the Brattle Street Church.

68 **Portuguese coin:** Cary, *Joseph Warren*, p. 24. Several years later in 1769, Cooper would marry John Singleton Copley and his bride Sukey Clarke. Warren and Copley were involved in similar social circles.

68 **much dancing and feasting:** Many wedding celebrations and dances took place even within colonial Boston. For one example, see Rowe, *Diary of John Rowe*, p. 119.

68 **"for encouraging the Soldiery":** Samuel Cooper to Benjamin Franklin, August 15, 1774, in National Archives.

68 **"men are born equal and free":** Cooper, *Sermon on the Commencement*.

68 **"no man could, with a better grace":** Oliver, *Origins and Progress*, pp. 43n34, 44–45.

68 **among the most ardent patriots:** Loring, *Hundred Boston Orators*, p. 48; See Joseph Warren Estate Inventory, Suffolk County Probate Records, p. 76:648.

69 **back in Roxbury:** Entry for Samuel Sumner, September 11, 1763, Warren Medical Ledger, Warren Papers.

69 **he continued to help his family run the farm:** Entry for Samuel Warren, Warren Medical Ledger, Warren Papers.

69 **Sugar Act:** In Britain the act was known as the American Revenue Act.

69 **reduced duties on molasses:** The duty on foreign molasses was halved, making it cheaper for distilleries to produce rum.

70 **"new taxations upon us":** Boston, *Report of the Record Commissioners*, pp. 121–22.

70 **"The Black Act takes place this day":** Rowe, *Diary of John Rowe*, p. 64. Negative connotations associated with the word *black* were prevalent in early New England, as witness the Black Act, the Black Regiment, Black Magic. Rowe's diary is one of the few surviving primary sources documenting events in Boston, almost daily, for more than a decade providing a rare glimpse into that world. However, the published editions of Rowe's

diary don't contain the entire text. Also, later on, Rowe altered at least one entry to seem more patriotic.

71 **"set people a thinking":** *The Rights of the British Colonies Asserted and Proved* (Boston, 1764), p. 54.

71 **a young boy was killed:** Entry for November 5, 1764, in Rowe, *Diary of John Rowe.* That day Warren treated several patients; see entries for James Allen, Andrew Oliver Esq., Capt. Duncan Ingraham, and Mr. Joshua Blanchard. Entry for November 6, 1764, Joseph Warren Medical Ledger, Warren Papers. This was the last time Warren treated Oliver, according to his surviving journals.

72 **"During these commotions":** Gage to Conway, January 16, 1765, in *Correspondence of General Gage,* pp. 1:80–81.

72 **"nerves much disordered":** For hatters, consistent exposure to mercury vapors usually led to mercury poisoning, which caused hallucinations and muscular tremors, consistent with Warren's diagnosis.

72 **"this laudable example":** Joseph Warren Medical Ledger, Warren Papers. Entries for his grandfather, Capt. Samuel Stevens, occured on October 3, 4, 5, 6, 7, 8, 26, 27, 28, 29, 30, 31, and November 1, 2, 1764; *Boston Evening-Post,* November 12, 1764.

73 **the core members:** See Warren Medical Ledgers, Vols. 1, 2, Warren Papers, for the entries mentioned above.

73 **"reducing [resetting] her shoulder":** Entry for Moorfield, "To Reducing Bone for Wife," September 7, 1774, Joseph Warren Medical Ledger, Warren Papers.

73 **"opening tumor[s]":** Entry for Capt. Deming, Joseph Warren Medical Ledger, Vol. II, Warren Papers.

73 **experimented with new treatments:** That Warren was experimenting with new treatments is evident from one of his journal entries from 1771. Thanks to Sharon Cotner from the Gualt Apothecary shop in Colonial Williamsburg. Information was also gleaned from part of Warren's ledger in possession of the author.

73 **"now first in business":** Edes, p. 8.

73 **"The remainder given":** Joseph Warren Medical Ledger, Warren Papers.

6

ACTS OF VIOLENCE

74 **house calls proved difficult:** Joseph Warren Medical Ledger, Warren Papers. The ledger lists many instances of Warren making house calls during the frigid months of January and February 1765.

74 **Freezing temperatures:** *Boston News-Letter,* January 17, 1765.

75 **"the ink freezes as I write":** Rowe, *Diary of John Rowe,* p. 75.

75 **sum of 1,150 pounds:** James Lloyd Medical Ledger, Harvard Countway Library of Medicine.

75 **behaved traitorously:** Wheelwright even sued two military officers for libel over accusations of treason and malfeasance against his country. James Otis defended the officers, who were ultimately assessed exorbitant fines, when the court ruled in favor of Wheelwright.

75 **rumors of his financial distress:** Hamilton, "Robert Hewes and the Frenchmen," pp. 195–210.

75 **owed more money:** Wheelwright died the following year in 1766. John Scollay, the father of Warren's future fiancée, Mercy Scollay, did not abscond but instead remained in Boston and auctioned off his personal possessions to pay his creditors. See entry for January 19, 1765, Rowe, *Diary of John Rowe*, p. 74. In addition to his "valuable Articles," Scollay sold two of his personal slaves. "Very bad accts Mr John Scollay shut up . . . Am like to be a large sufferer by Scollay"; *Boston Post-Boy*, November 18, 1765. See *Boston Post-Boy*, November 18, 1765.

76 **effects of the financial meltdown:** Rowe also mentioned the bankruptcies of John Dennie, Peter Bourne, Wm Haskings & Co., and Joseph Scot. See his diary pp. 74–75.

76 **"horror and dread":** James Otis to George Johnstone, et al., Boston January 25, 1765, *Massachusetts Historical Society Proceedings* 43 (1909–10): 205.

76 **remained blank:** Various entries for 1764–68, Warren Medical Ledger, Warren Papers.

76 **"all the edifices and buildings":** Warren to Bowes, Suffolk County Deeds, July 24, 1765, pp. 105:18–19 and 107:86–88. They borrowed 656 pounds 13 shillings and 4 pence from Bowes and 133 pounds from Hancock.

76 **"the Westerly part of Boston":** Warren to Campbell, Suffolk County Probate Records, p. 106:61. The land was described as being "Easterly on Spring Street there measuring Forty feet, South on land of Knight Leverett there measuring Eighty five feet, Westerly on land of Josias Byles there measuring Forty feet, Northerly on land of Joseph (R)icks there measuring Eighty five feet." The property was described "as of a good Estate of Inheritance." Likely, it was a piece of land that Elizabeth inherited from her father. Richard Hooton's will, Suffolk County Probate Records, p. 63:392, refers to "a piece of land at New Boston" valued at twenty pounds. New Boston was also known as West Boston.

76 **Andrew Campbell:** Warren had other dealings with Campbell over the years. In 1768 Campbell paid Warren notes for the settlement of the Wheelwright estate totaling 30 pounds 18 shillings. Campbell also paid Warren 10 pounds 14 shillings for part of a piece of land in 1767. Additionally, Warren had an account with Campbell for which he owed him 2 pounds 16 shillings between June 21, 1770, and September 25, 1771. See Estate of Doct Joseph Warren Deces'd to And'w Campbell, Ch. M.2.3.929, settled May 7, 1783, Rare Manuscripts Division, Boston Public Library.

77 **"to unite in a Petition":** *Boston Gazette*, July 8, 1765.

78 **Loyal Nine:** The group's nine original members were likely Henry Bass, a cousin of Samuel Adams, Benjamin Edes the printer, George Trott a

jeweler, Joseph Field a ship captain, Thomas Crafts a painter, distillers Thomas Chase and John Avery, and braziers Stephen Cleverly and John Smith. Two possible lists of members exist.

78 **friends, Masonic brothers, and patients:** Zobel, *Boston Massacre*, p. 38.

78 **"seem'd to touch":** Stoll, *Samuel Adams*, p. 42.

78 **jackboot with a green sole:** The boot symbolized former Prime Minister Lord Bute and the green sole represented Prime Minister George Grenville.

78 **marched to Andrew Oliver's house:** Rowe, *Diary of John Rowe*, p. 89.

79 **Governor Bernard fled:** Castle William was where Loyalist refugees would later seek safety from Whig violence real and imagined.

79 **The mob broke the windows:** *Boston Gazette*, October 21, 1765. The article listed the notes and treasurer receipts taken from Hallowell's property "to acquaint the Possessor or Possessors, that they will be of no use to them payment being immediately stopped."

79 **"nothing remaining but":** George Pomeroy Anderson, "Ebenezer MacKintosh: Stamp Act Rioter and Patriot," *Publications of the Colonial Society of Massachusetts* 26 (1927): 33.

79 **Mackintosh as the suspected ringleader:** "Capt. McKintosh & others tried before Mr. Justice Dana & Justice Storey for the 5 of Nov. affair." Rowe, *Diary of John Rowe*, p. 76; *The Correspondence of General Thomas Gage with the Secreteries of State, 1763–1775* (New Haven, 1931), pp. 1, 79.

80 **"merchants in general":** Gage to Conway, December 21, 1765, in *Correspondence of General Gage*, p. 1:79; Fischer, *Paul Revere's Ride*, p. 38.

80 **at least four patients:** On August 26, Warren saw as patients Mrs. Soper (he extracted a tooth for a boy at another location but entered the service under Soper's account), Samuel Pemberton, Ebenezer Seaver, and Mrs. Mary Minot. He also loaned cash to Minot. Warren Medical Ledger, Warren Papers.

80 **"to suppress the like disorders":** *Boston Evening-Post*, September 2, 1765.

80 **"the town remained the whole night":** *Boston Post-Boy*, November 11, 1765. Prior to the rioting a boy was killed in the South End when a wagon wheel crushed his skull.

81 **"wooden horse":** Hoerder, *Crowd Action*, pp. 51, 207.

81 **tarring and feathering:** This was the act of forcibly pouring boiling hot tar over an individual—either over clothing or directly on the flesh—covering them with feathers, then parading them through the streets in humiliation.

81 **"We endeavor to keep":** Henry Bass to Samuel P. Savage, December 19, 1765, in *Proceedings of the Massachusetts Historical Society* 44 (1911): 689.

81 **rejoined St. Andrew's Lodge:** The lodge had purchased the Green Dragon Tavern, which became a center of revolutionary activity for the next decade. The Green Dragon was advertised as having "a very large convenient Chamber, suitable for a Fire Club, or other societies." *Boston Gazette*, September 7, 1761.

81 **"grievous and unconstitutional Tax"**: As was the custom of the times, authors used pen names (like "B.W.") to mask their identity.

82 **"Never has there been"**: Warren to Edmund Dana, March 19, 1766, in Frothingham, *Life and Times*, p. 22. News from Britain took at least six weeks to reach the colonies by sea. The day before he wrote this letter, unknown to Warren, Parliament had repealed the Stamp Act.

83 **dismissed George Grenville**: Grenville had tried to prevent the king's mother being named regent if her son became unfit to fulfill his duties.

83 **frame the repeal in terms**: R. Baldwin, "An authentic Copy of Lord CHATHAM's proposed Bill, entitled A Provisional Act for settling the Trouble in AMERICA, and for asserting the Supreme Legislative Authority and superintending Power of GREAT-BRITAIN over the COLONIES." *London Magazine, Or, Gentlemen's Monthly Intelligencer*, January 1, 1775, p. 44:71.

83 **"hushed into silence"**: Entry for November 11, 1766, in John Adams, *Diary*, Adams Family Papers.

84 **"designed by this act"**: Warren to Dana, March 19, 1766.

84 **"such a supposition"**: Bailyn, *Ideological Origins*, p. 101. Three groups comprised the Whig Party: conservatives, moderates, and radicals, of which the latter constituted the minority in the 1760s.

84 **"power-hungry cabal"**: Bailyn, *Ideological Origins*, pp. 150–51.

84 **"Independence, it is true"**: Oliver, *Origins and Progress*, p. 148.

85 **"The revolution was in the minds"**: Adams to Jefferson, August 24, 1815, in National Archives.

86 **Sam Adams would not become one of Dr. Warren's patients**: In contrast to the many misspelled words and sloppy handwriting in many diaries, account books, and letters of the time, Warren's first medical ledger reveals beautiful penmanship and meticulous spelling. Misspelled words are few and far between. Therefore it is curious that when Warren entered Samuel Adams's name in his ledger for the first time, he misspelled the surname as "Adames." Since claims abound that Adams was Warren's mentor, it's hard to believe that Warren would misspell the name of his mentor. While pure conjecture, the spelling could indicate that in 1768 Warren was on more of an equal footing with Adams than most historians have realized, or perhaps that the two were not as close as has been asserted. It could also have been a simple oversight on Warren's part. Entry for Samuel Adams, Joseph Warren Medical Ledger, Warren Papers.

86 **"fortune was equal to his"**: Letter from William Palfrey to John Wilkes, Oct. 21, 1769, *Proceedings of the Massachusetts Historical Society* 47 (1913–14): 211.

86 **"subscribers towards Mr. Adams's debt"**: "Notes on Ante-Revolutionary Currency and Politics," *New England Historical and Genealogical Register* (1860): 14:261–62.

86 **donation of over thirteen pounds**: Warren had failed to pay the annual rent of 24 pounds on the building he leased for his office in 1765. He also made a purchase in July 1765 for "cloathes." Estate of Dr. Joseph Warren

to O. Wendell, Rare Manuscript Division, Boston Public Library. And in May 1766, he sold a half-acre of his land in Roxbury lying "easterly eight rods by the public road leading to Braintree" to John Cheesman for just over thirteen pounds. Suffolk County Probate Records, pp. 108:212–13. Warren likely used the money from the sale to assist Adams.

86   **vengeful political charlatan and freeloader:** The Loyalist supporter Peter Oliver observed that Samuel Adams "with his oily tongue had duped a man [John Hancock] whose brains were shallow and his pockets deep, and ushered him to the public as a patriot too: He filled his head with importance and emptied his pockets." The statement is a somewhat bitter exaggeration, but Adams did rely upon the financial assistance of others on several occasions. See Oliver, *Origins and Progress,* p. 164. Also of note, Adams was given a large loan by his father, which he lost after making bad financial decisions.

87   **"a curious employment":** Entry for September 6, 1769, John Adams, *Diary and Autobiography,* ed. Butterfield.

87   **"If the Devil himself were":** Zobel, *Boston Massacre,* p. 110.

87   **"the happiness of this province":** *Boston Gazette,* June 2, 1766.

88   **"in a state of insanity":** *Boston Gazette,* June 9, 1766.

88   **"worthless treacherous man":** *Boston Gazette,* June 16, 1766. Other "Paskalos" letters appeared in *Boston Gazette,* November 10 and December 8, 1766.

88   **alleged healing properties:** *Connecticut Courant,* June 30, 1855. The *Courant* also republished the original article from "the files of our old Connecticut Courant." (That article also appeared in *Newport Mercury,* August 18, 1766.) The 1855 *Courant* newspaper article paid homage to Warren, concluding that "Stafford Springs will seem more palatable from the fact that Warren drank from them."

88   **more "Yankee" than most:** Fischer, *Paul Revere's Ride,* pp. 10–12. See also Ms. N-1731, box 2, John Collins Warren Papers. Genealogical information is listed in folder 2. John Hancock spent time in London and attended the coronation ceremony of George III. Paul Revere's father was an immigrant from France. Dr. Benjamin Church studied medicine in London, where he met and married his wife. Josiah Quincy, Jr., traveled to London for health reasons and to connect with other patriot leaders and sympathizers. Dr. Thomas Young left Boston in 1774. William Molineux was born in England. Samuel and John Adams were delegates to the Continental Congress, spending extended periods of time in Philadelphia as crucial events unfolded in Massachusetts.

89   **Hutchinson appointed Warren:** That Hutchinson appointed Warren as the administrator indicates that Warren was a man of considerable standing within the community. In 1765, Charles Ward Apthorp was "trustee" for Wheelwright's estate. *Boston Gazette,* May 20, 1765, and *Boston Post-Boy,* September 16, 1765.

89   **Warren . . . was of no relation:** Why Hutchinson appointed Warren as administrator is somewhat puzzling. But in 1767, Warren was on good

terms with Hutchinson, who was also close to Dr. James Lloyd. This fact is amazing considering what the Whigs had done to Hutchinson in 1765. That Hutchinson sought Warren's allegiance is further supported by the fact that Warren would receive the coveted almshouse physician appointment in 1769. Also, in a private communication with J. L. Bell he offered an additional possibility that also makes sense: Wheelwright's principle creditor was Charles Ward Apthorp, whose main attorney was William Molineux. Thus Hutchinson choosing Warren to represent the Wheelwright estate might have put him at odds with another Whig activist.

89 **"all persons indebted":** Versions of this notice appeared in the *Boston Post-Boy,* May, 15, 29, August 21, 28, and September, 11, 1769; *Boston News-Letter,* August 17, 31, 1769; *Boston Chronicle,* August 10-14, 1769; *Boston Evening-Post,* September 4, 1769.

89 **"lasted four days":** *Boston Evening-Post,* December 18, 1769. *New York Gazette,* October 16, 1769.

7

UNSHEATH THY QUILL

90 **Joseph Warren, was baptized:** Church in Brattle Square, *Manifesto Church,* p. 184.

90 **notes and cash payments:** Warren likely used the money to pay off the debts on the farm mortgages he and Samuel had borrowed in 1765.

91 **"happy coalition":** Palmer et al., *St. Andrew's Lodge,* p. 270.

91 **largest number of mourners:** Rowe, *Diary of John Rowe,* p. 141.

91 **Miles Whitworth and Thomas Young:** Whitworth's first name is also spelled Myles in Boston Town Meeting records.

91 **"There is nothing in this account":** *Boston Gazette,* May 25, 1767.

92 **"I would just hint to you":** *Boston Gazette,* July 27, 1767.

92 **he could be fair and impartial:** Apparently the rift between Young and Warren had healed by 1771. That spring Young had Warren assist him in "the most diligent endeavor to free the bowels" of a sickly man. *Boston Evening-Post,* June 3, 1771.

92 **"for granting certain duties":** *Boston Evening-Post,* September 14, 1767. The Townshend Acts called for (1) an American import tax on paper, painter's lead, silk, glass and tea; (2) establishment of an American board of commissioners of the customs to supervise a tightened customs policy and oversee the collection of money (and enforce the acts without trial by jury); (3) revision of the vice-admiralty courts (which resolved disputes between merchants and seamen). The revenue raised was supposed to go to the salaries of colonial judges, governors, and other royal appointees—thus insulating them from local pressure. The writs of assistance were first introduced in Massachusetts in 1751 to enforce the Acts of Trade.

92 **"an imposition on America":** Rowe, *Diary of John Rowe,* 146.

92 **the nonimportation agreement garnered:** The subscription lists were

discovered by Karen Nipps, head of the Rare Book Cataloging Team at the Houghton Library in July 2012. Notable signatures included those of Paul Revere, John Rowe, William Dawes, Jr., John Scollay, Daniel Malcolm, Thomas Young, and John Gill. Also of interest are the numerous signatures of future Loyalists, such as Adino Paddock, but in 1767 that political boundary was not yet clearly defined.

93 **"an open opposition"**: Schlesinger, *Prelude to Independence*, p. vii.

93 **"To the memory of the glorious"**: Stoll, *Samuel Adams*, p. 69; Rowe, *Diary of John Rowe*, p. 167.

93 **"associations and assemblies"**: Hutchinson to Lord Hillsborough, October 19, 1769, *Atlantic Monthly*, Vol. 12, p. 600.

94 **a "herd of fools and knaves"**: Mein, *Sagittarius's Letters*, p. 58.

94 **"I was solicited to go"**: Frothingham, *Life and Times*, pp. 114–15, 51.

95 **"the man in whose fortunes"**: *Massachusetts Historical Society Proceedings* 47 (1913–14): 200.

95 **"men totally abandoned"**: *Boston Gazette*, February 29, 1768.

95 **"The liberty of the press"**: *Boston Gazette*, March 7, 1768.

95 **"to find all orders"**: *Boston Gazette*, March 14, 1768.

96 **"the iron rod of oppression"**: Letter from Joseph Warren to John Wilkes, April 13, 1769, *Massachusetts Historical Society Proceedings* 47 (1913–14): pp. 199–200.

96 **Hancock's sloop *Liberty* was seized:** The *Liberty* was towed by the fifty-gun British warship HMS *Romney*.

96 **"a great uproar"**: *The American Gazette*, London, 1770, pp. 449–50.

97 **Warren told Hallowell:** Cary, *Joseph Warren*, p. 76.

97 **"invaluable rights and liberties"**: Ibid., p. 78.

97 **more than two thousand soldiers:** The 14th and 29th Regiments from Halifax, and the 64th and 65th Regiments of Foot from Ireland were dispatched to Boston.

97 **gathered at their homes:** "From the year 1768, a number of politicians met at each other's houses to discuss publick affairs, and to settle upon the best methods of serving the town and country. Many of these filled publick offices. But the meetings were private, and had a silent influence upon the publick body." Eliot, *Biographical Dictionary*, p. 472.

98 **"We see Boston surrounded"**: Tudor, *Deacon Tudor's Diary*, pp. 27–28.

98 **"broke up and rushed"**: Cary, *Joseph Warren*, p. 83.

98 **"the king will reward"**: Gage to Dalrymple, September 25, 1768, Vol. 81, American Series, Gage Papers.

98 **burned his private papers:** Cary, *Joseph Warren*, pp. 80–83. When British troops marched on King Street to Boston Common on October 1, Warren treated a Miss Lucy Whitaker, and someone named White, who lived in Wing's Lane, among several other patients that day. See Joseph Warren Medical Ledger, Warren Papers.

98   **Green Dragon Tavern:** Palmer et al., *Lodge of St. Andrew,* p. 195.

99   **"grand master of Masons in Boston":** Ibid., p. 197.

99   **"the Barraks provided":** Tudor, *Deacon Tudor's Diary,* p. 28.

99   **"debauchery and licentiousness":** "Extract of a Letter from Boston," dated Dec. 22," *Boston News-Letter,* April 27, 1769.

99   **Richard Ames:** *Boston News-Letter,* November 3, 1769.

100 **"It is well known indeed":** Samuel Adams writing as "Vindex," *Boston Gazette,* December 24, 1770.

100 **"Disturbances . . . and some tumults":** *Essex Gazette,* June 20, 1769.

101 **"damn incendiary":** Rowe, *Diary of John Rowe,* p. 176.

101 **"the king had been graciously":** Nicolson, *"Infamas Govener,"* p. 203; *Boston Gazette,* August 7, 1769.

102 **"who not only deserted":** *New York Gazette,* October 16, 1769.

102 **"be looked upon with an eye":** *Boston Evening-Post,* August 14, 1769; *Boston Gazette,* August 14, 1769; *Essex Gazette,* June 20, 1769.

102 **"misrepresents me":** *Boston Gazette,* September 4, 1769.

102 **"The general cry":** *Essex Gazette,* September 12, 1769.

102 **fractured wrist:** Otis "received many very heavy blows on his head, and one particularly on his forehead, that instantly produced a copious discharge of blood." *Boston Post-Boy,* September 11, 1769.

102 **made him almost unrecognizable:** The British Coffee House stood opposite the Bunch of Grapes, a Whig tavern.

103 **torrential rains:** Rowe, *Diary of John Rowe,* p. 192.

103 **"behaved very madly":** Ibid., pp. 199, 201.

103 **"country for the recovery":** *Boston Evening-Post,* May 14, 1770.

103 **George Gailer, a sailor:** Gailer was associated with Hancock's sloop, *Liberty,* which customs officials had seized in 1768.

104 **"that people might see":** William Dunlap, *A History of New York, for Schools* (New York, 1837), p. 105. Peter Oliver explained the procedure for tarring and feathering: "First, strip a Person naked, then heat the Tar until it is thin, and pour it upon the naked Flesh, or rub it over with a Tar Brush, *quantum sufficit.* After which, sprinkle decently upon the tar, whilst it is yet warm, as many Feathers as will stick to it. Then hold a lighted Candle to the Feathers, and try to set it all on Fire, if it will burn so much the better. But as the Experiment is often made in cold Weather; it will not then succeed—take also an Halter, and put it round the Person's Neck, and then cart him the Rounds." Oliver, *Origins and Progress,* p. 94.

104 **"much terror":** Rowe, *Diary of John Rowe,* p. 194.

8
FROM RED FIELDS TO CRIMSON COBBLESTONES

105 **a song traditionally attributed to Warren:**

"A SONG ON LIBERTY"

THAT Seat of science, ATHENS, and Earth's great Mistress ROME,
   Where now are all their Glories, we scare can find their Tomb's
Then guard your Rights, AMERICANS! nor stoop to lawless Sway,
   Oppose, oppose, oppose, oppose,—my brave AMERICA.

Proud ALBION bow'd to *Caesar*, and num'rous *Lords* before,
   To *Picts*, to *Danes*, to *Normans*, and many Masters more:
But we can boast AMERICANS! we never fall a Prey:
   Huzza huzza huzza huzza for brave AMERICA!

We led fair FREEDOM hither, when lo the *Desart* smil'd,
   A Paradise of Pleasure, was open'd in the Wilds;
Your Harvest bold AMERICANS! no Power shall snatch away,
   Assert yourselves, yourselves, yourselves, my brave AMERICA.

Torn from a World of Tyrants, beneath this western Sky,
   We form'd a new Dominion, a *Land* of LIBERTY;
The World shall own their Masters here, then hasten on the Day,
   Huzza, huzza, huzza, huzza, for brave AMERICA.

GOD bless this maiden Climate, and thro' her vast Domain,
   Let Hosts of Heroes cluster, who scorn to wear a Chain:
And blast the venal Sycophant, who dare our Rights betray,
   Preserve, preserve, preserve, preserve my brave AMERICA.

Lift up your Heads my Heroes! and swear with proud Disdain,
   The Wretch who would enslave you, shall spread his Snares in vain;
Should EUROPE empty all her force, wou'd meet them in Array,
   And shout, and shout, and shout, and shout, for brave AMERICA.

Some future Day shall crown us, the Masters of the Main,
   And giving Laws and Freedom to subject FRANCE and SPAIN;
When all the ISLES o'er Ocean spread, shall tremble and obey,
   Their Lords, their Lords, their Lords, their Lords, of brave AMERICA.

See, *Printed Ephemera: Three Centuries of Broadsides and Other Printed Ephemera.*
Library of Congress, Rare Book and Special Collections Divisions. While
the song has been traditionally attributed to Warren, J. L. Bell located
copies of this "New Massachusetts Liberty Song" attributing Warren as
the author dating back to 1807 (within the lifetime of Warren's contemporaries and earlier than the previous available sources), thus making it all
the more likely that Warren indeed wrote the piece. I have been unable
to find any source document disputing or claiming someone other than

Warren to be the author of this version. After "The New Massachusetts Liberty Song" was first played at Concert Hall in Boston on February 13, 1770, it was later mentioned in the *Virginia Gazette,* January 1, 1774, and then in the *Massachusetts Spy* in May 1774.

106 **"highly proper that":** *Boston Gazette,* December 18, 1769.

107 **"cut slugs":** *Boston Evening-Post,* February 26, 1770.

107 **"his body was opened":** *Boston Evening-Post,* February 26, 1770.

107 **"wilfully and feloniously shot":** Zobel, *Boston Massacre,* p. 177.

107 **"the largest perhaps":** Ibid, p. 178.

108 **"The little corpse":** *Boston Gazette,* March 5, 1770.

108 **"stationed in our very bowels":** Adams, *Writings of Samuel Adams,* p. 1:392.

108 **"government here":** Dalrymple to Gage, October 28, 1769, Vol. 88, American Series, Gage Papers.

108 **"The people shouting, huzzaing":** *The Trial of the British Soldiers of the 29 Regiment of Foot . . .* (Boston, 1824), p. 99.

108 **firing into the crowd:** The five victims were Crispus Attucks, Samuel Gray, James Caldwell, Patrick Carr, and Samuel Maverick. Christopher Monk, the sixth and final victim, died in 1780 due to complications from his wounds.

108 **While some of the rioters dispersed:** Earlier in the day, Warren had been signing deeds with Benjamin Cudworth for property that was being mortgaged to them. See Thomas Hudson and Mary Carter mortgages to Benjamin Cudworth and Joseph Warren, Suffolk County Deeds, March 5, 1770. Thanks to J. L. Bell for sharing this source. Given that Warren was in Boston, he was certainly in the vicinity of King Street and if not present during the incident, would have been summoned in the massacre's immediate aftermath.

108 **an illuminated moon:** That evening was the first-quarter moon.

109 **"It is supposed":** *Boston Gazette,* March 12, 1770.

109 **slaughter in London:** "A more dreadful tragedy has been acted by the soldiery in King-Street, Boston . . . than . . . exhibited in St. George's Field, London." *Boston Gazette,* March 12, 1770.

110 **commemorative engraving:** The original engraving had been made by John Singleton Copley's half-brother, Henry Pelham. Revere copied that original and made several minor changes to Pelham's engraving to exaggerate the brutality of the British soldiers. Pelham then wrote a scathing letter to Revere: "When I heard that you was cutting a plate of the late Murder. I thought it impossible, as I knew you was not capable of doing it unless you coppied it from mine and as I thought I had entrusted it in the hands of a person who had more regard to the dictates of Honour and Justice than to take the undue advantage you have done of the confidence and trust I reposed in you. But I find I was mistaken . . . If you are insensible of the Dishonour you have brought on yourself by this Act, the World will not be so. However, I leave you to reflect upon and consider of one of the most dishonorable Actions you could well be guilty of." Copley and

Pelham, *Letters*, p. 83. Revere is best remembered for his engraving and for his midnight ride, but in both instances other men were responsible for instigating his actions.

110 **"the most important one ever":** James Bowdoin, Joseph Warren, Samuel Pemberton, *A Short Narrative of the Horrid Massacre in Boston*, Boston, 1770. Incredibly, in her seminal book, *The Boston Massacre*, Zobel never mentions Warren's involvement with the massacre narrative, attributing it solely to Bowdoin. See p. 213.

110 **"advised and urged":** *Josiah Quincy, Memoir of the Life of Josiah Quincy, Junior of Massachusetts Bay: 1744–1775*, Boston, 1875, pp. 27–28. Loyalist Robert Auchmuty was the senior defense council and Sampson Salters Blowers, a younger attorney, helped in the jury selection.

111 **"tarred and feathered in 1770":** *Mr. Parker Cooke's Book Before Commissioner Wilmot. Evidence in the Claim of Owen Richards, February 9, 1784*, Vol. 2 of *Ontario Archives Report Year 1904, Proceedings of the Loyalist Commissioners* (London, 1784), p. 1160.

111 **"There was a very great hallooing":** Rowe, *Diary of John Rowe*, p. 202.

111 **"Sunk down Speechless":** Colin Nicolson, "A Plan 'To Banish All the Scotchmen': Victimization and Political Mobilization in Pre-Revolutionary Boston," *Massachusetts Historical Review*, Vol. 9, 2007 p. 81.

111 **"the designs of particular persons":** Bailyn, *Ordeal of Hutchinson*, p. 164.

111 **"a motley rabble":** Smith, *John Adams*, p. 1:124.

112 **"intended to quit all":** Stoll, *Samuel Adams*, 95; Hosmer, *Life of Hutchinson*, p. 224.

112 **"Farewell, Politicks":** Entry for April 20, 1771, in John Adams, *Diary*, Adams Family Papers.

112 **to treat Christopher Monk:** Portion of Joseph Warren's missing Medical Ledger from 1771. Author's collection.

113 **"the more martial virtues":** Cary, *Joseph Warren*, p. 100.

113 **an annual oration:** On March 5, 1771, prior to Lovell's official commemorative massacre oration delivered on April 2, Dr. Thomas Young delivered a popular speech about the event at the Boston Manufactory House.

113 **"to revive the memory":** *Boston News-Letter*, February 21, 1771.

113 **"Seiders pale ghost":** *Boston Gazette*, March 11, 1771. The Seider display showed the young boy putting his finger into his fatal wound. Perhaps Revere intended to highlight Seider's martyrdom with a display similar to Caravaggio's *The Incredulity of St. Thomas*, which showed a "doubting" Thomas putting his finger into the wound of Jesus Christ. Revere's close relationship with artists like Copley and Pelham, together with his father's European background, make this scenario plausible, but it depends on what art would have been available in Boston.

114 **He understood the importance:** "Dr. Warren, whose popularity was increasing, undertook it." *Boston Evening-Post*, February 17, 1772. See also Loring, *Hundred Boston Orators*, p. 57.

114 **"the esteem and regard":** Eliot, *Biographical Dictionary*, p. 314.

114 **their third child, Mary:** The Warrens' daughter Mary was baptized at the Brattle Street Church on March 26, 1769. She had died by the time their next daughter was born; she was also named Mary and was baptized at the same church. Some histories incorrectly list March 26, 1769, as the baptism of Richard Hooton Warren, one of the couple's two sons, who was born in 1770. Mary very possibly died from a dysentery outbreak in 1769 that killed scores of Bostonians.

114 **"it was with much difficulty":** *Connecticut Journal*, March 9, 1772.

114 **"mighty revolutions":** Joseph Warren, *An Oration Delivered March 5th, 1772*, 2nd ed. Boston, 1772. Massachusetts Historical Society.

116 **"received the unanimous applause":** Frothingham, *Life and Times*, p. 178.

116 **"the fervor, which is":** Ibid, p. 178.

9

A TIME TO MOURN

117 **almshouse physician:** John Greenleaf, Waste Book 1766–1772, MSS. L80, Vol. 4, Greenleaf Papers. Greenleaf had Warren's almshouse account listed between May 5, 1769, and May 6, 1772.

117 **he made 730 visits:** Joseph Warren Medical Ledger, Warren Papers.

118 **"glazed":** Green, *Account of Percival and Ellen Green*, p. 62.

118 **"a Negro Boy":** Ibid., p. 61.

118 **property in West Boston:** Warren and Elizabeth purchased the land in West Boston "together with the Houses and all Buildings standing thereon" from Benjamin Leigh (a patient of Warren) and John Allman. It was situated "southerly on the land of Hugh McDaniel Deceas'd and there measures one hundred fifty nine feet; Westerly on Allen's Highway so called and there measures One hundred six feet: Northerly on Land of Nathaniel Cunningham Deceas'd, and there measures One hundred and thirty four feet, Easterly on Leverett's Street so called and there measures One hundred and fifty five feet." Warren and Elizabeth mortgaged the "House and Premises . . . as colateral security" for payment on the note.

For additional income, Warren leased a small property in New Boston to Richard Palmes for just over thirty pounds a year, from April 1771 through at least December 1772. When Palmes failed to pay the money he owed, Warren sued him for the eighteen months' back rent and the costs associated with the suit, which carried into February 1773. Suffolk County Court Records, pp. 603:111–13.

By December 24, 1778, Bowdoin had taken full possession of the West Boston property, which he then sold to Benjamin Goldthwaite, exactly a decade after the Boston Massacre on December 5, 1780. Folder 1738, Warren Papers.

118 **"2 elbow pieces, 1 draw":** Estate of Doc.t Joseph Warren Esq. to Wil-

liam Crafts, Ch.M.23.923, Rare Manuscript Division, Boston Public Library. Crickets were small wooden footstools. Thanks to Cary Carson, and Jeff Klee, at Colonial Williamsburg Foundation, for their assistance with this term.

119 **lead, "blew" and olive:** "The Estate of Doc.t Joseph Warren Esq. to Sam Harris," Miscellaneous, p. 943, Rare Manuscript Division, Boston Public Library.

119 **carpets were so expensive:** Carpets in eighteenth-century America were items of extreme luxury.

119 **eight-day mahogany clock:** It has been claimed that "the clock's provenance before 1873" is undocumented, as "no receipt or inventory spells out its connection to Warren." See Newell, Stelling, and Swanson, *Curiosities of the Craft*, p. 221. But Willard had engraved his own name, place of manufacture (Roxbury), and the number 228 on the clock's face. The number helped experts narrow the date of manufacture to 1772–74. The clock passed to Warren's brother, Ebenezer, and remained in the possession of the family until 1872. It was then removed from the house in Foxborough and was purchased by the Grand Lodge of Massachusetts on August 29, 1873. *Springfield Republican*, December 17, 1872. Today the clock is on display at the Scottish Rite Masonic Museum and Library in Lexington, Massachusetts. The *Springfield Republican* article is proof that the clock belonged to Joseph Warren.

120 **eight-day clocks, were expensive:** Eight-day clocks had to be wound every eight days and were more expensive than thirty-hour clocks, which had to be wound every day.

120 **several paintings:** Many decades later the paintings and the grandfather clock were nearly destroyed by two separate house fires, but were fortunately saved, although at the cost of a servant boy's life. Previous historians were unable to pinpoint the "family fire," only alluding to it in vague terms. Here is what we know.

After the deaths of Elizabeth and Joseph, the paintings came into the possession of Dr. John Warren. By the time General Warren's youngest daughter, Mary, married her second husband, Judge Richard English Newcomb, her uncle John Warren had already given her the paintings, since she was the only surviving child at the time of the marriage. See entries for October 1851, John Collins Warren Journal, John Collins Warren Papers.

After Mary's death in 1826, the paintings remained in the parlor of the Newcomb family. Mary's only surviving son, Joseph Warren Newcomb, inherited them, along with other Warren family heirlooms after his father, Judge Richard English Newcomb, passed away. "Judge Newcomb in his will refers to the portraits . . . as the property of his son, Joseph Warren Newcomb." See Thompson, *History of Greenfield*, p. 2:1036. (Other existing Warren artifacts are his medicine chest, dressing table, and candle stand, which are in possession of current Joseph Warren descendants.)

Joseph Warren Newcomb married Sarah Wells Alvord on October 3, 1830, and they had two children. Sarah died on March 6, 1836. The paintings remained in the possession of the Alvord family, who suffered two ruinous fires. The first occurred on December 22, 1847: "The house of the late Elijah Alvord [Sarah Wells Alvord Newcomb's father] was destroyed by fire." Thompson, *History of Greenfield Shire Town*, p. 1:329. The second fire, in 1856, likely caused by a "defect in the chimney," destroyed most of Joseph Warren's remaining papers and heirlooms, "but a small portion of the contents of the dwelling were salvaged." Fortunately the paintings were retrieved: "The portrait of Gen Joseph Warren, which was highly valued by the family, was saved by Major Reed." The fire claimed the life of a servant: "A little colored boy, named Charles Taylor, living in the family of Mrs. Alvord, perished in the flames. He was once in a place of safety, but during the hurry and confusion it is supposed he went back into the building to save some of the clothing (among other items) and was suffocated by the smoke." *Springfield Republican*, January 11, 1856.

The fires devastated the Alvords financially, and Sarah's brother Daniel wrote to General Warren's great-nephew, Dr. J. Mason Warren, offering to sell him both portraits for $1,700 so they could remain in the Warren family. See Daniel W. Alvord to Dr. J Mason Warren, January 20, 1857, John Collins Warren Papers. Two years before, Alvord had written to a Mr. Thompson offering to sell both paintings for $5,000. The letter was forwarded to Dr. John Collins Warren, who offered $2,500 for the pair or $100 "for the lady." Entry for March 10, 1856, John Collins Warren Journal. Prior to that, in 1851, Alvord had written to Dr. John Collins Warren offering to sell the paintings for a total of $1,500. Entry for October 20, 1851, John Collins Warren Journal.

The paintings returned to the Warren family, and by the latter half of the nineteenth century they were in the possession of Dr. Buckminster Brown and his wife, Sarah Alvord Brown—cousins and Warren descendants. Sarah was a direct descendant of Gen. Joseph Warren, and Buckminster Brown was a lineal descendant of Dr. John Warren. They married in 1864. Upon their deaths, he in 1891 and she in 1895, the Warren painting and the Elizabeth Hooton paintings were donated to the Boston Museum of Fine Arts, where they reside today. See Buckminster Brown's will, Suffolk County Probate Records, pp. 653:7–9.

At this writing, the trusteeship has passed to Carolyn M. Matthews, M. D. The Daniel Alvord letter is significant because it helps prove that Elizabeth Hooton's painting was painted not by Copley, as scholars and historians believed for centuries, but by Henry Pelham, Copley's half-brother. Alvord explicitly wrote that Copley had painted Joseph Warren and "that of Madame [Elizabeth] Warren by Pelham in my possession." Since Alvord's sister had married General Warren's grandson and both families had been close both politically and socially in Greenfield for decades, these facts would have been known by both families. Copley scholar Jules Prown reexamined the Hooton painting and suggested it might have been painted by someone other than Copley. The Alvord letter helps prove that theory correct, identifying the true artist as Henry Pelham.

120 **Copley portrait:** The painting, like its subject, remains steeped in intrigue. The oils have cracked with age, fabricating a puzzle that must be pieced

together, and the glossy facade creates a dichotomy of space and time, separating the eighteenth-century doctor from his present-day audiences. But looking beyond the surface, Warren and his colonial world become tangible. The meaning of the doctor's facial expression remains elusive—one might even call it a *Mona Lisa* smile. Initially, his gaze appears steady, without any trace of emotion. But as one looks more closely, the right side of Warren's mouth seems to crease into a grin of sorts, or perhaps a smirk.

Copley scholars disagree as to the portrait's date—some claim it was painted in 1764, while others date it as late as 1774, the year of Copley's permanent departure to London. It is unlikely that the painting was created after 1772, given Warren's hectic schedule and the vitriol between himself and Copley's family. Particularly damaging to the relationship between the families was the incident on the wharf involving the merchant Richard Clarke (Copley's father-in-law) and the rift between Copley's half-brother Henry Pelham and Warren's close friend Paul Revere regarding the Boston Massacre engraving. Most likely the painting was completed in the early 1770s.

120 **"the best works":** Flexner, *John Singleton Copley,* inscription.

120 **he would deliver Copley's son:** Copley's son became Lord Lyndhurst in Britain; see *Age* (Philadelphia), October 31, 1863.

121 **black broadcloth coat:** Black was the traditional color worn by doctors, particularly in Europe. Warren's coat is mentioned in his estate inventory. Suffolk County Courthouse Records, p. 76:647.

121 **grisly amputations:** In 1847 Warren's nephew would help introduce anesthesia to the world.

121 **sumptuary laws:** Sumptuary laws were "made for the purpose of restraining luxury or extravagance, particularly against inordinate expenditures in the matter of apparel, food, furniture, etc." *Black's Law Dictionary,* 6th ed. (1999), p. 1436. According to at least one contemporary, the colonists in Boston were notorious for their bad teeth, which may help explain the lack of smiling in their portraits.

121 **a bucolic scene:** Like the symbolism of the pillar and fabrics, the outside view was likely a representation, not based on an actual scene.

121 **It appears smooth:** Shaving was an important part of a gentleman's grooming: "Did not go to church this forenoon occasioned by the barber not coming to shave me." Entry for September 23, 1764, Rowe, *Diary of John Rowe,* p. 63. Copley usually painted his sitter's imperfections, including warts, moles, and birthmarks, so we may assume that Warren's portrait accurately represents his appearance.

121 **bathing was generally limited:** Most days colonists would "sponge themselves down," using a small washbasin or shaving bowl, rather than take a full-immersion bath, which some peruke shops provided. An advertisement for a "cold bath" appeared in the June 20, 1763, issue of *Boston Gazette.* Many stores advertised diverse soaps. These facts help dispel modern notions that the colonists were consistently foul smelling or dirty from a lack of bathing and washing.

121 **heavy nasal twang:** The twang can be inferred from the way he spelled certain words, such as "mahagany" for *mahogany*. Joseph Warren Medical Ledgers, Warren Papers.

122 **"a pretty, tall, genteel":** John Adams to Abigail Smith, April 13, 1764, Adams Family Papers, MHS.

122 **"the ladies pronounced":** The average height of men in colonial times was somewhere between five-seven and five-eight—only slightly shorter than today's average. Gordon, *Rise, Progress, and Establishment*, p. 1:357.

122 **Peruke shops:** John Piemont and John Haslett were two peruke makers in Boston. See their advertisements in *Boston Evening-Post*, February 18, 1760, and *Boston Post-Boy*, May, 19, 1760.

122 **his pigeon-winged wig:** White wigs were formal. For a custom fit, a head would usually be shaved. The styles were designed so that one could wear a cocked hat. Wigs had to be maintained, an additional expense—they had to be washed, combed, stiffened, and then curled with heating irons and hairpins. That Warren owned a wig is shown in Copley's painting, He also wore a wig at the Battles at Lexington and Concord, where a bullet that grazed the side of his head shot a hairpin.

122 **indicative of social standing:** Likely, Warren's wig was made from human hair. Town doctors often wore a wig called a "frizzed bob" or a "physical bob" that came in different colors; its short fluffy curls appeared more like a modern-day afro. Warren wore wigs throughout his life, which was also a testament to his high, formal position in society as a doctor and Whig leader. At a minimum, wigs cost at least around 2 pounds 3 shillings, the equivalent of a month's wages for a typical laborer. Depending on the type, a wig could cost upward of twenty pounds, making it an expensive indulgence. Usually wigs worn by magistrates were the priciest.

122 **ostentatious carriage:** Warren owned several horses and in 1774 accepted "one saddle and bridle . . . in payment of part of a debt." Ms. N-1731, 1774 folder, John Collins Warren Papers.

122 **"At the Sign of the Golden Key":** Ch.M.2.3.863 document, Boston Public Library; *Boston News-Letter*, July 10, 1760. Many thanks to Dr. Kimberly Alexander for conversations on eighteenth-century clothing and Warren's wardrobe as well as additional information about Abraham.

123 **decisive measures:** In a 1771 series of inflammatory articles, one in particular that referred to Governor Hutchinson as "a monster" and "USURPER," were published in the *Massachusetts Spy*, under the pseudonym, Mucius Scaevola. Questions surrounding the identity of the author have long been debated. Some claim the author to be Joseph Greenleaf and others claim it to be Warren. Evidence points in favor of Greenleaf, not Warren. For a detailed explanation of Greenleaf authorship, see J. L. Bell's blog for December 13, 2017. For the particular article mentioned above see, *Massachusetts Spy*, November 14, 1771.

123 **"agreed who should be":** Eliot, *Biographical Dictionary*, pp. 472–73.

124 **"attest how large a credit":** Frothingham, *Life and Times*, p. 190.

124 **"Above all things, I must avoid"**: Entry for November 21, 1772, in John Adams, *Diary*, Adams Family Papers.

124 **"rather a cautious man"**: Frothingham, *Life and Times*, p. 219.

125 **"doctrine of independence"**: Thomas Hutchinson to Richard Jackson, December 8, 1772, in *Hutchinson Letter Books*, p. 27:431, Massachusetts Archives.

125 **"Head of Wing's-Lane"**: *Boston Gazette*, May 23, 1757. Previous scholarship has asserted that on the night of April 18, 1775, Warren dispatched Paul Revere on his midnight ride from the house he was renting from the Green family on Hanover Street.

My research disproves this assertion. In fact, Warren lived in two different houses on Hanover Street, and Warren dispatched Revere from a home he was renting from Peter Chardon, years after he left the Green property.

Back in 1734, Joshua Green had purchased a house and property on Hanover Street on three-quarters of an acre, from Governor Belcher for 3,600 pounds (Belcher Esq. to Green, Suffolk County Deeds, p. 50:113). This was the Green house.

Meanwhile in August 1747 Benjamin Colman purchased a different but adjacent house on Hanover Street from his father, John Colman, for "five shillings" (Colman to Colman, Suffolk County Deeds, p. 74:49). This house "front[ed] south easterly on Hanover Street and there measuring thirty seven feet south westerly on the land of Joseph Green" (Peter Chardon's will and a rent receipt). In 1752 Peter Chardon purchased this house from Benjamin Colman (Colman to Chardon, Suffolk County Deeds, p. 80:159). This was the Chardon house. They shared a boundary line; see copy of Peter Chardon's will in Joseph Warren Papers.

Joseph Warren lived in both houses on Hanover Street, at different times.

In 1770 he began renting the Green house and stayed there at least until December 31, 1771. He rented not only the house but its furnishings. In January 1772, he purchased an item of furniture—"a lolling chair" for 3 pounds and 12 shillings. Green, *Account of Percival and Ellen Green*, p. 51. It is unlikely that Warren would have purchased an item of furniture from Green while still renting furnishings and space from Green. I can find no evidence that he lived in the Green house beyond January 1772.

After he left the Green property in January 1772, Warren could have moved from the Green property into his house in West Boston. But Richard Palmes rented that house from April 16, 1771, through at least December 16, 1772, so Warren was unlikely to have gone there, especially considering that a large-scale renovation was occurring at that time. He most likely moved to the Chardon house. See Green, *Account of Percival and Ellen Green*, p. 62.

He definitely lived in Chardon's house between November 2, 1774, and April 1775. It was large enough to accommodate his family and his medical practice and its location adjacent to the Green house enabled a quick and smooth transition while he remained in a area familiar to his clientele.

He rented the Chardon house for just over 53 pounds a year as compared to the 40 pounds he paid to Green in December 1771. Chardon rent receipt, Ch.M.2.3.859, Boston Public Library; Green, *Account of Percival and Ellen Green*, p. 62. When his estate was being settled in 1783, Warren still owed more than one hundred pounds for the Chardon rental.

Warren was living at the Chardon house on the evening of April 18, 1775, when he dispatched Revere. He left to fight in the Battles of Lexington and Concord, in the next days, and did not return.

Both properties soon changed hands. In October 1772, the Green family sold the property to John Hancock (a "parcel of Land situate in Hanover Street . . . containing by estimation three quarters of an acre more or less butted + bounded as follows . . . towards the northeast on land late of John Coleman Esq. deceased now of Peter Chardon Esq. and in the possession of Moses Gill." Green to Hancock Esq., Suffolk County Deeds, pp. 122:104–5).

As for the Chardon house, in 1778 Chardon conveyed it and the land to his daughter, Sarah. In May 1794, that house ("a large brick building on Hanover St. + bounded W. by land of Gov. Hancock") was sold to a Lydia Osborne, for 1,350 pounds. She became a member of the Boardman family. According to Clough's 1798 Atlas, the Boardman family had two lots on Hanover at the head of Wing's Lane and off the corner of Cold Lane (also known as Portland Street as seen by the Rev. Colman's 1747 purchase).

In 1835, the old Green house property ("on the north side of Hanover Street, west of Portland Street.") became the site of a new hotel, American House. Thwing, *Crooked and Narrow Streets*, pp. 84–85. American House stood on the corner of Hanover and Portland streets (Cold Lane) and had three storefronts on the ground level; 38, 40, and 44 Hanover Street. The entrance to American House was 42.

In 1844, during a Whig convention held in Boston, a large banner was displayed in Hanover Street that read, "The residence of Dr. Joseph Warren, quitted by him forever on April 19, 1775, to take part in the battle of Lexington." See *American and Commercial Daily Advertiser* (Baltimore), September 23, 1844.

From 1837 to 1874, the proprietor of the American House was Lewis Rice. In 1849 Rice bought the old Chardon property, next door to American House, from the Boardmans. He had the house demolished in order to renovate and expand American House over that property. The hotel was "rebuilt, enlarged and elegantly furnished." That expansion was completed in 1851.

Now American House stood on both properties where Warren had lived. See lithographs of American House by Pendleton's Lithography, http://catalog.bostonathenaeum.org/vwebv/holdingsInfo?bibId=414126, and John Henry Bufford, http://catalog.bostonathenaeum.org/vwebv/holdingsInfo?bibId=419990.

In 1898, State Society of the Sons of the American Revolution placed a small bronze tablet above the entrance of American House. The inscription, which informed passersby that the site was formerly the home of Gen. Joseph Warren, was written by Dr. Samuel A. Green, a Green family descendant, physician, historian, and twenty-eighth mayor of Boston. See *New York Tribune*, April 6, 1898. American House closed in 1916 but reopened in 1918. It was eventually razed. Prior to its destruction, its precious "relics" were auctioned but fetched little interest and even less money. See *Boston Herald*, August 1935. The John F. Kennedy Federal Building now stands on the site of the former American House.

125 **The Chardon house was close:** Green, *An Account of Percival and Ellen Green*, pp. 51–52, 61–63.

125 **"appointing him Grand Master":** Palmer et al., *Lodge of St. Andrew*, p. 37; Warren's youngest brother John eventually served as Grand Master of St. Andrews, when that lodge joined with St. John's Lodge, forming the Massachusetts Grand Lodge.

125 **he granted charters:** *Boston News-Letter*, April 3, 1772.

125 **"in procession from":** Palmer et al., *Lodge of St. Andrew*, p. 199.

126 **initials J A to J W:** The porringer handle remains in the possession of Warren's direct descendants. I was fortunate to visit the family compound and view several Warren family heirlooms.

126 **bracelet made from his hair:** *New-Bedford Mercury*, July 26, 1857.

126 **"free will and accord":** Suffolk County Courthouse, *Warren to Warren*, Vol. 133, pp. 209–10. For the sum of twenty shillings Joseph and Elizabeth gave Ebenezer Warren "One half of a Wharf at the North part of said Boston commonly known by the name of Hootons Wharf." April 10, 1773.

127 **"If fading Lilies, when":** *Boston Gazette*, May 3, 1773.

127 **a gold mourning ring:** "The outer rim of the ring is chased in black and bears this inscription: 'E. Warren, obt. 27 Apr. 1773, aet 26,'" *Providence Evening Press*, June 14, 1875.

128 **Mourning jewelry was quite popular:** I believe that this also helps disprove assertions that Warren married Elizabeth for pecuniary gain. The ring has never before been known to historians, and current direct Warren family members were unaware of its existence. Many thanks to Janine Skerry and Corinne Brandt from the Colonial Williamsburg Foundation for sharing their knowledge of mourning jewelry with me. Also, private conversations with Jessica Regan from the Metropolitan Museum of Art and Phyllis Magidson from the Museum of the City of New York were helpful in uncovering additional information about the mourning ring.

128 **Warren's mourning ring:** Sadly, the Warren's two eldest children, Elizabeth and Joseph, would have scant memories of their mother as they matured into adults, and Richard and Mary, the couple's youngest son and daughter, age three and one, respectively, would have almost no recollection of their mother as they grew up.

128 **Warren, now thirty-one:** The extreme lack of primary source documents regarding Warren and his children has led to past historians miscalculating the number of children he had. See French, *First Year*.

129 **"upon an especial occasion":** Palmer et al., *Lodge of St. Andrew*, p. 199.

129 **Both men had lost their fathers:** Warren was fourteen when his father died in 1755. Revere was nineteen when his father died in 1754.

129 **silversmith's social standing:** Another radical leader, Dr. Thomas Young, said of Revere that "no man of his rank and opportunities in life, deserves better of the community."

10

A BITTER CREW

130 **responsibility for writing instructions:** On April 9, 1773, the correspondence committee voted to create a subcommittee to produce such a draft. The first member was Dr. Church, followed by Warren, Molineux, Appleton, and Young. Subsequently the official town meeting choose an official committee for the same task, which was led by Warren.

130 **significant and growing influence:** In relation to Warren's rise within the Whig ranks, his appearance on Boston's annual committees to prepare instructions is as follows: in 1770, he was listed third of five members (no instructions committee in 1771), fourth out of nine in 1772, and first in 1773 and 1774.

130 **"Committees all over Massachusetts":** Cary, *Joseph Warren*, pp. 125–27.

131 **no longer treating Boston's elite:** The last entry Warren made in his medical ledger referencing those Loyalist families was Thomas Hutchinson in the summer of 1767. Warren's clientele between late 1768 and early 1773 remains unclear due to the absence of a ledger for this period. But by 1774, those names no longer appeared in his ledger book.

132 **"their lives and fortunes":** Frothingham, *Life and Times*, pp. 239–40.

133 **"the infernall yell":** Copley and Pelham, *Letters*, p. 200–202. The original writing of the sentence read "the infernall yell of the Children of Satan," before Pelham erased the latter part.

133 **"attended constantly":** L. F. S. Upton, "Proceedings of Ye Body Respecting the Tea," *William and Mary Quarterly* 22, no. 2 (1965): 300.

133 **"Lodge held its meeting":** Warren attended every St. Andrews Lodge meeting, except for three, between May 1769 and March 3, 1775.

134 **"Lodge closed on account":** Palmer et al., *Lodge of St. Andrew*, p. 274.

134 **"chief Speakers":** Upton, "Proceedings of Ye Body Respecting the Tea," p. 300.

134 **"hideous yelling":** Ibid., pp. 297–300, esp. 298.

134 **"was conducted with":** Henry Bromfield to Messrs. Flight and Halliday in London, December 17, 1773, in *Henry Bromfield Letterbook*, 1773, New England Historic Genealogical Society (NEHGS). William Molineux was another patriot leader at the scene of the Tea Party.

134 **underscoring the need for disguise:** "It is a little surprising that the names of the tea-party were never made public: my father, I believe, was the only person who had a list of them, and he always kept it locked up in his desk while living." See Boardman, Edes, and Leach, *Pioneer Printer in*

Maine. Peter Edes was the son of Benjamin Edes, Warren's friend, compatriot, and printer of the *Boston Gazette.*

135 **"Rally Mohawks! Bring out your axes":** Palmer et al., *Lodge of St. Andrew,* p. 170. Warren was directly involved with the actions leading up to the Tea Party in a variety of roles. While I strongly suggest that he was directing and present during at least a portion of the actual dumping of the tea in the harbor, it remains doubtful as to whether he was physically involved with the actual destruction of the tea on board the vessels that night.

136 **"so bold, so daring":** Entry for December 17, 1773, in John Adams, *Diary,* Adams Family Papers.

137 **Coercive Acts:** The Administration of Justice Act granted the governor power to move trials of accused royal officials to Britain, which colonists believed would give those officials unchecked powers to intimidate. The Quartering Act allowed the governor to provide housing for troops. The Quebec Act, which extended the territory of the colony of Quebec far west of the Mississippi, further angered colonists, particularly Bostonians, since it also recognized Roman Catholicism, reviving inherent fears and hatred of a resurgent popish French presence in North America.

137 **"We have this day received":** Frothingham, *Life and Times,* p. 300–301.

137 **"into operation amid":** Frothingham, *History of the Siege of Boston,* p. 7.

137 **Solemn League and Covenant:** Frothingham, *Life and Times,* pp. 300–301.

138 **"rude and brutal behavior":** Hutchinson, *Diary and Letters,* p. 1:130.

138 **"generally expected and hoped":** Oliver, *Origins and Progress,* p. 114.

139 **a gentleman's daughter:** In 1897 a fire screen "worked by" Mercy Scollay from 1760 was featured in an exhibit by the Massachusetts Daughters of the American Revolution. Fire screens were often intricately sewn and used as decorative pieces in the eighteenth century. See *Catalogue of a Loan Collection,* p. 40. Although the catalogue incorrectly listed Mercy's name as "Nancy," it did note that she was "engaged to Gen. Warren at the time he was killed at Bunker Hill, and his children, he being a widower, were placed under her care." Mercy continued to sew and embroider into the 1820s.

140 **New England female patriots:** Mercy Otis Warren was a staunch patriot and political writer, and the wife of James Warren, a distant relative and Whig colleague of Joseph Warren. She was also the sister of James Otis, Jr. She was tied closely to the most powerful radical leaders and was herself a staunch opponent against various British policies. Her writings have at times been incorrectly attributed to Mercy Scollay. Mercy Otis Warren would author one of the earliest histories of the American Revolution, *History of the Rise, Progress and Termination of the American Revolution,* in 1805. Her portrait which was painted by John Copley currently hangs next to Joseph Warren's in the Museum of Fine Arts, Boston. She died at the age of eighty-six in 1814.

140 **"heart bleeds for the calamity":** This letter is the earliest known piece to exist in her hand and has never been identified or appeared in any published work on Warren. Mercy Scollay to Mary Bruce Strange, June 1, 1774, Photostats Collection, 1501–1950, Massachusetts Historical Society.

140 **"the ruin of this <u>once</u> flourishing"**: Ibid.

140 **"Thank Heaven! We can supply"**: Ibid.

141 *"But now the sound"*: Ibid.

141 **"never feel the pangs"**: Ibid.

141 **"if we sent over"**: "The Boston Port Bill," in Force, *American Archives, Fourth Series*, p. 1:41.

141 **the Fourth King's Own Regiment**: On July 4 and 5, the 38th and Fifth Regiments landed in Boston, and on August 9 the 23rd Regiment also arrived. The following day the New York Artillery landed.

141 **"there is now an open"**: Frothingham, *History of the Siege of Boston*, p. 7.

141 **"lenient measures"**: Fischer, *Paul Revere's Ride*, p. 37.

142 **"I am for dying rather than"**: *Boston Evening Post*, June 6, 1774. Frothingham believed the language in this article to be "characterized by Warren's vehement spirit." While it cannot be absolutely certain that Warren was the author, I also attribute the piece to him in terms of the language.

142 **"The celebrated Colonel Putnam"**: Warren to Samuel Adams, August 15, 1774, in Frothingham, *Life and Times*, pp. 339–40.

142 **"the cause of Boston"**: Washington to George William Fairfax, June 10–15, 1774. National Archives.

143 **"prevent those unwarrantable"**: Frothingham, *History of the Siege of Boston*, p. 9.

143 **"many colonists had little"**: Gordon S. Wood, *Radicalism of the American Revolution*, pp. 110–11.

143 **"like men"**: *Boston Evening Post*, June 6, 1774.

143 **"All trade, commerce"**: Cary, *Joseph Warren*, p. 141.

144 **"the mistress we court"**: Warren to Samuel Adams, June 15, 1774, in Frothingham, *Life and Times*, p. 317.

144 **"highly expedient and necessary"**: Entry for June 17, 1774, in *Journals of Massachusetts House*, pp. 287–90.

144 **attend a continental congress**: Frothingham, *Life and Times*, p. 325.

11

RESOLVED

146 **"prevents it being"**: Rowe, *Diary of John Rowe*, pp. 278, 280.

147 **"belonging to the Province"**: Ibid., pp. 283, 284.

147 **Mandamus Council**: Rather than being appointed by the lower house, the councilors of the upper house were now appointed by London under a writ of mandamus. The upper house thus came to be called the Mandamus Council.

147 **"to take some step"**: Thomas Oliver was the last Royal Lieutenant Governor of Massachusetts. Some histories incorrectly claim that it was Peter Oliver who went to Gage that day. These two Oliver men were not brothers.

147 **"I doubt whether a man":** Warren to Samuel Adams, September 4, 1774, in Frothingham, *Life and Times*, pp. 357–58.

148 **"it is natural for the People":** *Boston News-Letter*, September 22, 1774. See also Peter Force, *American Archives, Fourth Series,* Vol. 1, 1837, pp. 780–81; Warren was likely the principle drafter of the committee letter.

148 **"desirous of accommodating":** Warren to Josiah Quincy, Jr., November 21, 1774, in Frothingham, *Life and Times*, pp. 394–96.

148 **"Our all is at stake":** Warren to Samuel Adams, September 4, 1774, ibid., pp. 357–58.

149 **"the selectmen and committee":** Warren to Samuel Adams, August 15, 1774, ibid., pp. 339–40.

149 **"stylish berlin":** *The Story of the Suffolk Resolves,* Milton, Massachusetts Historical Commission, 1973, pp. 4–5. Also see Frothingham, *Life and Times*, p. 342.

149 **"have very important":** Warren to Samuel Adams, August 21, 1774, in Frothingham, *Life and Times*, pp. 343–44.

149 **Mr. Richard Woodward in Dedham:** Richard Woodward acquired the property when he married the widow of the elder Dr. Nathaniel Ames, Deborah. Woodward was not on good terms with the younger Dr. Nathaniel Ames and others in the Ames family; It has been recently suggested that Warren fathered an illegitimate child with a teenage girl named Sally Edwards and placed her in the home of Dr. Nathaniel Ames, his Harvard friend, in Dedham. Warren had an account with Ames. In Ames's ledger his entry for Warren has a line that reads "his fair incognita pregnans" (a phrase Ames used in other ledger entries for people other than Warren). Another reason cited as Warren's possible paternity was that following Warren's death, Mercy Scollay referred to a Sally Edwards as a "vixen" in a November 26, 1776, letter. Under Warren's account, Ames documented that room and board were paid for Sally Edwards after the birth of her child and for other expenses such as a "gauze cap for the Child's christening" and for "cloathing."

But several factors suggest that the girl Warren sent to Ames's was not his illegitimate child. Ames specialized in delivering babies, so it made sense that Warren would send a pregnant girl to him, particularly outside of the explosive situation in Boston. Ames's account books are filled with entries of children being delivered, making Ames a natural candidate to help the pregnant girl and keep her under his care outside Boston. Also, if Warren was trying to hide an indiscretion, he would not have been likely to choose Ames, since Ames was close friends with Mercy Scollay's brother John. At the time of conception, Warren would have been busy drafting the Suffolk Resolves, handling his patient load, and engaged with Mercy, which would have left little time for other activities.

Warren's Sally Edward's account with Ames was continued posthumously and eventually settled by Warren's medical students "W. Eustis" and "Dr. Townsend" on April 15, 1779. Ames even noted that "This Acc't was paid & contracted chiefly after Dr. Warren's heroic death." The fact that they made payments on Warren's behalf suggests that Sally Edwards had possibly been with one of them or with someone in their circle, or possibly that she was being helped out of charity. That Ames continued to provide for and look after Sally and her daughter for several more years, suggests a paternity other than Warren.

In 1783, when Warren's brothers were settling his estate, they paid Dr. Ames approximately twenty-five pounds for services rendered, which came several years after the Sally Edwards account had been settled by Warren's medical students. See Ames's medical ledger at the Dedham Historical Society. Yet, neither side of the argument has irrefutable proof.

150 **Suffolk Resolves:** For another source indicating Warren as the primary drafter of the Resolves, see the *American Magazine of Useful and Entertaining Knowledge*, 1835.

150 **"so closely parallels Warren's":** Cary, *Joseph Warren*, p. 153.

150 **Warren drafted the resolves:** Frothingham, *Life and Times*, p. 361.

151 **"pay all due respect":** Ibid., pp. 529–34.

151 **"The colonies had grown up":** John Adams to Hezekiah Niles, February 13, 1818, National Archives.

152 **"a certain degree of jealousy":** Samuel Adams to Warren, September 25, 1774, in Frothingham, *Life and Times*, pp. 377–79.

152 **approved and adopted:** On September 6, the Congress in Philadelphia had received reports of a British military attack on Boston, giving rise to a potential war scenario in New England.

152 **"This was one of the happiest":** Entry for September 17, 1774, in John Adams, *Diary and Autobiography*, p. 2:134–35.

152 **extralegal congress:** Under the Massachusetts Government Act, Gage dissolved the town meeting, so patriots created a Provincial Congress as an extralegal governing body, meeting in Concord. The first Provincial Congress adjourned on December 10, after the delegates agreed to reconvene elsewhere. The second Provincial Congress met on February 1, 1775, in Cambridge. *Journals of Each Provincial Congress*, p. 6.

153 **"The treatment which the":** Warren to Samuel Adams, September 29, 1774, in Frothingham, *Life and Times*, p. 382.

153 **Josiah Quincy, Jr., whose health:** Upon his return, Quincy died at sea, within sight of his homeland.

153 **William Molineux died:** *Essex Gazette*, October 24, 1774.

154 **"a most infamous disturber":** Oliver, *Origins and Progress*, p. 117.

154 **"the first leader of dirty matters":** Rowe, *Diary of John Rowe*, p. 286.

154 **"It is the united voice":** Warren to Josiah Quincy Jr., November 21, 1774, Frothingham, *Life and Times*, pp. 394–96.

154 **"The New England Governments":** George III to Lord North, November 18, 1774, in Donne, *Correspondence of George the Third*, pp. 214–15.

155 **"constantly busied in helping":** Warren to Samuel Adams, August 29, 1774, in Frothingham, *Life and Times*, p. 360.

155 **a Committee of Safety:** During the English Civil War, the Long Parliament called its action committee the Committee of Safety; it oversaw the war effort.

156 **"It is the opinion":** Lord Dartmouth to General Gage, January 27, 1775. Thomas Gage Papers. Gage did not receive the letter until mid-April.

156 **Dr. Benjamin Church:** Church was the Harvard roommate of John Hancock, which likely also contributed to the implicit trust many of the Whigs placed in him. Warren was a friend and Harvard classmate of Church's younger brother, which perhaps clouded his judgment about Benjamin Church.

156 **"Friends of Warren":** Loring, *Hundred Boston Orators*, p. 48.

156 **"an affray happened":** Rowe, *Diary of John Rowe*, p. 289.

156 **"disperse the Congress":** Warren to Samuel Adams, Feb. 10, 1775, Frothingham, *Life and Times*, pp. 414–15.

157 **"the event, which I confess":** Warren to Arthur Lee, Feb. 20. 1775, Frothingham, *Life and Times*, pp. 418–19.

157 **"Many men who would":** Brown, *Stories about General Warren*, p. 37.

157 **"took every opportunity":** Ibid. p. 31.

157 **"To-morrow an oration":** Frothingham, *Life and Times*, p. 427.

158 **"A single horse chair":** *Rivington's New York Gazette*, March 16, 1775.

158 **intent on disrupting:** At least one hundred British officers were in attendance, possibly as many as three hundred. See "Old Bostonian," *Columbian Centinel*, September 12, 1821; Hutchinson, *Diary and Letters*, pp. 528–29.

158 **"of the obligation I am under":** Joseph Warren, An *Oration Delivered March Sixth, 1775*. Boston, Edes and Gill.

159 **"Our Liberty must be preserved; it is far dearer than life":** Warren, *Oration Delivered March Sixth, 1775*.

160 **"It has always been a wonder":** "Old Bostonian," *Columbian Centinel*, September 12, 1821. Following the conclusion of Warren's oration, Samuel Adams spoke and when he referred to the massacre perpetrated at the behest of Captain Preston, one British officer exclaimed, "Fie," an English expression of extreme disgust. It was misheard as "Fire," causing panic to ensue, as scores of people rushed to exit from the windows. "Extract of a Letter," *Rivington's New-York Gazeteer*, March 23, 1775.

160 **"this day . . . a most seditious":** "A British Officer in Boston in 1775," *The Atlantic Monthly*: April 1877, Vol. XXIX, No. CCXXIV, p. 897.

160 **"the Americans would be compelled":** *Boston Evening-Post*, March 6, 1775. Frothingham suggests this piece was written by Warren.

160 **"skill in Chemistry":** *An Oration delivered March 15th 1775 from the Coffee House by Doctor Thomas Bolton* (manuscript copy), Miscellaneous Bound Manuscripts, MHS.

160 **home of John Hancock:** *New-York Journal*, March 30, 1775.

161 **"American liberty or democracy":** *Journals of each Provincial Congress*, p. 132; *Norwich Packet* (Connecticut), March 16, 1775.

161 **"Hancock, Adams and hundreds":** Hutchinson, *Diary and Letters,*
pp. 528–29. The colonel mentioned that only Hancock and Adams were
to be cut down, had Warren made any negative comments about the king.
Ostensibly, Warren would have been targeted as well, given he was delivering the oration. This remark was made following Warren's death.

161 **His trusted friend and colleague:** Warren paid Dr. Dix just over thirty
pounds for the repairs. The two were friends and colleagues; when Dr. Dix
encountered problems in exhuming a corpse, he turned to Warren for advice and assistance. Thomas, *Celebration,* p. 136.

161 **"should arrive before any":** Warren to Dr. Elijah Dix, February 25,
1775, in Leffingwell, *Catalogue of Autograph Letters and Historical Documents.*

161 **He also informed Dix:** Warren to Dr. Elijah Dix, April 10, 1775, ibid.

12

JOSEPH WARREN'S RIDE

164 **"I was one of upwards":** Fischer, *Paul Revere's Ride,* p. 51.

164 **William Dawes:** Dawes is buried in Forest Hills Cemetery, near Warren.

165 **Second Church of Boston:** This was the second Congregationalist church
in Boston, established ca. 1650. Crocker, *Reminiscences and Traditions,* p. 14.

165 **"Gen Warren had directed":** Brown, *Stories about General Warren,* p. 37.

165 **"cannon and other artillery":** J. L. Bell, *The Road to Concord,* Westholme
Publishing, 2016. See Chapter 2.

166 **"immediately set off":** Letter Paul Revere to Jeremy Belknap, circa
1798. Manuscript Collection, Massachusetts Historical Society.

166 **two lanterns lit:** One lantern was to indicate if the British forces were
coming by land.

166 **"seeming to thirst":** "Narratives of the Excursion of the King's Troops,"
April 19, 1775, in Massachusetts, *Journals of Each Provincial Congress,*
pp. 662–63.

167 **under Warren's instructions:** Warren was the top radical leader remaining in Boston, and Revere took his orders that night directly from
Warren. It is unlikely that Revere would have made the decision to alert
any militia officers without specific instructions from Warren, or at the
very least discussing it with him.

167 **"He assured me it was":** Frothingham, *Life and Times,* p. 457.

168 **"sudden arrest":** Fischer, *Paul Revere's Ride,* p. 91.

168 **"I assure you, I":** Maj. John Pitcairn to Lord Sandwich. March 4, 1775,
in William Bell Clark, edt, *Naval Documents of the American Revolution,* 1964,
Vol. 1, p. 125.

168 **"We were fired on":** Barker, *British in Boston,* p. 35.

169 **"from his ardor":** Brown, *Stories about General Warren,* pp. 50–51.

169 **"I can with truth":** Washington to John Augustine Washington, May 31,
1754, National Archives.

170 **"They fought like bears"**: *History of Middlesex County*, Massachusetts, Philadelphia, 1890, p. 830.

170 **"Your Excellency, I believe knows"**: Warren to General Gage, April 20, 1776, in Frothingham, *Life and Times*, p. 467.

170 **"The barbarous murders"**: Ibid., p. 466.

170 **"an army of 30,000"**: Massachusetts, *Journals of Each Provincial Congress*, p. 148.

171 **"the troops of Britain, unprovoked"**: "Narratives of the Excursion of the King's Troops," April 19, 1775. Ibid., pp. 662–63.

171 **"a profound secret"**: Massachusetts, *Journals of Each Provincial Congress*, p. 159.

171 **"to purchase every kind"**: Ibid., p. 165.

171 **"as I shall keep several horses"**: Warren to Mercy Scollay, May 10, 1775, in Leffingwell, *Catalogue of Autograph Letters and Historical Documents*, p. 224.

172 **"Any sum of money"**: *Celebration by the Inhabitants of Worcester, Mass., of the Centennial Anniversary of the Declaration of Independence*, p. 136; letter from Dr. Joseph Warren to Dr. Elijah Dix, May 13, 1775.

172 **"Much the greater parts"**: Andrew Elliot to unidentified recipient, draft letter, May 31, 1775, Massachusetts Historical Society, Collections Online.

172 **"order, and attend his duty"**: Massachusetts, *Journals of Each Provincial Congress*, p. 178.

173 **"ten horses, two hundred"**: Ibid., p. 185.

173 **"be forwarded this way"**: Frothingham, *Life and Times*, p. 490.

173 **"The repeated intelligence"**: Warren to Joseph Reed, May 15, 1775. Ibid., pp. 486–87.

173 **"he will but gratify"**: Warren to Arthur Lee, May 16, 1775. Ibid., p. 488.

173 **Warren personally delivered**: Massachusetts, *Journals of Each Provincial Congress*, p. 243.

173 **"made a harangue"**: John Adams, *Works*, p. 3:277; Frothingham, *Life and Times*, pp. 491–92.

173 **"obey any person of whom"**: Frothingham, *Life and Times*, p. 485.

174 **"small arms to do"**: Ibid., p. 493.

174 **"I love,—I admire"**: Ibid., p. 496.

174 **Battle of Noddle's Island:** The engagement is also called the Battle of Chelsea Creek.

174 **Hog's Island, located:** Hog Island and Noddle's Island no longer exist; the water around them was filled in, and both land masses are now part of East Boston.

175 *Cerberus* **docked in Boston Harbor:** In Greek mythology, Cerberus was the vicious three-headed dog that guarded the gates of Hades.

175 **"Yesterday arrived the three"**: Frothingham, *Life and Times*, p. 496.

175 **organizing a provincial army:** The New England men who turned out on April 19 were militia companies and served for a short term. Follow-

ing the battles of Lexington and Concord, the Provincial Congress had to reorganize the militia units into an army enlisted through the end of 1775; some men left, some remained on new terms, and others arrived. Also, the troops that came from other New England colonies after April were not militia but those other colonies' armies.

176 **obtain a copper plate:** *Journals of Each Provincial Congress*, pp. 186, 200, 203; Frothingham, *Life and Times*, pp. 483–84.

176 *"Diseases incident to Armies":* This book was given to Dr. Nathaniel Ames as part of a payment to settle Warren's account with him. See Ames's Medical Ledger.

176 **Dr. Isaac Foster:** Foster was born in 1740 and graduated from Harvard in 1758. Being a year apart, Warren and Foster almost assuredly knew each other at Harvard and their medical training with Lloyd likely overlapped since a medical apprenticeship lasted two years.

176 **"was conducted with the utmost":** Frothingham, *Life and Times*, p. 501.

176 **"the parties passed an hour":** *New England Chronicle*, June 8, 1775.

177 **"misguided fellow countrymen":** *Journals of Each Provincial Congress*, p. 346.

177 **took unnecessary risks:** Several sources mention Warren accompanying Putnam that day, including Frothingham, *Life and Times*, p. 497, and Tentindo and Jones, *Battle of Chelsea Creek*, p. 39.

177 **"wait on the Hon. Joseph Warren, Esq.":** Massachusetts, *Journals of Each Provincial Congress*, p. 333.

13
HILL OF LAMENTATIONS

178 **"My God, I never saw such a carnage of the human race":** Morse and Parish, *Compendious History*, p. 342.

178 **"gentleman of undoubted veracity":** French, *First Year*, p. 209.

179 **"decided that possession":** *Journals of Each Provincial Congress*, p. 569.

179 **received secret dispatches:** Crocker, *Reminiscences and Traditions*, p. 41.

180 **attended a war council:** Warren signed Ward's commission.

180 **a steady stream of cannon fire:** Entry for June 17, 1775, in Samuel A. Green, "The Diary of Amos Farnsworth," *Proceedings of the Massachusetts Historical Society*, 2nd series (January 1898): 74–103, esp. 83–84.

180 **"The first man who fell":** Hudleston, *Gentleman Johnny*, p. 63. But the British field artillery attack was largely ineffectual due to the fact that oversize, twelve-pound balls had been sent to load six-pounders. Eventually General Howe ordered that grapeshot be used instead.

180 **"Raw lads and old men":** Lee and Langworthy, *Life and Memoirs of Lee*, pp. 44–45.

180 **"many of our young country people":** Peter Brown to Sarah Brown, June 25, 1775, Massachusetts Historical Society, Collections Online.

180 **marched in procession:** At one point during the 1700s, the Long Wharf extended as far as two hundred feet into the ocean.

180 **"Grenadiers & Light Infantry":** Frothingham, *Centennial*, p. 29; Lt. J. Waller to unidentified recipient, June 21, 1775, Massachusetts Historical Society, Bunker Hill Exhibit.

181 **"I wish the Americans":** Frothingham, *Centennial*, p. 9.

181 **"any man who shall quit":** Howe, *General Howe's Orderly Book*, p. 2. The "Orderly Book . . . presents every detail of the administration and discipline of the English Army in the siege of Boston."

181 **"Between 3 and 4 oclock":** Barker, *British in Boston*, p. 61.

181 **"Warren for several years was":** Knapp, *Biographical Sketches*, p. 116.

182 **"a most awful, grand":** Samuel Paine to Dr. William Paine, June 22, 1775, *Proceedings of the American Antiquarian Society*, Massachusetts, 1909, Vol. 19, pp. 435–38.

182 **"like a thunder cloud":** Dearborn, *Account of the Battle*, p. 6.

182 **"The dead lay as thick":** John Fellows, *The Veil Removed*, New York, 1843, p. 120.

182 **huzzahs and cheers:** Frothingham, *Life and Times*, p. 515.

182 **"light colored coat":** Willard, *Letters on American Revolution*, p. 150; Drake, *Bunker Hill*, p. 50.

183 **easily identifiable:** Dearborn, *Account of the Battle*, p. 6. One commanding phrase shouted within the redoubt was "there," "see that officer," "let us have a shot at him."

183 **"set them an example":** Swett, *History of Bunker Hill*, p. 34.

183 **"Our first fire was":** Bancroft, "Colonel Bancroft's Personal Narrative," p. 61.

184 **mounted Breed's Hill:** The hill's terrain, which was strewn with stones, small fences, and other impediments, was uneven but was partially camouflaged by tall grass.

184 **British troops pressed up Breed's Hill:** An 1818 source claimed that "General Warren, the 'leader,' was 'everywhere aiding and encouraging his men.'" Frothingham, *History of the Siege*, p. 378.

184 **"trees stone walls, and rails":** Lt. J. Waller to unidentified recipient, June 21, 1775, Massachusetts Historical Society, Bunker Hill Exhibit.

184 **"advanced in open order":** Frothingham, *History of the Siege*, p. 143; *Rivington's Gazette*, August 3, 1775.

184 **"terrible desperation piled":** Swett, *History of Bunker Hill*, p. 34.

184 **"too great a confidence":** Commager and Morris, *Spirit of 'Seventy-Six*, p. 135.

184 **"wounded and dying, exerting":** Swett, *History of Bunker Hill*, p. 34.

185 **"mowed them down":** Jeremy Belknap, "Extracts from Dr. Belknap's Note-books," *Proceedings of the Massachusetts Historical Society* 14 (1875–76): 92.

185 **"now ensued one":** Drake, *Bunker Hill*, p. 40.

185 **howls of British war cries:** Frothingham, *History of the Siege*, p. 383.

185 **"their bayonets into all":** Samuel Paine to Dr. William Paine, June 22, 1775, in *Proceedings of the American Antiquarian Society*, Massachusetts, 1909, Vol. 19, pp. 435–38. Samuel Paine was a classmate of Joseph Warren's youngest brother, John Warren, at Harvard. In reference to General Warren, Paine wrote, "The Rebels lost a vast many, among whom was Doct. Warren, a noted Rascal.": Beacon Hill is almost two miles from Breed's Hill. See also "Account of Adjutant Waller, Royal Marines," in Drake, *Bunker Hill*, pp. 28-30.

185 **"fought gallantly":** "Judge Prescott's Account of the Battle of Bunker Hill," *Proceedings of the Massachusetts Historical Society* 14 (1875–76): 68–78, esp. 77.

185 **"more like devils than men":** *Massachusetts Spy*, June 28, 1775.

186 **overwhelmed and exhausted:** Dearborn, *Account of the Battle*, p. 5.

186 **"'twas streaming with blood":** Lt. J Waller to unidentified recipient, June 21, 1775, Massachusetts Historical Society, Bunker Hill Exhibit.

186 **drop and crawl:** Eleazer French reputedly "had an arm shot off during the action, and picking it up, bore it as a trophy from the bloody field." Nason, *History of Dunstable*, p. 114.

186 **"lingered to the last":** Swett, *History of Bunker Hill*, p. 45.

186 **"After performing many feats":** James Warren to John Adams, June 20, 1775, in *Warren-Adams Letters*, pp. 62–64; Swett, *History of Bunker Hill*, p. 45; Dearborn, *Account of the Battle*, p. 6. Henry Dearborn, a patriot soldier, saw Warren's corpse toward the end of the battle: "As he appeared to be much better dressed than our men generally were, I asked a man who was passing me, if he knew who it was. He replied 'it is Dr. Warren.'" On the day of the battle, most of the participants were unaware that Warren had been appointed a major general. For many, this information came to light after the battle had been fought; *Pennsylvania Journal*, June 28, 1775. Regarding the exact spot where Warren fell, one 1875 newspaper account reads: "A granite slab in Concord street nearly opposite the High School is inscribed 'Here fell Warren, June 17, 1775,' but the best authorities are of the opinion that this is not historically accurate. Mr. Frothingham expresses the belief that the General had reached a spot in front of the present residence of Dr. Lyon on the southwest side of the monument grounds. The rail fence ran across at this point." *Daily Graphic*, June 1, 1875.

187 **"immediately [stabbed] him":** *London Evening Post*, July 13–16, 1776. "Some recent acts of cruelty have been exercised by the troops in America. The cases have been reported to the Congress; the members of which assembly were deliberating on the measures of retaliation, when the last advices were transmitted from America. The soldier who so inhmanly (sic) ran Doctor Warren through the body, with his bayonet, is taken by the Provincials, among other prisoners. He was discovered by a comrade, who is also taken."

187 **"His whole soul seemed":** Jonathan Williams Austin to John Adams, July 7, 1775, Papers of John Adams, Series 3, Vol. 3, Adams Family Papers.

187 **"Major General Warren"**: Oliver, *Origin and Progress,* p. 126.

187 **giving his life for the patriot cause:** While Warren refused official command of the battle, he undoubtedly led provincial troops throughout the fighting. According to Frothingham, *Siege of Boston,* several accounts mention Warren as a leader. In a 1779 letter, Governor Trumbull named "General Warren as the commanding officer"; Edmund Burke, *An Impartial History of the War in America* (1780), attributed to "General Warren the command" of battle; in Charles Stedman's *The History of the Origin, Progress, and Termination of the American War* (1794), the only American officer named is "Doctor Warren, who commanded in the redoubt," p. 1:128.

187 **"in possession of his body"**: John Chester and Samuel Webb to Joseph Webb, June 19, 1775, in Ford, *Boston in 1775,* p. 12.

188 **"murdered worthy"**: James Warren to John Adams, June 20, 1775, in *Warren-Adams Letters,* pp. 62–63. James Warren wrote the word "murdered" and then crossed it out.

188 **attire was now covered:** "Dr. John Warren . . . has related that, when the dead body of the general was discovered after the battle, his right hand was covered with blood, though there was no wound upon it, occurring as if he had raised his hand to the back of his head, on the right side, when the ball fractured his skull." See James Spear Loring, *The Hundred Boston Orators Appointed by the Municipal Authorities and Other Public Bodies, From 1770-1852,* Boston, 1852, p. 66.

188 **looted his personal items:** A missive was found in Warren's coat pocket when the British were stripping his clothes. It was written by Lemuel Hedge, Warren's former Harvard classmate, who was suspected of being a Tory; he had written to Warren pleading his innocence. He was later disarmed and confined in his town of Warwick. Shipton, *Sibley's Harvard Graduates* XIV (1756–60): 440.

188 **"off his head"**: Benjamin Hichborn to John Adams, December 10, 1775, John Adams Papers, Series 3, pp. 3:323–24, Adams Family Papers. In a separate report, a rumor from a deserting British soldier was told to Abigail Adams of an attempt by royal troops to decapitate Warren. Abigail Adams to John Adams, July 31–2 August 1775, Adams Family Papers. Thus John Adams received two separate accounts related to Warren's mutilation and beheading. I mention these two accounts to help underscore the disdain felt from both sides of the conflict. Although Warren's body was uncovered April 1776, the corpse was significantly disfigured from both British abuses and from nature taking its toll. Warren's brothers immediately left the scene. That two separate reports regarding attempts of beheading were circulated, lead me to believe that there was some form of mutilation committed upon Warren's head after he died, but not decapitation. Moreover, Gage would have taken great pains to cover any such abuses.

188 **"He was buried hastily"**: Warren, *Life of John Warren,* p. 74. Various posthumous accounts assert that Warren was buried with at least one other slain patriot. See letter, Lt. Walter S. Laurie to John Roebuck, June 23,

1775; see also *Virginia Gazette*, May 11, 1776, and *Reminiscences Related to General Warren*, p. 7.

188 **"streets were filled":** Henry Hulton letter, June 20, 1775, in Hulton, *Letters of a Loyalist Lady*, p. 99.

189 **"The horrors and devastations":** John Chester and Samuel Webb to Joseph Webb, June 19, 1775, in Ford, *Boston in 1775*, p. 9.

189 **"The loss we have sustained":** General Gage to Lord Barrington, June 26, 1775, in Commager and Morris, *Spirit of 'Seventy-Six*, p. 134.

189 **"My God, I never saw":** Morse and Parish, *Compendious History*, p. 342.

189 **waited for tents and provisions:** Although he survived the fighting at Lexington and Concord, Major Pitcairn was fatally shot on Breed's Hill and reportedly died in the arms of his son, a lieutenant in the king's army.

189 **"lying in heaps on the ground":** John Winthrop to John Adams, June 21, 1775, in *Collections of the Massachusetts Historical Society*, Vol. IV, Fifth Series, Heath papers, Boston, 1878, pp. 292–94.

189 **worth five hundred:** Gordon, *History of the Rise, Progress*, pp. 2:49–50.

189 **"the officers and soldiers":** *Pennsylvania Packet*, July 31, 1775.

190 **"Doctor Warren, president":** Walter S. Laurie to John Roebuck, June 23, 1775, *New England Quarterly*, Bunker Hill, Tory Propaganda, and Adam Smith, Vol. 25, No. 3 (Sep. 1952), pp.363–74.

190 **forbade his troops to desecrate:** Howe, *General Howe's Orderly Book*, p. 44. The "Orderly Book . . . presents every detail of the administration and discipline of the English Army in the Siege of Boston."

190 **"I wish this cursed place":** Letter from General Gage to Lord Barrington, June 26, 1775, in *Correspondence of Thomas Gage*, pp. 686–87.

14
FOUNDING MOURNERS

191 **"I feel great distress":** Ford, *Journals of Continental Congress*, p. 2:92. By the time of Washington's appointment, the Congress had also moved to raise an army in northern New York, pay for the army outside Boston, and send companies of riflemen from the middle colonies—issues the delegates from Massachusetts had pushed for and achieved.

192 **"His commission is made out":** John Hancock to Warren, June 18, 1775, Edmund C. Burnett Edt. *Letters of the Members of the Continental Congress*, Washington D.C., 1921, Vol. 1, p. 134. Warren's successor in the Provincial Congress would receive the letter when it arrived.

192 **"If any should be disaffected":** Samuel Adams to Warren, June 20, 1775, in *Warren-Adams Letters*, MHS 1917, Vol. 1, p. 64.

192 **"We find a great many":** Hancock and the Adams cousins would not return to Massachusetts until August 11, 1775. John Adams to Joseph Warren, June 21, 1775. *Warren-Adams Letters*, MHS 1917, Vol. 1, p. 65.

193 **an express rider carrying news:** Governor Trumbull was the father of Warren's Harvard classmate.

193 **"He is now gone":** *Warren-Adams Letters*, p. 74. See also Jonathan Williams Austin to John Adams, July 7, 1775; papers of John Adams, Series 3, Vol. 3, Adams Family Papers.

194 **"the greatest loss sustaind":** John Bromfield to Jeremiah Powell, June 21, 1775, Miscellaneous Bound Manuscripts MHS. Note the reference to Warren as "Dr." and not "General."

194 **"inexpressible grief":** James Warren to Mercy Warren, June 18, 1775, in *Warren-Adams Letters*, MHS 1917, Vol. 1, p. 59.

194 **"We learn from one":** Abigail Adams to John Adams, July 31, 1775, in National Archives.

195 **that he had survived:** *London Evening Post*, July 13, 1776.

195 **"The death of our truly amiable":** Fowler, *Samuel Adams*, p. 141; Frothingham, *Life and Times*, p. 521.

195 **"Warren's death doubled":** Fowler, *Samuel Adams*, p. 140.

195 **"The day; perhaps the decisive":** Ellis, *American Creation*, p. 28.

196 **"For God's sake my Friend":** John Adams to James Warren, July 6, 1775, John Adams Papers, Vol. 3, Adams Family Papers. Adams incorrectly believed that Warren had accepted the post of chief surgeon of the Provincial Army.

196 **"Godlike Warren":** *New England Chronicle*, July 13, 1775.

196 **"if he had lived":** Catherine Barton Mayo, ed., "Additions to Thomas Hutchinson's History of Massachusetts Bay," *AAS Proceedings* 59 (1949): 11–74, esp. 45.

196 **"Washington" would have:** Oliver, *Origin and Progress*, p. 128.

196 **"respectable . . . virtuous":** Hulton, *Letters of a Loyalist Lady*, pp. 97–100.

197 **"I have often passed Doct Warren's":** *Copley-Pelham Letters*, pp. 344–47.

197 **"to see an irregular peasantry":** George Johnstone, *Governor Johnston's Speech on American Affairs on the Address to the King's Speech, 1776* (Edinburgh, 1885), p. 20. Johnstone, a former governor of West Florida, made this speech to members of Parliament in 1776.

197 **"open and avowed rebellion":** Force, *American Archives*, Series 4, pp. 3:240–41.

197 **"received the melancholy":** John Collins Warren Journal, pp. 44–46, John Collins Warren Papers.

198 **"without a tree or a green shrub":** At least 123 trees had been cut down for the war effort. See Drake, *Town of Roxbury*, p. 214.

198 **the Warren family refused:** This newspaper article was found tucked in the fold of the Warren family book that rested upon the night table of Warren Wildrick, General Warren's fourth great-grandson, for more than four decades. *Boston Evening Post*, February 8, 1858.

199 **Warren's four orphaned children:** The children's nicknames were Betsey (Elizabeth), Jose or Josie (Joseph), Dickie (Richard), and Polly (Mary).

199 **"to take all possible care":** Worcester Fire Society, *Reminiscences*, p. 25.

199 **mansion estate in West Boston:** James Bowdoin to Warren, July 1770, Warren MSS II, Massachusetts Historical Society.

200 **To her dismay:** Mercy Scollay to Dr. Dix, Aug. 17, 1775, Mercy Scollay Papers, 1775–1824, Cambridge Historical Society; George Washington had referenced buying several mattresses on October 1, 1775, but that was for a "field bed." When Washington left Cambridge in April 1776 he left all the furniture behind.

200 **"religiously bound by the promise":** Mercy Scollay to John Hancock, May 21, 1776. John Hancock Family Papers, reel 2, Massachusetts Historical Society.

200 **"nothing can be done":** Mercy Scollay to Dr. Dix, Aug. 17, 1775, Mercy Scollay Papers.

201 **"which their Papa had hope for":** Mercy Scollay to John Hancock, May 21, 1776. John Hancock Family Papers.

201 **"My eyes are surcharged":** Ibid.

201 **"This day I visit Charlestown":** "Being One of the Party by permit from the General I had an opportunity of seeing everything just as it was left about two hours before by the enemy." "Record of the service of Dr. John Warren in Revolution, April 19, 1775–May 11, 1776." Vol. 1A, box 1, March 17, 1776. John Collins Warren Papers; John Collins Warren, March 21, 1776. Ibid.

202 **"a corpse began to appear":** *Massachusetts Spy*, April 12, 1776.

202 **"person buried in trousers":** *Virginia Gazette*, May 11, 1776.

202 **"two artificial teeth":** Ibid. The article stated that the location of the body and the particulars of the burial were "agreeable to the account given by one who was well acquainted with that circumstance"; several other accounts verify Warren's March 1776 exhumation. "Though the body which our savage enemies scarce privileged with earth enough to hide it from the birds of prey, was disfigured, when taken up, yet it was sufficiently known by two artificial teeth, which were set for him a short time before his glorious exit." *New England Chronicle*, April 25, 1776; "When disinterred in 1776, for removal to Boston, the remains were identified by an inspection of the teeth, upon which an operation had been performed, the evidence of which remained." *Salem Observer*, July 29, 1848; "Ten months after, a native of Great Britain, who was in Boston at the time of the battle, came to his friends and told them he could point out the spot where the general was buried. He was offered a reward if his information should be correct, and two brothers of the general, with some other gentlemen, accompanied him to the field. A sexton commenced digging on the spot he pointed out, and a corpse soon began to appear. The brothers, unable to remain longer, retired, having informed the other gentlemen that their brother might be distinguished by a particular false tooth. He was identified accordingly." *Weekly Messenger* (Boston), May 13, 1819; other accounts began to claim that Paul Revere had wired in the false teeth for Warren, starting with the *Independent Chronicle & Boston Patriot*, August 10, 1825,

"Col. Revere who set the artificial tooth . . ."; more than eighty years after the actual event, Sumner also mentioned Revere and the artificial tooth. See *Reminiscences Related to General Warren*, p. 7. But some of the testimonies in Sumner's work are questionable—it also claimed that the body buried with Warren was wearing a frock. But Paul Revere did perform dental work on Warren: Revere's February 1773 ledger entry reads, "To taking out bicuspid 0.40." Weinberger, *Introduction to Dentistry*, pp. 2:116–17.

202 **dental evidence:** *General Evening Post* (London), August 17, 1776, noting that "the following accounts are taken from the Boston Gazette."

202 **they lay in state:** Placing Warren's remains in state not only honored the martyred general but also, by highlighting the viciousness of tyrannical Great Britain, served as valuable propaganda to bolster the patriot resistance.

202 **"Hon. General Ward":** *Providence Gazette*, May 4, 1776. The ceremony was in King's Chapel because the minister and most members of that Anglican church had left Boston. Since the Old South Meetinghouse had been used by the British as a riding stable, the Old South congregation moved into the Chapel.

202 **"Col. Phiney's regiment":** *Virginia Gazette*, May 11, 1776.

202 **moving funeral dirge:** Abigail Adams to John Adams, April 10, 1776. Adams Family Papers.

202 **Perez Morton:** *Salem Gazette*, November 29, 1831. Morton was a patriot and lawyer.

EPILOGUE

203 **"distress [that] . . . rendered me":** Mercy Scollay to John Hancock, May 21,1776, *John Hancock Family Papers*.

203 **etched her name:** Worcester Fire Society, *Reminiscences*, p. 25.

203 **engraved his own name:** Watertown, *Watertown's Military History*, p. 71. Lovers often exchanged "scribbling rings," with centered uncut diamonds. They used them to etch their names and often romantic messages on windows, mirrors, and other glass. Lovers also gave each other "poesey rings" as a promise of love and affection; they were usually engraved with a sentiment.

203 **"the curtain is drop'd":** Mercy Scollay to Mrs. Dix, May 10, 1776. Mercy Scollay Papers.

204 **"mama mourns":** Scollay to Dr. Elijah Dix, April 26, 1776. Mercy Scollay Papers.

204 **"very ungenerously treated":** Scollay to Mrs. Dix, May 10, 1776. Mercy Scollay Papers.

204 **"it would be a fresh opening":** Scollay to Hancock, May 21, 1776, *John Hancock Family Papers*. For a time young Elizabeth was living in the house of Mrs. Charles Miller. According to Samuel Adams, Mercy Otis Warren, wife of James Warren, "was very solicitous that the eldest daughter should

spend the winter her and desired me to propose it to miss. I did so; but I could not prevail upon her. She said that Mrs. Miller . . . did not incline to part with her; and that it would be a breach of good manners, and ungrateful for her, to leave Mrs. Miller against her inclination. She very prettily expressed her obligations to both those ladies, and thus prevented my saying any more." Frothingham, *Life and Times*, p. 544, and Warren, *Life of John Warren*, p. 88.

204 **"tenderness for me unabated"**: Scollay to Hancock, May 21, 1776, *John Hancock Family Papers*.

204 **"the old lady is my fast friend"**: Scollay to Mrs. Dix, May 21, 1777, Mercy Scollay Papers. Mary Warren, General Warren's mother, eventually remarried. She went to live with her new husband, Deacon John Adams, in the neighboring town of Milton. He passed away on what would have been Joseph Warren's forty-ninth birthday in 1790. Deacon John Adams was born in Milton on February 26, 1709. He married his first wife Sarah Swift on May 19, 1730. Sarah gave birth to at least twelve children and died at the age of sixty-eight on November 16, 1774. Adams was eighty-one when he died in 1790. See Adams, *Genealogical History of Henry Adams*, p. 510.

204 **"be educated befitting"**: Scollay to Hancock, May 21, 1776, *John Hancock Family Papers*.

204 **"take particular care of the education"**: Benedict Arnold to Dr. Townshend August 6, 1778, Warren, *Life of John Collins Warren*, Vol. 2, p. 56.

205 **"fidelity to our departed friend"**: Samuel Adams to Mercy Scollay, March 18, 1777, in MHS Collections Online. In a December 20, 1779, letter, Adams wrote, "I think it does not appear that Betsey has been altogether friendless and 'deserted,' or that the others are in danger of 'suffering irreparably on account of their education.' Yet, as I am very desirous that they should have the greatest advantage in their growth into life, I shall, among other friends, think myself much obliged to any gentleman who, from pure and unmixed motives, shall add to those which they now enjoy." Frothingham, *Life and Times*, p. 544.

205 **"the departed hero should laugh"**: Scollay to Mrs. Dix, May 21, 1777, Mercy Scollay Papers.

205 **"The pains you have taken"**: Mercy Scollay to Benedict Arnold, July 7, 1780, Library of Congress. This letter has never been cited in any of the works on Warren. The amount of money noted in this letter that Arnold gave Mercy for Warren's children is much larger than previous research documents have shown.

205 **name his favorite horse:** Thanks to Nat Philbrick for relaying this information in a private conversation.

205 **"I greatly rejoice to hear"**: Mary Warren to John Warren, August 6, 1778, in *John Warren Papers*, Massachusetts Historical Society.

206 **John eventually adopted:** Frothingham, *Life and Times*, p. 543; Richard and Mary Warren were with Mercy Scollay from 1776 to 1780.

206 **"deserves the greatest praise"**: Frothingham, *Life and Times*, p. 543.

206 **"no gentlemans daughter":** Samuel Adams to Elbridge Gerry and James Lovell, in Warren, *Life of John Warren*, p. 88. See also, Frothingham, *Life and Times*, p. 543.

206 **"satisfied that I have":** Scollay to Arnold, July 7, 1780, Library of Congress.

206 **Warren's son Joseph was educated:** Mercy took particular interest in Joseph's early education since she noticed the young boy could barely read at the age of eight. She partially blamed this on his desire to not attend school, which apparently Mary Stevens Warren tolerated out of pity for her youngest grandson. Scollay Papers.

206 **first of Warren's children to die:** Jane T. Paine (daughter of Ebenezer Warren) to J. Sullivan Warren (grandson of John Warren), September 8, 1858, John Collins Warren Papers; Joseph Warren still has a cenotaph in Rock Hill Cemetery. His remains were moved to Forest Hills Cemetery on September 28, 1860.

207 **Mary "Polly" Warren:** Paine to Warren, September 8, 1858, John Collins Warren Papers. Mary Warren Newcomb died of consumption on February 7, 1826, and was buried in Federal Street Cemetery in Greenfield.

207 **son married the granddaughter:** Richard English Newcomb's daughter and wife died in the first week of August, and the son perished in the last week of September. Their son John Adams was named after his brother, who had died two years earlier. See Severance, Kellogg, and Thompson, *History of Greenfield*; in the spring of 2016 I visited the Federal Street Cemetery in Greenfield (with George Wildrick, General Warren's fifth great-grandson), where the family were all buried.

207 **many painful losses:** Mercy's father died in 1790, and her mother followed in 1793.

207 **Warren's unrecognized widow:** One source indicates that Mercy Scollay married Maj. Edward Carnes in 1780. But other sources indicate that Carnes, who died in 1782, was married to another woman at the time of his death. Carnes was possibly involved in the settling of Warren's estate.

207 **"my sands are running low":** Mercy Scollay letter, January 28, 1824, Mercy Scollay Papers.

207 **She died during the blustery winter:** Mercy died the same year as John Adams and Thomas Jefferson, who both died on July 4, 1826.

207 **"whose whole life has been":** Mercy Scollay letter, March 14, 1791, Mercy Scollay Papers.

208 **Vine Lake Cemetery:** The thirty-two-acre public cemetery, founded in 1651, is cared for by the Vine Lake Preservation Trust.

WARREN'S LEGACY

209 **Dr. John Collins Warren:** The Warren Museum was established at the Harvard Medical School in 1847, when John Collins Warren donated his personal collection of anatomical models. The museum is one of the few

medical museums founded in the nineteenth century that still exists; today it is known as the Warren Anatomical Museum. The museum's collection was housed in Gordon Hall for most of the twentieth century, then slipped gradually into storage in the 1990s. By 1998, the museum's fifteen thousand specimens were stored in warehouses off site. Several years ago Fortress Fine Arts Express was hired to move part of the collection, but many workers quit or opted out because they could not stomach the pickled fetuses or monstrous births that Collins Warren had chemically preserved in jars. Many nineteenth-century physicians liked to collect unusual items such as anatomical malformations. After Collins Warren passed away, his son Jonathan Mason Warren was to move into his home, but Mason Warren's wife refused until the house was cleared of all morbid objects. Mason Warren wanted the house to remain exactly as his father had left it, minus the objectionable collection pieces. Finally he and his wife moved in. After Mason Warren passed away, the house was demolished in 1877, and his widow moved into their former home at 6 Park Street. Arnold, *Memoir of Jonathan Warren*, p. 316.

209 **avid and meticulous collector:** June 1853–1855, box 15 of 23, John Collins Warren Papers.

209 **"very neat and in good order":** John Collins Warren Journal, Vol. 89. John Collins Warren Papers.

209 **"took high rank":** Warren, *Life of John Collins Warren*, p. 1:415.

209 **Large paintings:** J. M. Warren letter, June 17, 1856, in box 16, John Collins Warren Papers. John Collins Warren had purchased a painting of General Warren in the widow Hancock's estate sale.

210 **"high brusque authoritative":** Rice, *Trials of a Benefactor*, p. 36.

210 **"almost touching the wall":** Arnold, *Memoir of Jonathan Mason Warren*, pp. 314–15. General Warren's remains were housed in the Minot tomb between 1776 and 1825.

210 **had glanced out his window:** The Franklin tomb holds the parents of Benjamin Franklin, who is buried in Philadelphia. In 1826 the stone monument was "in a state of dilapidation," so Dr. John Collins Warren raised $940 to construct a twenty-foot granite pyramid to replace the old structure. See Franklin Bache to Dr. Warren, January 27, 1827, *Proceedings of the Massachusetts Historical Society* 45 (1912), p. 487.

210 **"with a view of preserving":** *Village Register* (Dedham, Mass.), May 10, 1822.

210 **Bunker Hill Monument Association:** Edward Everett professed that "the Bunker-Hill Monument owes its existence" to John Collins Warren "more than any other individual." Moreover, "I can truly say, that intimately as I was associated with him, in the early part of the undertaking, as a member of the Executive Committee, I never saw him in the slightest degree attempt to make the monument in any way minister to family feeling. I am sure that he was a member of the committee by whom the name General Warren was least frequently mentioned." Warren, *Life of John Collins Warren*, Vol. II, p. 309. This is to say, not that Collins Warren failed to

be an advocate of General Warren, but that he prioritized honoring the battle and all its participants, not solely his uncle.

210 **placement of the markers:** Entry for July 26, 1849, John Collins Warren Journal, Vol. 86, John Collins Warren Papers.

210 **"either to the state":** Entry for June 4, 1850, John Collins Warren Journal, Vol. 87. Ibid.

210 **once again planning:** Sixty-four tombs were built under St. Paul's Church, where it was decreed that "no tomb should be appropriated for the interment of strangers or of any person in consideration of payment thereof." *Saturday Evening Gazette*, August 5, 1865. In 1825, John Collins Warren removed the remains of his father, John Warren—who had died in 1815—and his uncle General Warren from the Old Granary Burial Ground and had them reburied in the underground crypt at St. Paul's.

210 **"Called on the Mayor":** Entry for August 1, 1855, John Collins Warren Journal, John Collins Warren Papers.

211 **purchased a new family plot:** Forest Hills Cemetery Records; entry for June 17, 1853, John Collins Warren Journal, Vol. 84, John Collins Warren Papers. Garden cemeteries gained popularity beginning in the 1830s as health issues surrounding burials, and their effects on drainage and air quality, became matters of public concern.

211 **within nine months he would be dead:** Warren, *Life of John Collins Warren*, Vol. 2, p. 264.

211 **"appearance was remarkable":** Rice, *Trials of a Benefactor*, p. 36.

211 **"Whatever place Dr. Warren":** Dr. Oliver W. Holmes, May 5, 1856, at a meeting of the Suffolk District Medical Society in Boston, made the remarks about the passing of Dr. John Collins Warren. May 1856 folder, John Collins Warren Papers.

211 **removed from the basement:** Three images were taken of General Warren's skull upon his exhumation. I believe John Collins Warren had the images taken in August 1855, during Joseph Warren's third exhumation, by Southworth and Hawes. (The competing firm was Whipple and Black.) The images were probably not taken in the photo studio. Most likely, since Joseph Warren was only temporarily exhumed, Collins Warren and his son Jonathan Mason hired the photographers to document where the bullet had struck—likely not transporting the skull to the studio but rather having the photographers come to them. As doctors, both father and son noted the fragile state of the skull and probably wanted to document the evidence immediately. The Southworth and Hawes studio was well known for its willingness to travel off site to take pictures. It was much easier to take a daguerreotype and leave the plate in the plateholder and develop it back in the studio. Although this procedure was possible with the wet plate process, it was much harder to accomplish out of studio. In 1855 daguerreotypes were being replaced by poster prints, but Southworth and Hawes clung to the daguerreotype process longer than other firms, believing it to be superior. So a photograph they took in 1855 stood a good chance of being a daguerreotype, especially if it were taken by Hawes.

Hawes also took the reenacted photo of the first operation that John Collins Warren performed with ether in 1846. As a token, Collins gave Hawes the very scalpel he used during the procedure. The photography studio was located on Tremont Street, very close to J. C. Warren's Park Street home, St. Paul's Church, and also Mass. General Hospital. Collins and Mason were friendly with both Southworth and Hawes and had hired them to take images both prior and after 1856. Collins's other son, J. Sullivan Warren, had hired Whipple and Black to take the memento mori image of John Collins Warren right after his death in May 1856. I find it unlikely that the images were taken in the summer of 1856, around the time of Joseph Warren's final burial. When Mason returned to New England from Europe in early July 1856, he was devastated to learn of the death of his father and his sister. Mason was ailing and despondent. His brother J. Sullivan had been handling all the family arrangements upon his return. Many thanks are due to photography historian David Silver, for conversation regarding photography in the nineteenth century.

212 **faded tin plate:** Frothingham, *Life and Times*, p. 525.

212 **"the bones were all found":** June 1853–1855, ms. N-1731, box 15, John Collins Warren Papers.

212 **"becoming enlarged":** Arnold, *Memoir of Jonathan Mason Warren*, p. 245.

212 **"the vase of pottery marked":** Appleton letter, August 1855 folder, June 1853–1855, ms. N-1731, box 15, John Collins Warren Papers.

212 **their final resting place:** June 1853–1855, ms. N-1731, box 15, John Collins Warren Papers. Much speculation has surrounded the whereabouts of Warren's remains between August 1855 and August 1856. An article in the *New London Daily Chronicle*, May 8, 1856, claimed that "a few weeks since, the late Dr. John C. Warren disinterred from the family tomb under St. Paul's church the remains of his uncle, General Joseph Warren. The skull was quite perfect, the chin still remaining. Behind one of the ears was seen an aperture, which indicated the place where the fatal ball entered. . . . The remains were placed in a stone urn, upon which an appropriate epitaph had been engraved. . . . The remains, with those of other members of the family were placed in Forest Hill Cemetery." This article also appeared in *Salem Register*, May 8, 1856, and *Richmond Whig* (Richmond, Va.), May 13, 1856. The description of the skull is remarkably similar to that written by William Appleton, Jr., in August 1855. It also describes the stone urn Collins had made specifically for General Warren. However, several newspaper articles mention that the remains of General Warren were kept at St. Paul's Church, as also indicated by the journal entries of James Sullivan Warren. "We are informed by the Sexton of St. Paul's Church that the remains of Gen. Joseph Warren are still deposited in the family tomb under that church. The report that they had been removed to Forest Hills Cemetery was therefore without foundation." *Boston Evening Transcript*, May 7, 1856; also see *Lowell Daily Citizen and News*, May 9, 1856, which declares, "The report that [Warren's remains] had been removed to Forest Hills was therefore incorrect." According to the burial records at Forest Hills Cemetery, General Warren was laid to rest there August 8, 1856. This is corroborated

by the journal entries of Dr, John Collins Warren's son, James Sullivan Warren, in July and August 1856. The entry of July 26, 1856, reads, "urn with remains dep at 2 Park Street." Therefore the remains and the urn were placed at the Park St. house of John Collins Warren less than two weeks prior to the Forest Hills burial. The entry for August 8 was written as follows, "Took Urns from St. Pauls tomb John W.—JCW—Joseph W—Mrs. SPW—Mrs. An W to tomb at Forest Hills . . . cont.d Gen Warrens skull and Dr. John W.s skull taken from 2 Park St. + placed in urn." Recent scholarship has claimed that General Warren's skull was kept at the house of Dr. John Collins Warren, 2 Park Street. The likely scenario is that Dr. John Collins Warren had his uncle's remains transferred from the coffin to the stone urn on August 3, 1855, where they remained deposited under St. Paul's church for another year until his son James Sullivan Warren transferred them to Forest Hills along with the other deceased relatives from St. Paul's. When General Warren's bones were removed from the coffin to the urn they were found to be moist and decomposing so the family sought to have them in an environment where they could dry. By at least May 1856, the remains were still at St. Paul's. Also of note is that most works of scholarship mistakenly cite that Jonathan Mason Warren continued the journal of his father Dr. John Collins Warren upon his death. However, this is incorrect since Mason was still in Europe at the time of his father's passing and did not return until July 3, 1856. Coincidentally, the next day Mason and Sullivan's sister Anna died and three days later was buried at Forest Hills—the first member of the family to be deposited in the vault at that cemetery. The journal was kept, and all the funeral arrangements were made by John Collins Warren's son, James Sullivan Warren.

212 **finally laid to rest:** It had "been doubted . . . where [W]arren's bones even were placed on their second interment." Austin, *Life of Gerry*, p. 86.

212 **postmortem journeys:** In colonial Boston in times of danger, "Town Born! Turn Out!" was the ancestral rallying cry. See Fischer, *Paul Revere's Ride*, for a more detailed description.

213 **"Future years will never know":** During the Civil War, Walt Whitman volunteered as a nurse at various camp hospitals. He later recollected stories told to him about patriot soldiers from the American Revolution who died on British prison ships anchored in New York's East River. For many years, during low tides, their bones and skulls would wash up along Brooklyn's shores, where "thoughtless boys would kick them about in play . . . finding bleached skeletons in great numbers." See Walt Whitman, *The Uncollected Poetry and Prose of Walt Whitman Much of Which Has Been But Recently Discovered with Various Early Manuscripts Now First Published*, ed. Emory Holloway (Garden City N.Y., 1921), p. 2:239. When the Marquis de Lafayette returned to tour America in 1824, Whitman was one of the boys who lined the streets to catch a glimpse of the old war hero. "Lafayette . . . took up the five-year-old Whitman, and pressing the child a moment to his breast, and giving him a kiss, handed him down to a safe spot" (p. 15). Whitman in later years became close with Colonel Fellows, a friend of Thomas Paine, author of *Common Sense*.

213 **unknown to most Americans:** Lee, *Funeral Oration in Honor of Washington.* This phrase, from Lee's eulogy, has become synonymous with Washington's honored legacy. Lee was a major general of the Continental Army and later governor of Virginia. His son was the Civil War general Robert E. Lee.

213 **"to preserve and diffuse":** John Trumbull to Thomas Jefferson, 1789, in McCoubrey, *American Art,* pp. 40–41.

214 ***Bunker-Hill: or the Death of General Warren:*** Jack Lynch, "Felled on the Field of Honor," *Colonial Williamsburg Journal,* Autumn 2005.

214 **Commemorations and odes:** *Diary* (New York), February 15, 1793; *Massachusetts Centinel,* June 14, 1788; *Essex Journal,* November 3, 1775.

214 **"We are not in circumstances":** "Extracted from a Boston paper, dated February 24, 1787," *Boston Traveler,* March 26, 1830.

214 **"in solemn silence":** *Massachusetts Spy,* December 17, 1794.

215 **"surprise, shame and indignation!":** *Boston Recorder,* April 26, 1823.

215 **"the illustrious Warren":** *Boston Patriot and Daily Chronicle,* May 14, 1818.

215 **"erecting a monument of American marble":** *Franklin Gazette,* February 23, 1818.

215 **gold headed cane:** *New-Bedford Mercury,* July 1, 1825.

215 **"our own deep sense of the value":** Webster, *Address Delivered,* p. 9.

215 **wave of Anti-Masonic feeling:** Warren, *Life of John Collins Warren,* p. 1:210.

215 **"anxious to take down":** Ibid.

216 **"dining at the Honorable Judge Prescott's":** Ibid., pp. 218–19.

216 **most of his personal and political papers:** Many of these were likely lost in the Alvord house fires mentioned earlier.

216 **"the papers and letters of General Warren":** Warren, *Life of John Collins Warren,* p. 1:217.

216 **Only two of his medical ledgers:** Mercy Scollay in a letter of May 10, 1776, wrote that Warren's brother John treated her "very ungenerously" since she had a "prior claim to the children" of the late general, which his brother John "was ignorant of, and was much surpriz'd that his brother should never mention such a design to him." Mercy Scollay Papers. I believe this is additional evidence that Warren never anticipated dying in battle or had a death wish as hypothesized by numerous historians.

216 **"the handwriting of Warren":** Ellis Ames to Ivers S. Adams. January 15, 1867, author's collection. In 1860 Warren's signature was sold at two different auctions, fetching twelve and twenty dollars. *New York Tribune,* August 25, 1860, and *Boston Traveler,* March 31, 1860. In 1869, at an auction in New York, Warren's autograph sold for $12.25—higher than any other signature listed. General "Mad" Anthony Wayne's was the next highest, selling at nine dollars. *Boston Journal,* March 17, 1869.

216 **"What did Gen. Warren do":** Brown, *Stories About General Warren,* preface. The author was a Warren family descendant.

216 **"the materials for the biography":** "Joseph Warren," in Sparks, *Library of American Biography,* p. 10:94.

217 **"beautiful white satin banner"**: *Liberator,* June 9, 1843.

217 **"What a name in the annals"**: John Quincy Adams, *Diary,* ed. Nevins, p. 551. Although Webster personally opposed the institution of slavery, he firmly believed that the preservation of the Union was paramount and thus compromised his own views in the hopes of saving the nation.

217 **"erection of a monument"**: *North America,* February 6, 1846.

218 **"either on Boston Common"**: Entry for February 2, 1846, John Collins Warren Journal, folder 82, John Collins Warren Papers.

218 **"No such compensation"**: *New Bedford Mercury,* December 25, 1846; *Augusta Chronicle,* December 22, 1846.

218 **"The City of Roxbury, Mass."**: *Boston Herald,* August 19, 1852.

218 **Three descendants**: *Albany Evening Journal,* June 12, 1857. Southworth and Hawes took a picture of the completed statue for the Bunker Hill Monument Association on June 16, 1857, prior to its removal from Dexter's studio. This fact serves as additional evidence that this firm was likely the photographers for the Warren skull daguerreotypes. See *Boston Traveler,* June 16, 1857.

218 **"Your cowardly northern Yankees"**: "An Enthusiastic Secessionist: A Woman's Letter," *Evening Post* (New York), June 20, 1861.

218 **"said he did not couple"**: *Boston Post-Boy,* December 19, 1859. The abolitionist John Brown led a raid against a federal armory in Harpers Ferry, Virginia, in October 1859. His plot to incite a slave revolt failed, and he was captured and hanged.

219 **"although urged as"**: *Commercial Advertiser,* November 24, 1865.

219 **first complete biography**: Since Warren's death more than 240 years ago, only two full-length biographies have been written about him. John Cary, author of the 1961 *Joseph Warren,* wrote that "though additional material has been uncovered since 1865, it has been largely on his professional and political life, and any biographer of Warren is confronted with the same difficulty of getting at his personal life that Frothingham faced. A personal, belletristic biography of Warren *cannot* be written, and this book is intended only as a new look at his public career." Condemned to obscurity even by his own biographers, Dr. Warren's personal side seemed destined to remain buried. At this writing, close to one thousand biographies have been written about George Washington.

219 **"remarkable that his biographical"**: *Public Ledger* (Philadelphia), December 21, 1865.

219 **"the more I study"**: *Boston Post,* June 27, 1859, p. 4.

219 **"more a life of Sam'l Adams"**: Ellis Ames to Iver S. Adams, January 15, 1867, author's collection.

219 **"the monument fever has broken"**: *Philadelphia Enquirer,* April 22, 1873.

219 **"putting up statues"**: *New York Tribune,* April 25, 1873.

220 **"such a proposition"**: *Boston Daily Advertiser,* April 30, 1874.

220 **"bones of Gen. Joseph Warren"**: *Salem Observer,* January 25, 1873.

220 **"The procession is to be"**: "Letter from Boston," *Providence Evening Press*, June 14, 1875.

220 **"prettily festooned"**: *Boston Journal*, June 18, 1875.

221 **"an old English chariot"**: "The Antiques and Horribles," *Boston Daily Advertiser*, June 16, 1875.

221 **"there were about 700 teams"**: *Connecticut Courant*, June 26, 1875. The Antiques and Horribles was a satirized version of the nation's oldest military organization, the Ancient and Honorable Artillery Company of Massachusetts established in the late 1630s. Since the company's members were allowed to dress in a variety of military uniforms, the older, paunchy ragtag group appeared humorously comical to many, which led to the playfully derisive appellation.

221 **wearing her great-grandfather's mourning ring**: *Boston Journal*, June 19, 1875. Warren Putnam Newcomb was the "great-great grandson of both the Revolutionary generals whose name he bears." Brown was described as having a "bodily distortion" which was a "striking physical contrast" to his "tall, fair wife." *Boston Herald*, December 27, 1891. Brown had suffered from Pott's disease as a child and as a result developed a pronounced hunchback. Brown dedicated himself to orthopedic surgery to help others suffering from similar circumstances.

221 **"balloon ascension"**: *Providence Evening Press*, June 14, 1875.

221 **placed above the entrance**: *Boston Herald*, April 2, 1898. The spot incorrectly designated the Green house that Warren had rented years earlier, rather than the Chardon house he rented in the spring of 1775.

222 **"a man who might have been"**: Ronald Reagan's First Inaugural Address, January 21, 1981. Reagan's first inaugural address was watched by 42 million viewers.

222 **excellent and informative**: Although the battle is known as Bunker Hill, the fighting took place less than a half mile away, on Breed's Hill. Surprisingly, the Breed's Hill engagement—one of the most significant in American history—has not only been mislabeled and overshadowed but also subjected to inaccuracies. As recently as 2008, one Pulitzer Prize–winning historian erroneously dated the battle at June 16. Other historians have mistakenly claimed that it was a "stunning victory" for the patriots.

222 *Liberty's Martyr* **by Janet Uhlar**: Uhlar's book was originally published in 2000 under the title *Bunker Hill*.

222 **extensively researched**: Samuel A. Forman, *Dr. Joseph Warren: The Boston Tea Party, Bunker Hill, and the Birth of American Liberty* (New York, 2012), p. 366.

224 **"When liberty is the prize"**: Warren to Stonington Committee, August 24, 1774, in Frothingham, *Life and Times*, p. 345.

224 **"a man whose memory"**: *Account of the Battle of Charlestown, July 25, 1775*, National Archives.

ACKNOWLEDGMENTS

THIS BOOK BEGAN AS A SENIOR THESIS PROJECT UNDER THE GUID-
ance of my mentor, Dr. Eric Foner, who then encouraged me to write
the definitive biography of Joseph Warren. I can't thank him enough
for his wisdom, encouragement, and advice over these many years.

I owe a great deal of thanks to many individuals and institutions
who helped make this book possible.

I want to acknowledge Sean P. Casey and Cecile W. Gardner
at the Boston Public Library; Cary Carson, Ronald Hurst, and Jeff
Klee at the Colonial Williamsburg Foundation; Sandra Waxman at
the Dedham Historical Society; Mary Warnement at the Boston Athenaeum; Timothy Salls at the New England Historic Genealogical
Society; Emily Curran at Old South Meeting House; Elizabeth Bou-
vier at the Massachusetts Archives in Boston; Gavin W. Kleespies at
the Cambridge Historical Society; Phyllis Magidson at the Museum
of the City of New York; Jessica Regan at the Metropolitan Museum

of Art; Caroline B. Carregal at the Massachusetts Medical Society; David L. Ostebur and Dominic Hall at the Francis A. Countway Library of Medicine; Walter H. Hunt at the Grand Lodge of Masons in Massachusetts; Catherine E. MacDonald and Jeff Mifflin at Massachusetts General Hospital; Lynn Smith at The Episcopal Diocese of Massachusetts; Daniel Hinchen, Anna Cook, and Sabina Beauchard at the Massachusetts Historical Society; Hilary Anderson Stelling at the Scottish Rite Masonic Museum & Library; and Elise M. Ciregna who was at Forest Hills Cemetery during my research visits. I would also like to acknowledge the helpful staffs at the Harvard University Archives, the American Antiquarian Society, the Bunker Hill Monument and Museum, and the National Archives. In particular, the Massachusetts Historical Society's entire staff were extremely helpful and welcoming hosts to me over the course of my many visits.

Individuals who also contributed and deserve thanks are Dr. Herb Sloan, whose lectures made my love of history even stronger with his impressive scholarship and dry sense of humor. The labyrinth of piled books in his office made many meetings with him all the more intriguing. Dr. Kimberley Alexander was generous with her time and extensive knowledge of eighteenth-century clothing and fashion. The late George C. Neuman spent many hours with me discussing the battle of Bunker Hill and period weapons. Forensic anthropologist for the city of New York, Dr. Bradley Adams, who had several conversations with me regarding Warren's skull, graciously indulged my questions and hypotheses. Photography historian David Silver shared his knowledge of the daguerreotype process. Peter S. Miller, local historian of Greenfield, Massachusetts, was kind enough to give me a tour around the area and show me everything Warren-related. Thanks are also due to Jack Authelet, the town historian of Foxborough, Massachusetts, for our conversations about Ebenezer Warren.

I must acknowledge the Colonial Williamsburg Foundation and its many dedicated employees and volunteers for allowing me access to their time machine, which transports me back to the eighteenth-century anytime I want. Their diligent attention to scholarship has been fodder for my imagination all these years. I have learned much. Having been a volunteer was my great pleasure and good fortune.

An enormous debt of gratitude is due to scholar, author, and now friend J. L. Bell, who read this manuscript and not only gave insightful opinions and comments, but also provided me with his impressive wealth of New England knowledge. A special thank-you is due to Sharon Cotner of Colonial Williamsburg's Pasteur & Galt Apothecary Shop. Sharon has been more than kind and giving of her time over the years, and tolerated my incessant queries and visits to the shop. She is a walking encyclopedia of eighteenth-century medicine and was able to translate the hieroglyphics that was Joseph Warren's medical ledgers into a comprehensible source of valuable information.

During my research I was fortunate to "discover" George C. Wildrick, Joseph Warren's fifth great-grandson and Warren family historian. Over the years, our New England and Virginia excursions and endless phone conversations helped breathe life back into Warren. His wife, Teri, has been kind enough to tolerate our shenanigans, and both she and George read the manuscript and provided me much help. Marcia Stoetzel has been extraordinary in her research efforts on my behalf. She managed to uncover so many of those "elusive" documents and has always made herself available to assist me. Bob Stoetzel graciously suffered through our spadework. I sincerely thank them both for their years of friendship. My friends Bob and John Sherman, descendants of one of the original subscribers of the Bunker Hill Monument Association, made me feel a special connection to this project. Their encouragement has been unwavering. Christian Kebekus has always been a welcome sounding board, and his presence and assistance on various research trips made them all the more seamless and enjoyable. Jason Posner, my dear friend since our days at Columbia University, has unselfishly lent his support in numerous ways. My uncle Tony Di Spigna, ever generous with his resources, weighed in with valuable artistic insight.

J. L Bell's blog, boston1775.blogspot.com, and Liz Covart's podcast, *Ben Franklin's World,* have become my go-to destinations for intellectual stimulation. Dr. Bruce M. Venter (and of course his wife, Lynne) and Dr. Edward G. Lengel also provide insightful period scholarship with their Annual Conference of the American Revolution, right in my backyard. I sincerely thank them for their dedication and the scholarship they provide the masses.

Of the many pleasures associated with writing this book, the most meaningful has been the friendships I have developed and also strengthened throughout the course of this project.

Much gratitude is due to Crown Publishing. Many thanks to Molly Stern for allowing Warren's story to be told. Kevin Doughten, my editor, has remained true to his word and as promised has followed me down every rabbit hole in the "Warren"—no matter how deep or thorny the terrain. His guidance and his dedication to this project was a blessing. I honestly could not have asked any more of him. His assistant, Jon Darga, has been a valuable asset and extremely helpful throughout the process. My copyeditor Janet Biehl and production editor Ada Yonenaka have been patient, and their judicious skills and fastidious attention to detail have defied all my expectations.

My agent, Betsy Lerner, believed in this project from the very beginning and I will always be grateful to her for opening this door.

I am humbled by the outpouring of support and help I have received throughout this project, and amazed by the breadth of knowledge that others have so graciously shared with me. Any errors in scholarship must be placed on my shoulders alone.

My family has always encouraged creativity and scholarship. I was lucky to have had four generations of incredible women in my life. Although both my grandmother and my mother passed away within a year of each other at the tail end of this project, making it a bittersweet conclusion, their courage and the strength of my sister helped sweep me across the finish line. Early on and for many years since, my father, a true renaissance man in every sense, gave me the "chariots of fire" to propel me past many other finish lines.

To my sweet little girl, Ava Elizabeth, who displayed a wisdom, patience, and understanding far beyond her years while her "daddy works on his book," always keeps me smiling. My wife, Jennifer, who has been my support network from the very beginning, your lust for life showers us all with the happiness we thrive on. You both continue to inspire me with your unconditional love that makes our journey magical, no matter the destination.

BIBLIOGRAPHY

Adams Family. Papers. Massachusetts Historical Society. Electronic Archive, http://www.masshist.org/digitaladams.

Adams, Andrew N., ed. *A Genealogical History of Henry Adams of Braintree, Mass., and His Descendants; also John Adams of Cambridge, Mass., 1632–1897*. Rutland, Vt., 1898.

Adams, John. *The Adams Papers; The Earliest Diary of John Adams*. Edited by L. H. Butterfield. Belknap Press, 1966.

———. *Autobiography*. Adams Family Papers.

———. *Diary*. Adams Family Papers.

———. *The Diary and Autobiography of John Adams*. Edited by L. H. Butterfield. Cambridge, Mass., 1961.

———. *The Works of John Adams, Second President of the United States*. Edited by Charles Francis Adams. Boston, 1851.

Adams, John Quincy. *The Diaries of John Quincy Adams*. Adams Family Papers.

———. *The Diary of John Quincy Adams*. Edited by Allan Nevins. New York, 1928.

Adams, Samuel. *The Writings of Samuel Adams*, Edited by Henry Alonzo Cushing. New York, 1904.

Ames, Nathaniel. "Diary of Dr. Nathaniel Ames." *Dedham Historical Register.* Vol. 1. Dedham, Mass., 1890.

———. *The Diary of Nathaniel Ames of Dedham, Massachusetts 1758–1822,* Edited by Robert Brand Hansen. Maine, 1998.

Anderson, Fred A. *A People's Army: Massachusetts Soldiers and Society in the Seven Years' War.* Chapel Hill, N.C., 1984.

Arnold, Howard Payson, *Memoir of Jonathan Mason Warren, M.D.* Boston, 1886.

Austin, James T. *The Life of Elbridge Gerry.* Boston, 1828.

Bacon, Edwin Monroe, *Washington Street, Old and New.* Boston, 1913.

Bailyn, Bernard. *The Ideological Origins of the American Revolution.* Cambridge, Mass., 1992.

———. *The Ordeal of Thomas Hutchinson.* Cambridge, Mass., 1974.

Baldwin, Christopher C. "Diary of Christopher C. Baldwin." *Archaeologia Americana: Transactions and Collections of the American Antiquarian Society* 8 (1901).

Bancroft. "Colonel Bancroft's Personal Narrative of the Battle of Bunker Hill," in S. T. Worcester, *Bi-Centennial of Old Dunstable.* Nashua, N.H., 1878.

Barber, Samuel. *Boston Common: A Diary of Notable Events, Incidents, and Neighboring Occurrences.* Boston, 1916.

Barck, Dorothy C., ed. *Papers of the Lloyd family of the Manor of Queens Village, Lloyd's Neck, Long Island, New York. 1654–1826.* 2 vols. New York, 1927.

Barker, John. *The British in Boston: The Diary of Lt. John Barker.* New York, 1924.

Batchelder, Samuel Francis. *Bits of Harvard History.* Cambridge, Mass., 1930.

Black, Henry Campbell. *Black's Law Dictionary,* 6th ed. 1999.

Boardman, Samuel Lane, Peter Edes, and John Leach, eds. *Pioneer Printer in Maine, a Biography: His Diary While a Prisoner by the British at Boston in 1775, with the Journal of John Leach, who was a Prisoner at the Same Time.* Bangor, Me., 1901.

Boston. *A Report of the Record Commissioners of the City of Boston, Containing the Boston Town Records, 1758–1769.* Boston, 1886.

———. *A Report of the Record Commissioners of the City of Boston, Containing the Selectmen's Minutes from 1764 through 1768.* Boston, 1889.

Brooks, Charles. *History of the Town of Medford, Middlesex County, Massachusetts.* Boston, 1886.

Brown, Rebecca Warren. *Stories About General Warren in Relation to the Fifth of March Massacre and the Battle of Bunker Hill by a Lady of Boston.* Boston, 1835.

Brown, Richard D. *Revolutionary Politics in Massachusetts: The Boston Committee of Correspondence and the Towns.* Cambridge, Mass., 1970.

Caramia, John A., Jr., "Wages and Prices," *Colonial Williamsburg Interpreter* 17, no. 2 (Summer 1996).

Cary, John H. *Joseph Warren: Physician, Politician, Patriot.* Urbana, Ill., 1961.

Chernow, Ron. *George Washington: A Life.* New York, 2010.

Church in Brattle Square. *The Manifesto Church: Records of the Church in Brattle Square.* Boston, 1902.

Commager, Henry Steele, and Richard B. Morris. *The Spirit of 'Seventy-Six: The Story of the American Revolution as Told by Participants.* New York, 1968.

Cooper, Samuel, *A Sermon on the Commencement of the Constitution,* October 25, 1780. Boston Commonwealth of Massachusetts: Printed by T. and J. Fleet and J. Gill. 1780.

Cooper, Wendy. *Hair: Sex, Society, and Symbolism.* New York, 1971.

Copley, John Singleton, and Henry Pelham. *Letters and Papers, 1739–1776.* Boston, 1914.

Crocker, Hannah Mather. *Reminiscences and Traditions of Boston.* Edited by Eileen Hunt Botting and Sarah L. Houser. Boston, 2011.

Dandridge, Danske. *American Prisoners of the Revolution.* Charlottesville, Va., 1911.

Dann, John C., ed. *The Revolution Remembered: Eyewitness Accounts of the War for Independence.* Chicago, 1983.

Daughters of the Revolution. *Catalogue of a Loan Collection of Ancient and Historic Articles.* Andover, Mass., 1897.

Daughters of the Revolution, Mary Warren Chapter, *Glimpses of Early Roxbury.* Roxbury, Mass., 1905.

Davis, Andrew McFarland. *Papers Relating to the Land Bank of 1740.* Boston, 1910.

Dearborn, Henry. *An Account of the Battle of Bunker's Hill.* Boston, 1818.

Donne, W. Bodham, ed. *The Correspondence of George the Third with Lord North from 1768–1783.* London, 1867.

Drake, Francis S. *The Town of Roxbury and Memorable Persons and Places.* Boston, 1905.

Drake, Samuel Adams. *Old Landmarks and Historic Personages of Boston.* Boston, 1873.

Drake, Samuel Adams, ed. *Bunker Hill; The Story Told in Letters from the Battle Field by British Officers Engaged.* Boston, 1875.

Dunlap, William. *A History of New York, for Schools.* New York, 1837.

An Elegiac Poem, Composed on the Never-To-Be-Forgotten Terrible and Bloody Battle Fought at an Intrenchment on Bunker-Hill. Broadside. Salem, Mass., 1775.

Eliot, John. *Biographical Dictionary Containing a Brief Account of the First Settlers, and Other Eminent Characters Among the Magistrates, Ministers, Literary and Worthy Men in New-England.* Boston, 1809.

Ellis, Joseph. *American Creation*. New York, 2007.

Emery, Sarah Anna. *Reminiscences of a Nonagenarian*. Newburyport, Mass., 1879.

Field, Edward. *The Colonial Tavern: A Glimpse of New England Town Life in the Seventeenth and Eighteenth Centuries*. Providence, R.I., 1897.

Fischer, David Hackett. *Paul Revere's Ride*. New York, 1995.

Flexner, James Thomas, *John Singleton Copley*. Boston, 1948.

Force, Peter. *American Archives: Fourth Series, Containing a Documentary History of English Colonies in North America*. Washington, D.C., 1837.

Ford, Worthington Chauncey, ed. *Boston in 1775, Letters from General Washington, Captain John Chester, Lieutenant Samuel B. Webb, and Joseph Barrell*. New York, 1892.

———. *Journals of the Continental Congress, 1774–1789*. Washington, D.C., 1904–37.

Fowler, William M., Jr. *Samuel Adams: Radical Puritan*. New York, 1997.

Franklin, Benjamin. *The Papers of Benjamin Franklin*. Edited by W. B. Wilcox. New Haven, Conn.: Yale University Press, 1959.

French, Allen. *The First Year of the American Revolution*. New York, 1968.

Frothingham, Richard, Jr. *The Centennial: Battle of Bunker Hill*. Boston, 1875.

———. *History of the Siege of Boston, and of the Battles of Lexington, Concord, and Bunker Hill*. Boston, 1851.

———. *Life and Times of Joseph Warren*. Boston, 1865.

Gage, Thomas. *The Correspondence of General Thomas Gage*. Edited by Clarence Edwin Carter. New Haven, Conn., 1931–.

———. Papers. Manuscript Division, William J. Clements Library, University of Michigan.

Galvin, John R. *Three Men of Boston: Leadership and Conflict at the Start of the American Revolution*. Washington, D.C., 1997.

Gardner, Samuel. "Diary for the Year 1759 kept by Samuel Gardner of Salem." *Essex Institute Historical Collections* 49 (1913): 1–22.

Gordon, William. *The History of the Rise, Progress, and Establishment, of the Independence of the United States of America*. New York, 1789.

Green, Samuel Abbott. *An Account of Percival and Ellen Green and of Some of Their Descendants*. Groton, Mass., 1876.

Greene, Lorenzo. *The Negro in Colonial New England*. New York, 1969.

Greenleaf, John. Papers. Boston Athenaeum.

Greenwood, Isaac J., ed. *The Revolutionary Services of John Greenwood of Boston and New York 1775–1783*. New York, 1922.

Hale, Richard Walden, Jr. *Tercentenery History of the Roxbury Latin School 1645–1945.* New York, 1945.

Hamilton, Edward P. "Robert Hewes and the Frenchmen. A Case of Treason?" *Proceedings of the American Antiquarian Society* 68, no. 2. (October 1958): 195–210.

Harrington, John. *The Last Words and Dying Speech of John Harrington: Aged 43 Years. Who Was Executed At Cambridge, March 17, 1757, for the Murder of Paul Learned.* Broadside. Boston, 1757.

Harvard University. Archives. Cambridge, Mass.

Hoerder, Dirk. *Crowd Action in Revolutionary Massachusetts 1765–1770.* New York, 1977.

Holyoke, Rev. Edward, et al. *The Holyoke Diaries, 1709–1856.* Salem, Mass., 1911.

Hosmer, James K. *The Life of Thomas Hutchinson, royal governor of the province of Massachusetts Bay.* New York, 1972 (c. 1896).

Howe, William. *General Sir William Howe's Orderly Book at Charlestown, Boston and Halifax, June 17, 1775, to 1776, 26 May.* Edited by Benjamin Franklin Stevens. London, 1890.

Hudleston, F. J. *Gentleman Johnny Burgoyne: Misadventures of an English General in the Revolution.* Indianapolis, Ind.,1927.

Hulton, Ann. *Letters of a Loyalist Lady, Being the Letters of Anne Hulton, Sister of Henry Hulton, Commissioner of Customs at Boston, 1767–1776.* Cambridge, Mass., 1927.

Hutchinson, Thomas. *The Diary and Letters of His Excellency Thomas Hutchinson, Esq.* Edited by Peter Orlando Hutchinson. Boston, 1884.

Johnstone, George. *Governor Johnston's Speech on American Affairs on the Address to the King's Speech, 1776.* Edinburgh, 1885.

Knapp, Samuel L. *Biographical Sketches of Eminent Lawyers, Statesmen, and Men of Letters.* Boston, 1821.

Lanning, Lt. Col. Michael Lee. *Defenders of Liberty: African Americans in the Revolutionary War.* New York, 2000.

Lee, Charles, and Edward Langworthy, *Life and Memoirs of the Late General Lee.* New York, 1813.

Lee, Henry. *A Funeral Oration in Honor of the Memory of George Washington.* New Haven, Conn., 1800.

Leffingwell, E. H. *Catalogue of Autograph Letters and Historical Documents Collected by the Late Prof. E. H. Leffingwell, of New Haven, Conn.* Boston, 1891(?).

Loring, James Spear. *The Hundred Boston Orators Appointed by the Municipal Authorities and Other Public Bodies, from 1770 to 1852.* Boston, 1852.

Marlowe, George Francis. *Coaching Roads of Old New England.* New York, 1945.

Marsh, Thomas. *Diary of Thomas Marsh, 1751.* HUG 1557.18, Harvard University Archives.

Mascarene, Margaret Holyoke. *Diary of Margaret Appleton Holyoke Mascarene, 1759.* HUM 92, Harvard University Archives.

Mather, Cotton. *Diary of Cotton Mather, 1709–1724.* Massachusetts Historical Society Collections, series 7, vol. 8 (1912).

McCoubrey, John W. *American Art: 1760–1960.* Englewood Cliffs, N.J., 1965.

McCullough, David, *John Adams.* New York, 2001.

Mein, John. *Sagittarius's Letters and Political Speculations. Extracted from the Public Ledger.* Boston, 1775.

Miller, John C. *Sam Adams: A Pioneer in Propaganda.* Stanford, Calif., 1964.

Morison, Samuel Eliot. *Three Centuries of Harvard, 1636–1936.* Cambridge, Mass., 1936.

Morse, Jedidiah, D.D., and Rev. Elijah Parish, A.M. *A Compendious History of New England, Designed for Schools and Private Families.* Charlestown, Mass., 1804.

Nason, Elias. *A History of the Town of Dunstable, Massachusetts: From its Earliest Settlement to the Year of Our Lord 1873.* Boston, 1877.

Nehama, Sarah, *In Death Lamented: The Tradition of Anglo-American Mourning Jewelry.* Boston, 2012.

Newell, Aimee E., Hilary Anderson Stelling, and Catherine Compton Swanson, *Curiosities of the Craft: Treasures from the Grand Lodge of Massachusetts Collection.* Lexington, Mass., 2003.

Nicolson, Colin. *The "Infamas Govener": Francis Bernard and the Origins of the American Revolution.* Boston, 2001.

"Notice of the Late James Lloyd, M.D." *New England Journal of Medicine and Surgery 2 (*1813): 127–30.

Oliver, Peter. *Origin and Progress of the American Rebellion: A Tory View.* Edited by Douglass Adair and John A. Schutz. 1871; San Marino, Calif., 1961.

Ormsby, John. *The Last Speech and Dying Words of John Ormsby: Who Was Appointed to Be Executed On Boston Neck . . .* Boston, 1734.

Otis, James. *The Rights of the British Colonies Asserted and Proved.* Boston, 1764.

Page, John. *Diary of John Page, 1757–1781.* HUD 757.68. Harvard University Archives.

Palmer, Ezra, ed. *The Lodge of St. Andrew and the Massachusetts Grand Lodge. Conditi et Ducati, Anno Lucis 5756–5769.* Boston, 1870.

Philbrick, Nathaniel. *Valiant Ambition: George Washington, Benedict Arnold, and the Fate of the American Revolution.* New York: 2016.

Provincial Congresses of Massachusetts. *The Journals of Each Provincial Congress of Massachusetts in 1774 and 1775 and of the Committee of Safety.* Boston, 1838.

———. *Journals of the House of Representatives of Massachusetts, 1773–1774.* Boston: 1891.

Rice, Nathan P. *Trials of a Public Benefactor.* New York, 1859.

Rose, Alexander. *Washington's Spies: The Story of America's First Spy Ring.* New York, 2006.

Rowe, John. *Letters and Diary of John Rowe.* Edited by Anne Rowe Cunningham. Boston, 1903.

Schlesinger, Arthur M., Jr. *Prelude to Independence: The Newspaper War on Britain 1764–1776.* New York: 1958.

Scollay, Mercy. Papers. Cambridge Historical Society.

Shipton, Clifford Kenyon. *Sibley's Harvard Graduates,* XIV, *The Classes of 1756–1760.* Boston, 1968.

Shurtleff, Nathaniel B. *Topographical and Historical Description of Boston.* Boston, 1891.

Smith, Page, *John Adams.* 2 vols. New York, 1962.

Sparks, Jared, *The Library of American Biography.* Boston, 1838.

Stoll, Ira. *Samuel Adams: A Life.* New York, 2008.

Sullivan, Thomas. *Journal of the Operations of the American War.* Philadelphia, 1804.

Sumner, William H. *Reminiscences Related to General Warren and Bunker Hill.* Boston, 1858.

Swett, Samuel. *History of Bunker Hill Battle: With a Plan.* Boston, 1827.

Taylor, James C., ed. *Founding Families: Digital Editions of the Papers of the Winthrops and the Adamses.* Boston, 2014, http://www.masshist.org/apde2/.

Tentindo, Vincent, and Marylyn Jones. *Battle of Chelsea Creek, May 27, 1775: Graves' Misfortune.* Revere, Mass., 1978.

Thayer, William Roscoe, *An Historical Sketch of Harvard University: From Its Foundation to May 1890.* Cambridge, Mass., 1890.

Thomas, Benjamin Franklin. *Celebration by the inhabitants of Worcester, Mass., of the Centennial Anniversary of the Declaration of Independence. July 4, 1876.* Worcester, Mass. 1876.

Thomas, Isaiah. *The History of Printing in America, with a Biography of Printers.* Albany, N.Y., 1874.

Thompson, Francis M., Charles Severance, and Lucy Kellogg. *History of Greenfield, Shire Town of Franklin County Massachusetts.* Greenfield, Mass., 1904.

Thwing, Annie H. *The Crooked and Narrow Streets of Boston 1630–1822.* Boston, 1920.

Thwing, Walter Eliot. *History of the First Church in Roxbury, Massachusetts 1630–1904.* Boston, 1908.

Truax, Rhoda. *The Doctors Warren of Boston: First Family of Surgery.* Boston, 1968.

Tudor, John. *Deacon Tudor's Diary; or, "Memorandoms from 1709, &c., by John Tudor, to 1775 & 1778, 1780 and to '93."* Edited by William A. B. Tudor. Boston, 1896.

Tufts, Joseph. *Don Quixote at College; or, History of the Gallant Adventures Lately Achieved by the Combined Students of Harvard University.* Boston, 1807.

Wallenborn, White McKenzie, M.D. *George Washington's Terminal Illness: A Modern Medical Analysis of the Last Illness and Death of George Washington.* Washington Papers, http://gwpapers.virginia.edu/history/articles/illness/.

Warren, Edward, M.D. *The Life of John Collins Warren M.D.* Boston, 1873.

Warren, John Collins. Papers. Massachusetts Historical Society.

Warren, Joseph. *An Oration Delivered March Sixth, 1775. At the Request of the Inhabitants of the Town of Boston, to Commemorate the Bloody Tragedy of the Fifth of March, 1770.* Boston, 1775.

———. Papers. Massachusetts Historical Society.

Washington, George. *George Washington's Expense Account.* Edited by Marvin Kitman. New York, 1970.

———. *George Washington's Rules of Civility and Decent Behavior.* London, 2013.

———. Papers. University of Virginia.

——— *The Writings of George Washington from the Original Manuscript Sources, 1745–1799.* Edited by John C. Fitzpatrick. Washington, D.C., 1931–44.

Watertown's Military History Authorized by a Vote of the Inhabitants of the Town of Watertown, Massachusetts. David Clapp & Son, Printers, 291 Congress Street, 1907.

Webster, Daniel. *An Address Delivered at the Laying of the Cornerstone of the Bunker Hill Monument.* Boston, 1825.

Weinberger, Bernhard Wolf. *An Introduction to the History of Dentistry.* St. Louis, 1948.

Wemms, William. *The Trial of the British Soldiers of the 29th Regiment of Foot, for the Murder of Crispus Attucks, Samuel Gray, Samuel Maverick, James Caldwell, and Patrick Carr, on Monday Evening March 5, 1770.* Boston, 1824.

Whitehill, Walter Muir. *Boston: A Topographical History.* Cambridge, Mass., 1959.

Willard, Margaret Wheeler, ed. *Letters on the American Revolution, 1774–1776.* Boston, 1925.

Wingate, Charles E. L. *Life and Letters of Paine Wingate.* Medford, Mass., 1930.

Winslow, Anna Green. *Diary of Anna Green Winslow: A Boston School Girl of 1771.* Edited by Alice Morse Earle. Boston, 1894.

Wood, Gordon S. *The American Revolution: A History.* New York, 2002.

Worcester Fire Society. *Reminiscences of Biographical Notices of Twenty-One Members,* 6th series. Worcester, Mass., 1899.

Young, Alfred F. *Liberty Tree: Ordinary People and the American Revolution.* New York, 2006.

Young. Edward J. *Subjects for Master's Degree in Harvard College, 1655–1791.* Cambridge, Mass., 1880.

Zobel, Hiller B. *The Boston Massacre.* New York, 1970.

INDEX